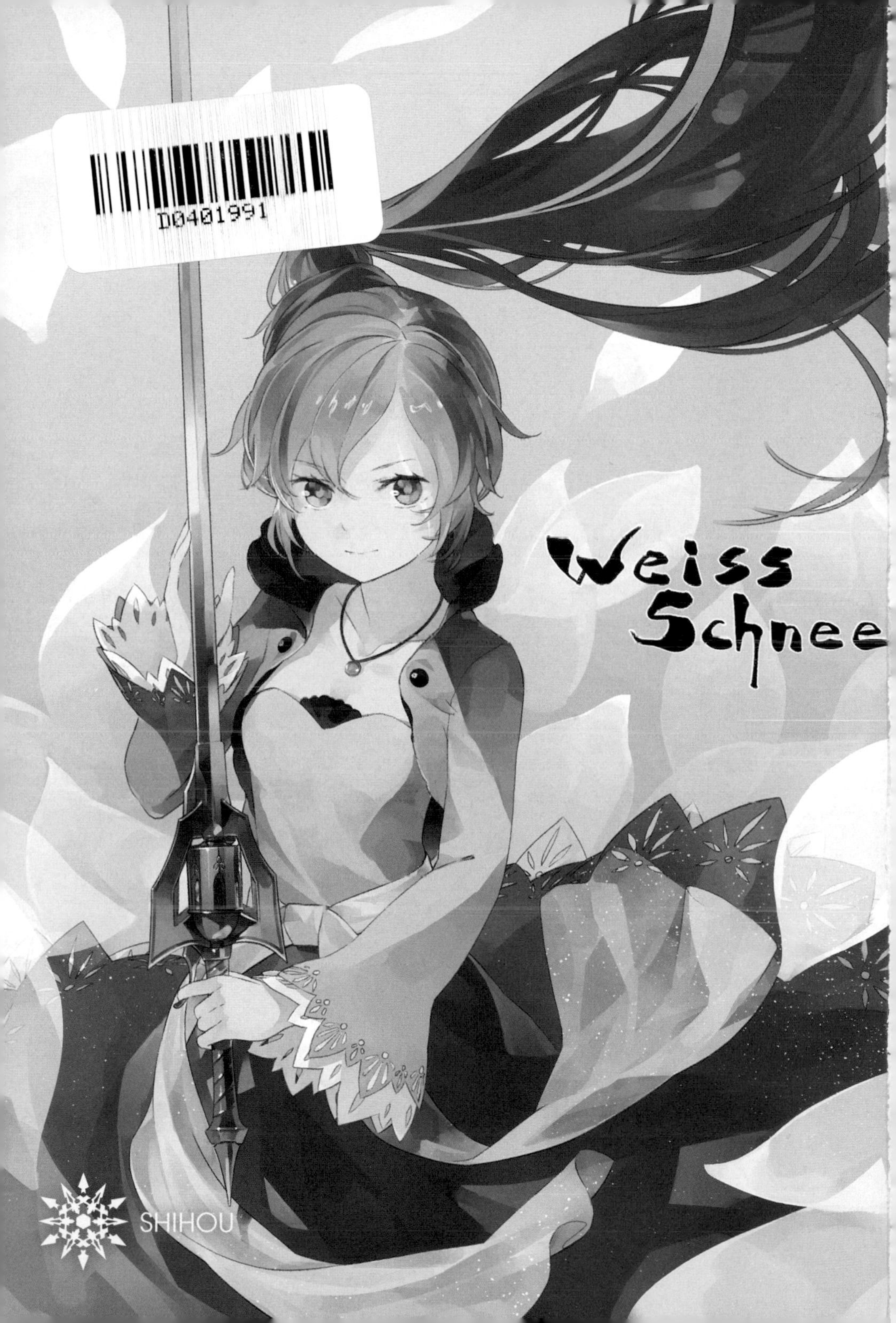

Weiss Schnee
SHIHOU

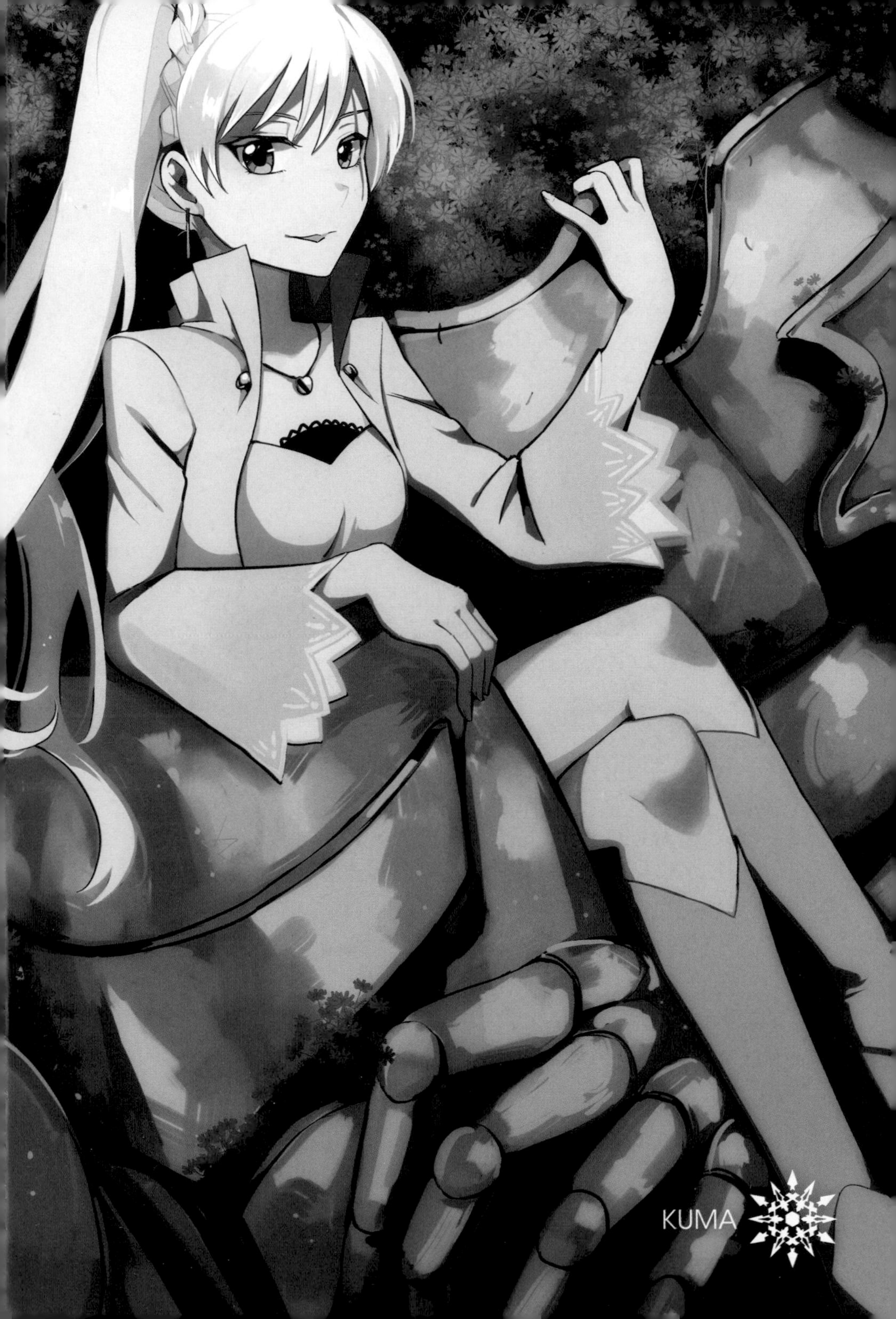
KUMA

My BFF

KaTe

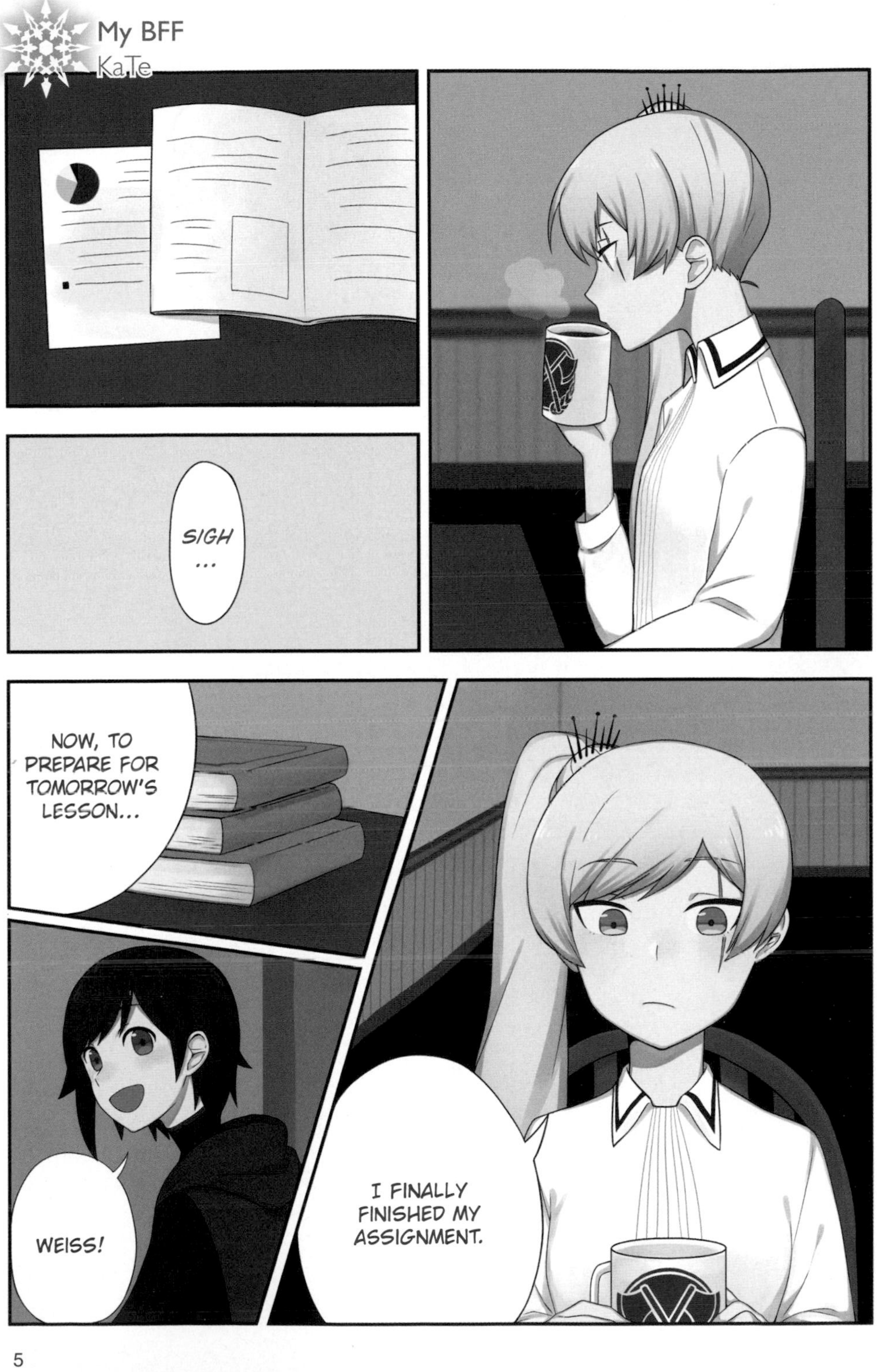
SIGH ...
I FINALLY FINISHED MY ASSIGNMENT.
NOW, TO PREPARE FOR TOMORROW'S LESSON...
WEISS!

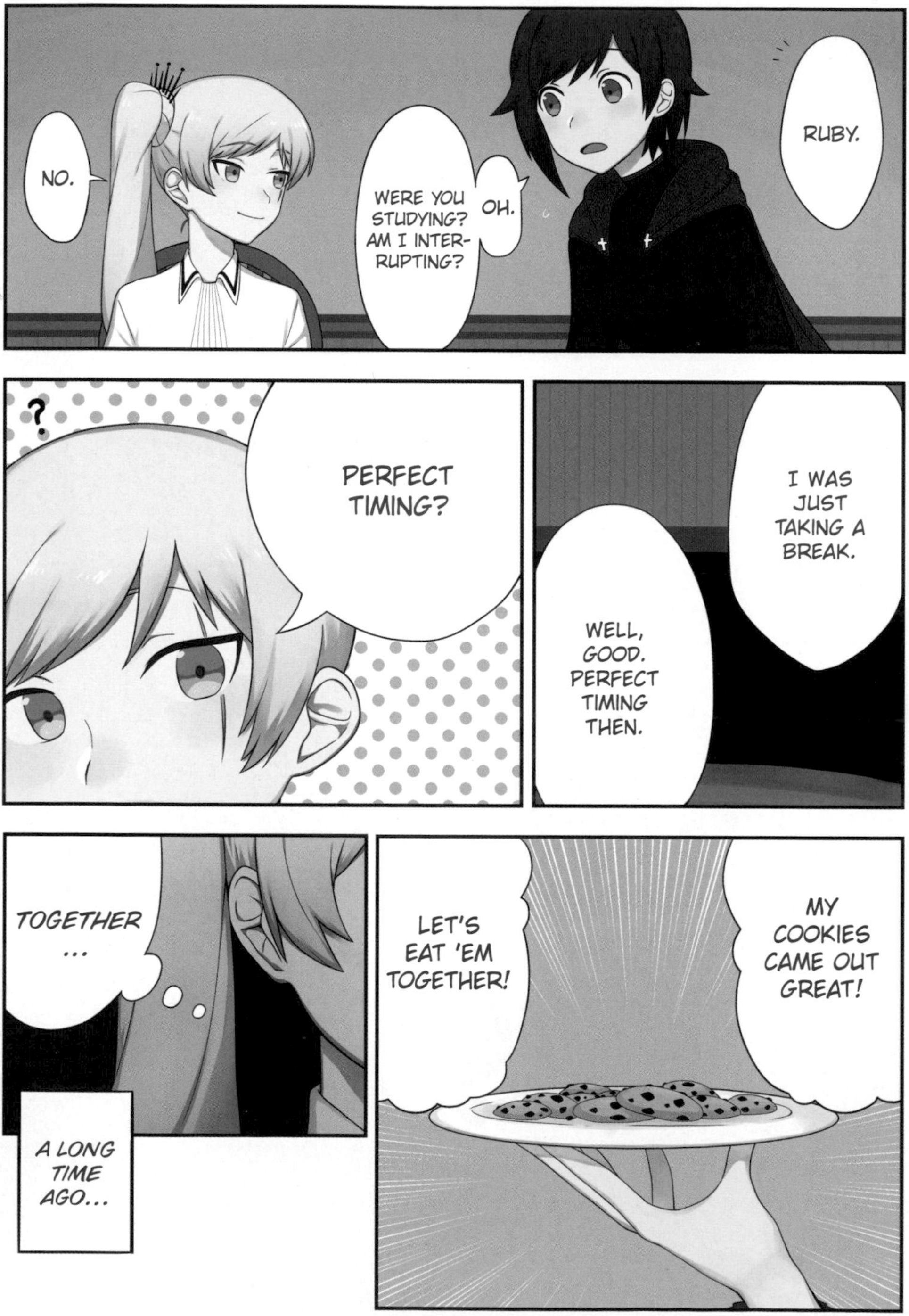
RUBY.
OH.
WERE YOU STUDYING? AM I INTER-RUPTING?
NO.
I WAS JUST TAKING A BREAK.
WELL, GOOD. PERFECT TIMING THEN.
PERFECT TIMING?
?
MY COOKIES CAME OUT GREAT!
LET'S EAT 'EM TOGETHER!
TOGETHER ...
A LONG TIME AGO...

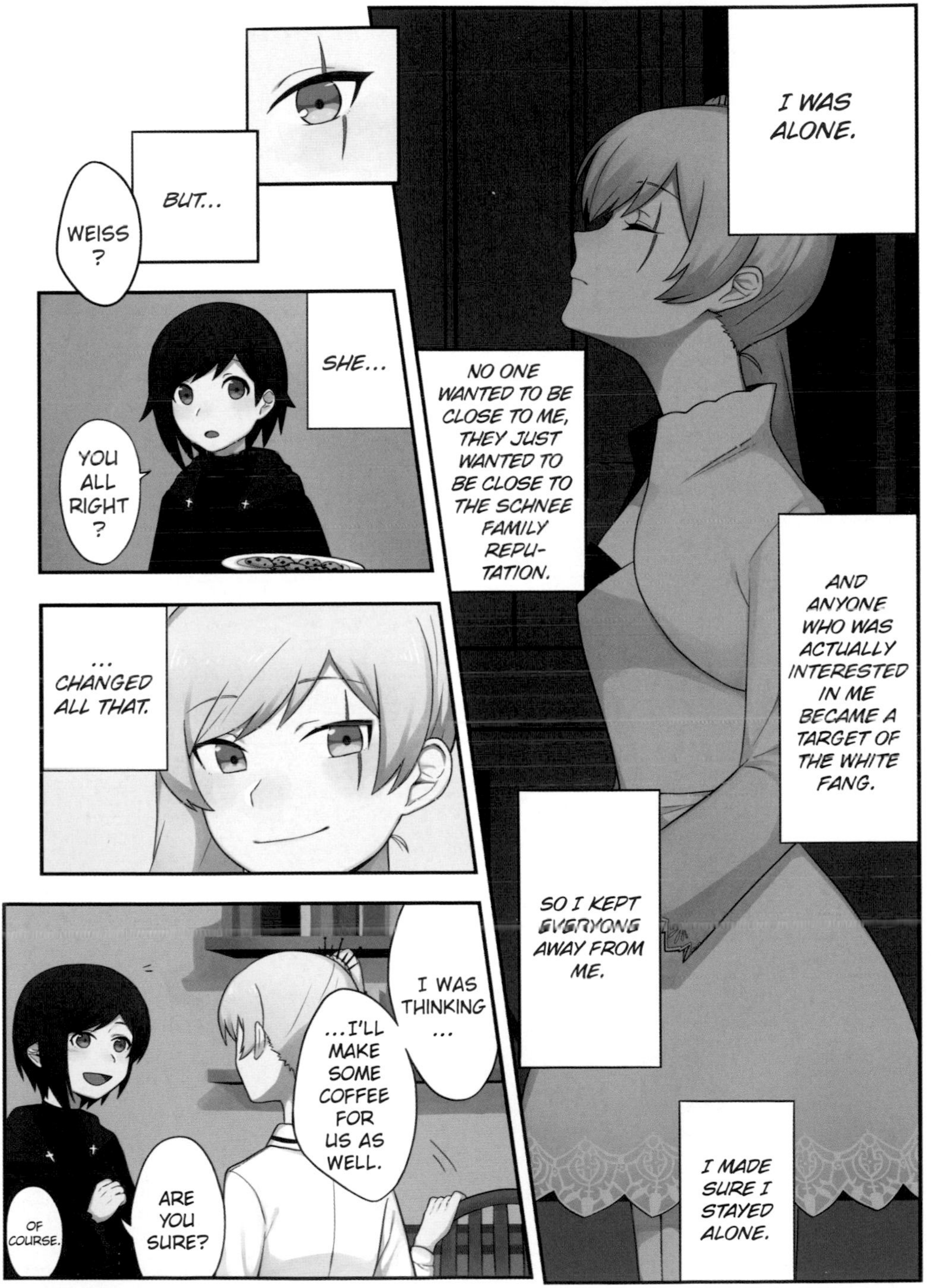
I WAS ALONE.
NO ONE WANTED TO BE CLOSE TO ME, THEY JUST WANTED TO BE CLOSE TO THE SCHNEE FAMILY REPUTATION.
AND ANYONE WHO WAS ACTUALLY INTERESTED IN ME BECAME A TARGET OF THE WHITE FANG.
SO I KEPT EVERYONE AWAY FROM ME.
I MADE SURE I STAYED ALONE.
BUT...
WEISS?
SHE...
YOU ALL RIGHT?
...CHANGED ALL THAT.
I WAS THINKING...
...I'LL MAKE SOME COFFEE FOR US AS WELL.
ARE YOU SURE?
OF COURSE.

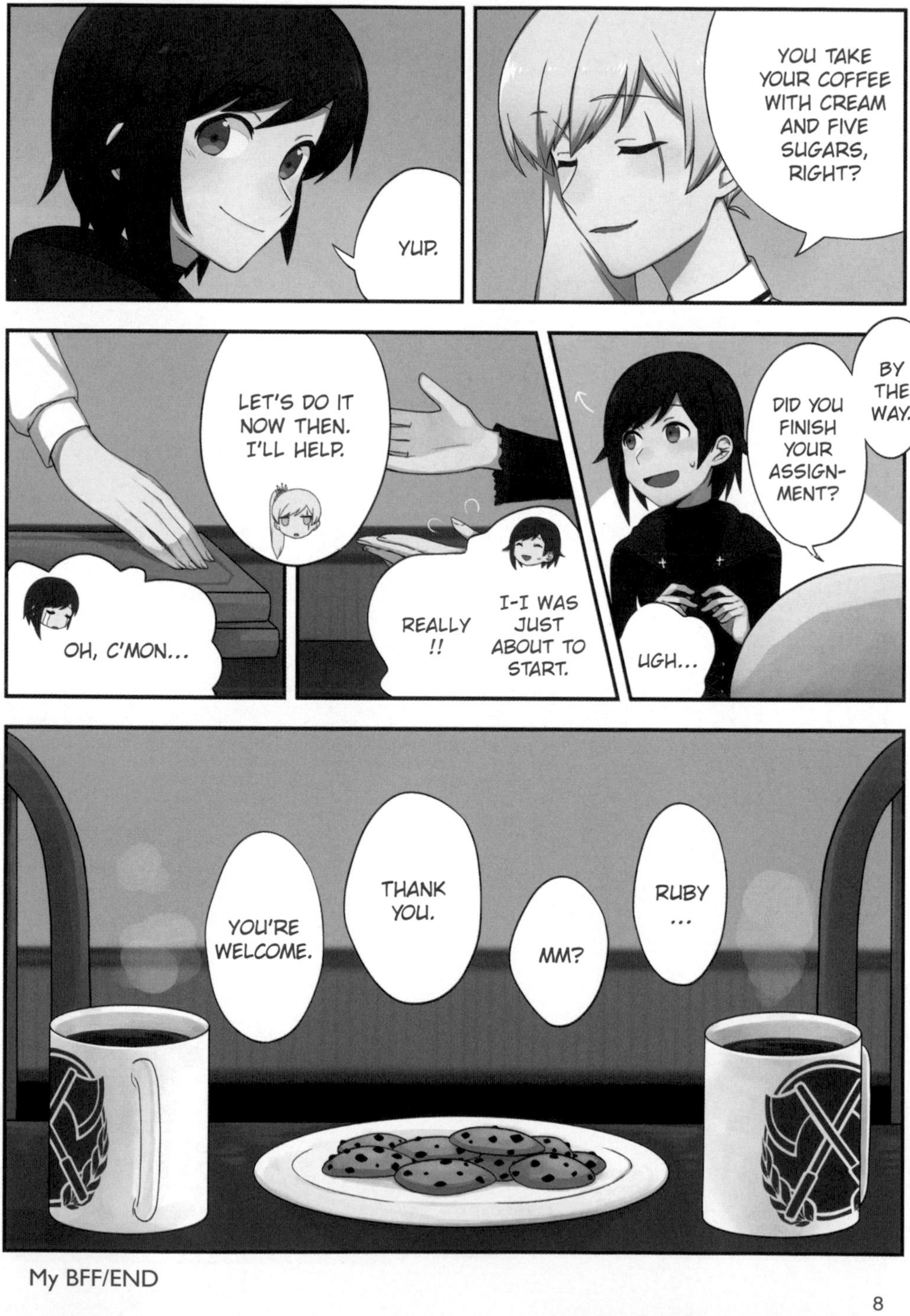
YOU TAKE YOUR COFFEE WITH CREAM AND FIVE SUGARS, RIGHT?
YUP.
BY THE WAY.
DID YOU FINISH YOUR ASSIGN-MENT?
UGH...
I-I WAS JUST ABOUT TO START.
REALLY !!
LET'S DO IT NOW THEN. I'LL HELP.
OH, C'MON...
RUBY ...
MM?
THANK YOU.
YOU'RE WELCOME.

My BFF/END

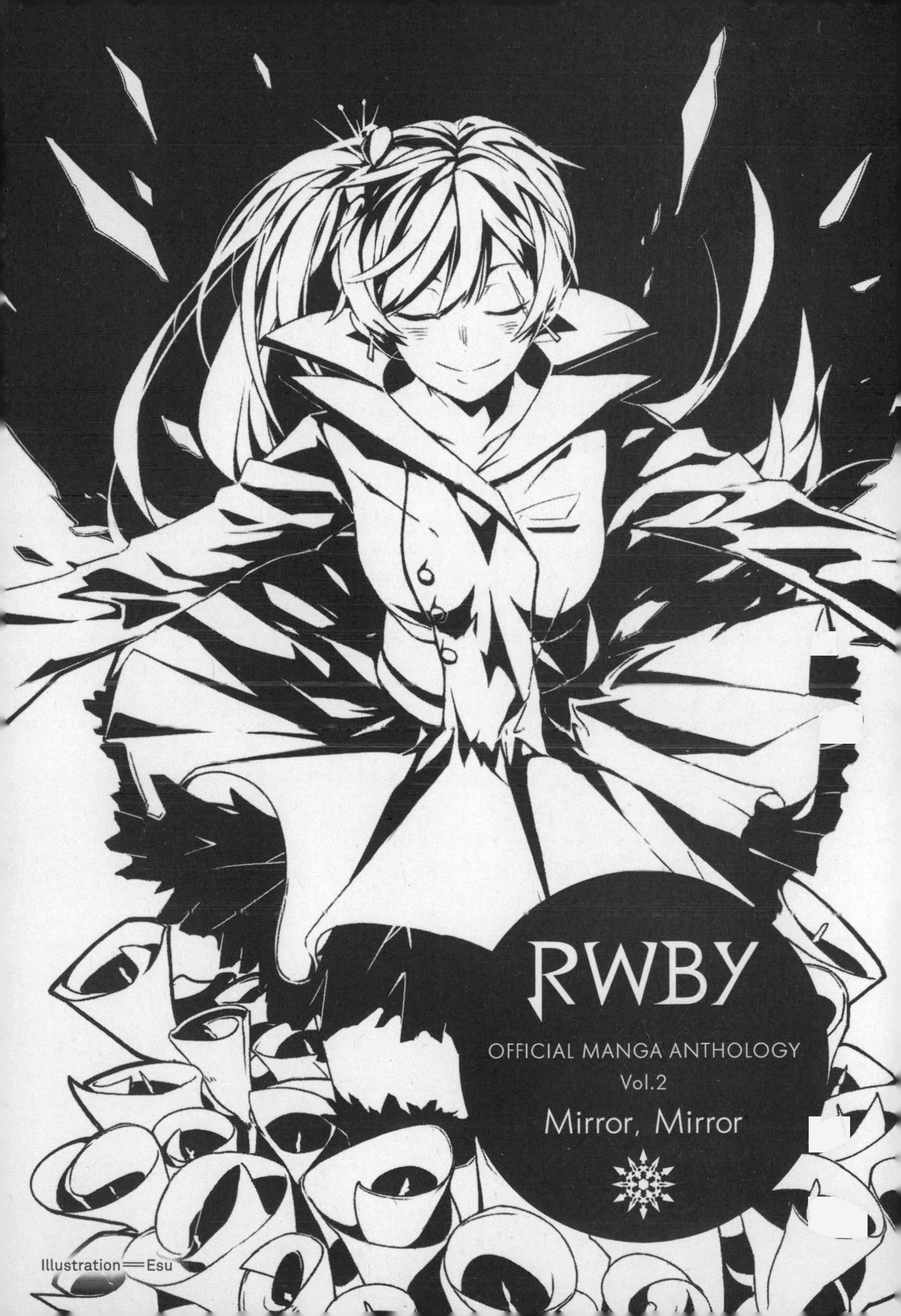
RWBY
OFFICIAL MANGA ANTHOLOGY
Vol.2
Mirror, Mirror
Illustration══Esu

RWBY

OFFICIAL MANGA ANTHOLOGY 2

Mirror, Mirror

CONTENTS

ILLUSTRATIONS

MANGA

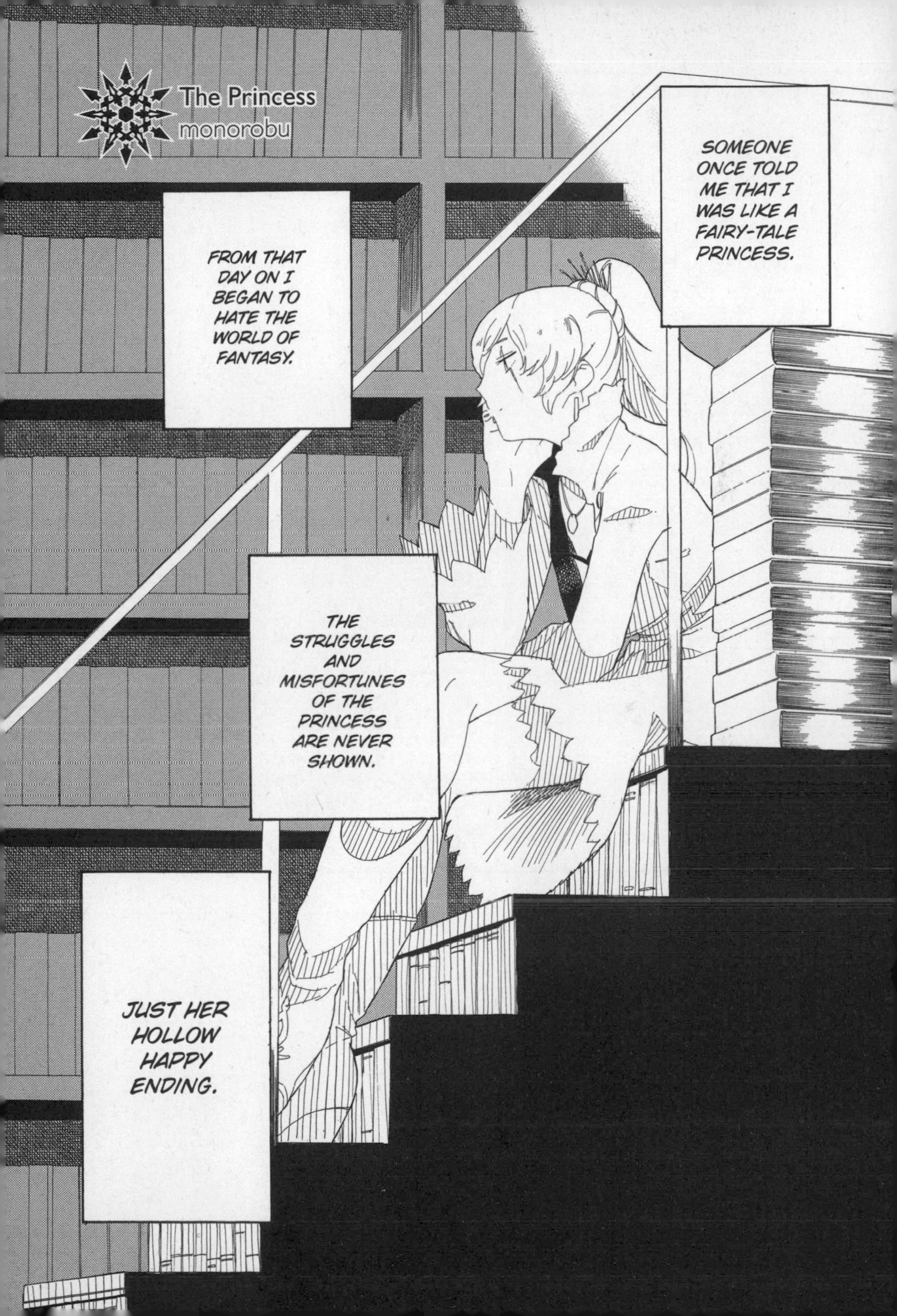
The Princess
monorobu
SOMEONE ONCE TOLD ME THAT I WAS LIKE A FAIRY-TALE PRINCESS.
FROM THAT DAY ON I BEGAN TO HATE THE WORLD OF FANTASY.
THE STRUGGLES AND MISFORTUNES OF THE PRINCESS ARE NEVER SHOWN.
JUST HER HOLLOW HAPPY ENDING.

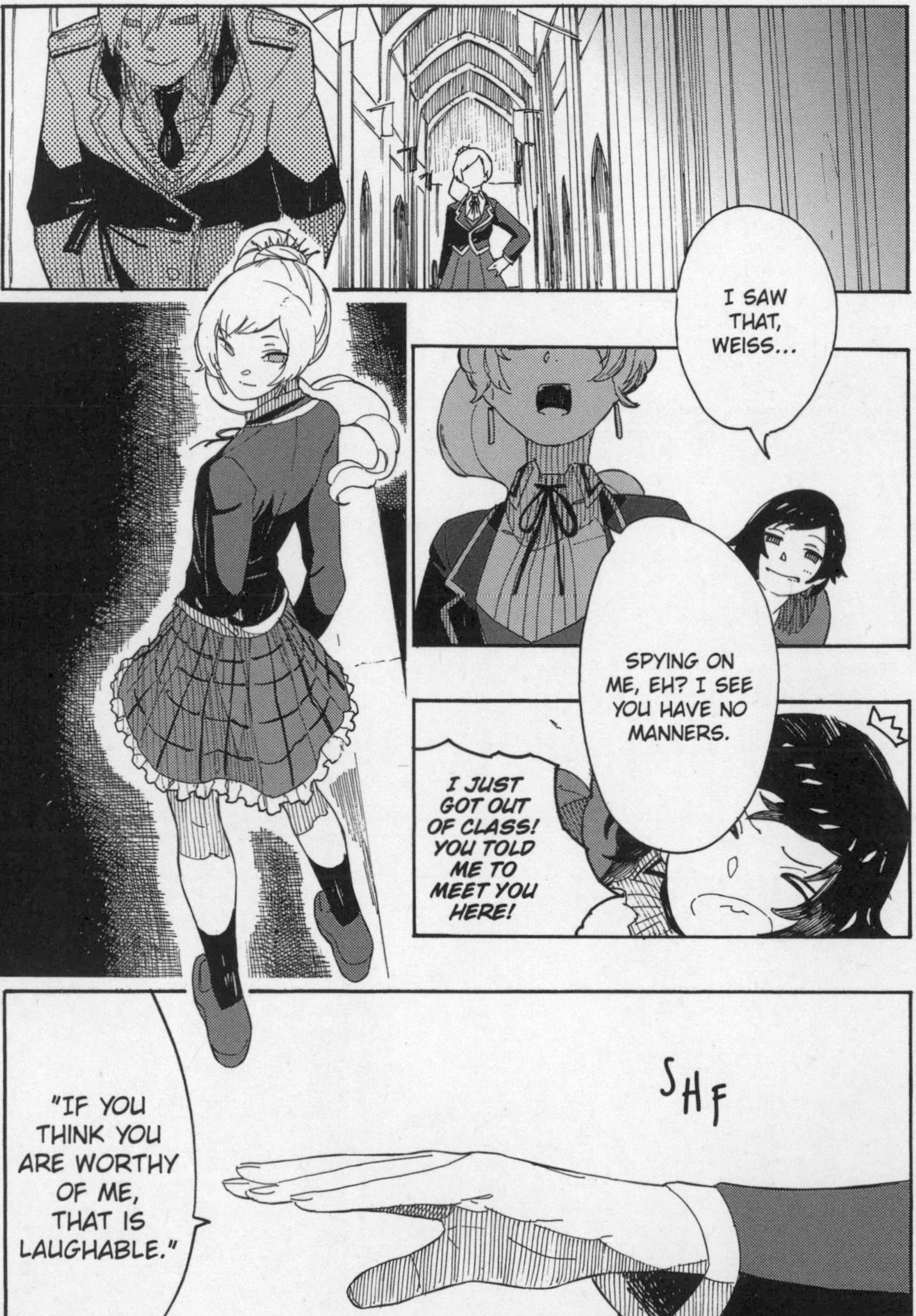
I SAW THAT, WEISS...
SPYING ON ME, EH? I SEE YOU HAVE NO MANNERS.
I JUST GOT OUT OF CLASS! YOU TOLD ME TO MEET YOU HERE!
SHF
"IF YOU THINK YOU ARE WORTHY OF ME, THAT IS LAUGHABLE."

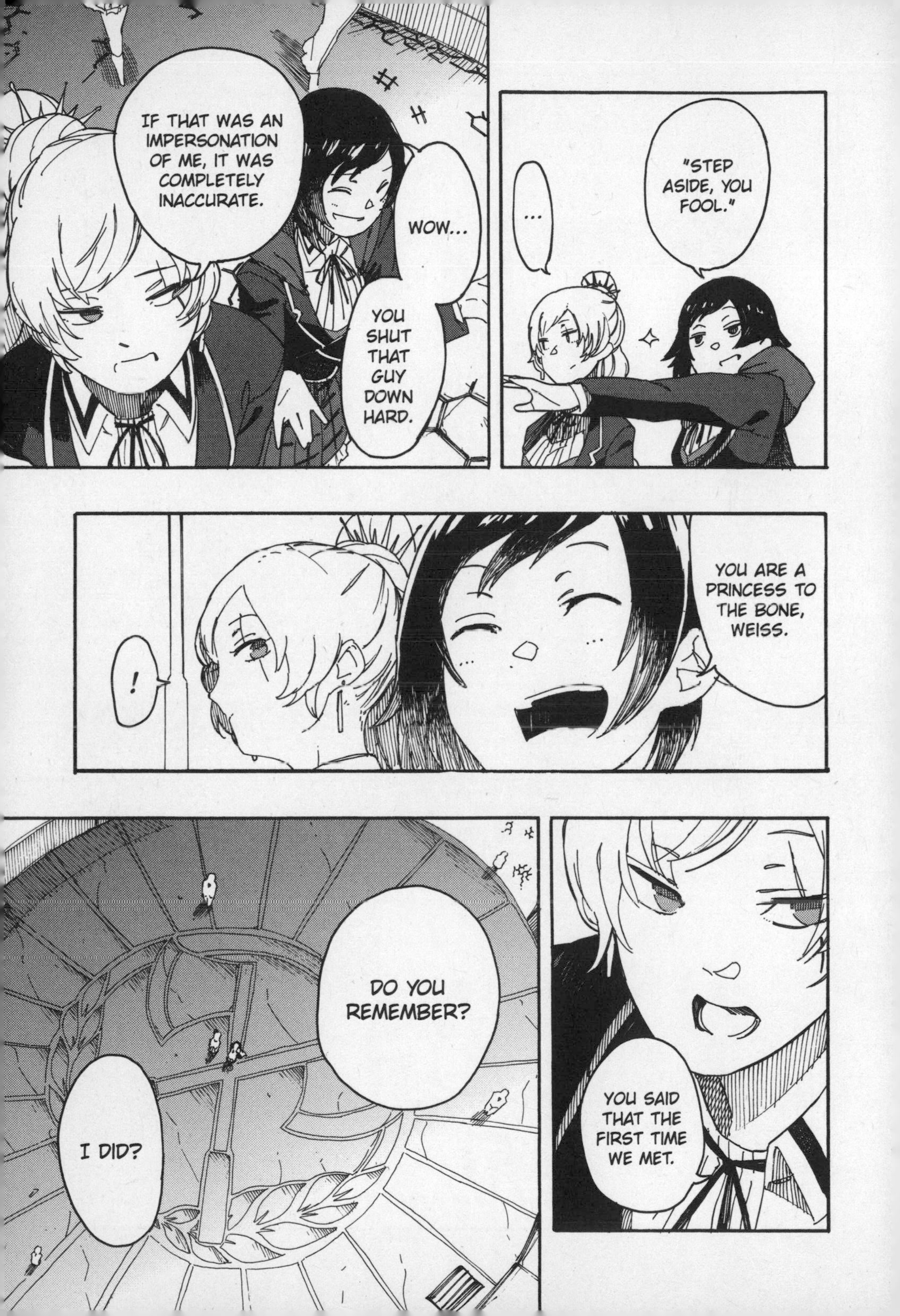
"STEP ASIDE, YOU FOOL."
...
WOW...
YOU SHUT THAT GUY DOWN HARD.
IF THAT WAS AN IMPERSONATION OF ME, IT WAS COMPLETELY INACCURATE.
YOU ARE A PRINCESS TO THE BONE, WEISS.
!
YOU SAID THAT THE FIRST TIME WE MET.
DO YOU REMEMBER?
I DID?

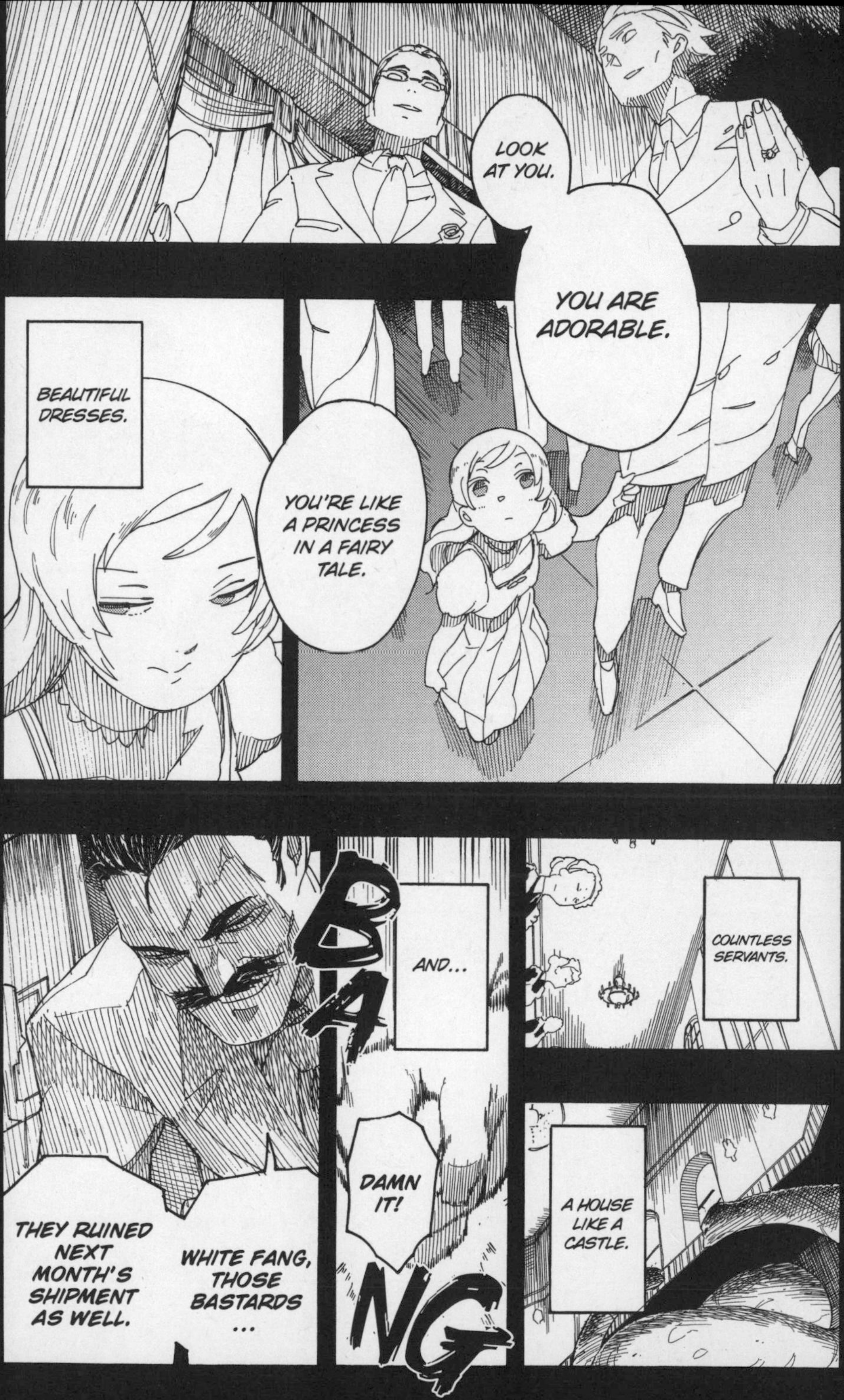
LOOK AT YOU.
YOU ARE ADORABLE.
YOU'RE LIKE A PRINCESS IN A FAIRY TALE.
BEAUTIFUL DRESSES.
COUNTLESS SERVANTS.
A HOUSE LIKE A CASTLE.
AND...
DAMN IT!
BANG
WHITE FANG, THOSE BASTARDS ...
THEY RUINED NEXT MONTH'S SHIPMENT AS WELL.

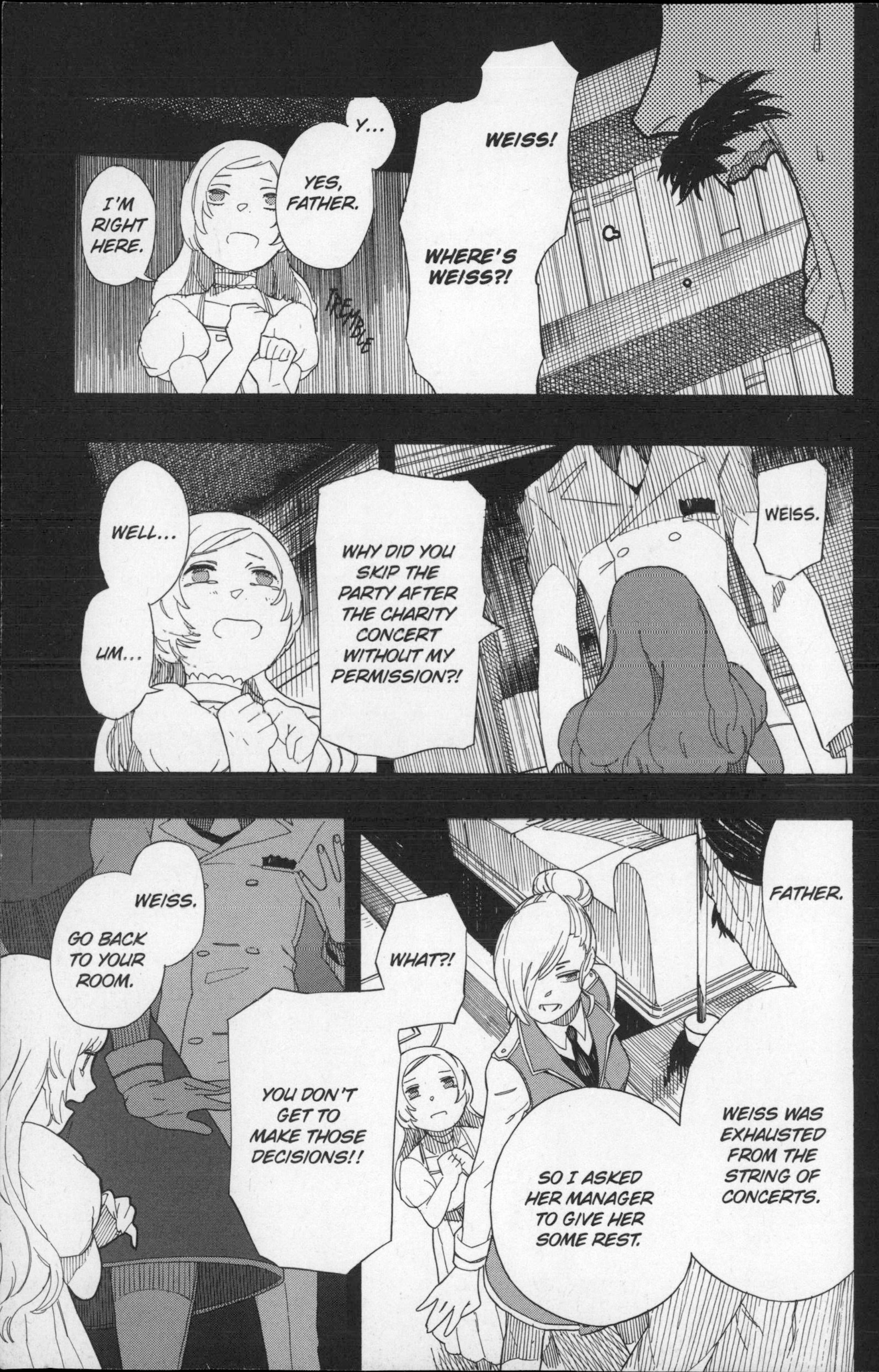
WEISS!
WHERE'S WEISS?!
Y...
YES, FATHER.
I'M RIGHT HERE.
TREMBLE
WEISS.
WHY DID YOU SKIP THE PARTY AFTER THE CHARITY CONCERT WITHOUT MY PERMISSION?!
WELL...
UM...
FATHER.
WEISS WAS EXHAUSTED FROM THE STRING OF CONCERTS.
SO I ASKED HER MANAGER TO GIVE HER SOME REST.
WHAT?!
YOU DON'T GET TO MAKE THOSE DECISIONS!!
WEISS.
GO BACK TO YOUR ROOM.

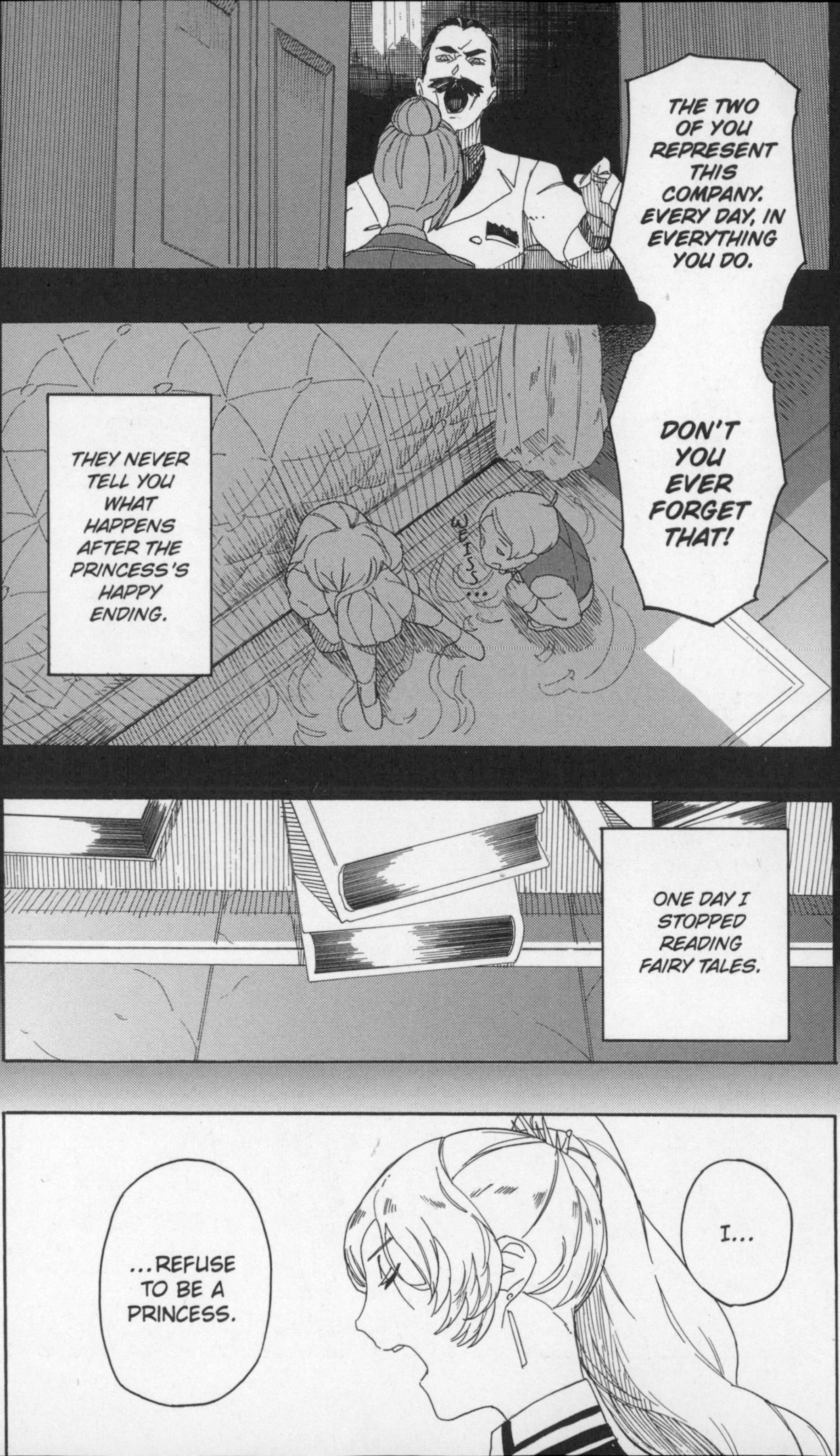
THE TWO OF YOU REPRESENT THIS COMPANY. EVERY DAY, IN EVERYTHING YOU DO.
DON'T YOU EVER FORGET THAT!
THEY NEVER TELL YOU WHAT HAPPENS AFTER THE PRINCESS'S HAPPY ENDING.
WEISS...
ONE DAY I STOPPED READING FAIRY TALES.
I...
...REFUSE TO BE A PRINCESS.

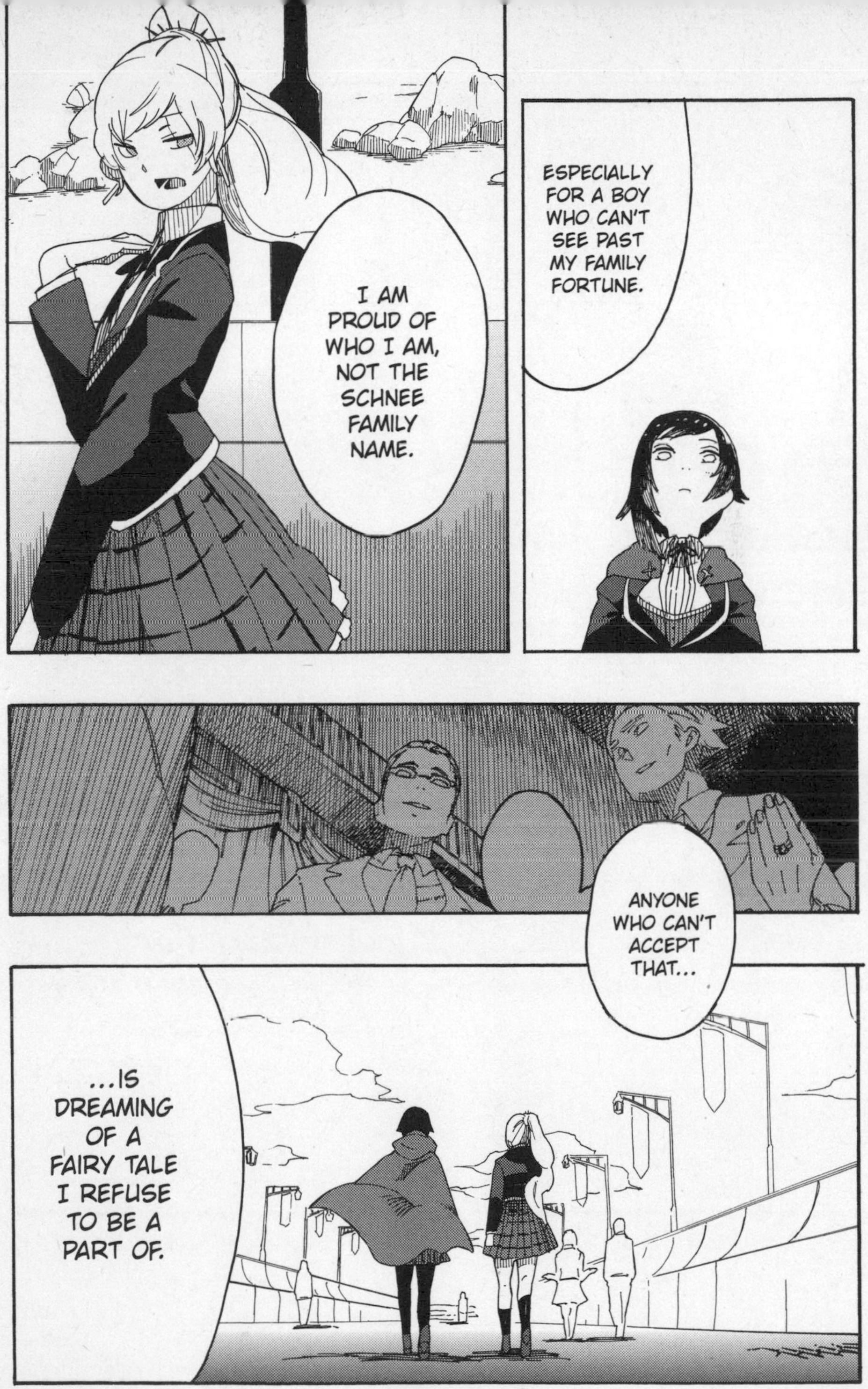
ESPECIALLY FOR A BOY WHO CAN'T SEE PAST MY FAMILY FORTUNE.
I AM PROUD OF WHO I AM, NOT THE SCHNEE FAMILY NAME.
ANYONE WHO CAN'T ACCEPT THAT...
...IS DREAMING OF A FAIRY TALE I REFUSE TO BE A PART OF.

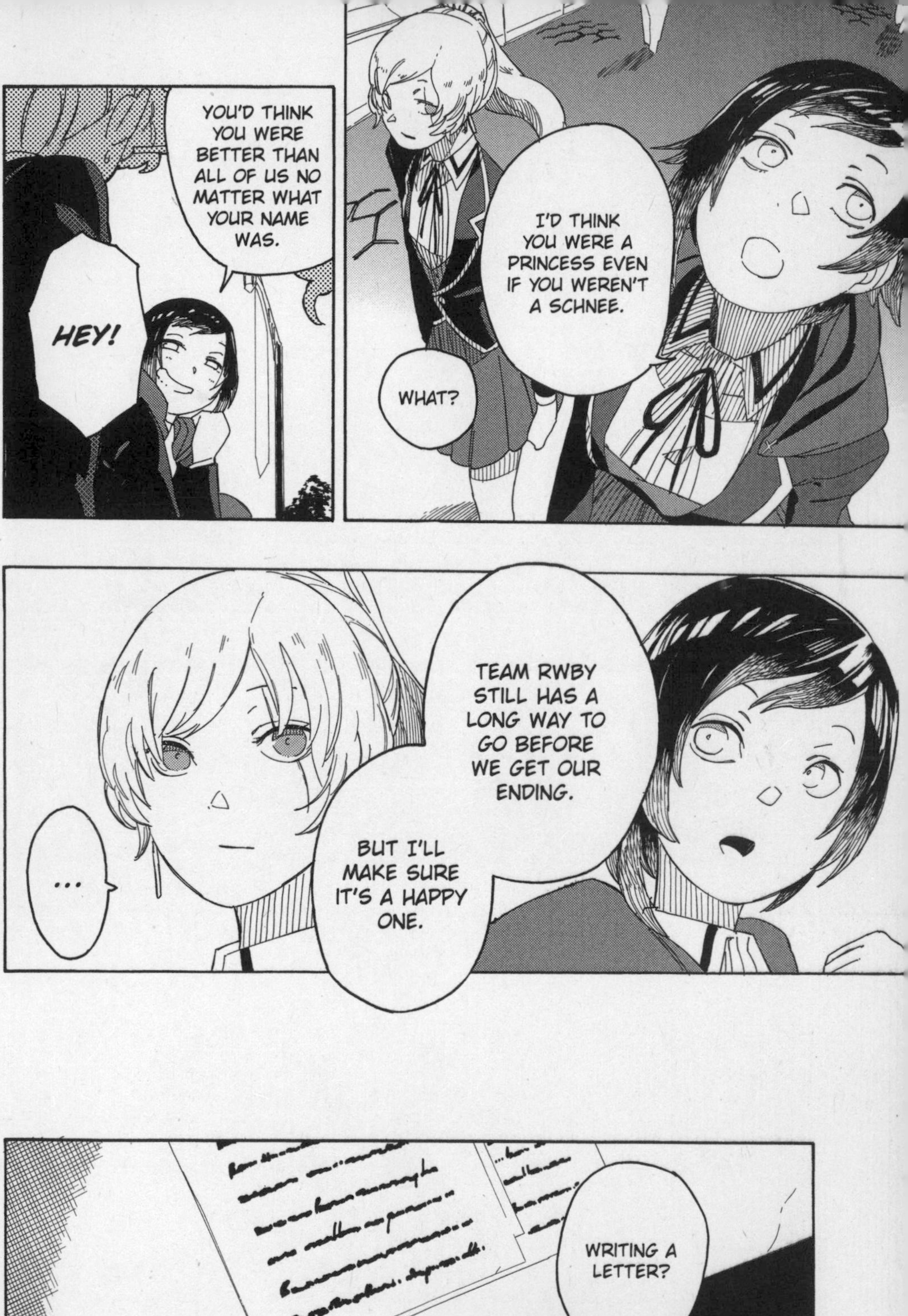
I'D THINK YOU WERE A PRINCESS EVEN IF YOU WEREN'T A SCHNEE.
WHAT?
YOU'D THINK YOU WERE BETTER THAN ALL OF US NO MATTER WHAT YOUR NAME WAS.
HEY!
TEAM RWBY STILL HAS A LONG WAY TO GO BEFORE WE GET OUR ENDING.
BUT I'LL MAKE SURE IT'S A HAPPY ONE.
...
WRITING A LETTER?

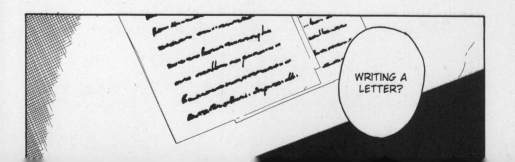

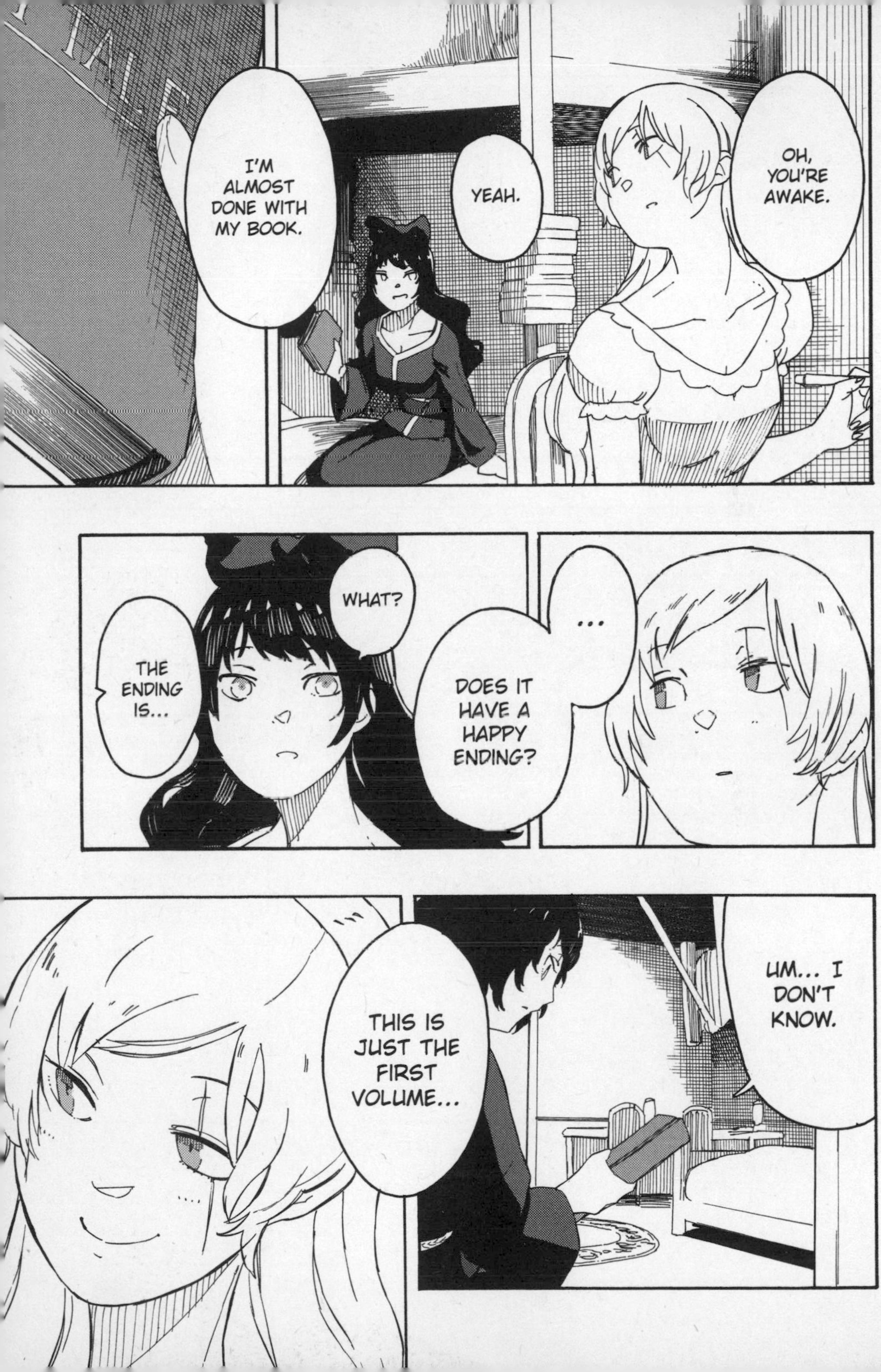
OH, YOU'RE AWAKE.
YEAH.
I'M ALMOST DONE WITH MY BOOK.
...
DOES IT HAVE A HAPPY ENDING?
WHAT?
THE ENDING IS...
UM... I DON'T KNOW.
THIS IS JUST THE FIRST VOLUME...

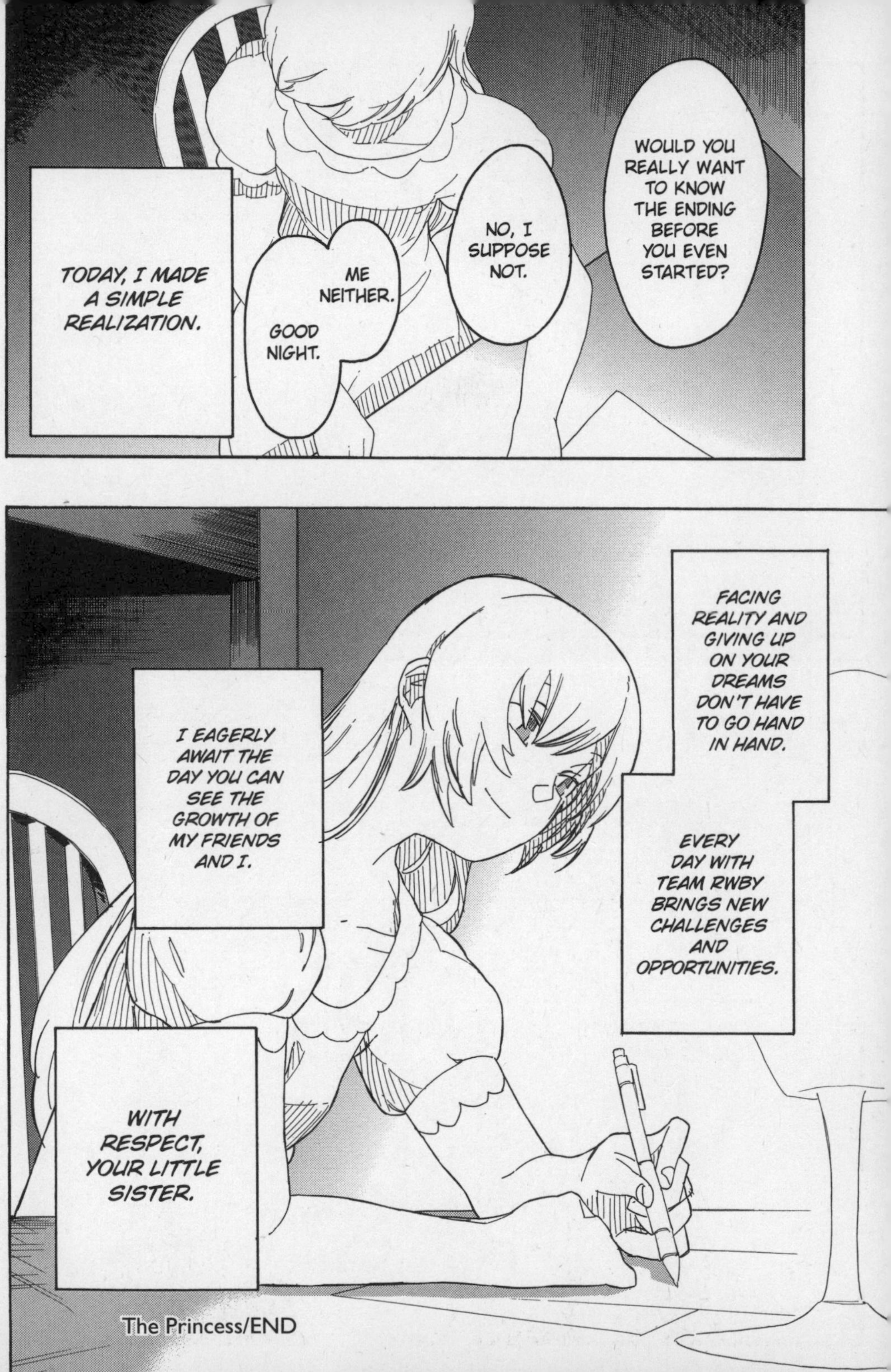
WOULD YOU REALLY WANT TO KNOW THE ENDING BEFORE YOU EVEN STARTED?
NO, I SUPPOSE NOT.
ME NEITHER.
GOOD NIGHT.
TODAY, I MADE A SIMPLE REALIZATION.
FACING REALITY AND GIVING UP ON YOUR DREAMS DON'T HAVE TO GO HAND IN HAND.
EVERY DAY WITH TEAM RWBY BRINGS NEW CHALLENGES AND OPPORTUNITIES.
I EAGERLY AWAIT THE DAY YOU CAN SEE THE GROWTH OF MY FRIENDS AND I.
WITH RESPECT, YOUR LITTLE SISTER.
The Princess/END

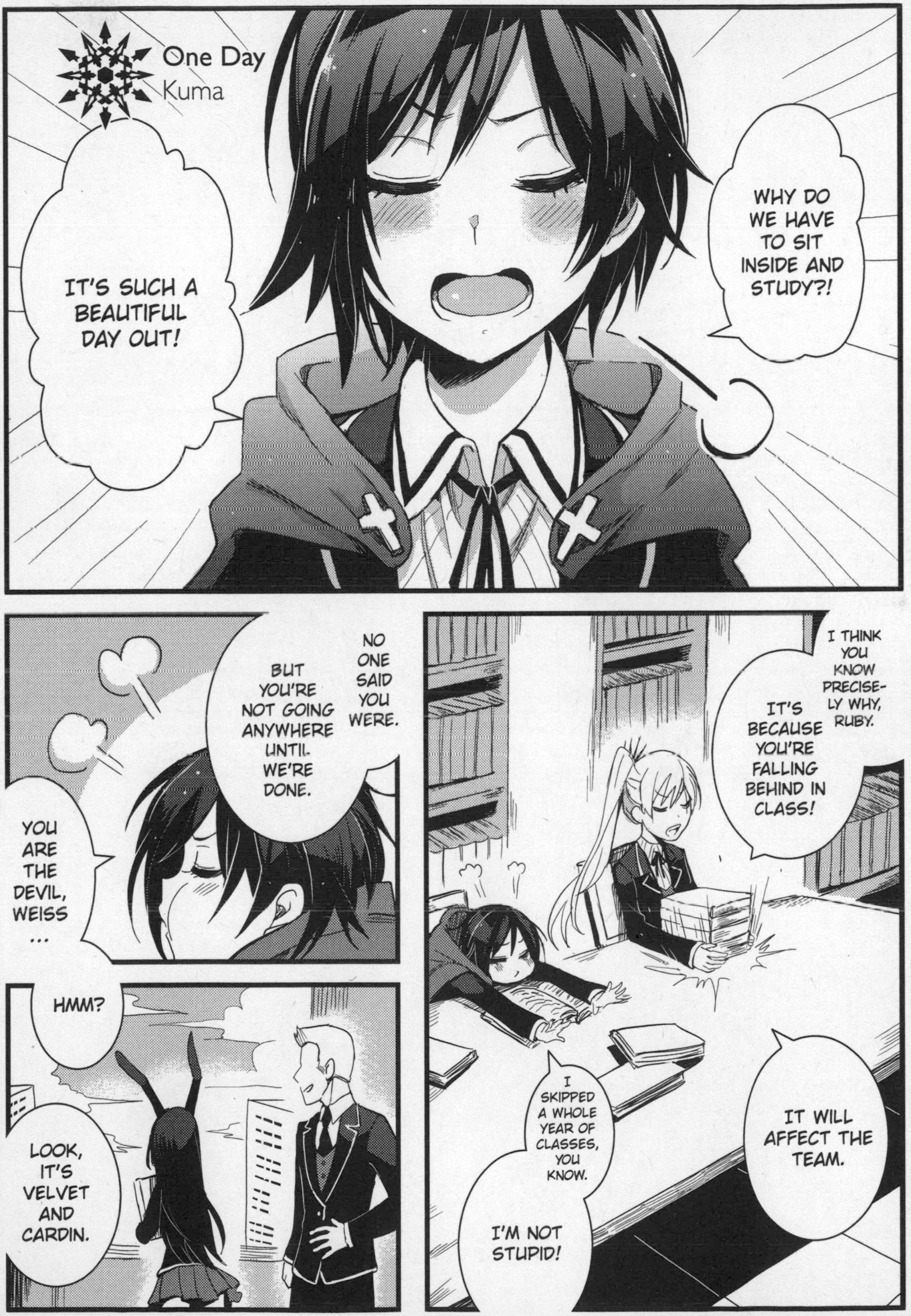
One Day
Kuma
WHY DO WE HAVE TO SIT INSIDE AND STUDY?!
IT'S SUCH A BEAUTIFUL DAY OUT!
I THINK YOU KNOW PRECISE-LY WHY, RUBY.
IT'S BECAUSE YOU'RE FALLING BEHIND IN CLASS!
IT WILL AFFECT THE TEAM.
I SKIPPED A WHOLE YEAR OF CLASSES, YOU KNOW.
I'M NOT STUPID!
NO ONE SAID YOU WERE.
BUT YOU'RE NOT GOING ANYWHERE UNTIL WE'RE DONE.
YOU ARE THE DEVIL, WEISS ...
HMM?
LOOK, IT'S VELVET AND CARDIN.

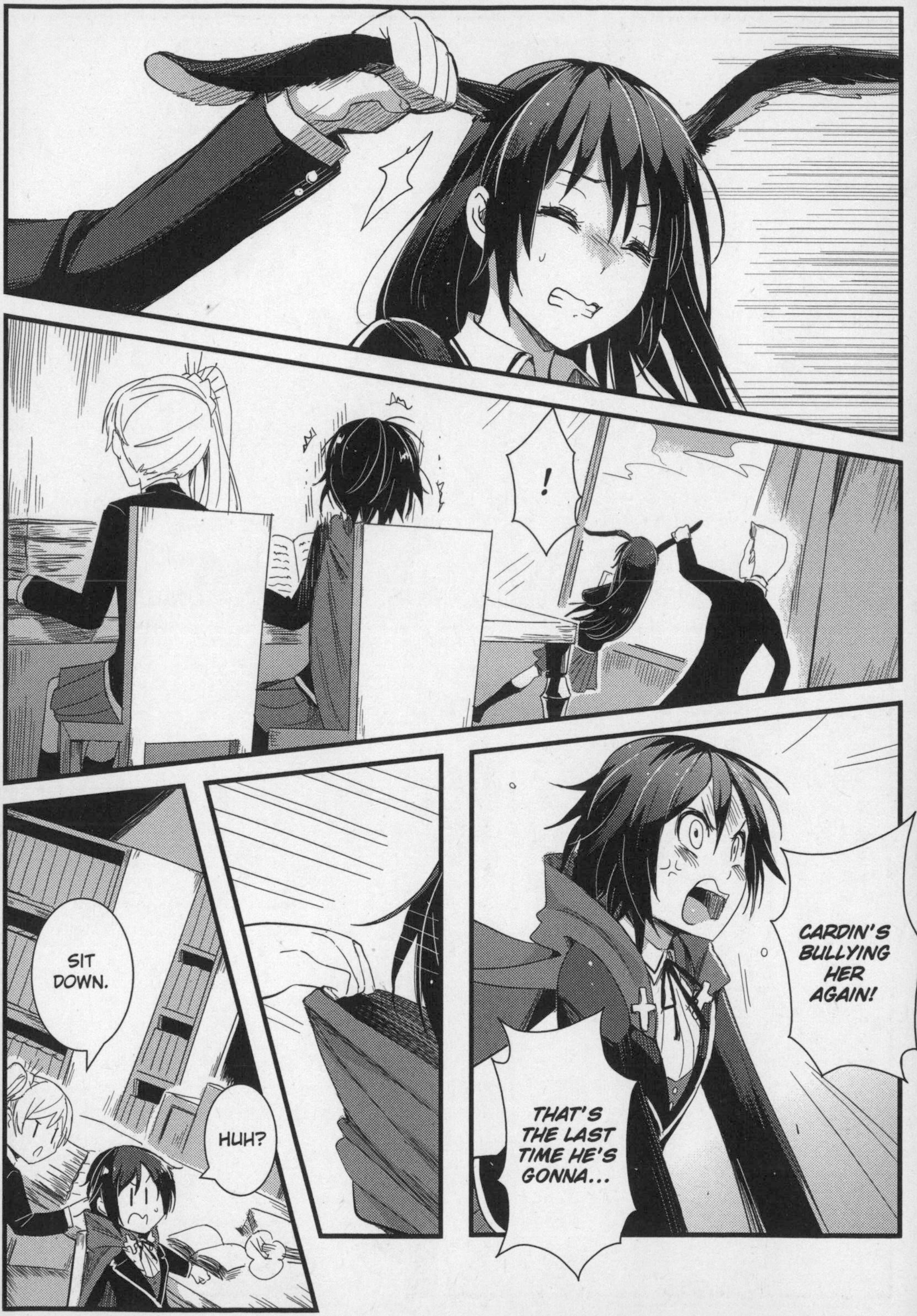
!
CARDIN'S BULLYING HER AGAIN!
THAT'S THE LAST TIME HE'S GONNA...
SIT DOWN.
HUH?

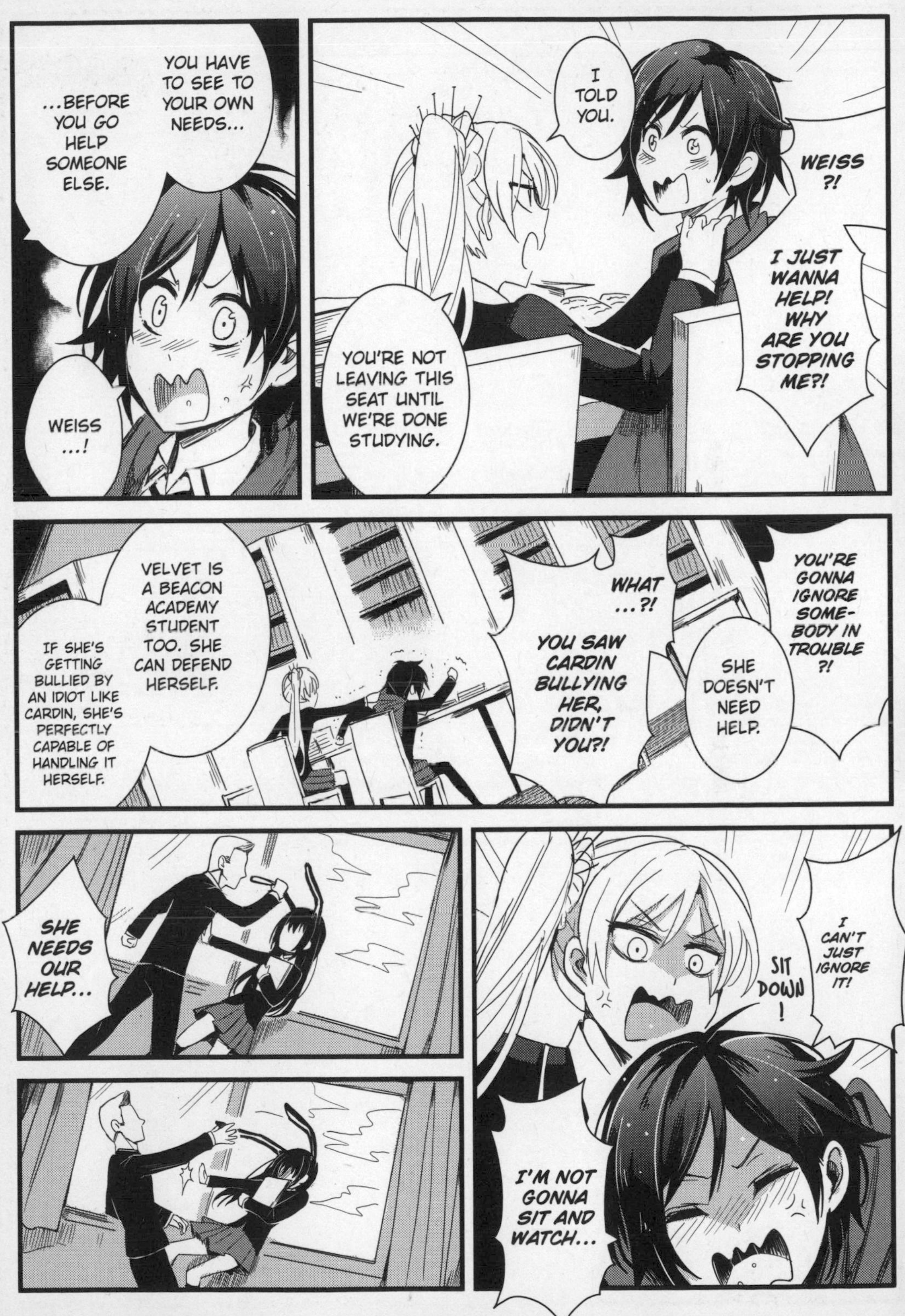
I TOLD YOU.
WEISS ?!
I JUST WANNA HELP! WHY ARE YOU STOPPING ME?!
YOU'RE NOT LEAVING THIS SEAT UNTIL WE'RE DONE STUDYING.
YOU HAVE TO SEE TO YOUR OWN NEEDS...
...BEFORE YOU GO HELP SOMEONE ELSE.
WEISS ...!
YOU'RE GONNA IGNORE SOME-BODY IN TROUBLE ?!
WHAT ...?!
SHE DOESN'T NEED HELP.
YOU SAW CARDIN BULLYING HER, DIDN'T YOU?!
VELVET IS A BEACON ACADEMY STUDENT TOO. SHE CAN DEFEND HERSELF.
IF SHE'S GETTING BULLIED BY AN IDIOT LIKE CARDIN, SHE'S PERFECTLY CAPABLE OF HANDLING IT HERSELF.
I CAN'T JUST IGNORE IT!
SIT DOWN !
I'M NOT GONNA SIT AND WATCH...
SHE NEEDS OUR HELP...

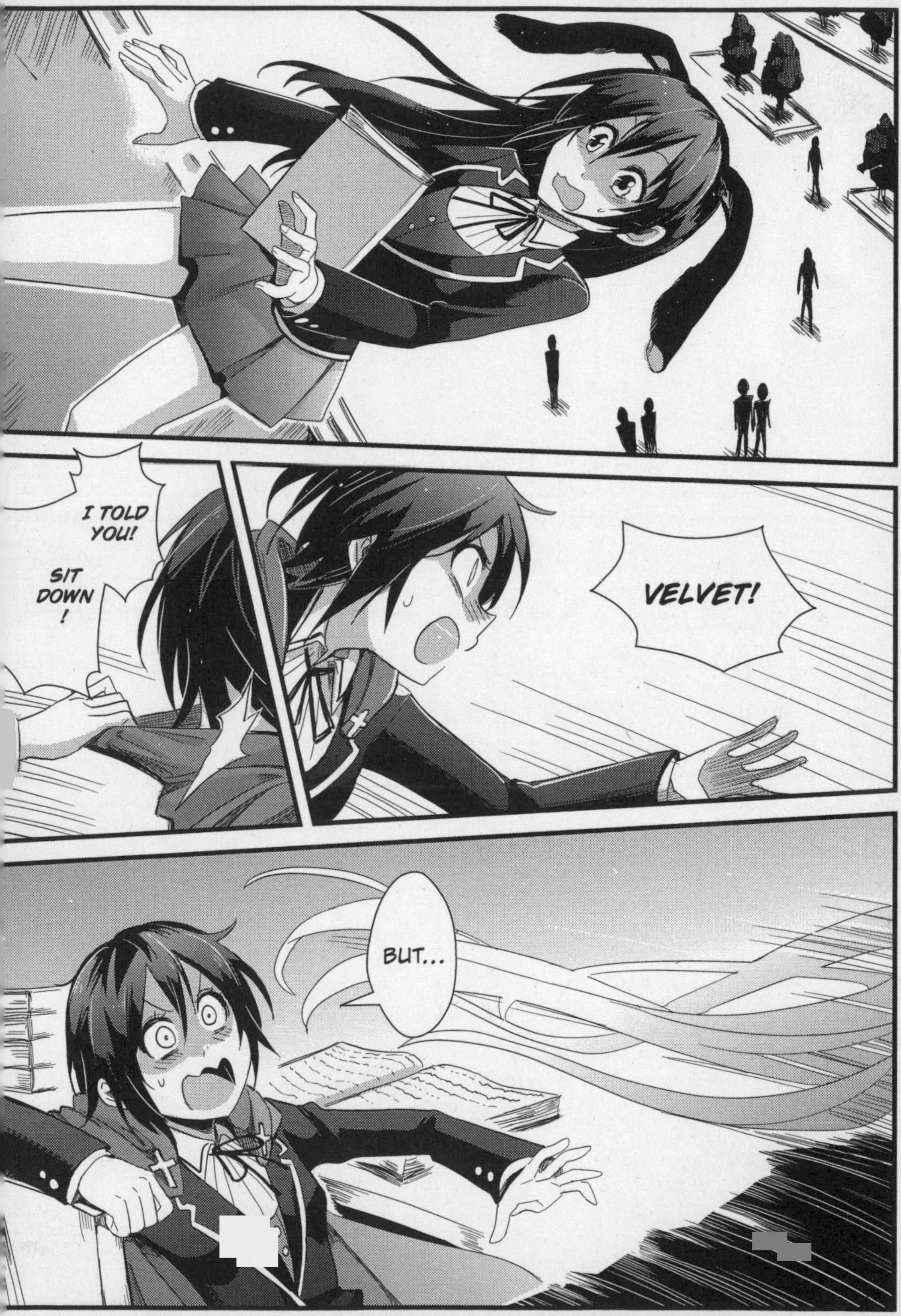
VELVET!
I TOLD YOU! SIT DOWN!
BUT...

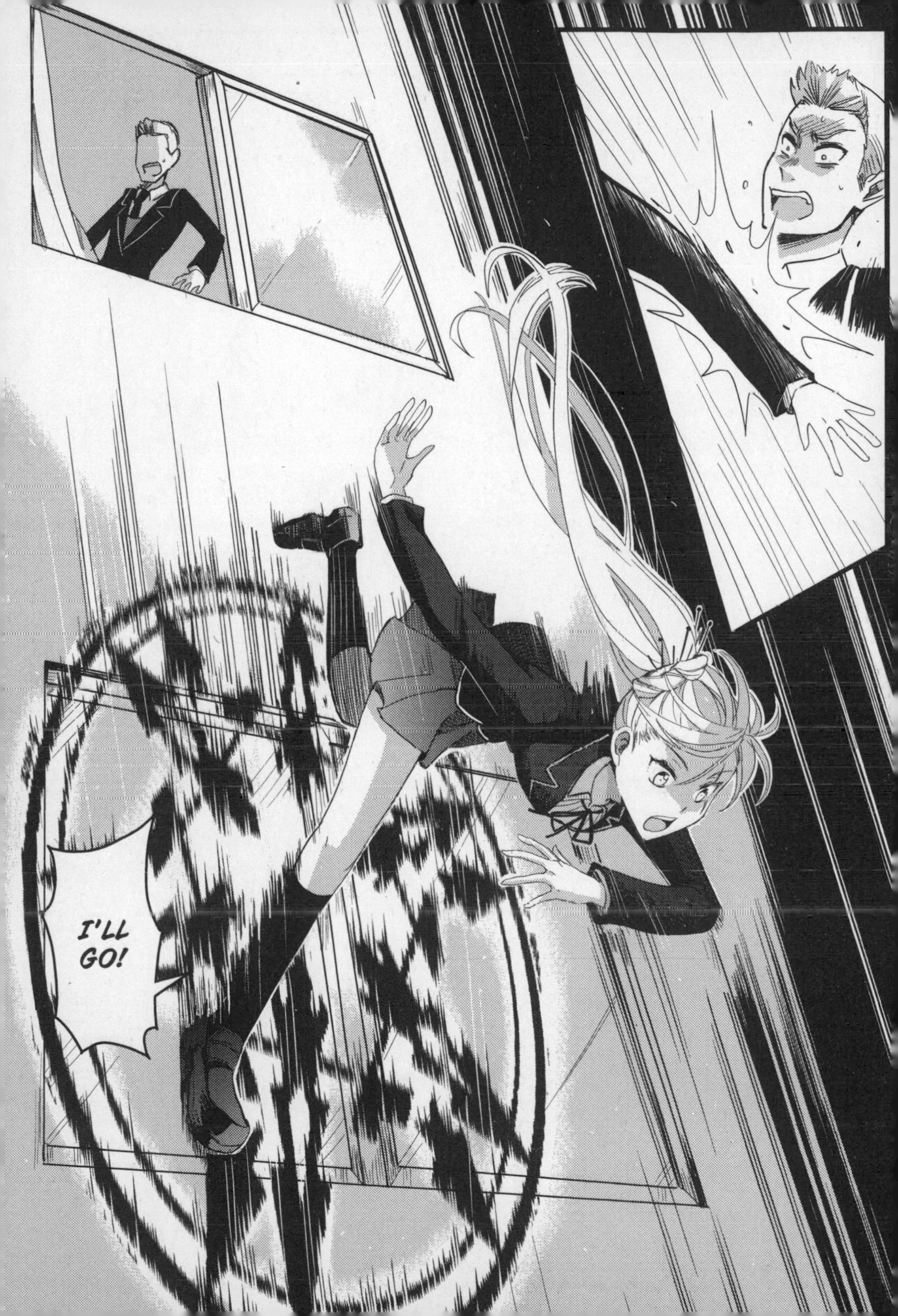
I'LL GO!

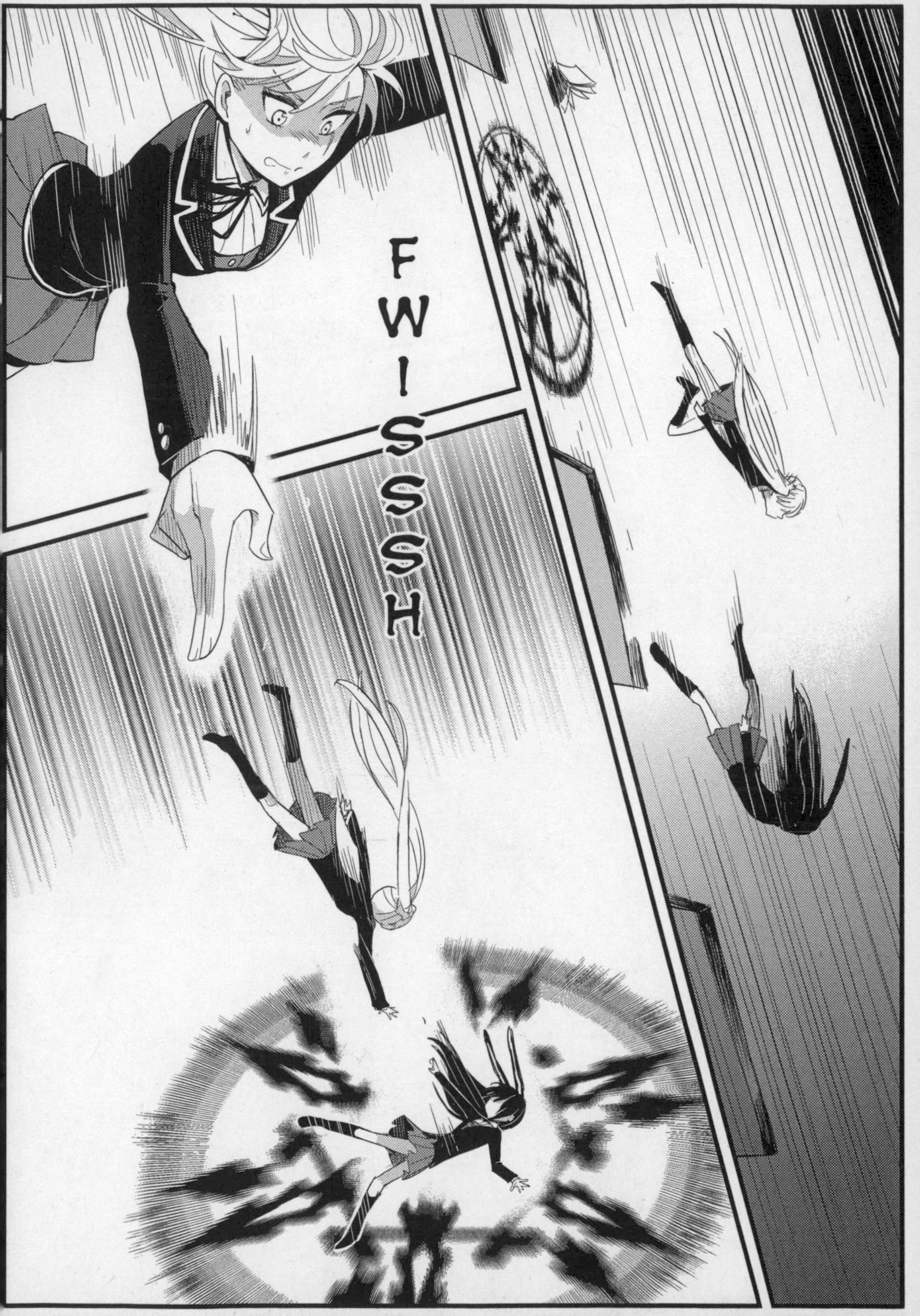
FWISSSH

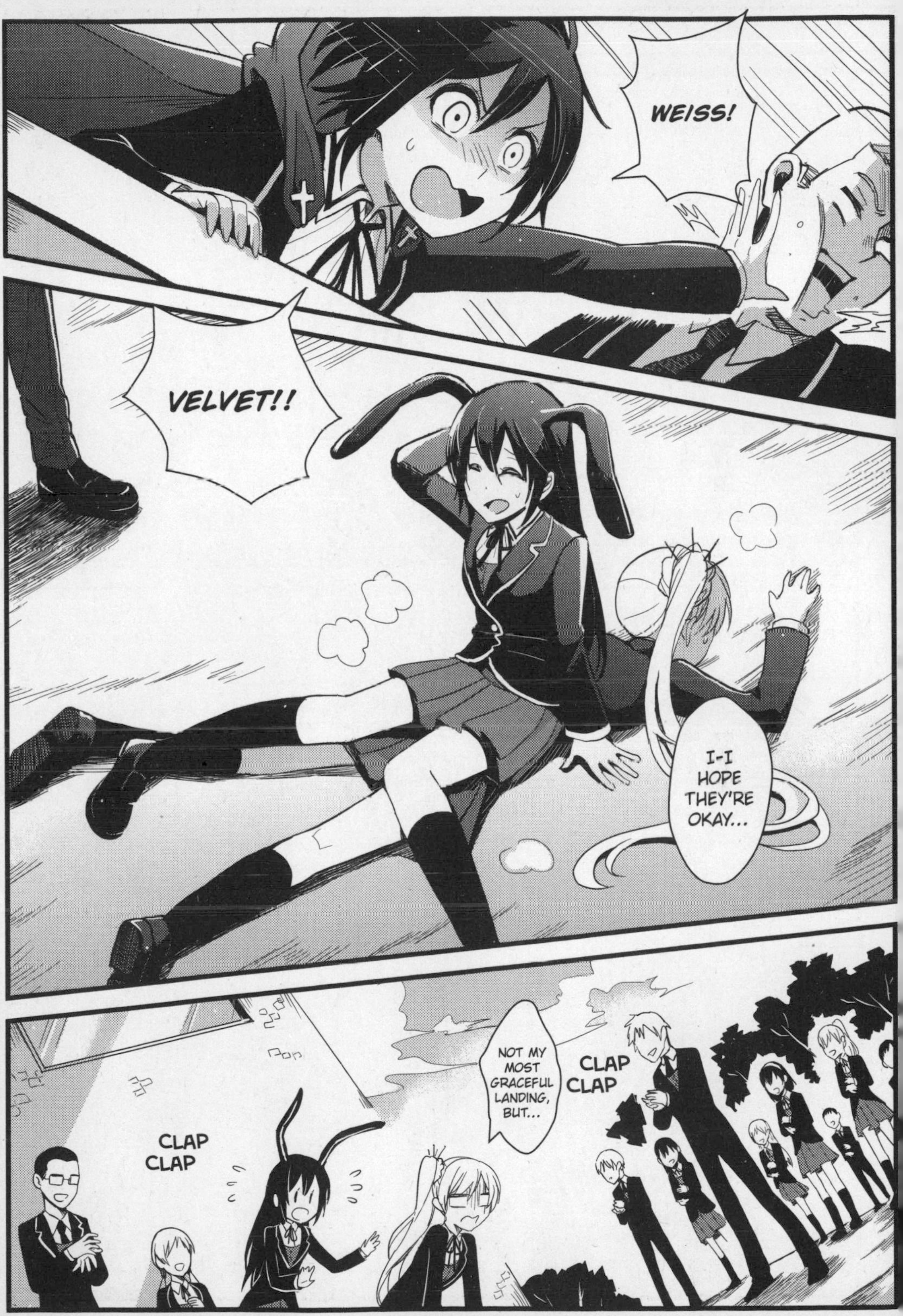
WEISS!
VELVET!!
I-I HOPE THEY'RE OKAY...
CLAP CLAP
NOT MY MOST GRACEFUL LANDING, BUT...
CLAP CLAP

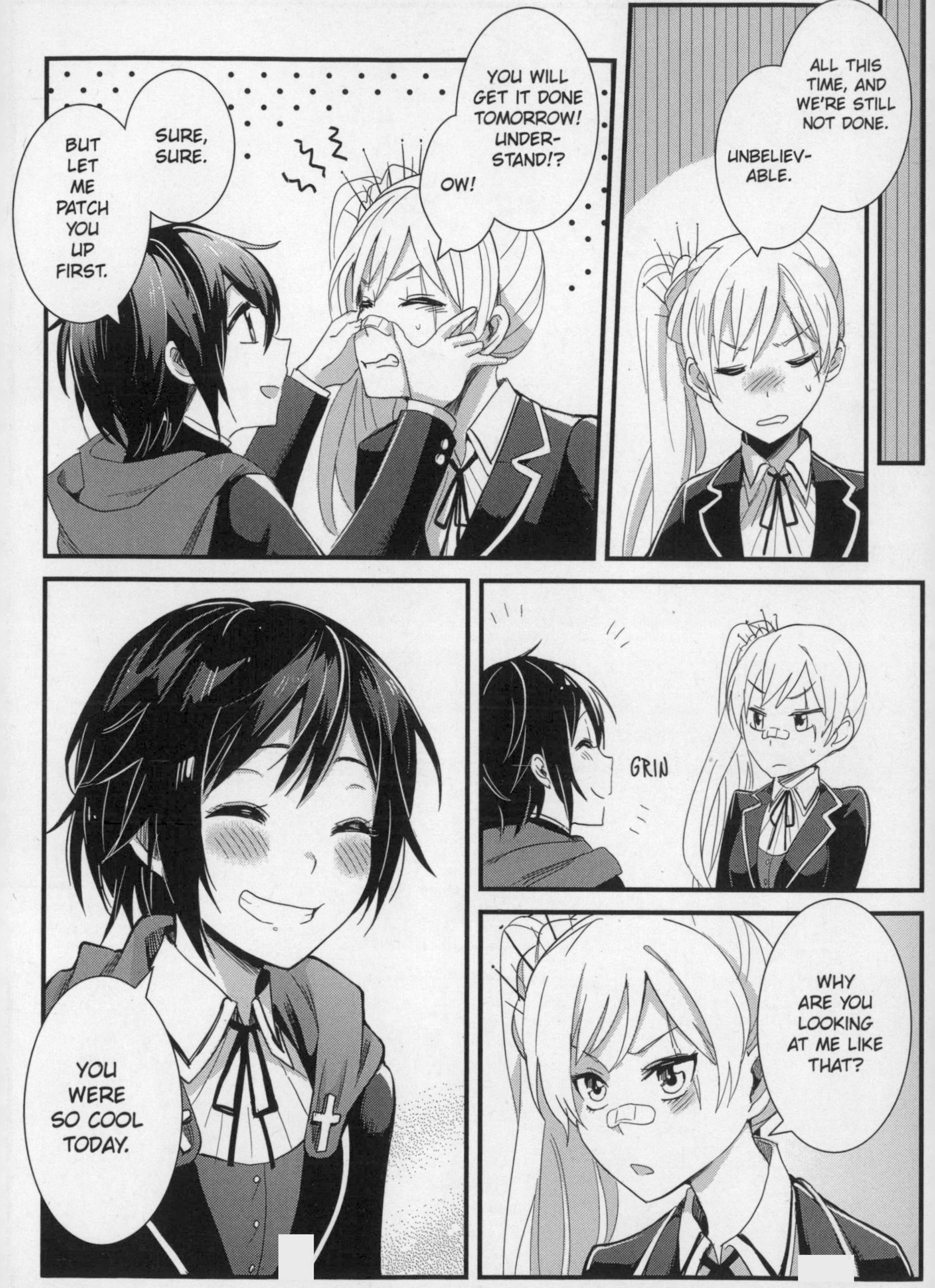
ALL THIS TIME, AND WE'RE STILL NOT DONE.
UNBELIEV-ABLE.
YOU WILL GET IT DONE TOMORROW! UNDER-STAND!?
OW!
SURE, SURE.
BUT LET ME PATCH YOU UP FIRST.
GRIN
WHY ARE YOU LOOKING AT ME LIKE THAT?
YOU WERE SO COOL TODAY.

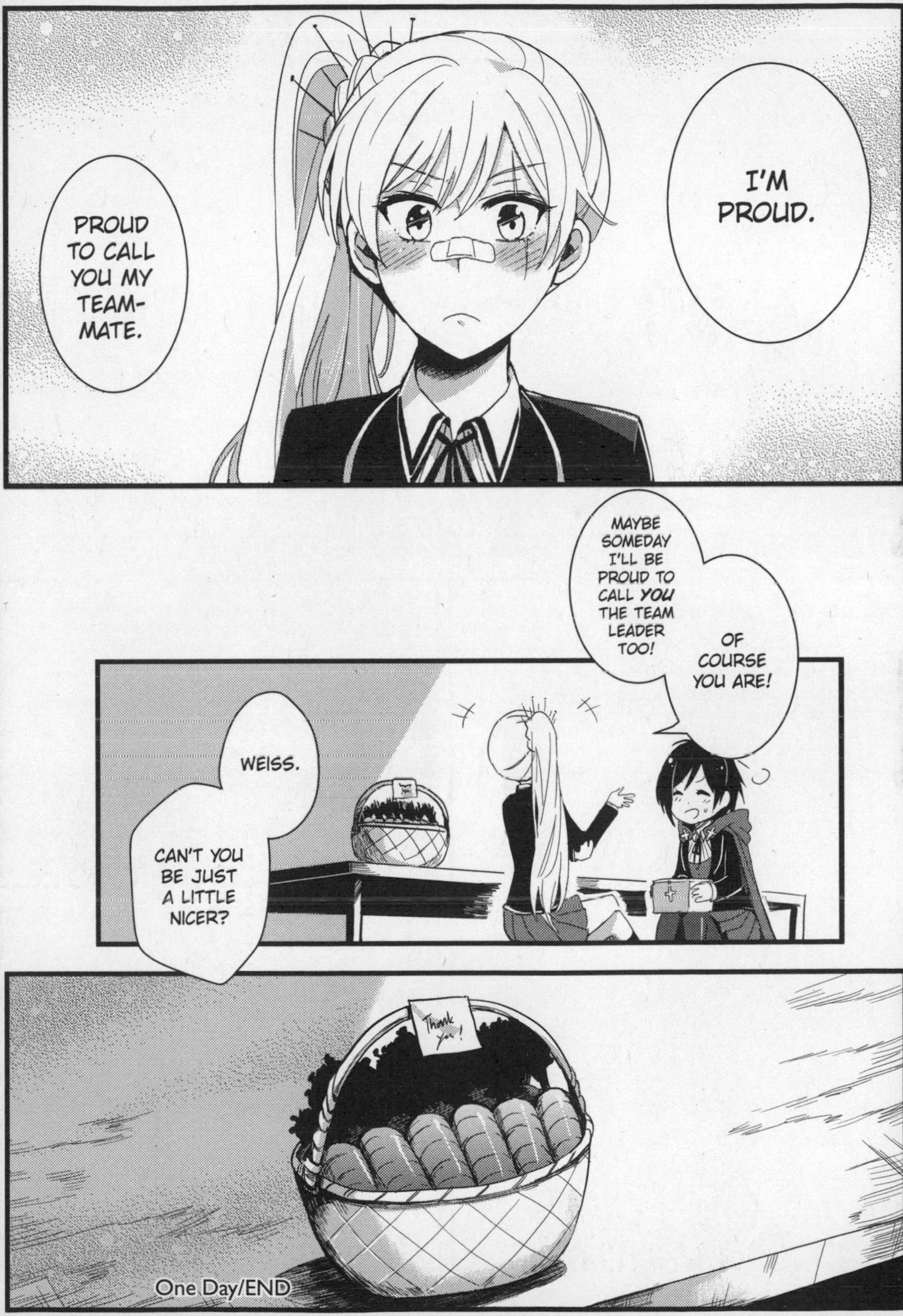
I'M PROUD.
PROUD TO CALL YOU MY TEAM-MATE.
MAYBE SOMEDAY I'LL BE PROUD TO CALL ***YOU*** THE TEAM LEADER TOO!
OF COURSE YOU ARE!
WEISS.
CAN'T YOU BE JUST A LITTLE NICER?
Thank you!
One Day/END

RWBY

OFFICIAL MANGA ANTHOLOGY
VOLUME 2 Mirror, Mirror

The Princess Makes Sweets

Mate

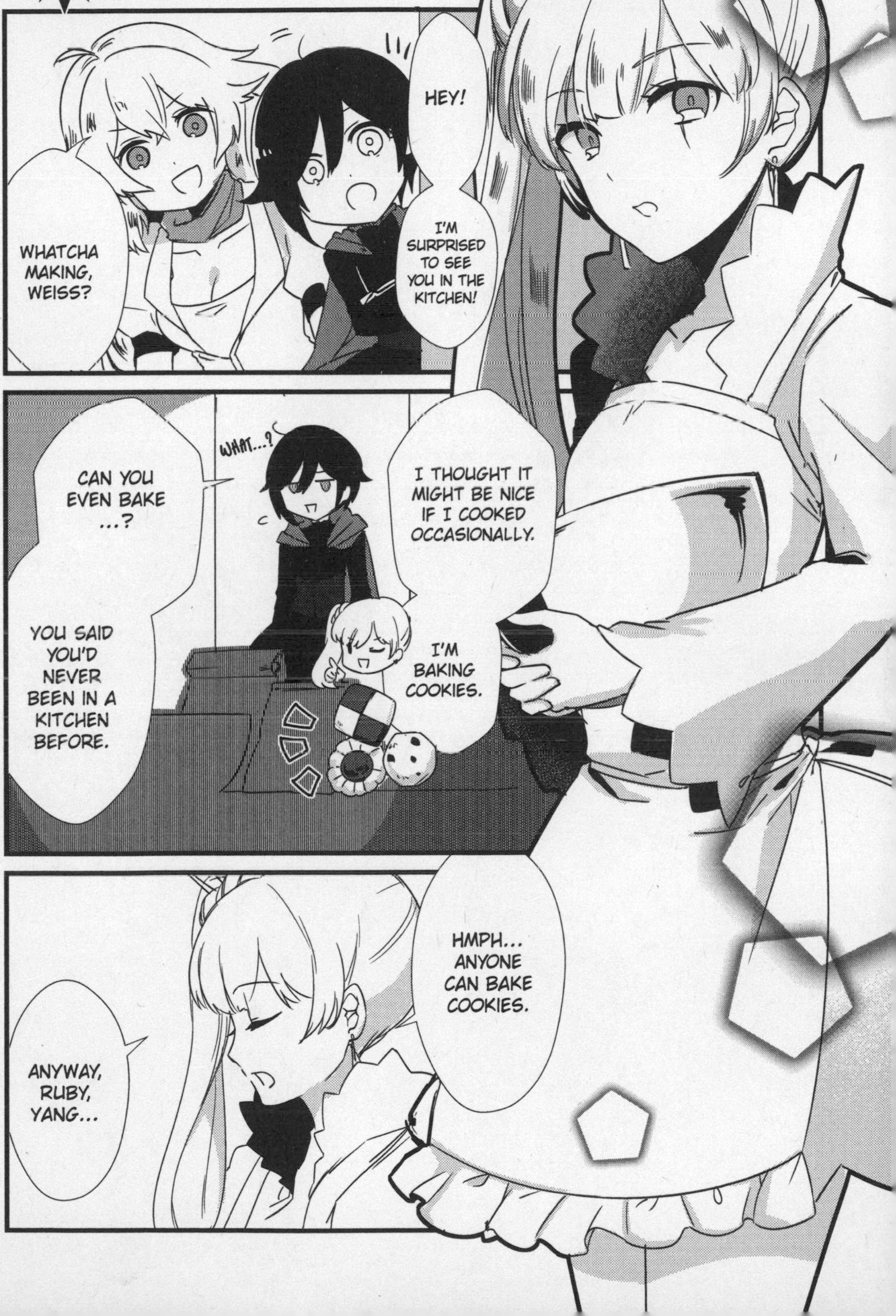
HEY!
I'M SURPRISED TO SEE YOU IN THE KITCHEN!
WHATCHA MAKING, WEISS?
I'M BAKING COOKIES.
I THOUGHT IT MIGHT BE NICE IF I COOKED OCCASIONALLY.
WHAT...?
CAN YOU EVEN BAKE ...?
YOU SAID YOU'D NEVER BEEN IN A KITCHEN BEFORE.
HMPH... ANYONE CAN BAKE COOKIES.
ANYWAY, RUBY, YANG...

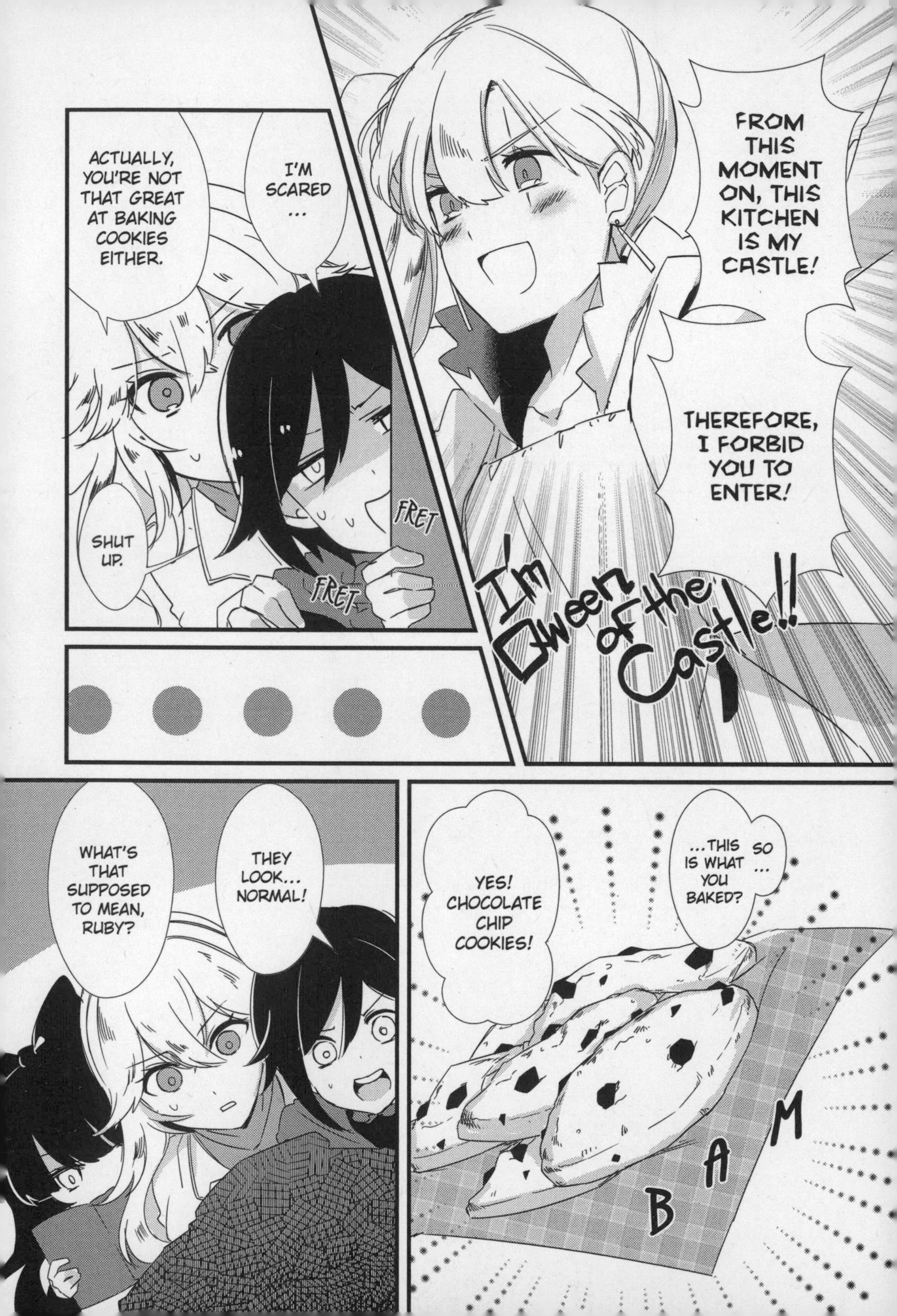
FROM THIS MOMENT ON, THIS KITCHEN IS MY CASTLE!
THEREFORE, I FORBID YOU TO ENTER!
I'm Qween of the Castle!!
I'M SCARED ...
ACTUALLY, YOU'RE NOT THAT GREAT AT BAKING COOKIES EITHER.
FRET
FRET
SHUT UP.
SO ...
...THIS IS WHAT YOU BAKED?
YES! CHOCOLATE CHIP COOKIES!
BAM
THEY LOOK... NORMAL!
WHAT'S THAT SUPPOSED TO MEAN, RUBY?

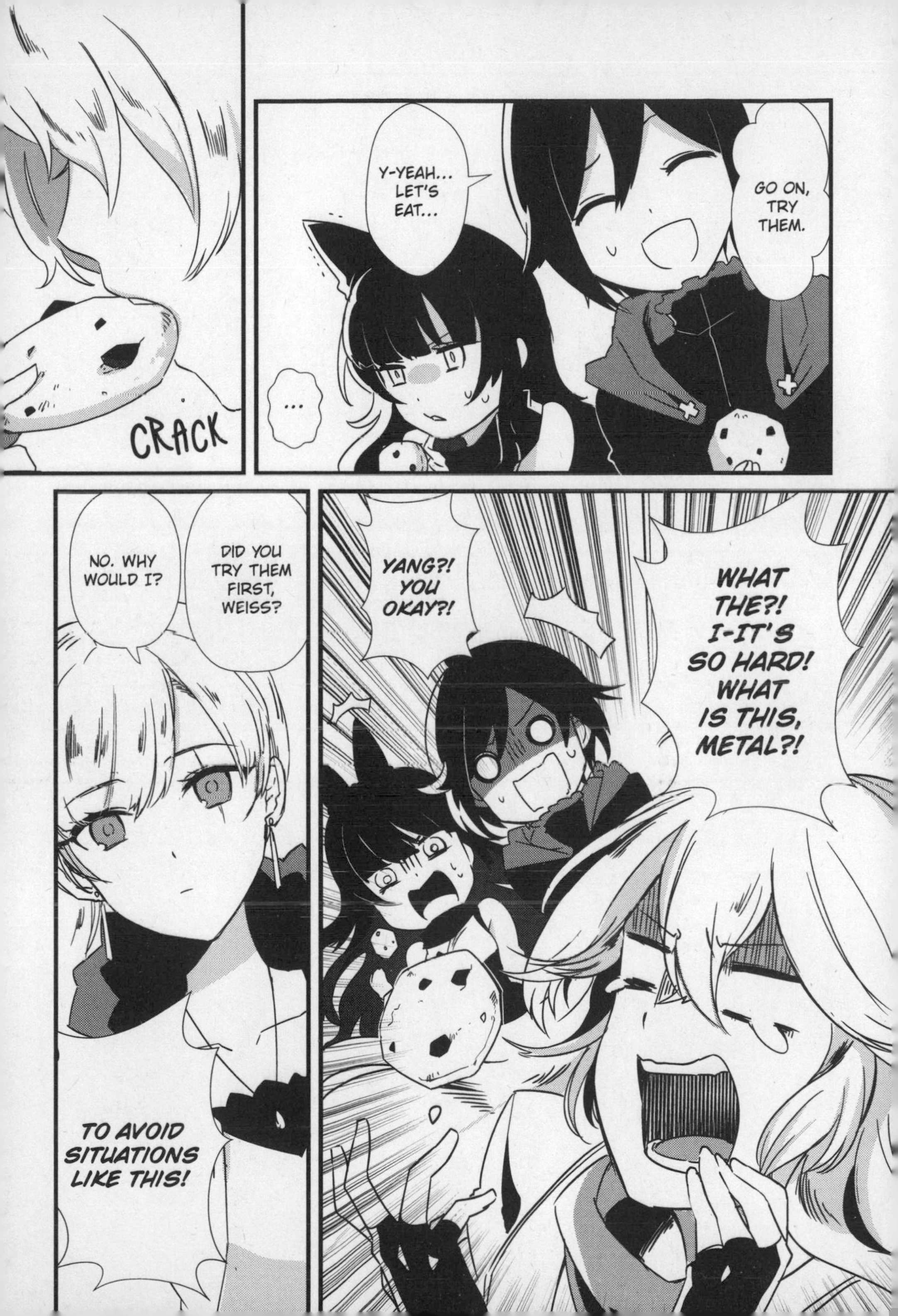
GO ON, TRY THEM.
Y-YEAH... LET'S EAT...
...
CRACK
WHAT THE?! I-IT'S SO HARD! WHAT IS THIS, METAL?!
YANG?! YOU OKAY?!
DID YOU TRY THEM FIRST, WEISS?
NO. WHY WOULD I?
TO AVOID SITUATIONS LIKE THIS!

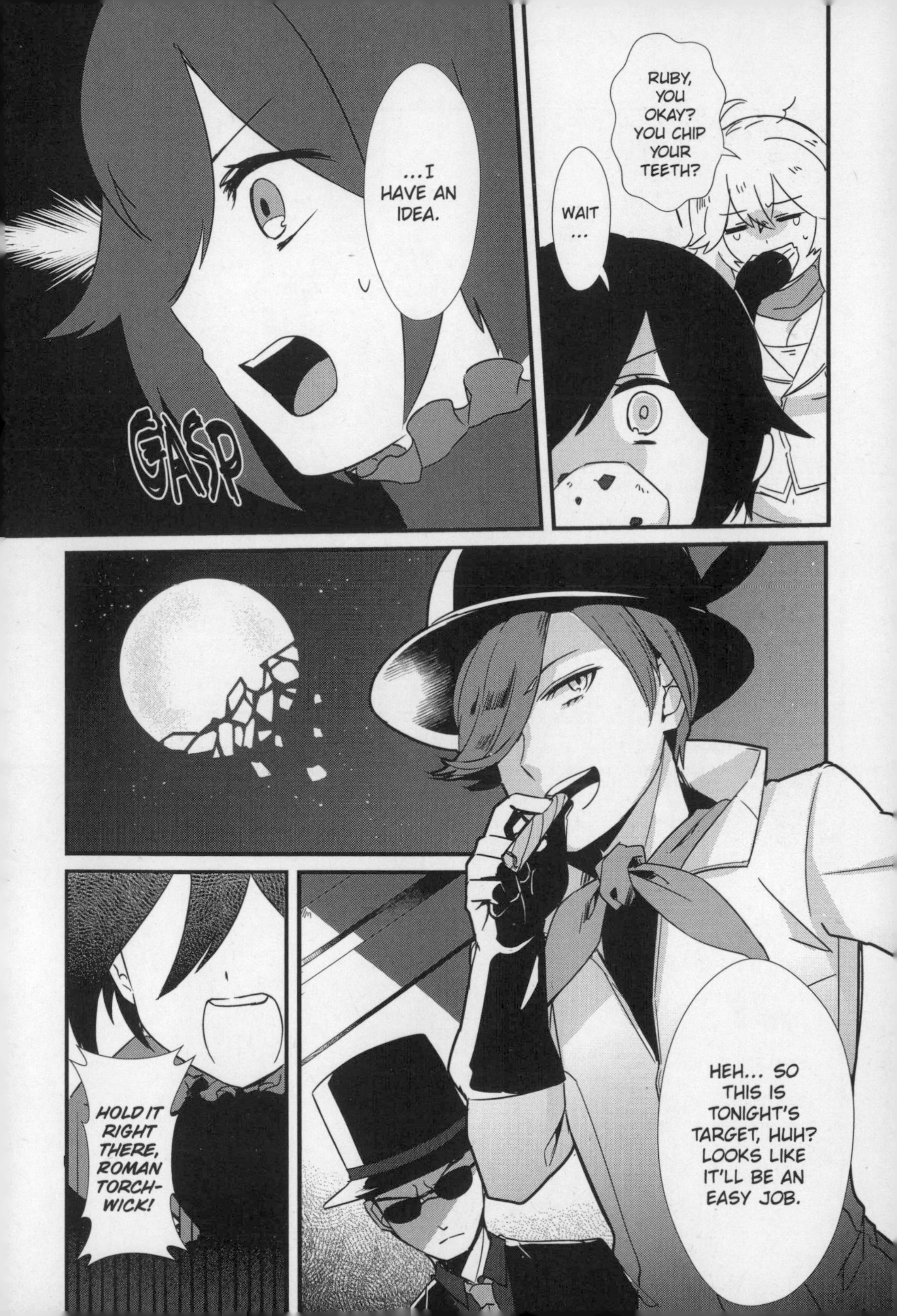
RUBY, YOU OKAY? YOU CHIP YOUR TEETH?
WAIT ...
...I HAVE AN IDEA.
GASP
HEH... SO THIS IS TONIGHT'S TARGET, HUH? LOOKS LIKE IT'LL BE AN EASY JOB.
HOLD IT RIGHT THERE, ROMAN TORCH-WICK!

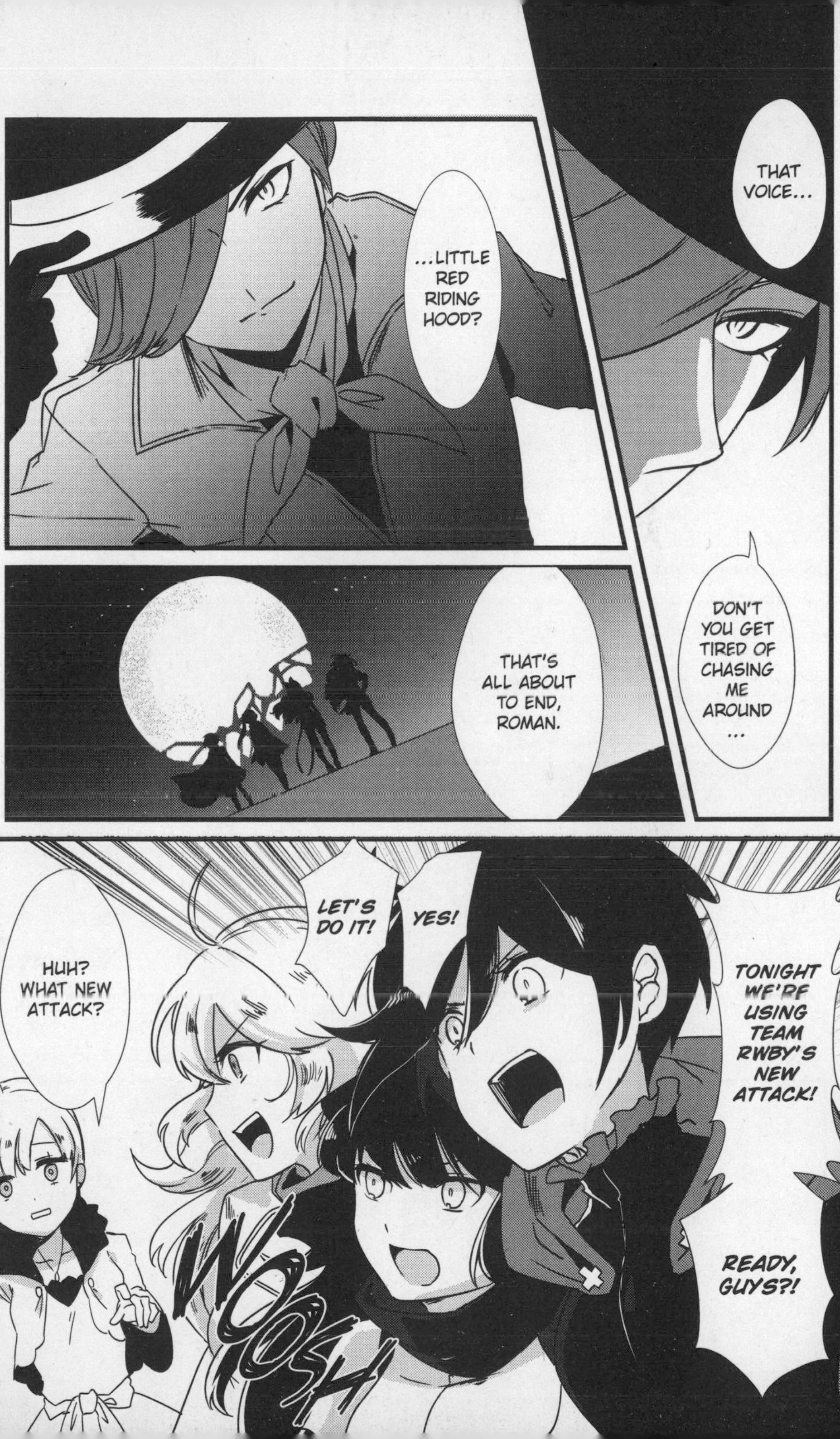
THAT VOICE...
DON'T YOU GET TIRED OF CHASING ME AROUND...
...LITTLE RED RIDING HOOD?
THAT'S ALL ABOUT TO END, ROMAN.
TONIGHT WE'RE USING TEAM RWBY'S NEW ATTACK!
READY, GUYS?!
YES!
LET'S DO IT!
HUH? WHAT NEW ATTACK?
WOOSH

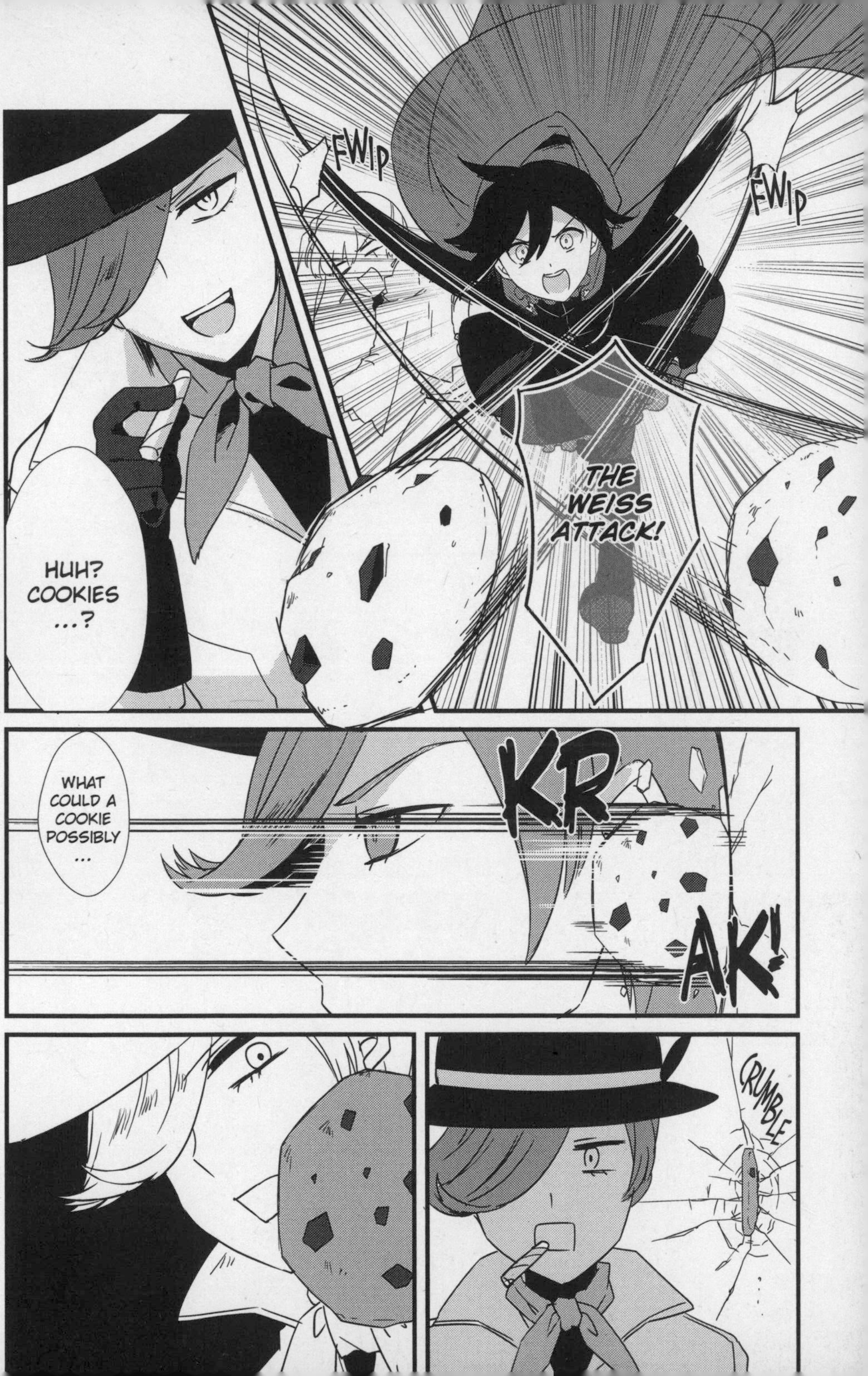
FWIP
FWIP
THE WEISS ATTACK!
HUH? COOKIES ...?
KR
AK!
WHAT COULD A COOKIE POSSIBLY ...
CRUMBLE

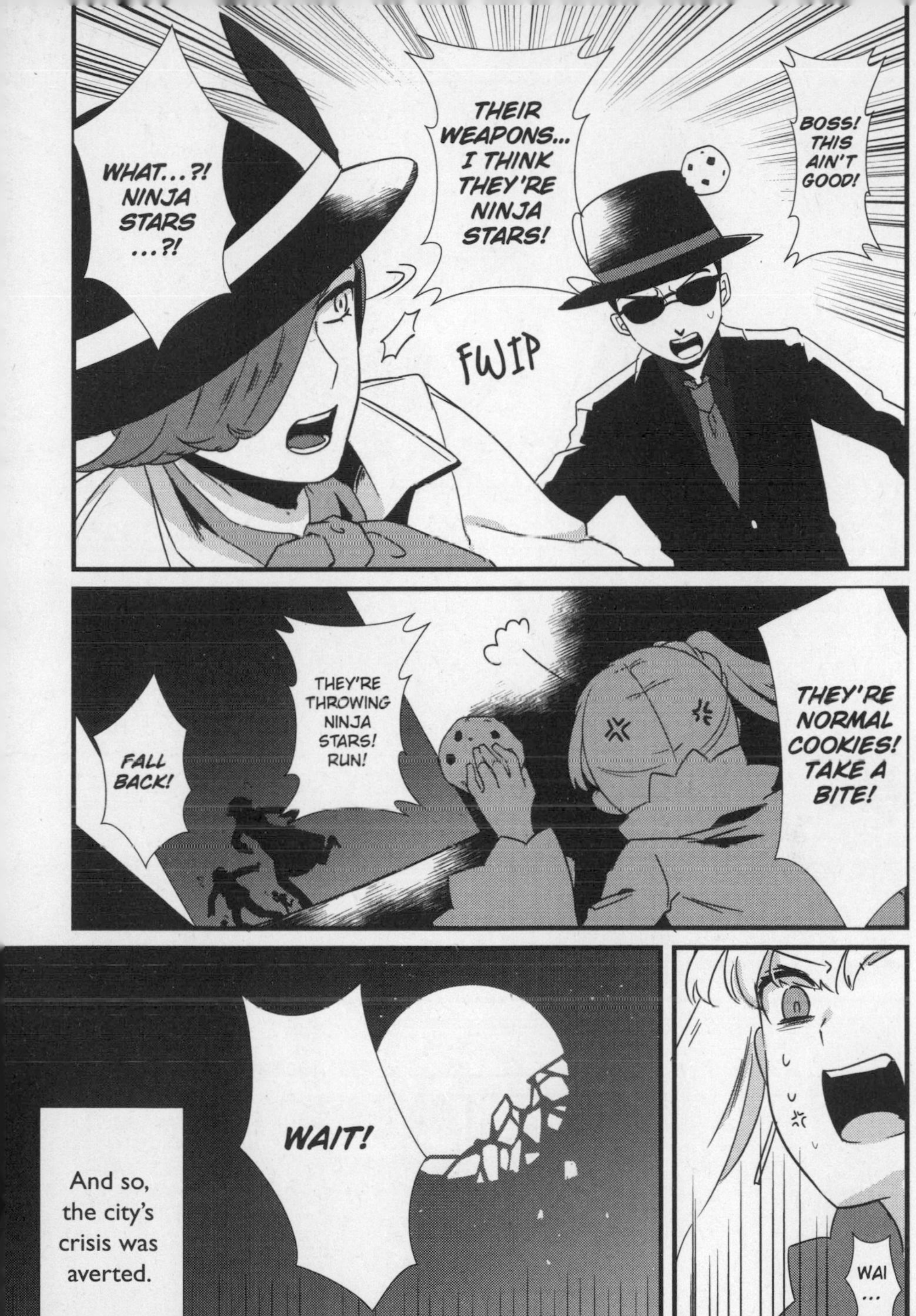
BOSS! THIS AIN'T GOOD!
THEIR WEAPONS... I THINK THEY'RE NINJA STARS!
FWIP
WHAT...?! NINJA STARS ...?!
THEY'RE NORMAL COOKIES! TAKE A BITE!
THEY'RE THROWING NINJA STARS! RUN!
FALL BACK!
WAI ...
WAIT!
And so, the city's crisis was averted.

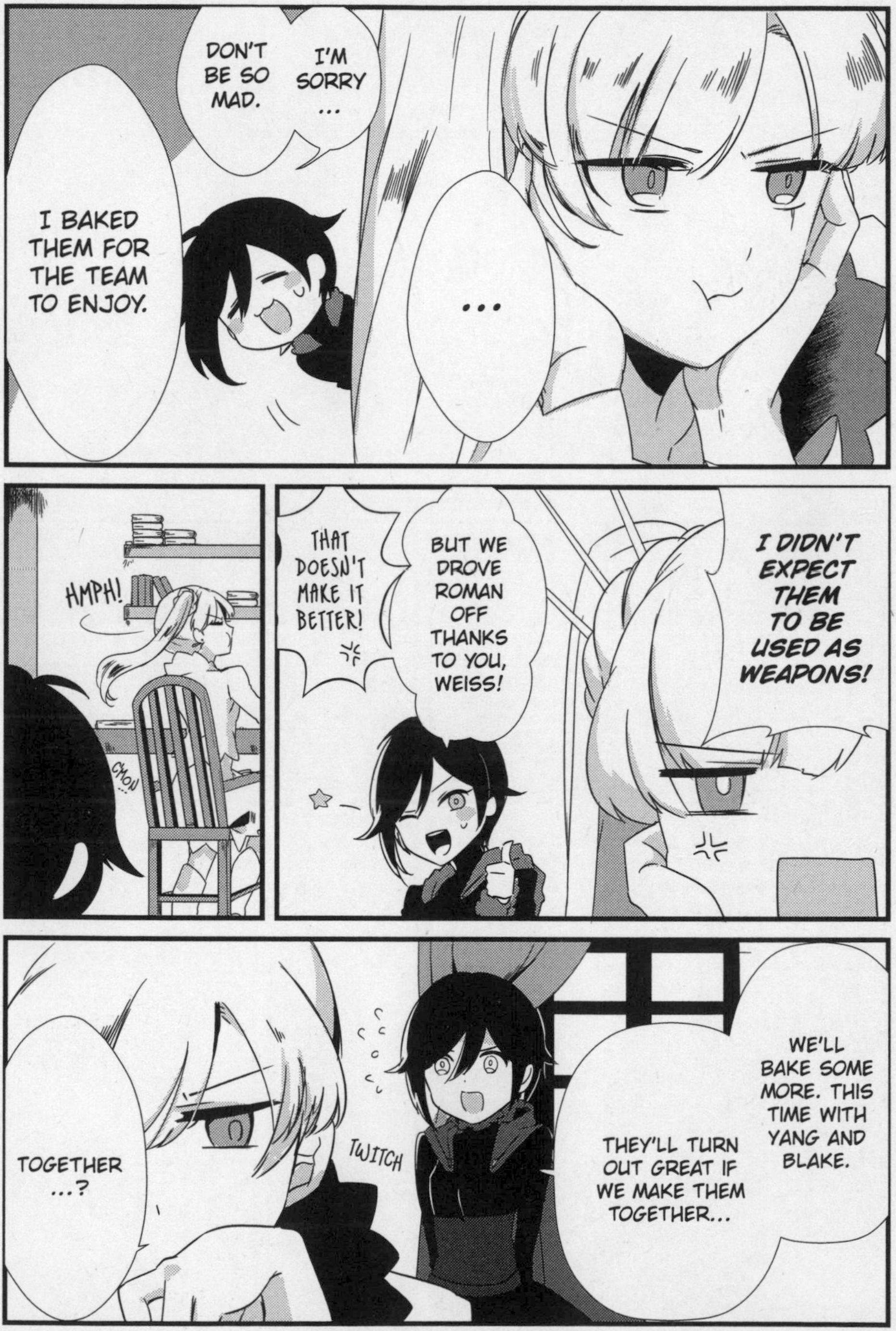
I'M SORRY ...
DON'T BE SO MAD.
...
I BAKED THEM FOR THE TEAM TO ENJOY.
I DIDN'T EXPECT THEM TO BE USED AS WEAPONS!
BUT WE DROVE ROMAN OFF THANKS TO YOU, WEISS!
THAT DOESN'T MAKE IT BETTER!
HMPH!
CHON...
WE'LL BAKE SOME MORE. THIS TIME WITH YANG AND BLAKE.
THEY'LL TURN OUT GREAT IF WE MAKE THEM TOGETHER...
TWITCH
TOGETHER ...?

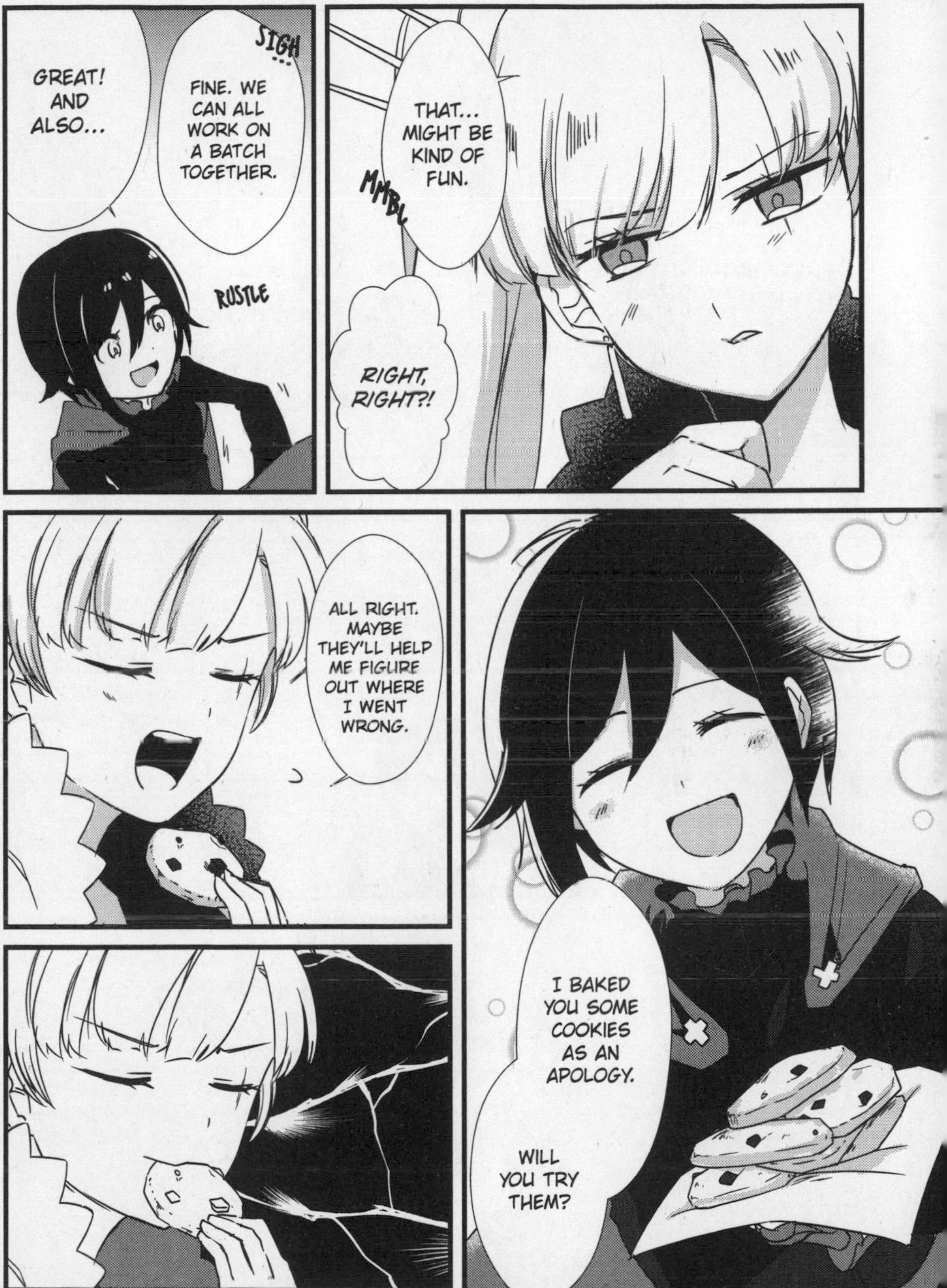
THAT... MIGHT BE KIND OF FUN.
MMBL
RIGHT, RIGHT?!
SIGH...
FINE. WE CAN ALL WORK ON A BATCH TOGETHER.
GREAT! AND ALSO...
RUSTLE
I BAKED YOU SOME COOKIES AS AN APOLOGY.
WILL YOU TRY THEM?
ALL RIGHT. MAYBE THEY'LL HELP ME FIGURE OUT WHERE I WENT WRONG.

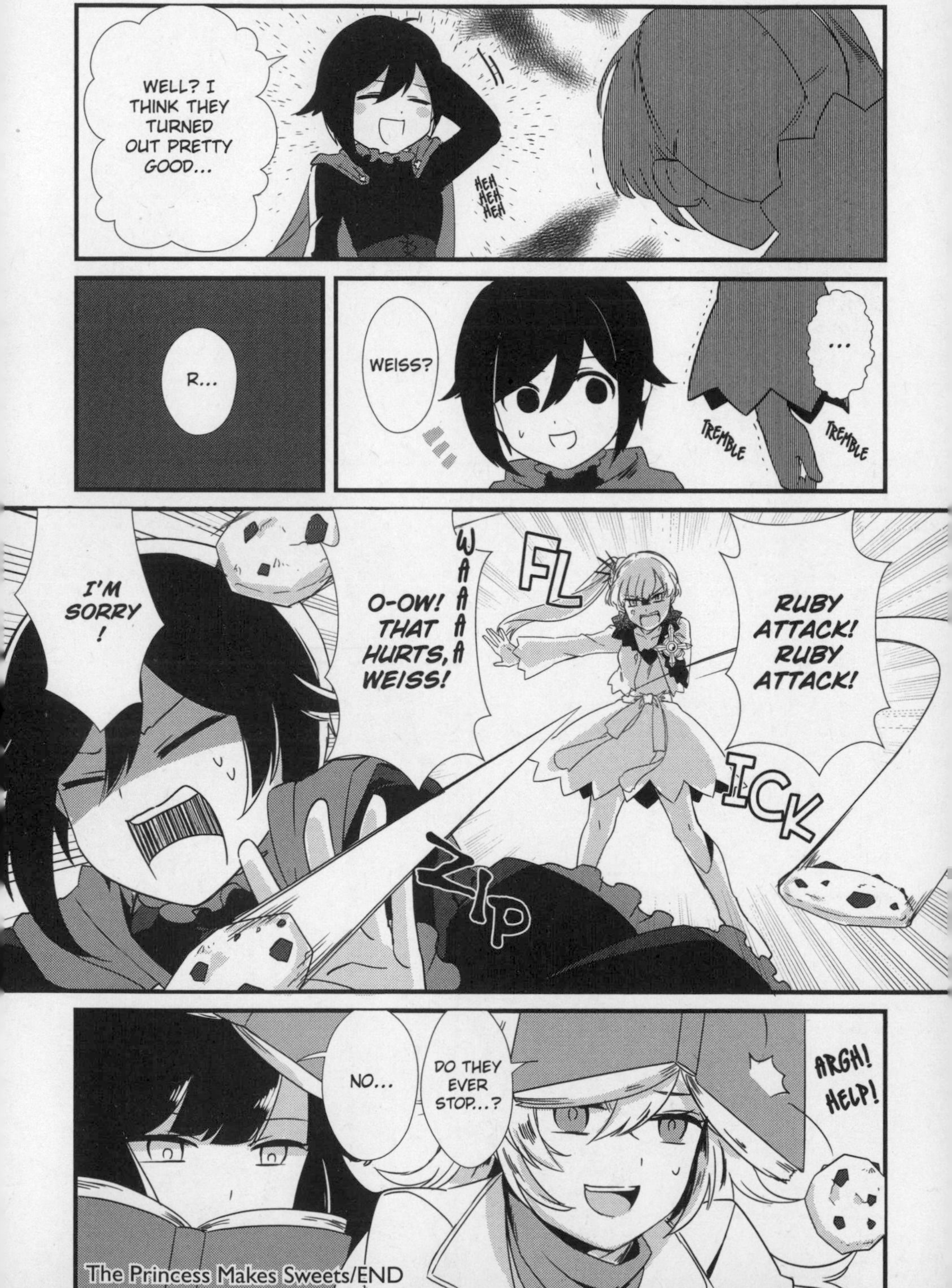
WELL? I THINK THEY TURNED OUT PRETTY GOOD...
HEH HEH HEH
...
TREMBLE
TREMBLE
WEISS?
R...
RUBY ATTACK! RUBY ATTACK!
FL
ICK
WAAAAAA
O-OW! THAT HURTS, WEISS!
ZIP
I'M SORRY!
ARGH! HELP!
DO THEY EVER STOP...?
NO...

The Princess Makes Sweets/END

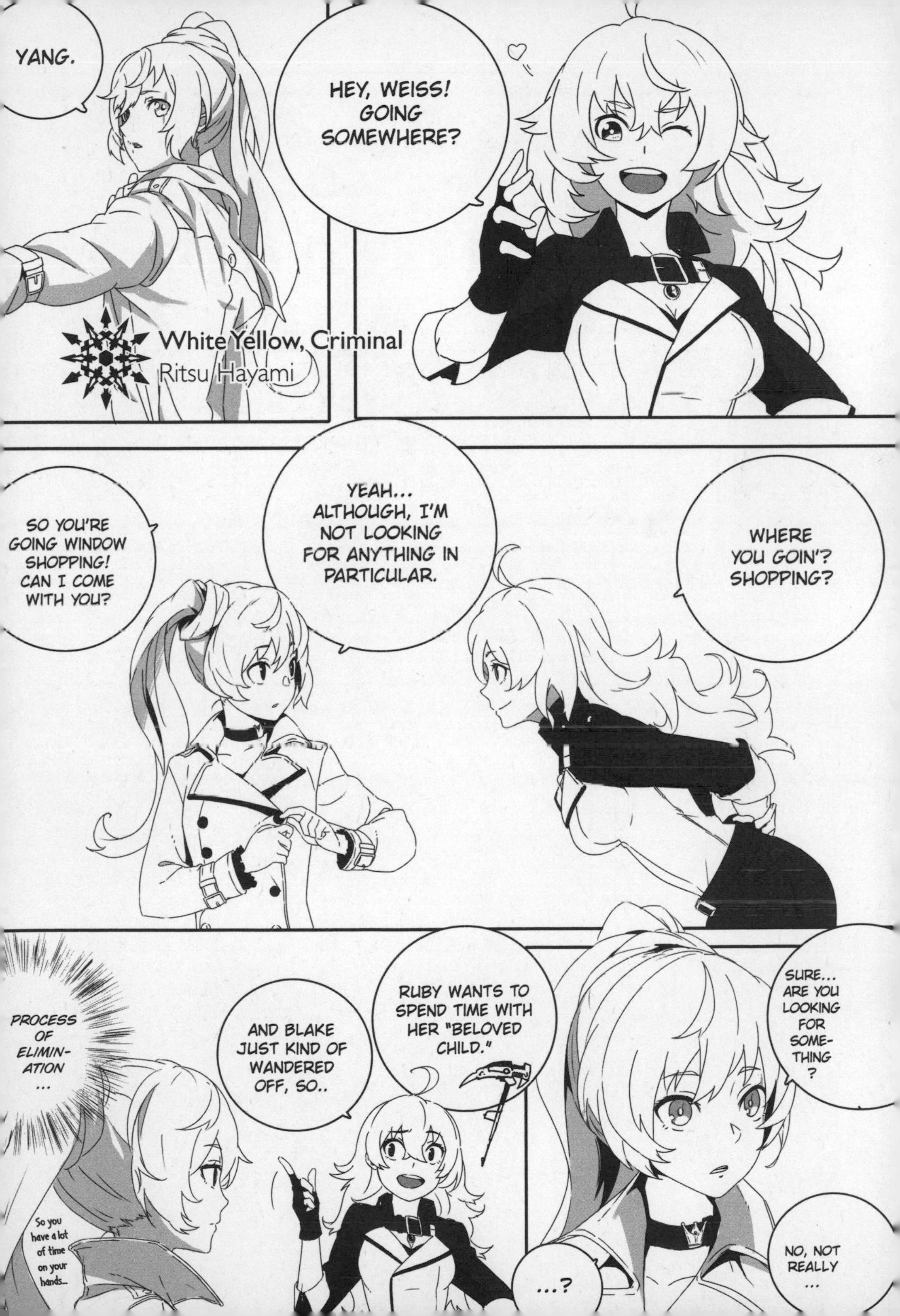
HEY, WEISS! GOING SOMEWHERE?
YANG.
White Yellow, Criminal
Ritsu Hayami
WHERE YOU GOIN'? SHOPPING?
YEAH... ALTHOUGH, I'M NOT LOOKING FOR ANYTHING IN PARTICULAR.
SO YOU'RE GOING WINDOW SHOPPING! CAN I COME WITH YOU?
SURE... ARE YOU LOOKING FOR SOME-THING?
NO, NOT REALLY ...
...?
RUBY WANTS TO SPEND TIME WITH HER "BELOVED CHILD."
AND BLAKE JUST KIND OF WANDERED OFF, SO..
PROCESS OF ELIMIN-ATION ...
So you have a lot of time on your hands...

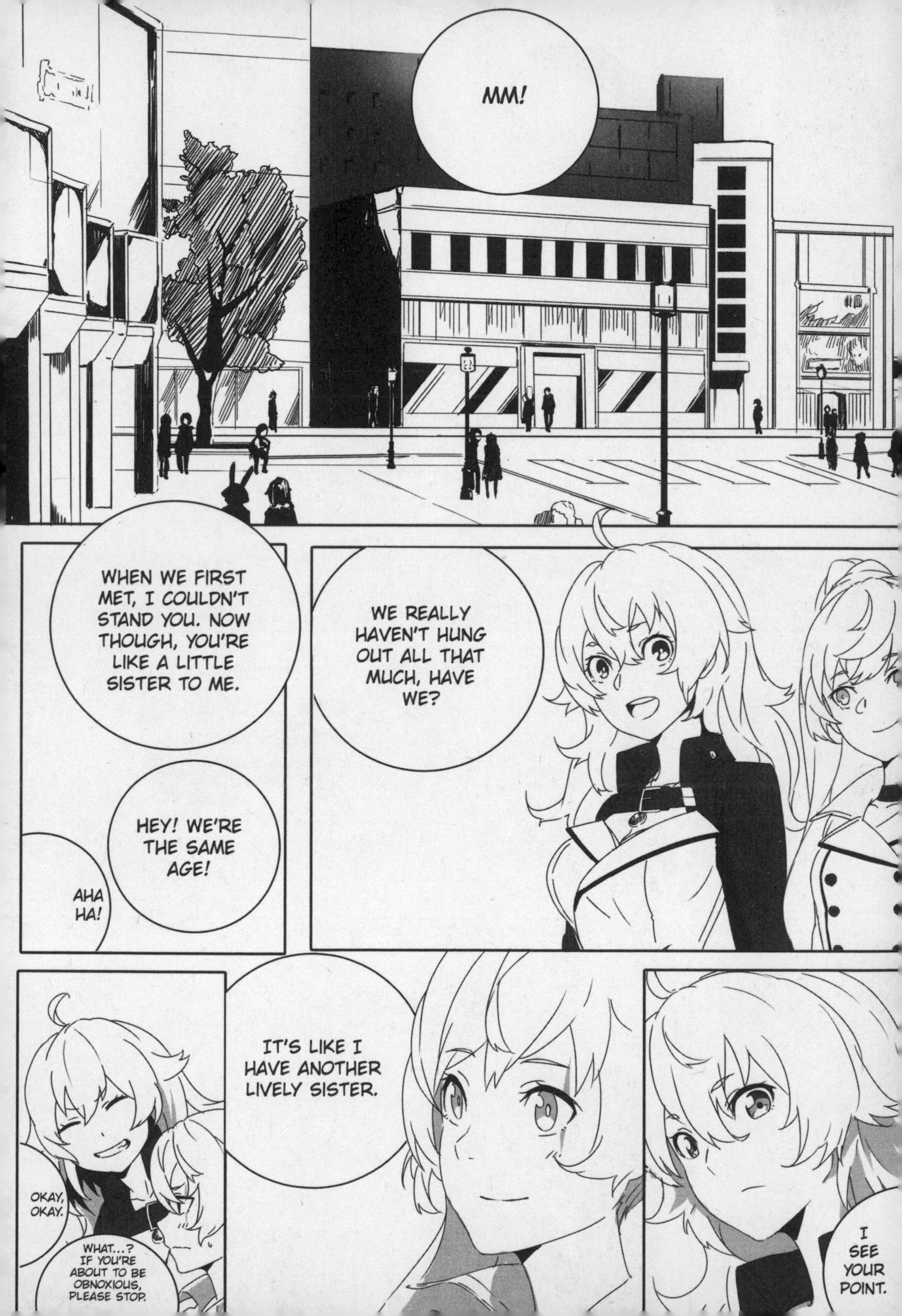
MM!
WE REALLY HAVEN'T HUNG OUT ALL THAT MUCH, HAVE WE?
WHEN WE FIRST MET, I COULDN'T STAND YOU. NOW THOUGH, YOU'RE LIKE A LITTLE SISTER TO ME.
HEY! WE'RE THE SAME AGE!
AHA HA!
I SEE YOUR POINT.
IT'S LIKE I HAVE ANOTHER LIVELY SISTER.
OKAY, OKAY.
WHAT...? IF YOU'RE ABOUT TO BE OBNOXIOUS, PLEASE STOP.

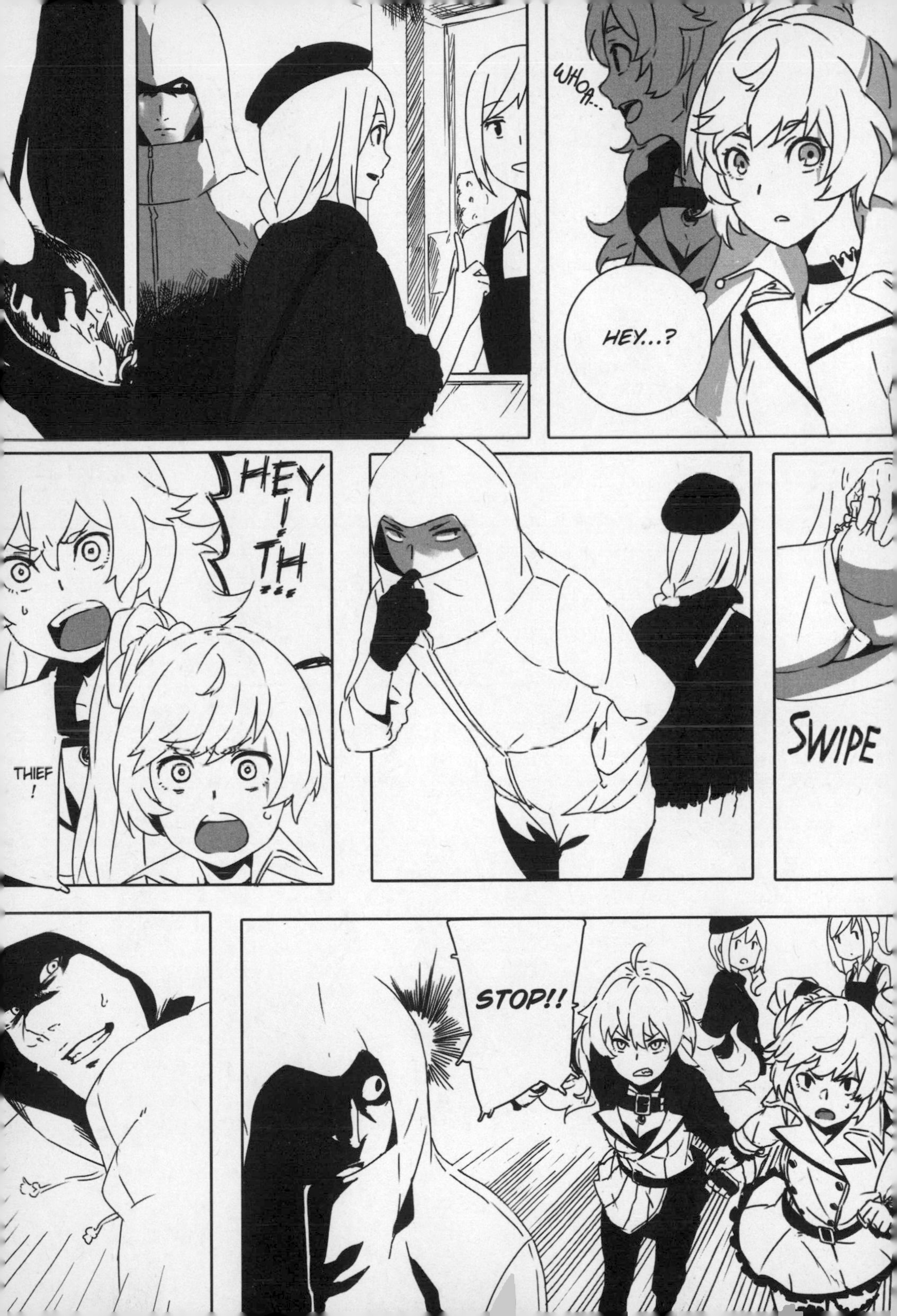
WHOA...
HEY...?
SWIPE
HEY! TH
THIEF!
STOP!!

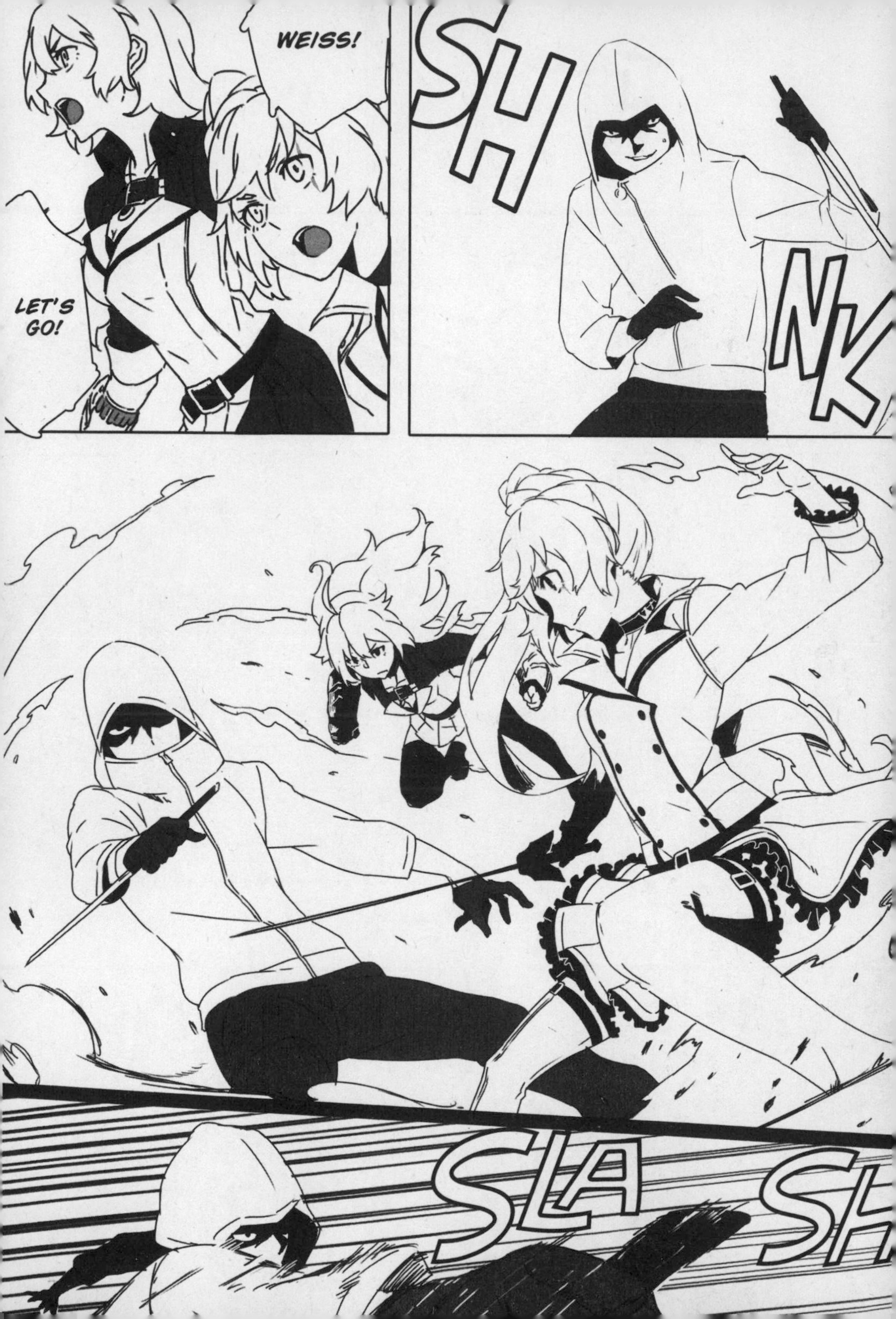
SHNK
WEISS!
LET'S GO!
SLA SH

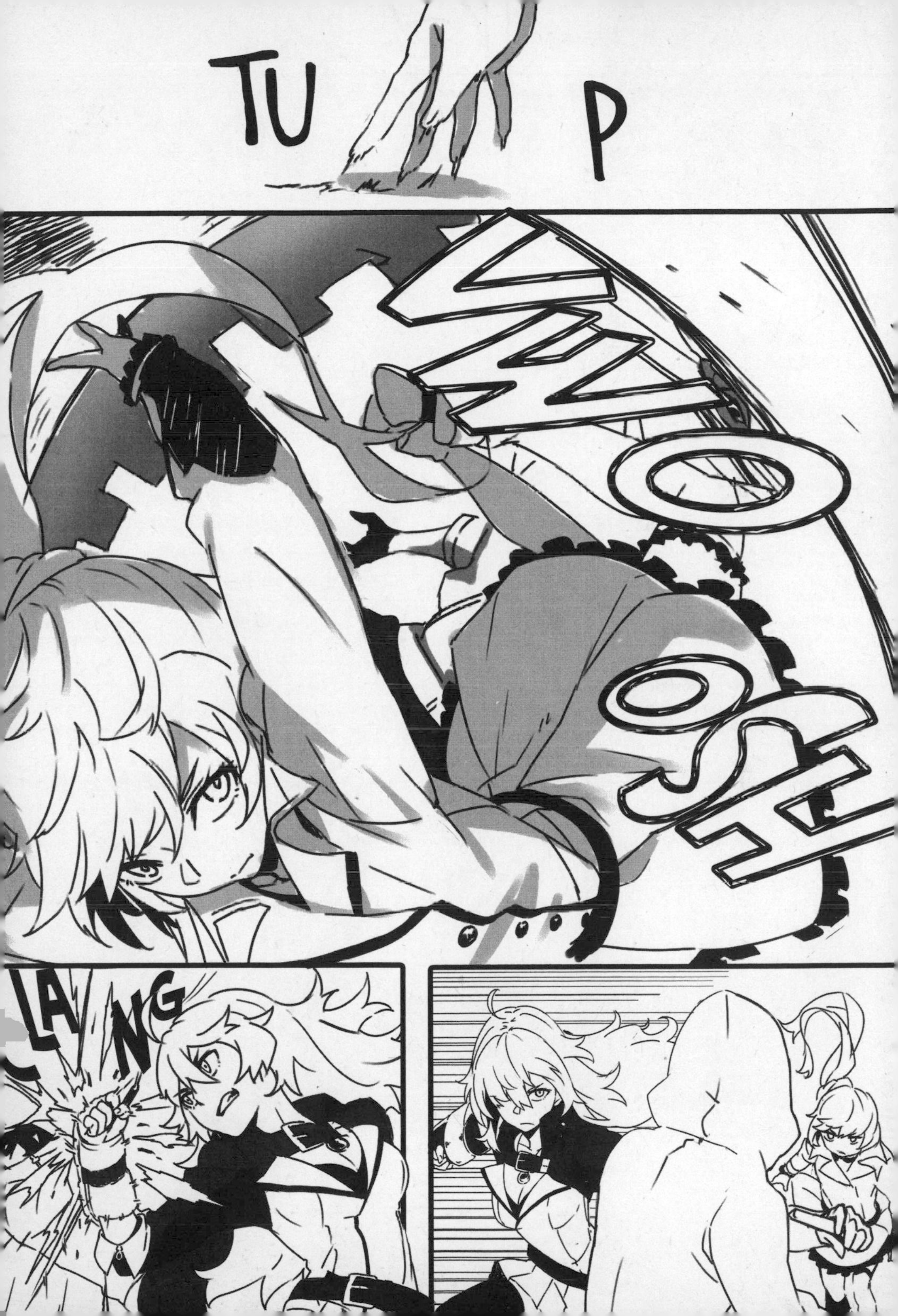
TU P
WHOOSH
CLANG

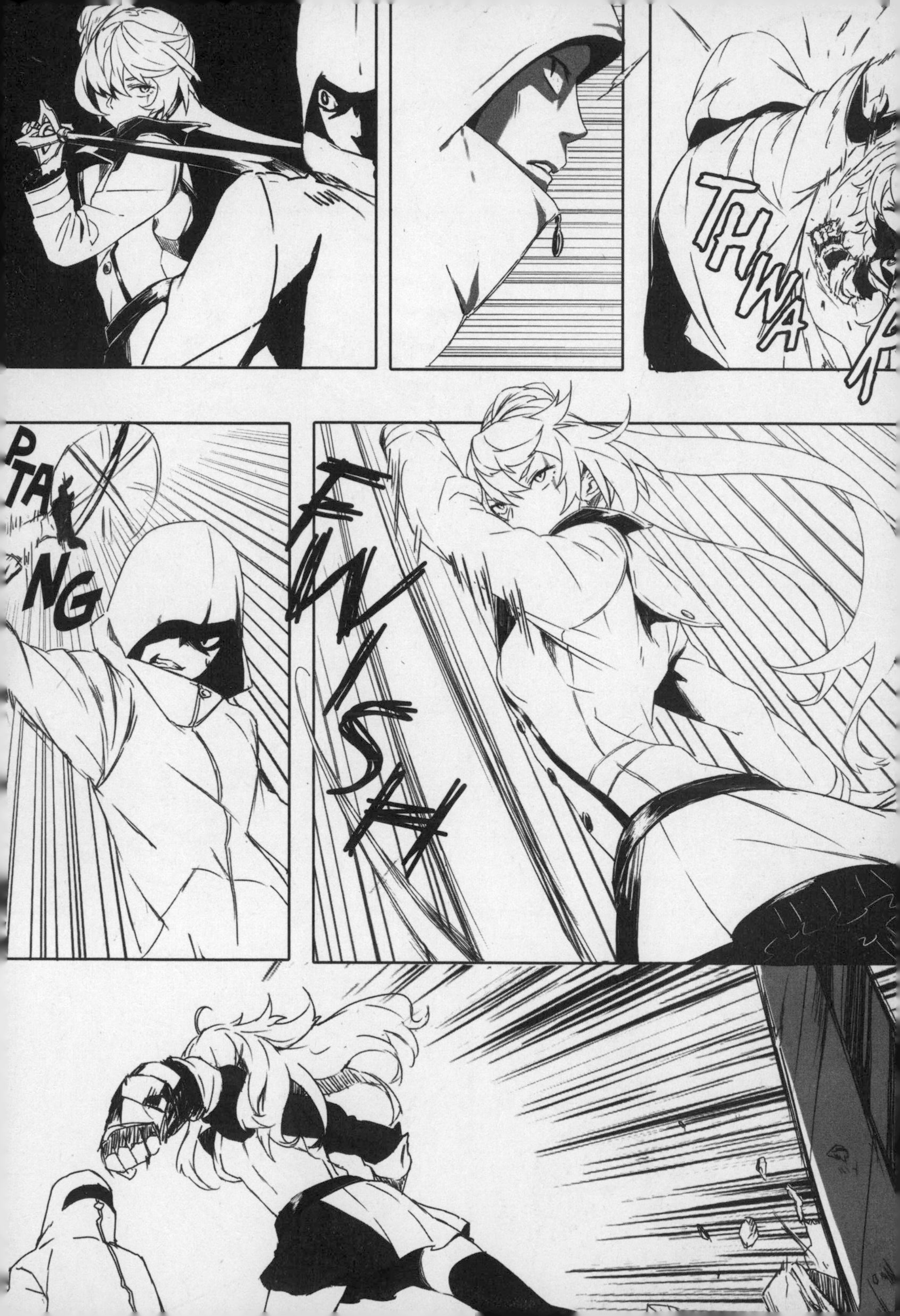
THWAP
FWISH
PTANG

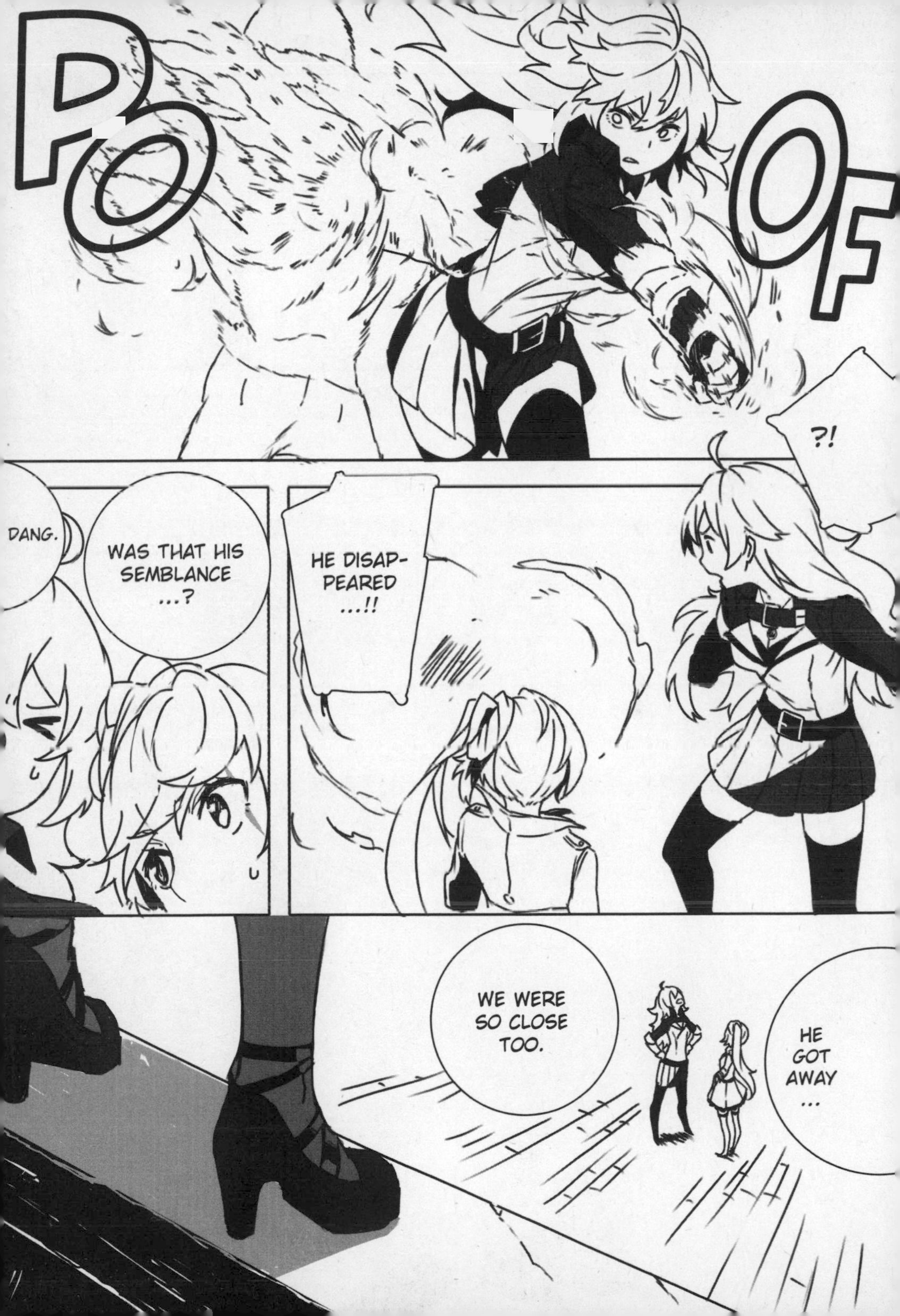
POOF
?!
HE DISAPPEARED ...!!
WAS THAT HIS SEMBLANCE ...?
DANG.
HE GOT AWAY ...
WE WERE SO CLOSE TOO.

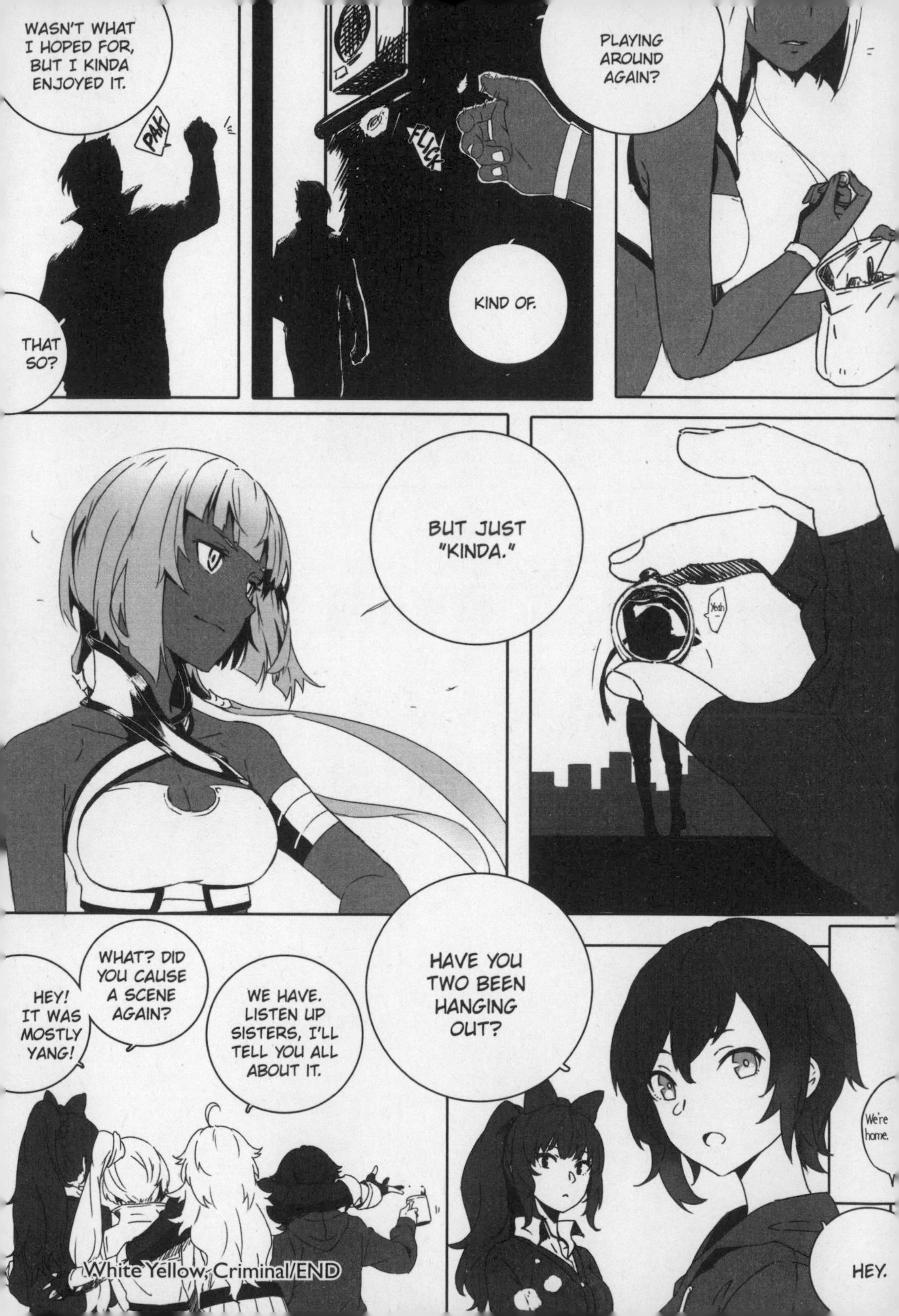
PLAYING AROUND AGAIN?
FLICK
KIND OF.
WASN'T WHAT I HOPED FOR, BUT I KINDA ENJOYED IT.
PAK
THAT SO?
Yeah
BUT JUST "KINDA."
We're home.
HEY.
HAVE YOU TWO BEEN HANGING OUT?
WE HAVE. LISTEN UP SISTERS, I'LL TELL YOU ALL ABOUT IT.
WHAT? DID YOU CAUSE A SCENE AGAIN?
HEY! IT WAS MOSTLY YANG!
White Yellow, Criminal/END

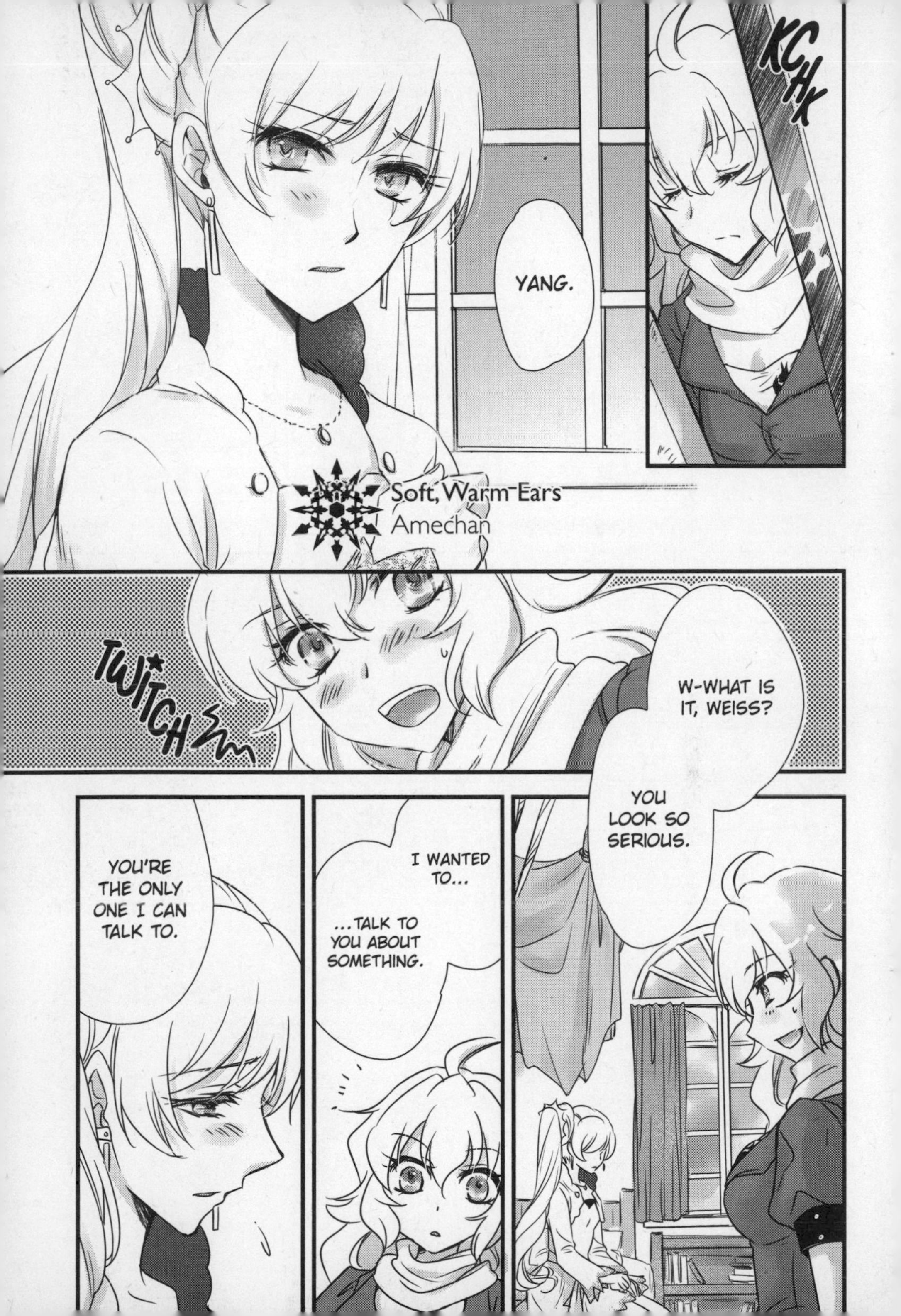
KCHK
YANG.
Soft, Warm Ears
Amechan
TWITCH
W-WHAT IS IT, WEISS?
YOU LOOK SO SERIOUS.
I WANTED TO...
...TALK TO YOU ABOUT SOMETHING.
YOU'RE THE ONLY ONE I CAN TALK TO.

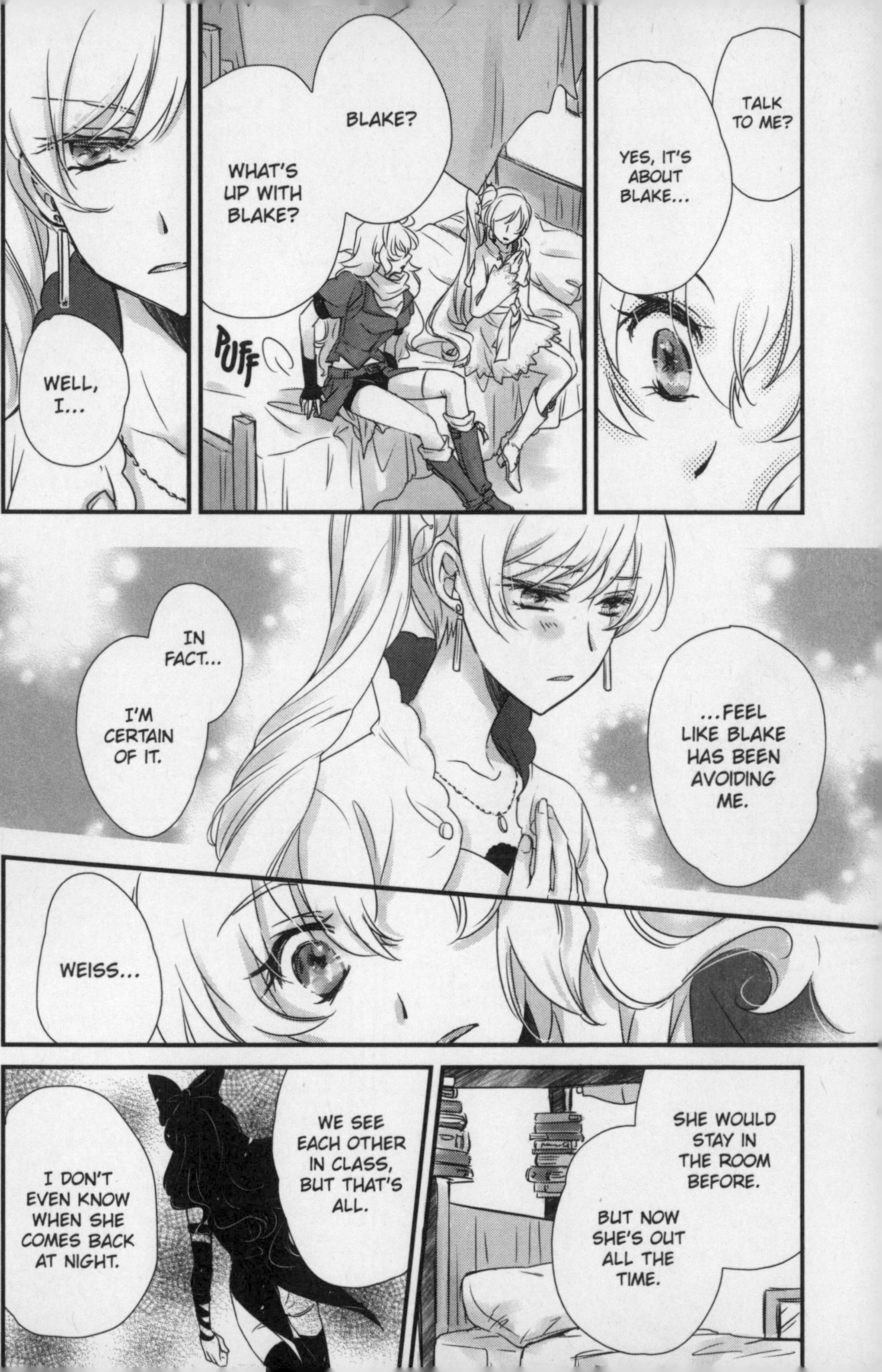
TALK TO ME?
YES, IT'S ABOUT BLAKE...
BLAKE?
WHAT'S UP WITH BLAKE?
PUFF
WELL, I...
...FEEL LIKE BLAKE HAS BEEN AVOIDING ME.
IN FACT...
I'M CERTAIN OF IT.
WEISS...
SHE WOULD STAY IN THE ROOM BEFORE.
BUT NOW SHE'S OUT ALL THE TIME.
WE SEE EACH OTHER IN CLASS, BUT THAT'S ALL.
I DON'T EVEN KNOW WHEN SHE COMES BACK AT NIGHT.

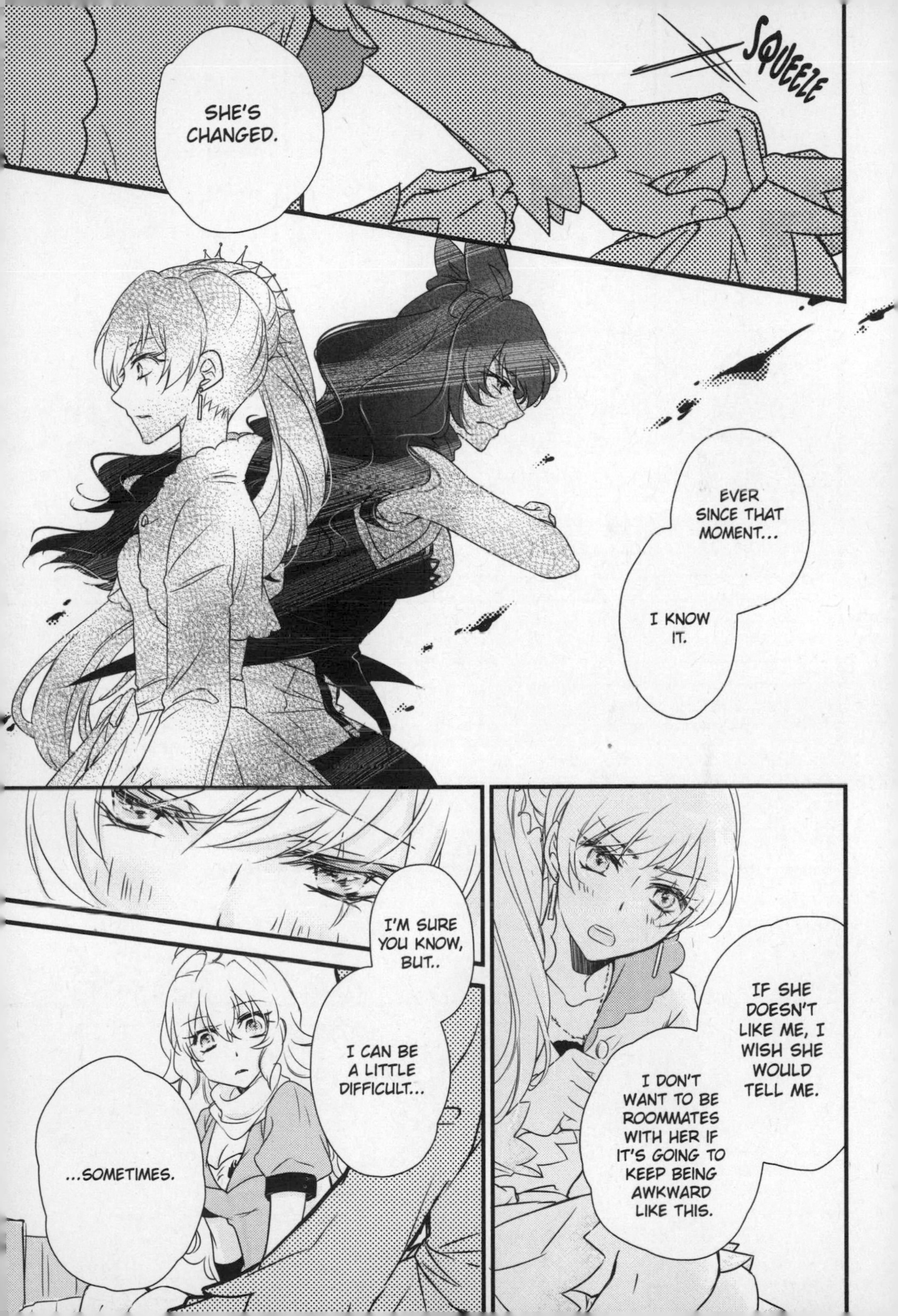
SQUEEZE
SHE'S CHANGED.
EVER SINCE THAT MOMENT...
I KNOW IT.
IF SHE DOESN'T LIKE ME, I WISH SHE WOULD TELL ME.
I DON'T WANT TO BE ROOMMATES WITH HER IF IT'S GOING TO KEEP BEING AWKWARD LIKE THIS.
I'M SURE YOU KNOW, BUT..
I CAN BE A LITTLE DIFFICULT...
...SOMETIMES.

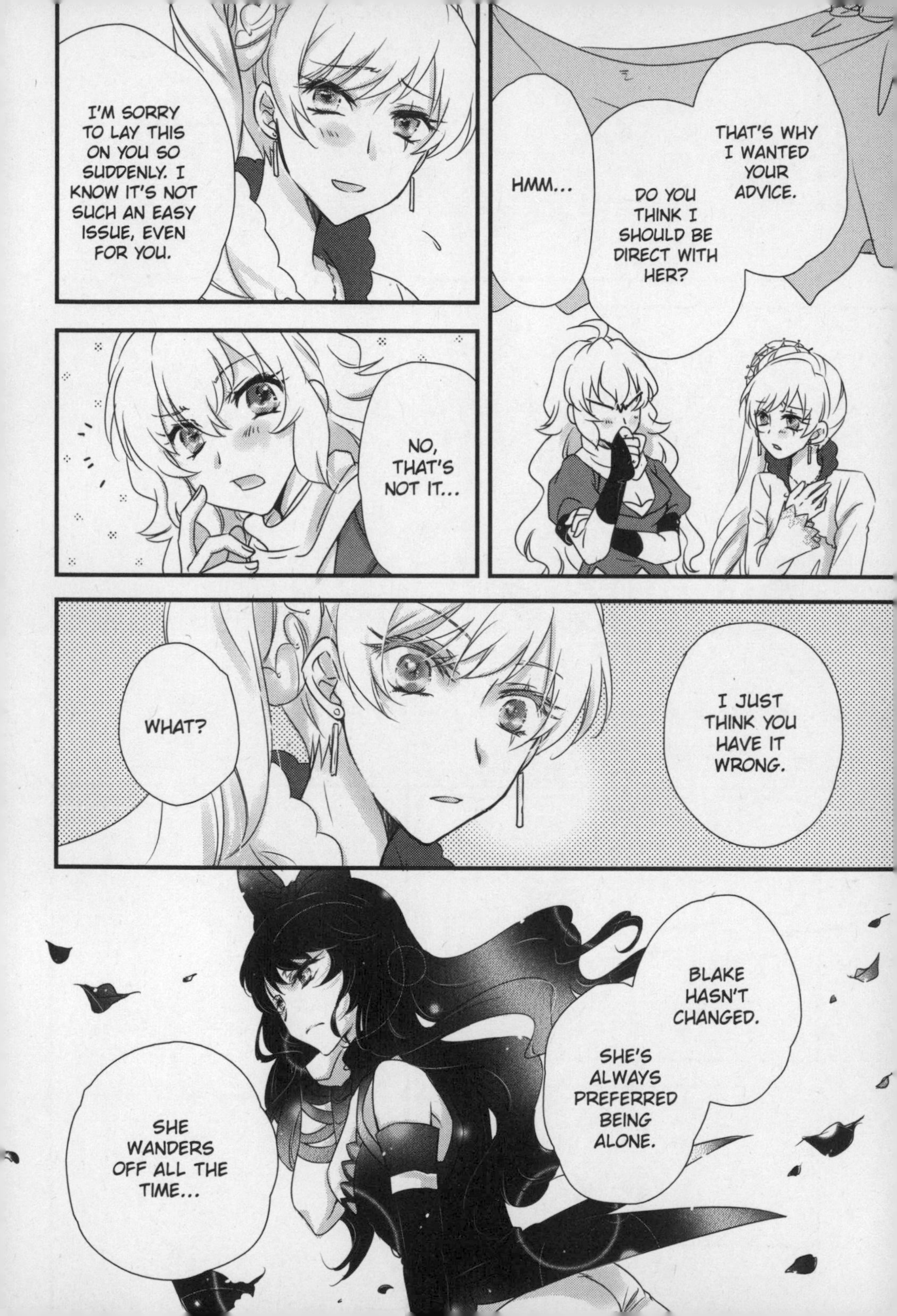
THAT'S WHY I WANTED YOUR ADVICE.
DO YOU THINK I SHOULD BE DIRECT WITH HER?
HMM...
I'M SORRY TO LAY THIS ON YOU SO SUDDENLY. I KNOW IT'S NOT SUCH AN EASY ISSUE, EVEN FOR YOU.
NO, THAT'S NOT IT...
I JUST THINK YOU HAVE IT WRONG.
WHAT?
BLAKE HASN'T CHANGED.
SHE'S ALWAYS PREFERRED BEING ALONE.
SHE WANDERS OFF ALL THE TIME...

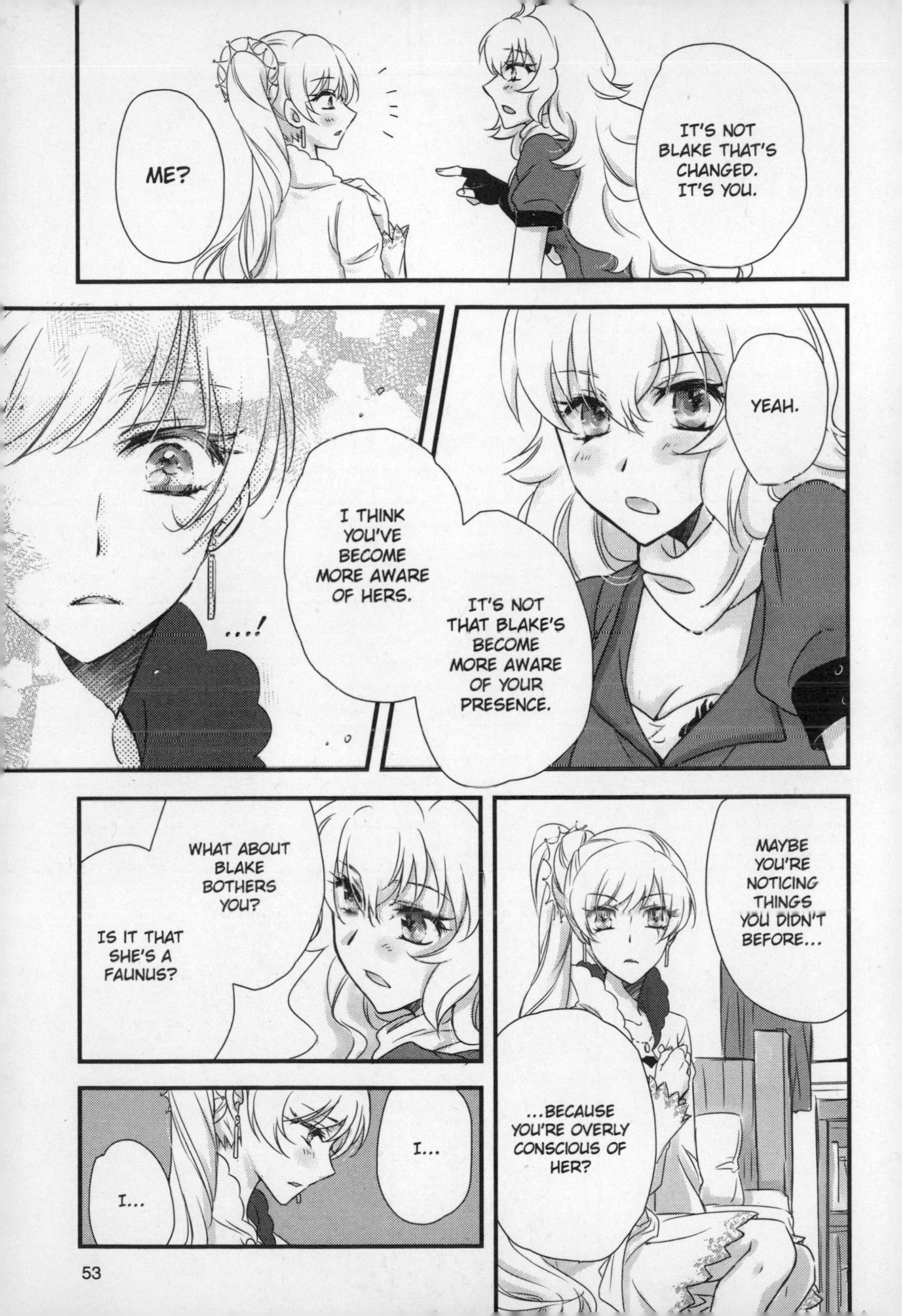
IT'S NOT BLAKE THAT'S CHANGED. IT'S YOU.
ME?
YEAH.
IT'S NOT THAT BLAKE'S BECOME MORE AWARE OF YOUR PRESENCE.
I THINK YOU'VE BECOME MORE AWARE OF HERS.
...!
MAYBE YOU'RE NOTICING THINGS YOU DIDN'T BEFORE...
...BECAUSE YOU'RE OVERLY CONSCIOUS OF HER?
WHAT ABOUT BLAKE BOTHERS YOU?
IS IT THAT SHE'S A FAUNUS?
I...
I...

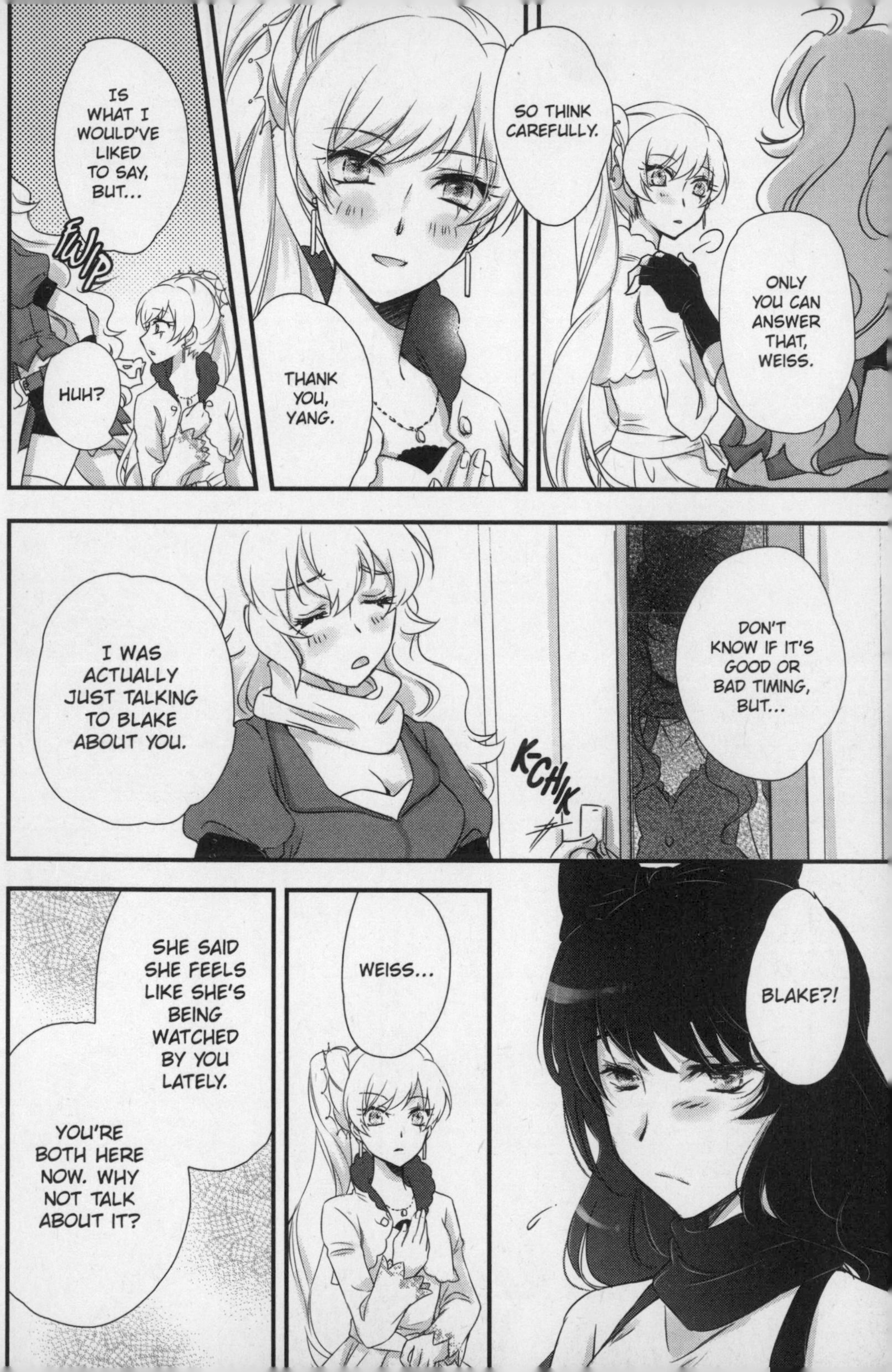
ONLY YOU CAN ANSWER THAT, WEISS.
SO THINK CAREFULLY.
THANK YOU, YANG.
IS WHAT I WOULD'VE LIKED TO SAY, BUT...
FWIP
HUH?
DON'T KNOW IF IT'S GOOD OR BAD TIMING, BUT...
K-CHIK
I WAS ACTUALLY JUST TALKING TO BLAKE ABOUT YOU.
BLAKE?!
WEISS...
SHE SAID SHE FEELS LIKE SHE'S BEING WATCHED BY YOU LATELY.
YOU'RE BOTH HERE NOW. WHY NOT TALK ABOUT IT?

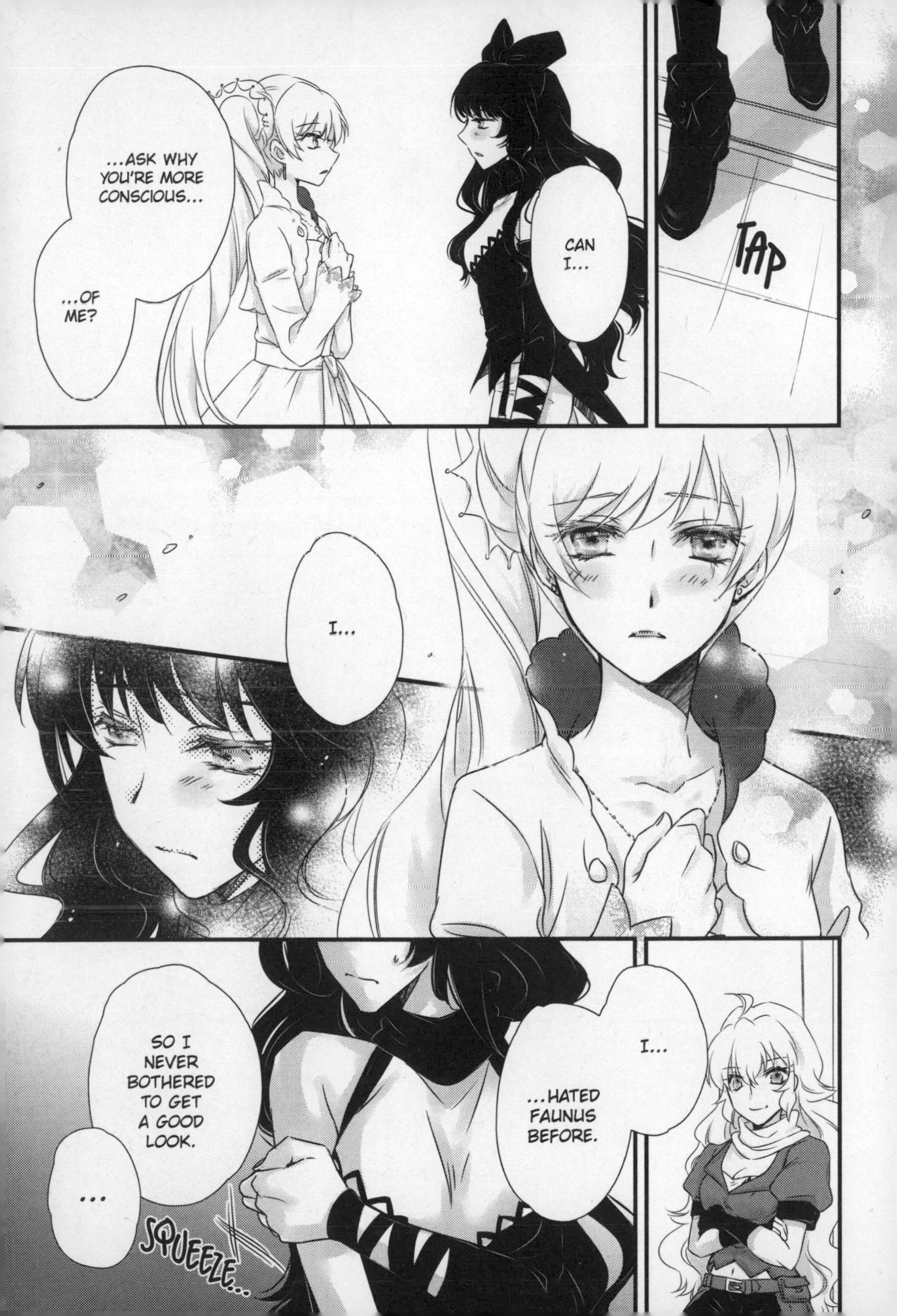
TAP
CAN I...
...ASK WHY YOU'RE MORE CONSCIOUS...
...OF ME?
I...
I...
...HATED FAUNUS BEFORE.
SO I NEVER BOTHERED TO GET A GOOD LOOK.
...
SQUEEZE...

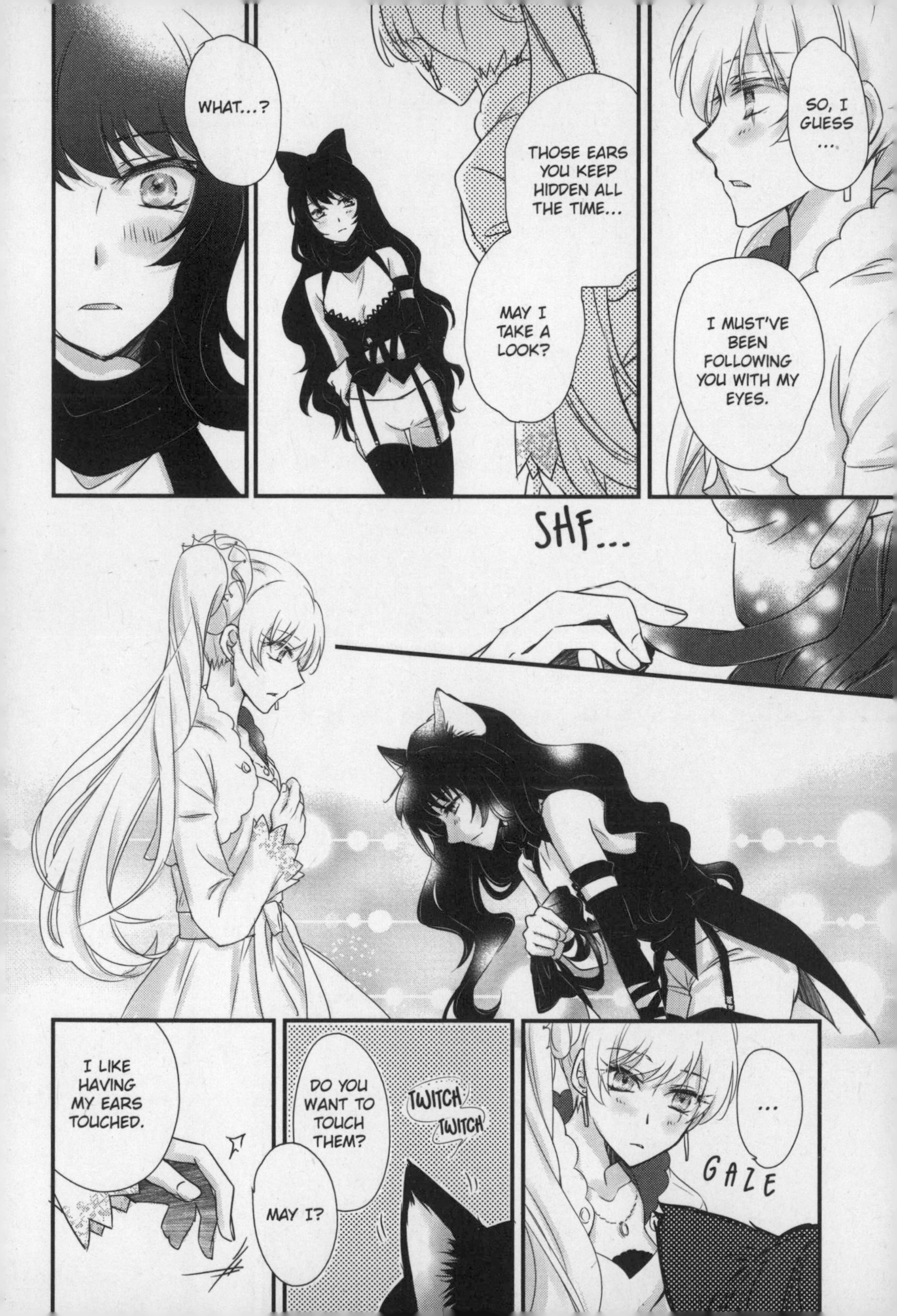
SO, I GUESS ....
I MUST'VE BEEN FOLLOWING YOU WITH MY EYES.
THOSE EARS YOU KEEP HIDDEN ALL THE TIME...
MAY I TAKE A LOOK?
WHAT...?
SHF...
...
GAZE
DO YOU WANT TO TOUCH THEM?
TWITCH TWITCH
MAY I?
I LIKE HAVING MY EARS TOUCHED.

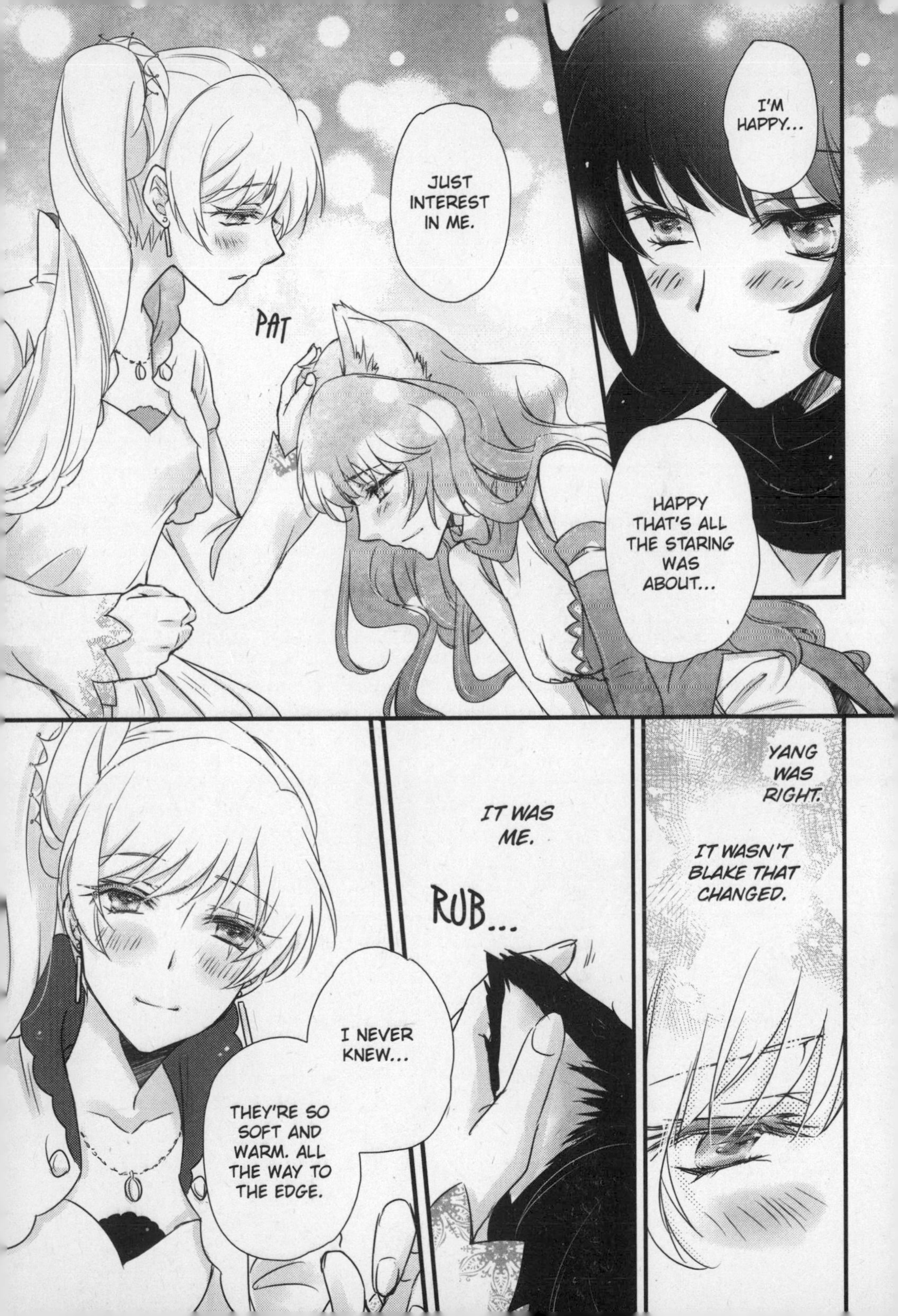
I'M HAPPY...
HAPPY THAT'S ALL THE STARING WAS ABOUT...
JUST INTEREST IN ME.
PAT
YANG WAS RIGHT.
IT WASN'T BLAKE THAT CHANGED.
IT WAS ME.
RUB...
I NEVER KNEW...
THEY'RE SO SOFT AND WARM. ALL THE WAY TO THE EDGE.

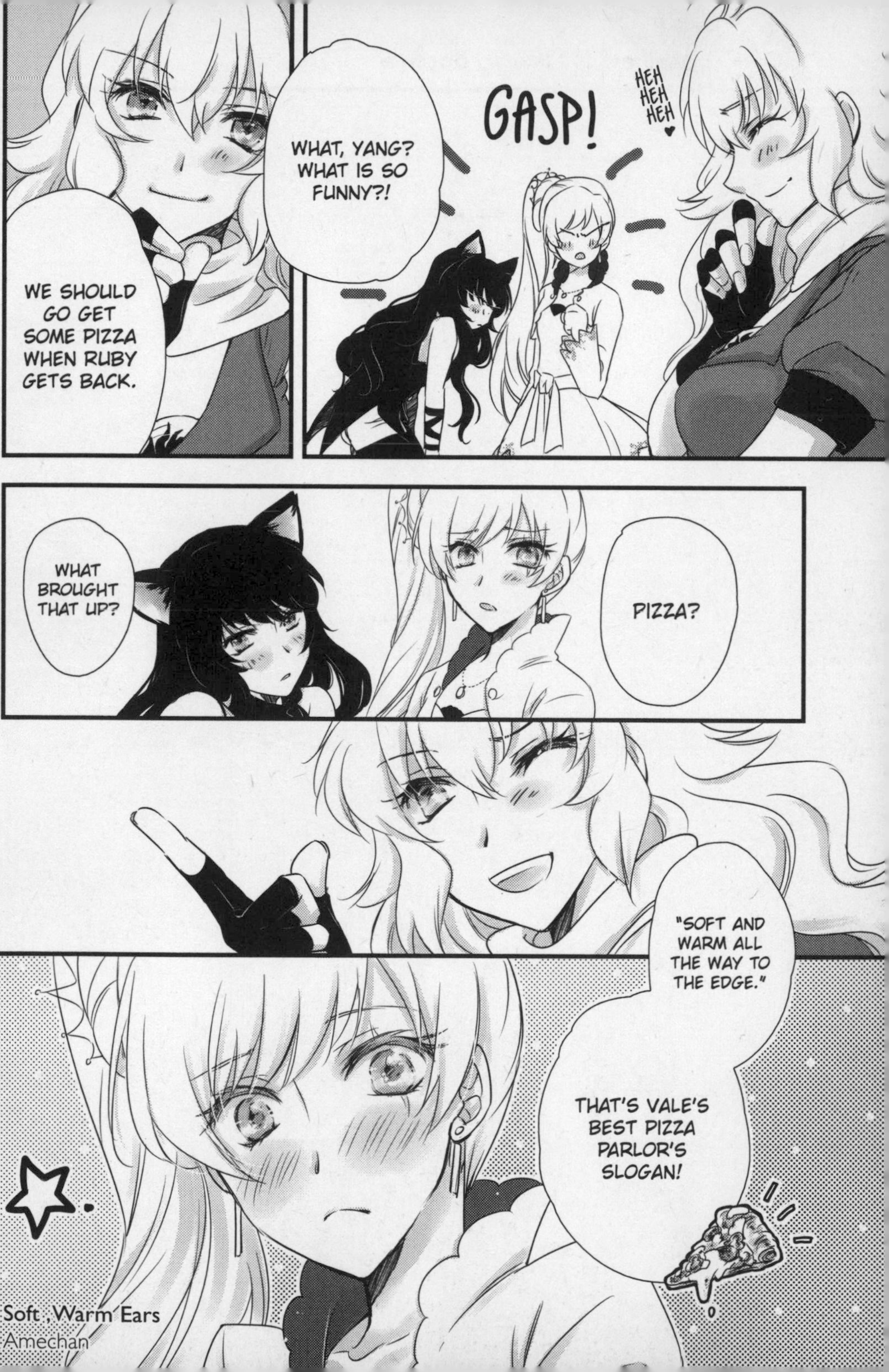
HEH HEH HEH
GASP!
WHAT, YANG? WHAT IS SO FUNNY?!
WE SHOULD GO GET SOME PIZZA WHEN RUBY GETS BACK.
PIZZA?
WHAT BROUGHT THAT UP?
"SOFT AND WARM ALL THE WAY TO THE EDGE."
THAT'S VALE'S BEST PIZZA PARLOR'S SLOGAN!

Soft, Warm Ears
Amechan

Happiness Is Next to Boredom

Rojine Kio

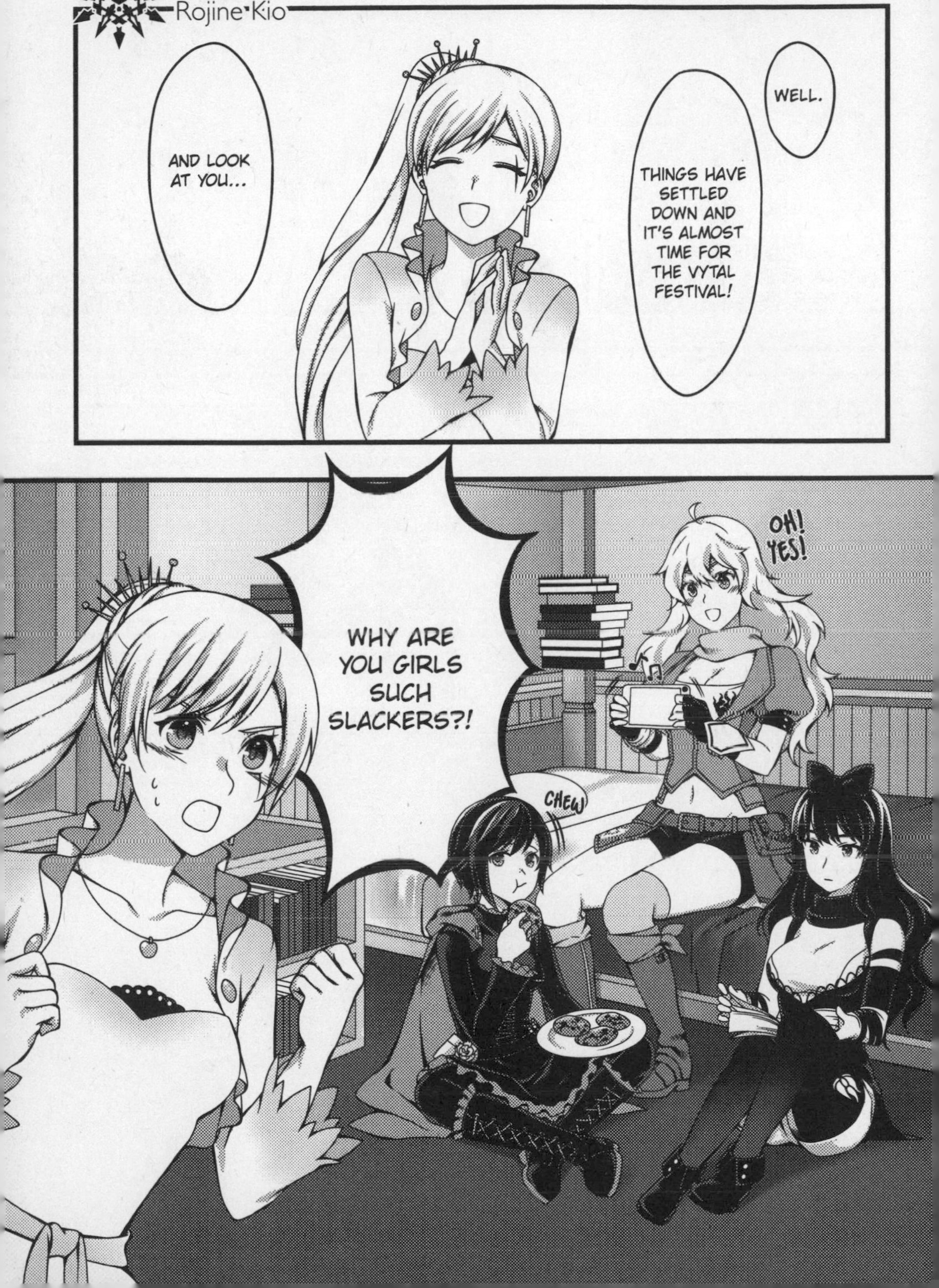
WELL.
THINGS HAVE SETTLED DOWN AND IT'S ALMOST TIME FOR THE VYTAL FESTIVAL!
AND LOOK AT YOU...
WHY ARE YOU GIRLS SUCH SLACKERS?!
OH! YES!
CHEW

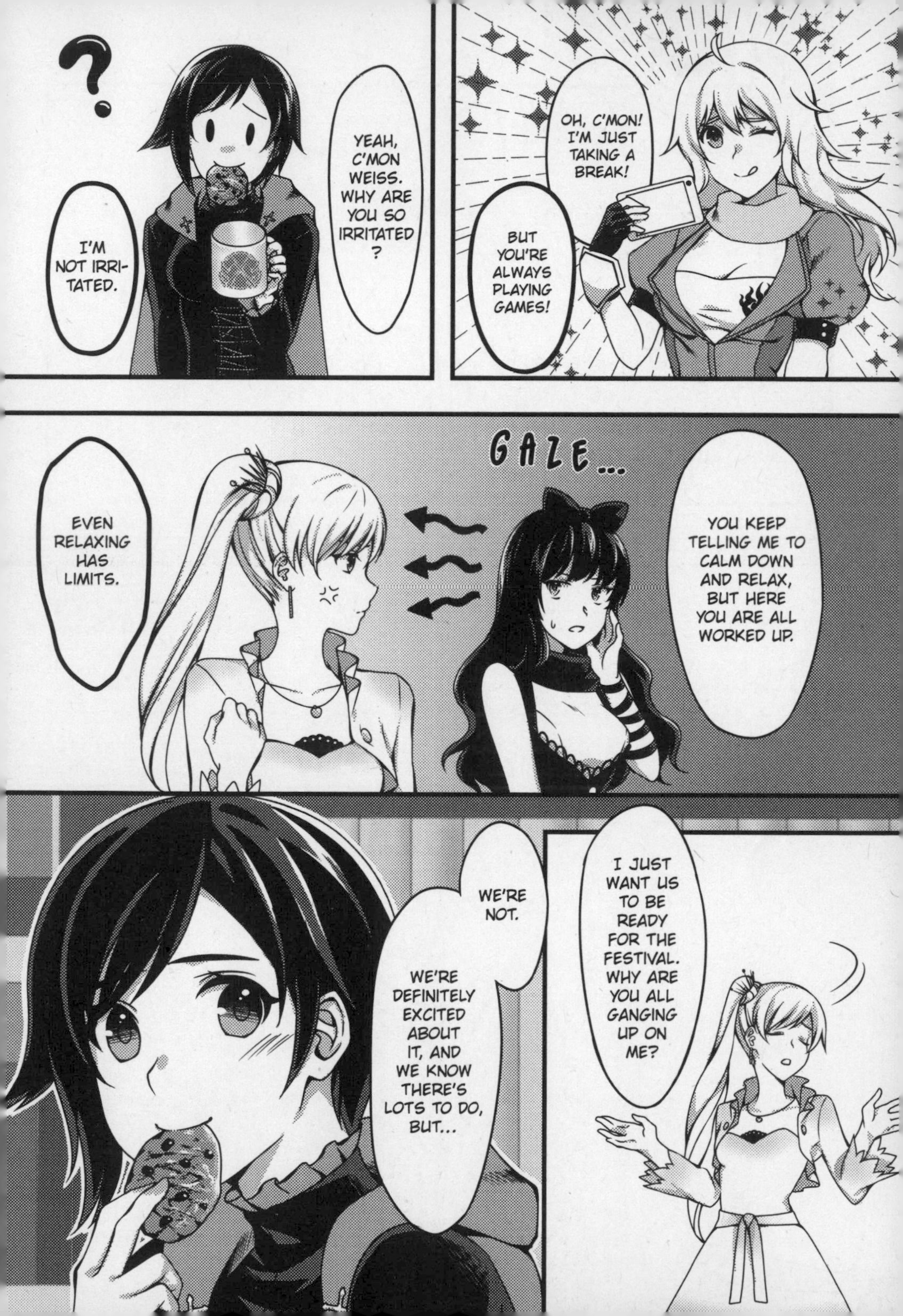
OH, C'MON! I'M JUST TAKING A BREAK!
BUT YOU'RE ALWAYS PLAYING GAMES!
YEAH, C'MON WEISS. WHY ARE YOU SO IRRITATED?
I'M NOT IRRITATED.
YOU KEEP TELLING ME TO CALM DOWN AND RELAX, BUT HERE YOU ARE ALL WORKED UP.
GAZE...
EVEN RELAXING HAS LIMITS.
I JUST WANT US TO BE READY FOR THE FESTIVAL. WHY ARE YOU ALL GANGING UP ON ME?
WE'RE NOT.
WE'RE DEFINITELY EXCITED ABOUT IT, AND WE KNOW THERE'S LOTS TO DO, BUT...

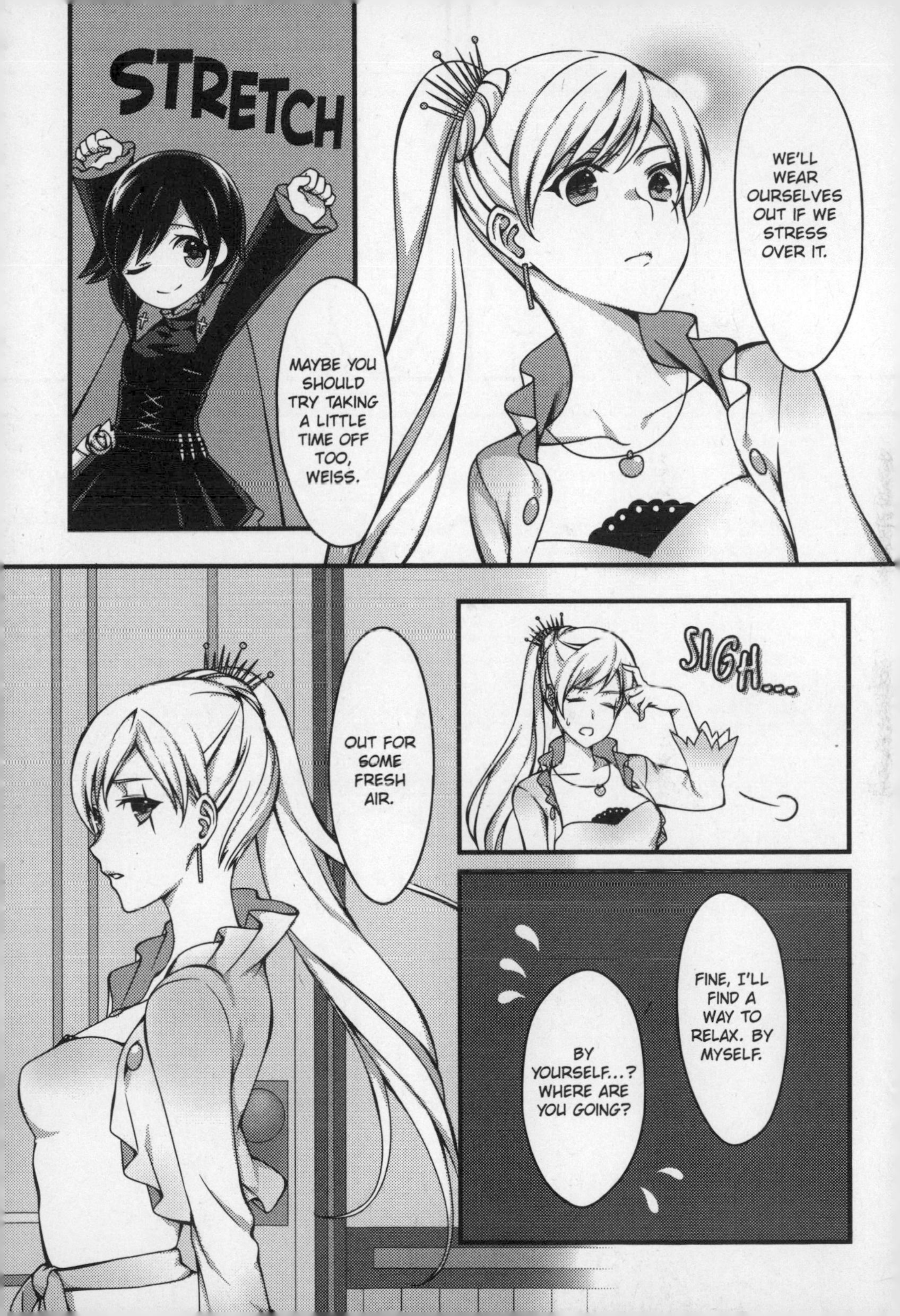
WE'LL WEAR OURSELVES OUT IF WE STRESS OVER IT.
MAYBE YOU SHOULD TRY TAKING A LITTLE TIME OFF TOO, WEISS.
STRETCH
SIGH...
FINE, I'LL FIND A WAY TO RELAX. BY MYSELF.
BY YOURSELF...? WHERE ARE YOU GOING?
OUT FOR SOME FRESH AIR.

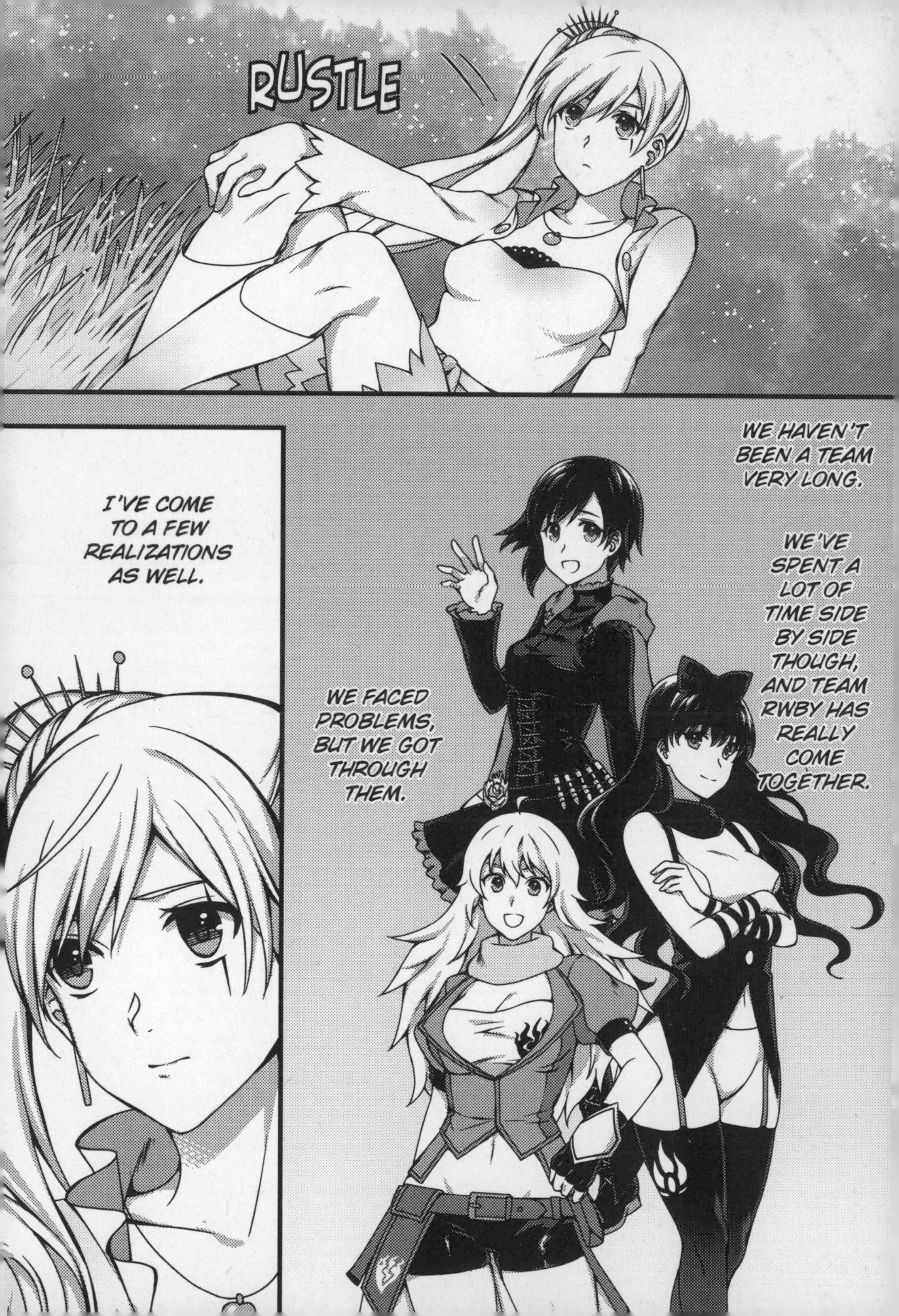
RUSTLE
WE HAVEN'T BEEN A TEAM VERY LONG.
WE'VE SPENT A LOT OF TIME SIDE BY SIDE THOUGH, AND TEAM RWBY HAS REALLY COME TOGETHER.
WE FACED PROBLEMS, BUT WE GOT THROUGH THEM.
I'VE COME TO A FEW REALIZATIONS AS WELL.

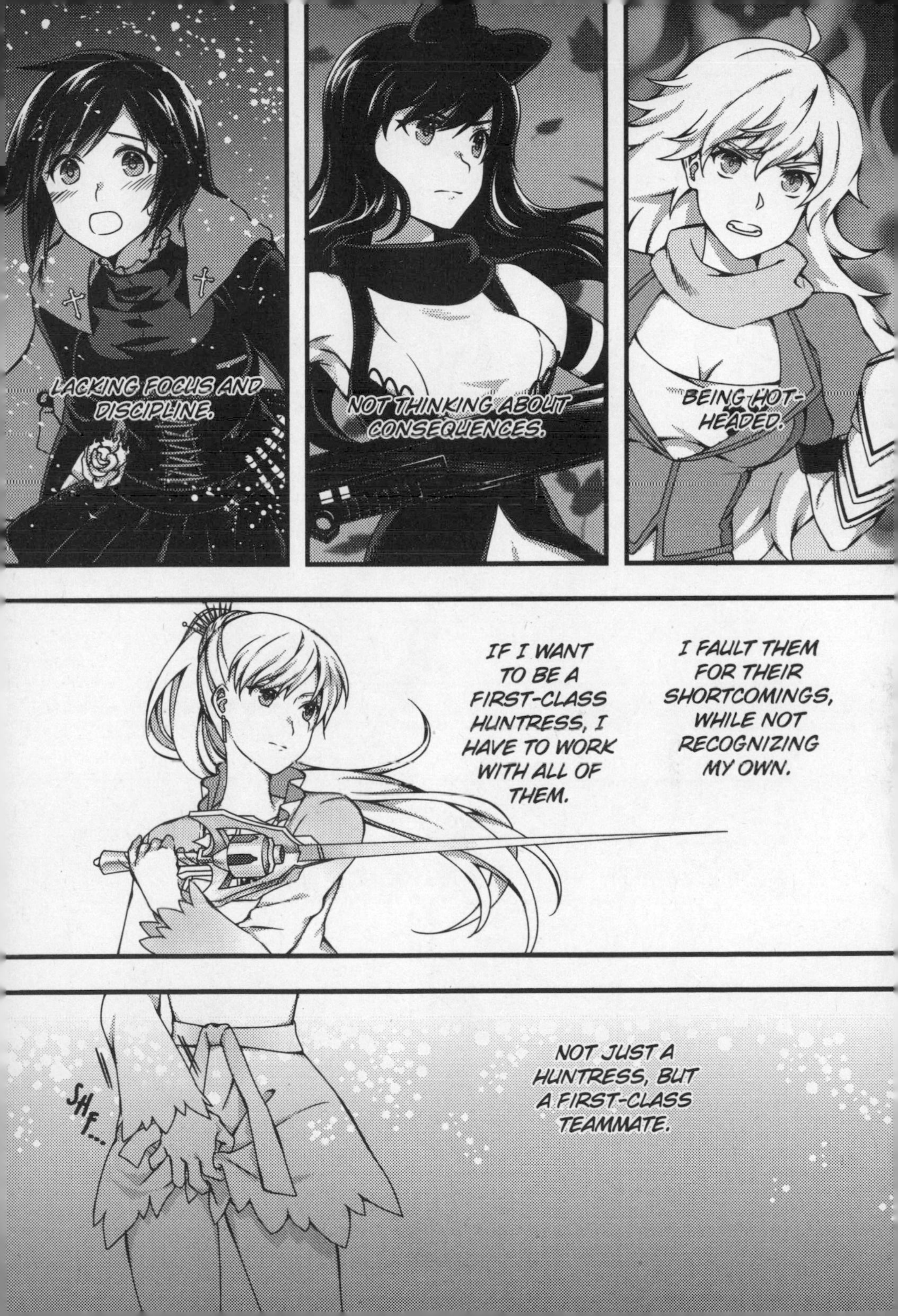
BEING HOT-HEADED.
NOT THINKING ABOUT CONSEQUENCES.
LACKING FOCUS AND DISCIPLINE.
I FAULT THEM FOR THEIR SHORTCOMINGS, WHILE NOT RECOGNIZING MY OWN.
IF I WANT TO BE A FIRST-CLASS HUNTRESS, I HAVE TO WORK WITH ALL OF THEM.
NOT JUST A HUNTRESS, BUT A FIRST-CLASS TEAMMATE.
SHF...

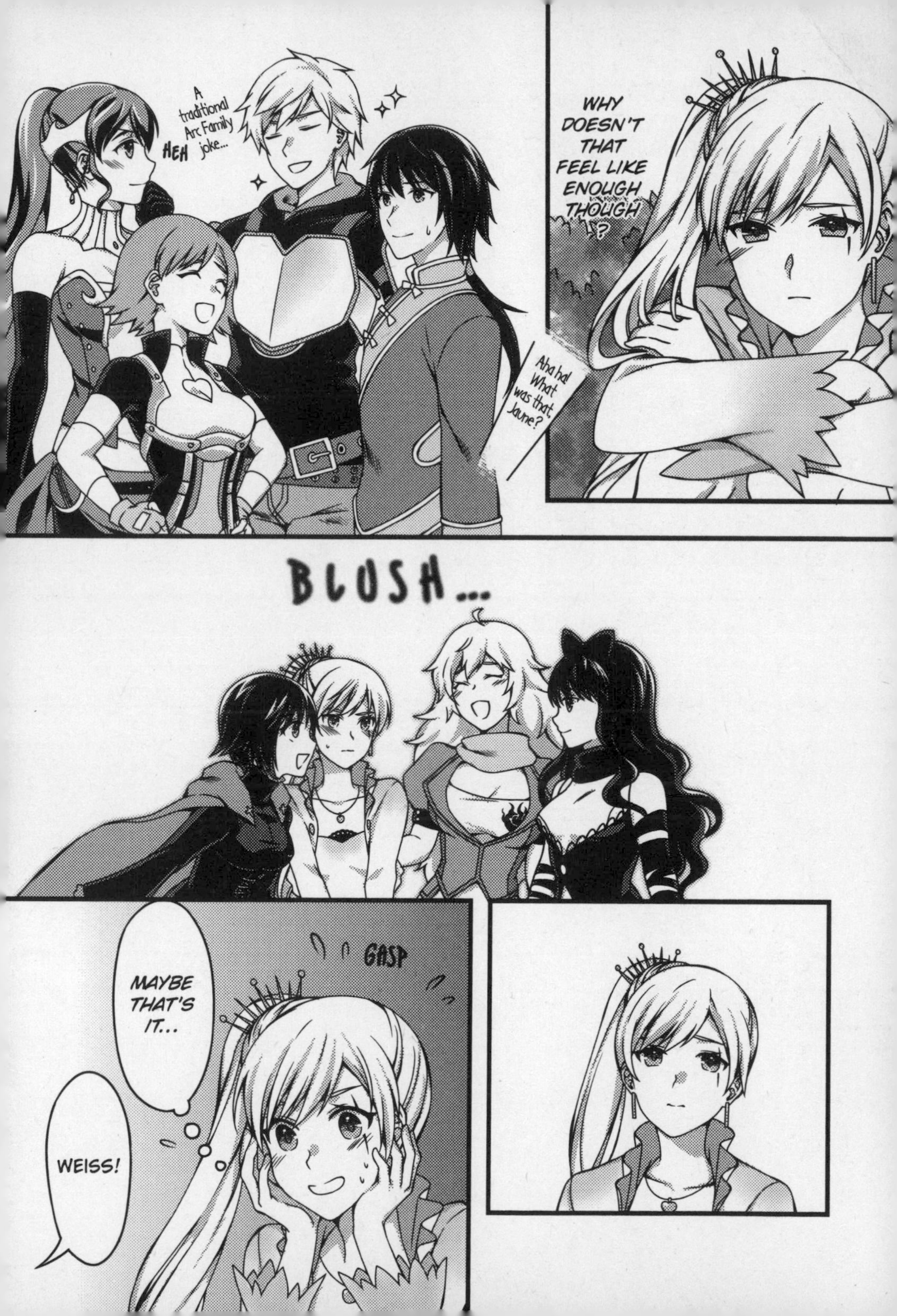
WHY DOESN'T THAT FEEL LIKE ENOUGH THOUGH?
A traditional Arc Family joke...
HEH
Aha ha! What was that, Jaune?
BLUSH...
GASP
MAYBE THAT'S IT...
WEISS!

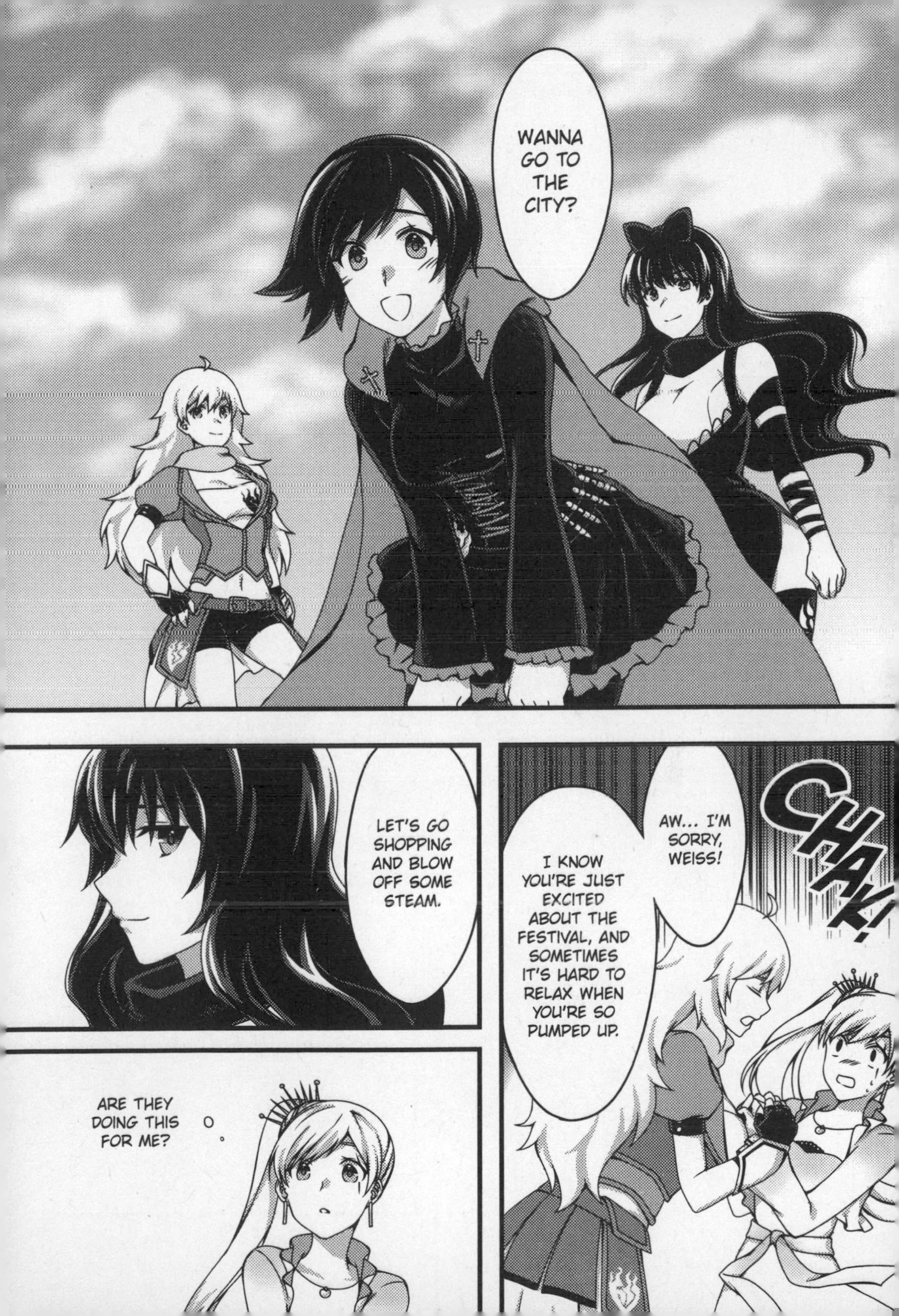
WANNA GO TO THE CITY?
CHAK!
AW... I'M SORRY, WEISS!
I KNOW YOU'RE JUST EXCITED ABOUT THE FESTIVAL, AND SOMETIMES IT'S HARD TO RELAX WHEN YOU'RE SO PUMPED UP.
LET'S GO SHOPPING AND BLOW OFF SOME STEAM.
ARE THEY DOING THIS FOR ME?

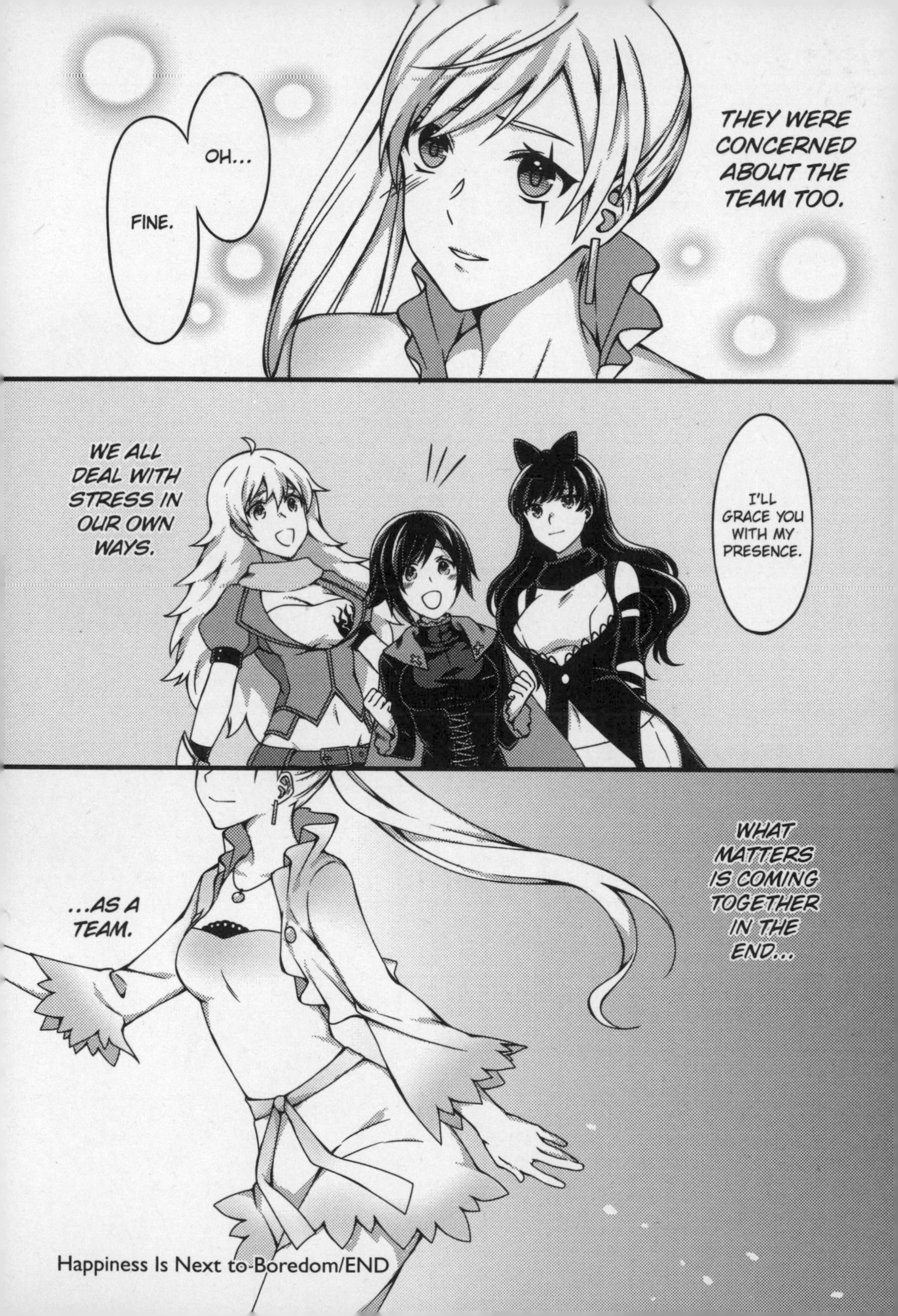
THEY WERE CONCERNED ABOUT THE TEAM TOO.
OH... FINE.
I'LL GRACE YOU WITH MY PRESENCE.
WE ALL DEAL WITH STRESS IN OUR OWN WAYS.
WHAT MATTERS IS COMING TOGETHER IN THE END...
...AS A TEAM.
Happiness Is Next to-Boredom/END

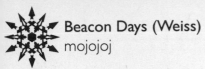

Beacon Days (Weiss)

mojojoj

Just Your Imagination

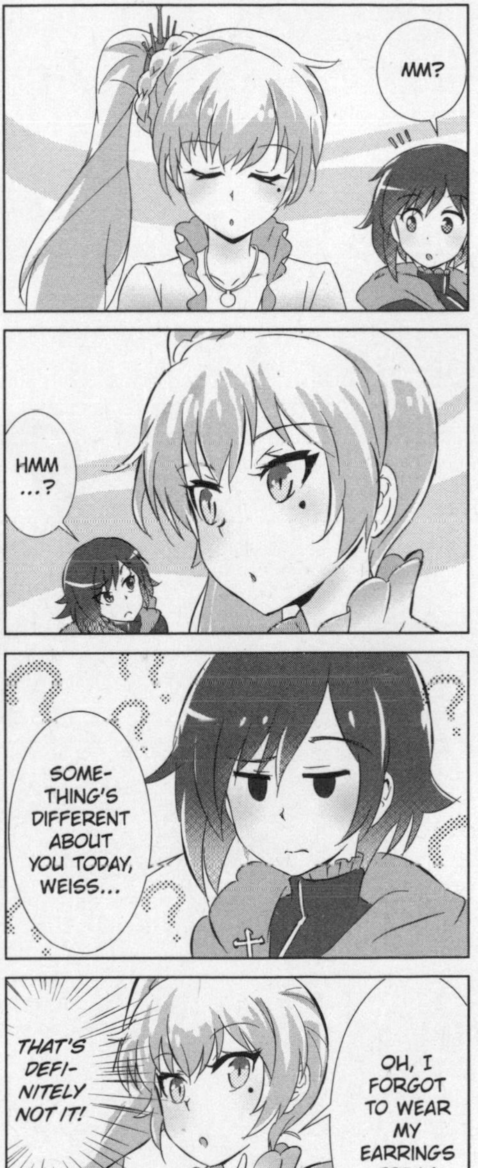
MM?
HMM ...?
SOME-THING'S DIFFERENT ABOUT YOU TODAY, WEISS...
OH, I FORGOT TO WEAR MY EARRINGS TODAY.
THAT'S DEFI-NITELY NOT IT!

High Costs

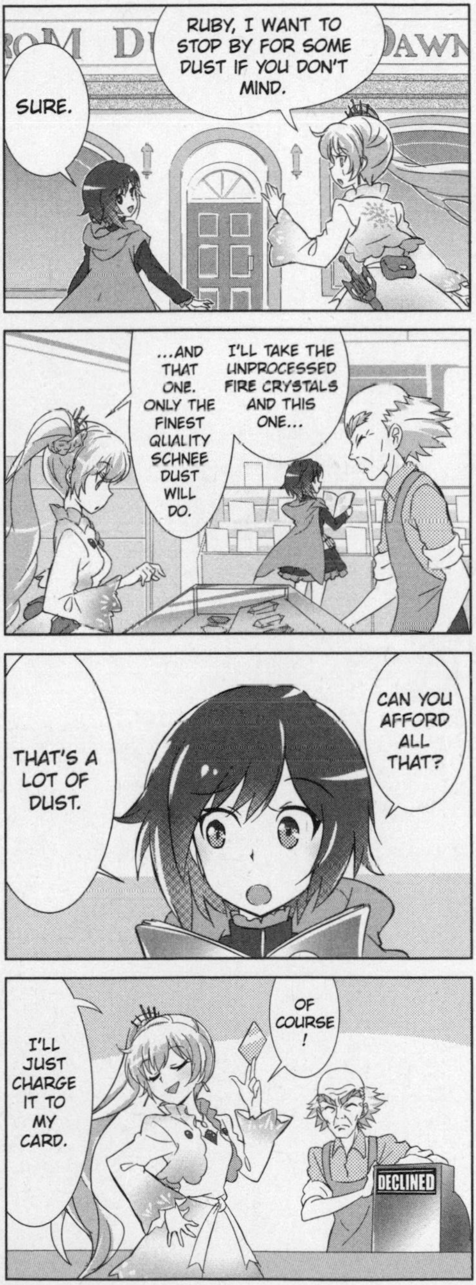
RUBY, I WANT TO STOP BY FOR SOME DUST IF YOU DON'T MIND.
SURE.
I'LL TAKE THE UNPROCESSED FIRE CRYSTALS AND THIS ONE...
...AND THAT ONE. ONLY THE FINEST QUALITY SCHNEE DUST WILL DO.
CAN YOU AFFORD ALL THAT?
THAT'S A LOT OF DUST.
OF COURSE!
I'LL JUST CHARGE IT TO MY CARD.
DECLINED

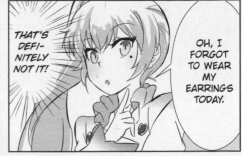

Guidance Counseling

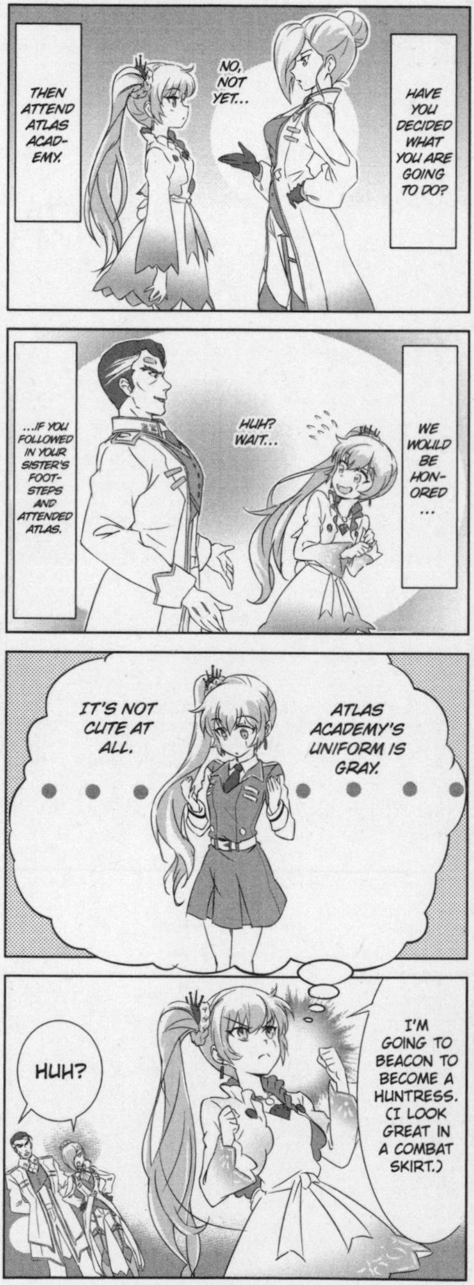
HAVE YOU DECIDED WHAT YOU ARE GOING TO DO?
NO, NOT YET...
THEN ATTEND ATLAS ACADEMY.
WE WOULD BE HONORED ...
HUH? WAIT...
...IF YOU FOLLOWED IN YOUR SISTER'S FOOTSTEPS AND ATTENDED ATLAS.
ATLAS ACADEMY'S UNIFORM IS GRAY.
IT'S NOT CUTE AT ALL.
I'M GOING TO BEACON TO BECOME A HUNTRESS. (I LOOK GREAT IN A COMBAT SKIRT.)
HUH?

A Day in the Life of the Snow Sisters

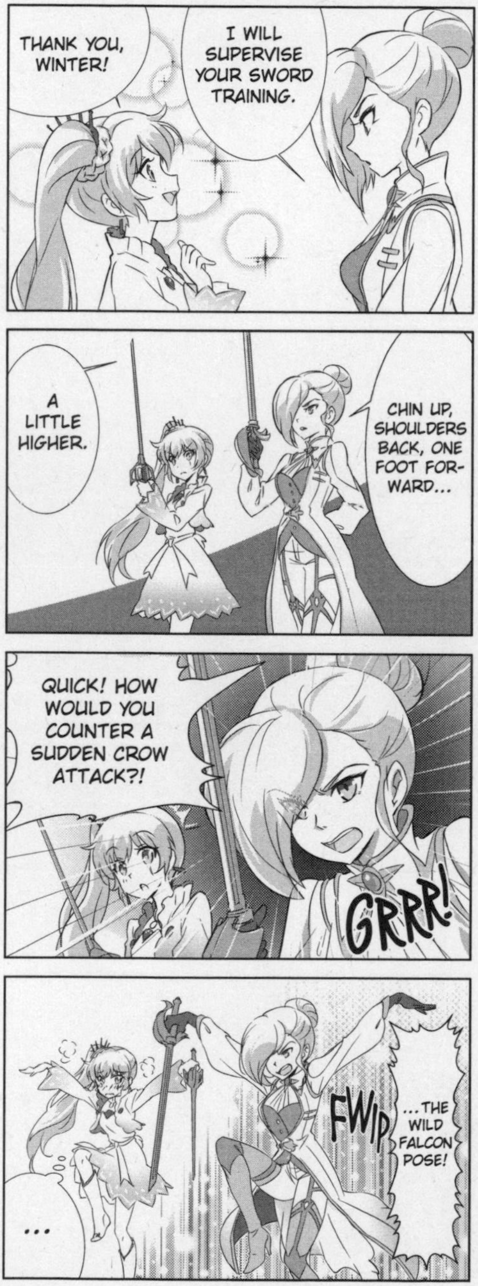
I WILL SUPERVISE YOUR SWORD TRAINING.
THANK YOU, WINTER!
CHIN UP, SHOULDERS BACK, ONE FOOT FORWARD...
A LITTLE HIGHER.
QUICK! HOW WOULD YOU COUNTER A SUDDEN CROW ATTACK?!
GRRR!
...THE WILD FALCON POSE!
FWIP
...

(BFF)

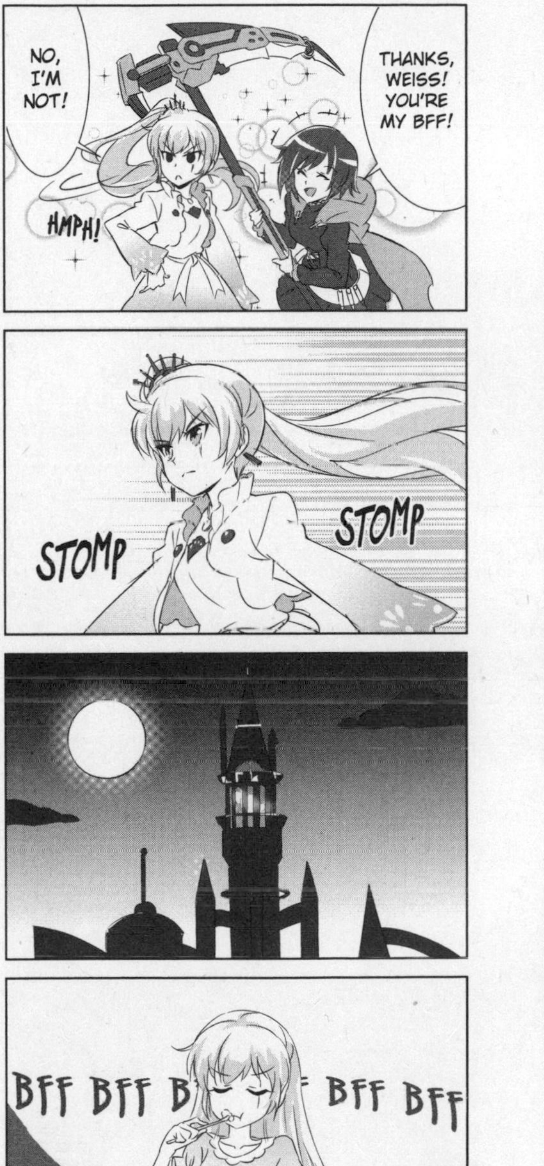
THANKS, WEISS! YOU'RE MY BFF!
NO, I'M NOT!
HMPH!
STOMP
STOMP
BFF BFF B
BFF BFF

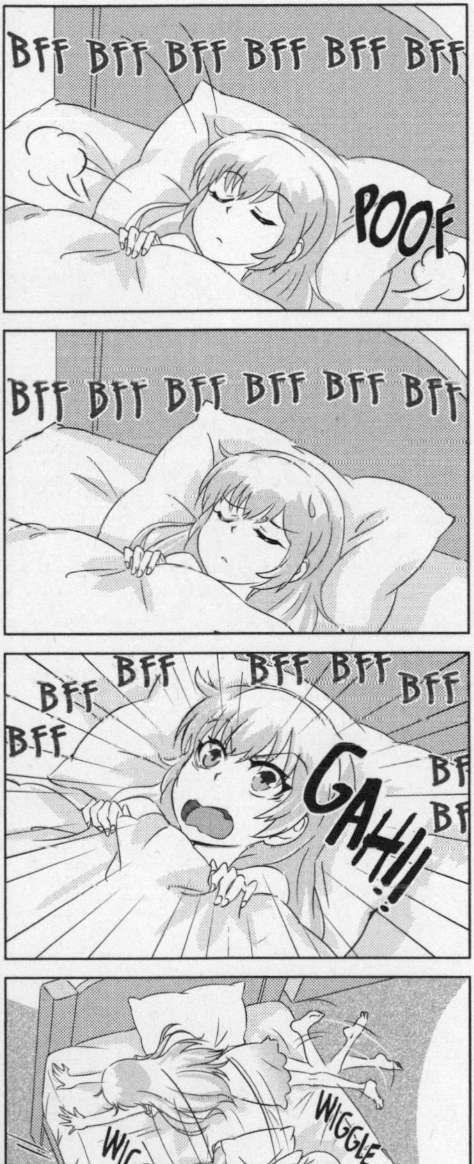
BFF BFF BFF BFF BFF BFF
POOF
BFF BFF BFF BFF BFF BFF
BFF BFF BFF BFF BFF BFF
BF
BF
GAH!!
WIGGLE
WIGGLE
Weiss!! Keep it down!!

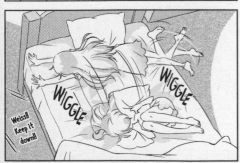

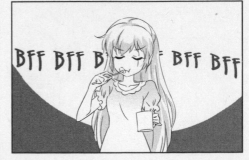

Hard Worker

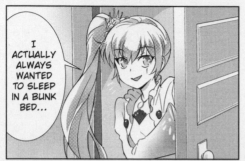

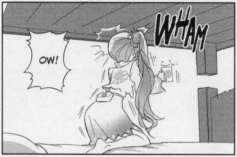

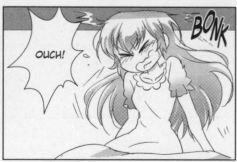

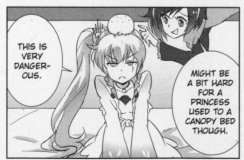

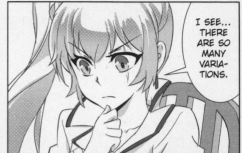

I SEE... THERE ARE SO MANY VARIA-TIONS.
HOP
WHAT'RE YOU READING SO INTENTLY?
OH, NOTHING!
A HUMAN-ITIES RESEARCH PAPER.
CREEP
REALLY? THAT SOUNDS FISHY.
CREEP
101 GREAT JOKES TO CRACK UP YOUR FRIENDS
I-I'M DEFINITELY NOT LYING.

Wish

I ACTUALLY ALWAYS WANTED TO SLEEP IN A BUNK BED...
WHAM
OW!
BONK
OUCH!
MIGHT BE A BIT HARD FOR A PRINCESS USED TO A CANOPY BED THOUGH.
THIS IS VERY DANGER-OUS.

Beacon Days (Weiss)/END

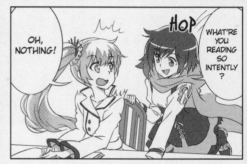

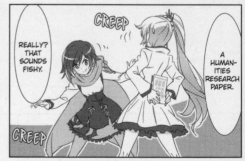

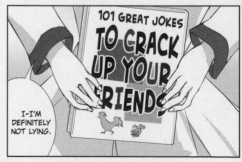

RWBY

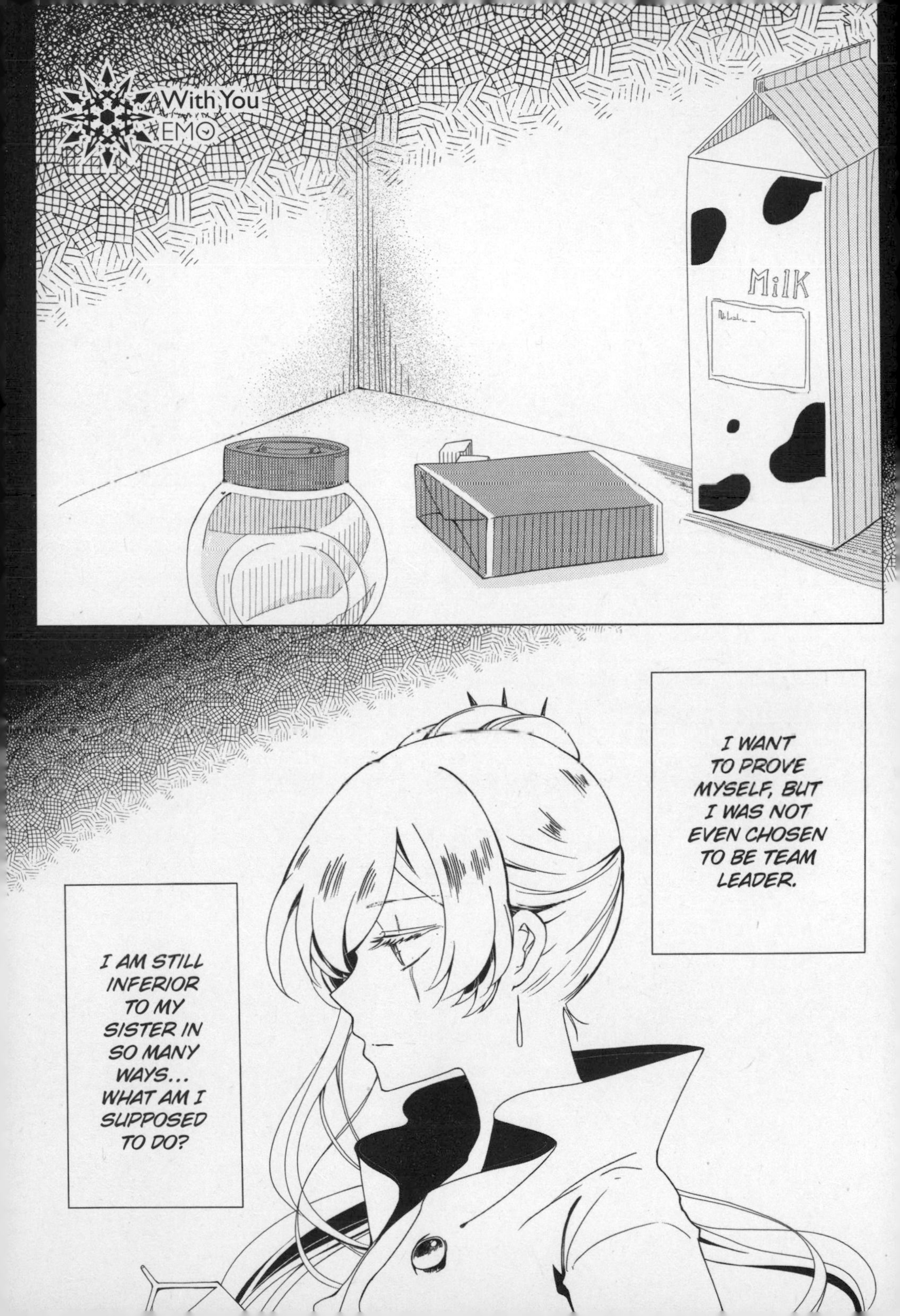
With You
EMO
MILK
I WANT TO PROVE MYSELF, BUT I WAS NOT EVEN CHOSEN TO BE TEAM LEADER.
I AM STILL INFERIOR TO MY SISTER IN SO MANY WAYS... WHAT AM I SUPPOSED TO DO?

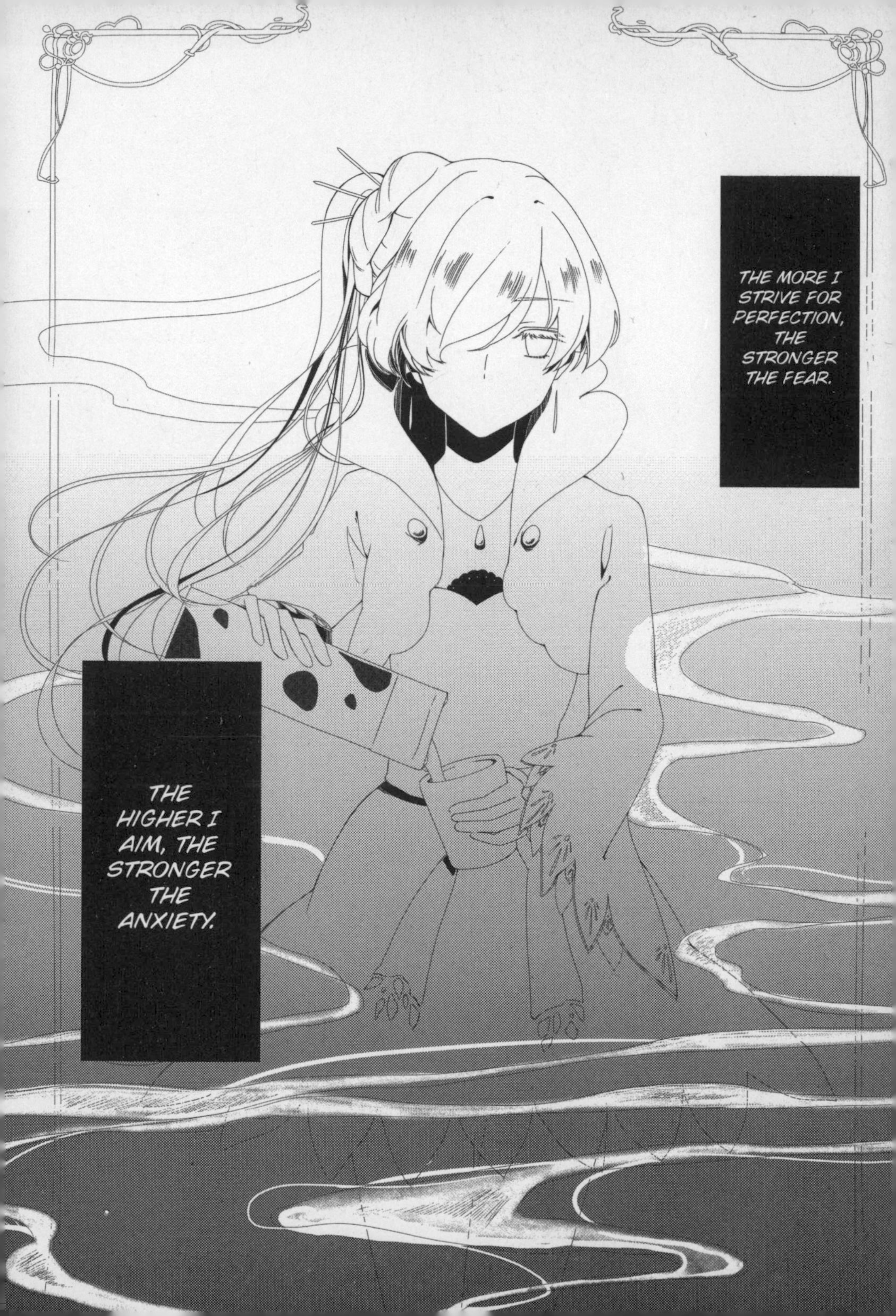
THE MORE I STRIVE FOR PERFECTION, THE STRONGER THE FEAR.
THE HIGHER I AIM, THE STRONGER THE ANXIETY.

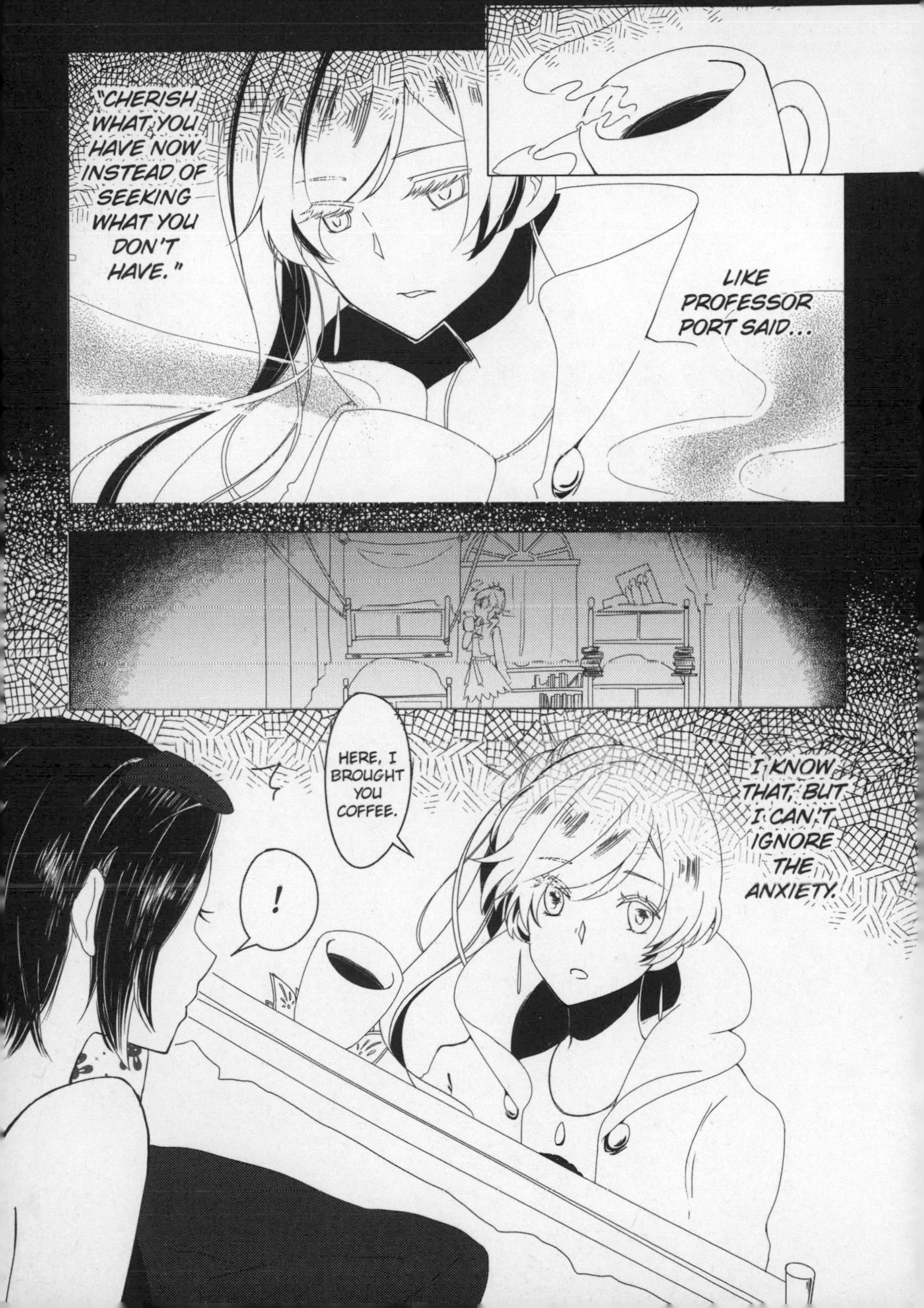
LIKE PROFESSOR PORT SAID...
"CHERISH WHAT YOU HAVE NOW INSTEAD OF SEEKING WHAT YOU DON'T HAVE."
I KNOW THAT, BUT I CAN'T IGNORE THE ANXIETY.
HERE, I BROUGHT YOU COFFEE.
!

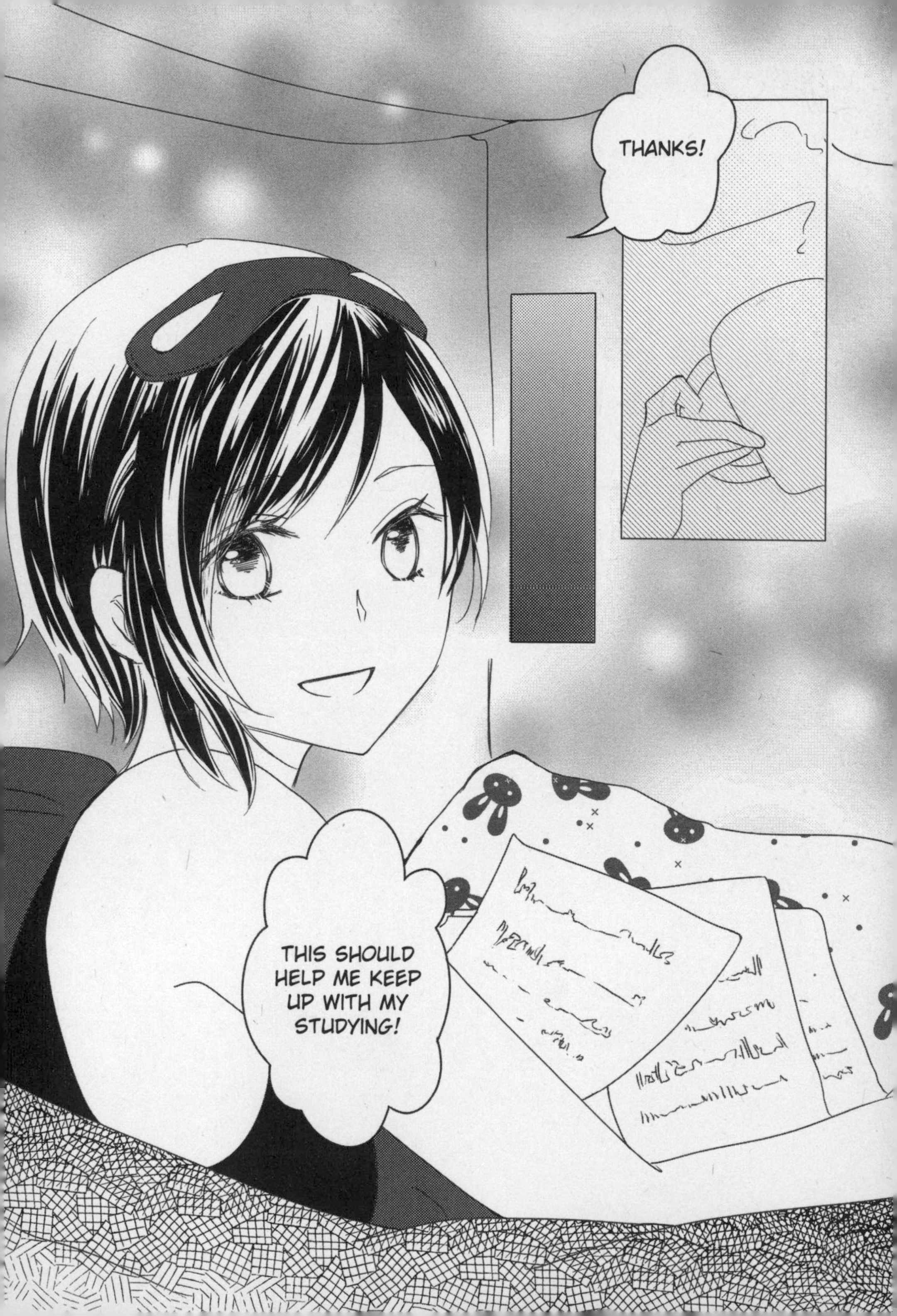
THANKS!
THIS SHOULD HELP ME KEEP UP WITH MY STUDYING!

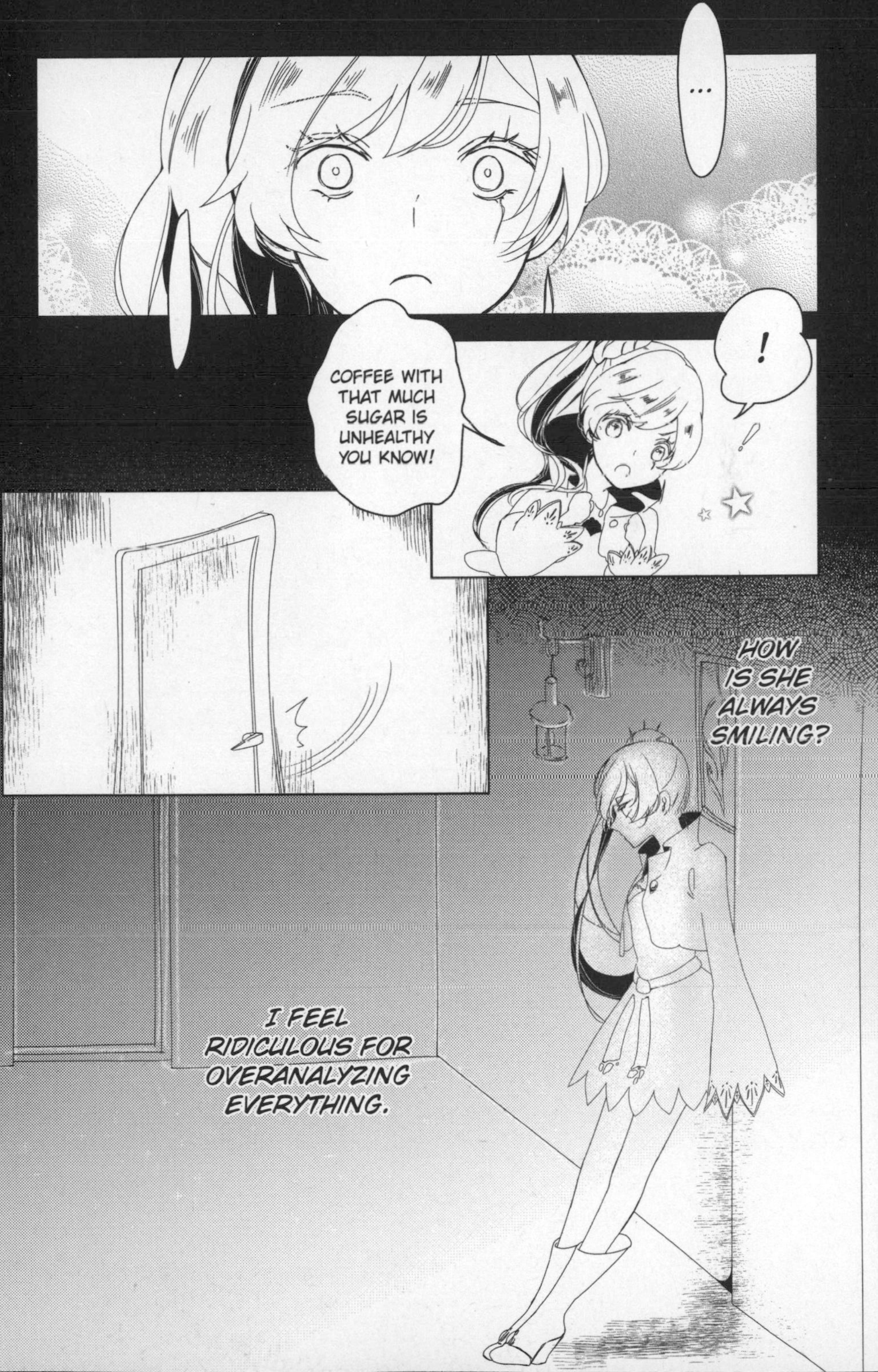
...
COFFEE WITH THAT MUCH SUGAR IS UNHEALTHY YOU KNOW!
!
HOW IS SHE ALWAYS SMILING?
I FEEL RIDICULOUS FOR OVERANALYZING EVERYTHING.

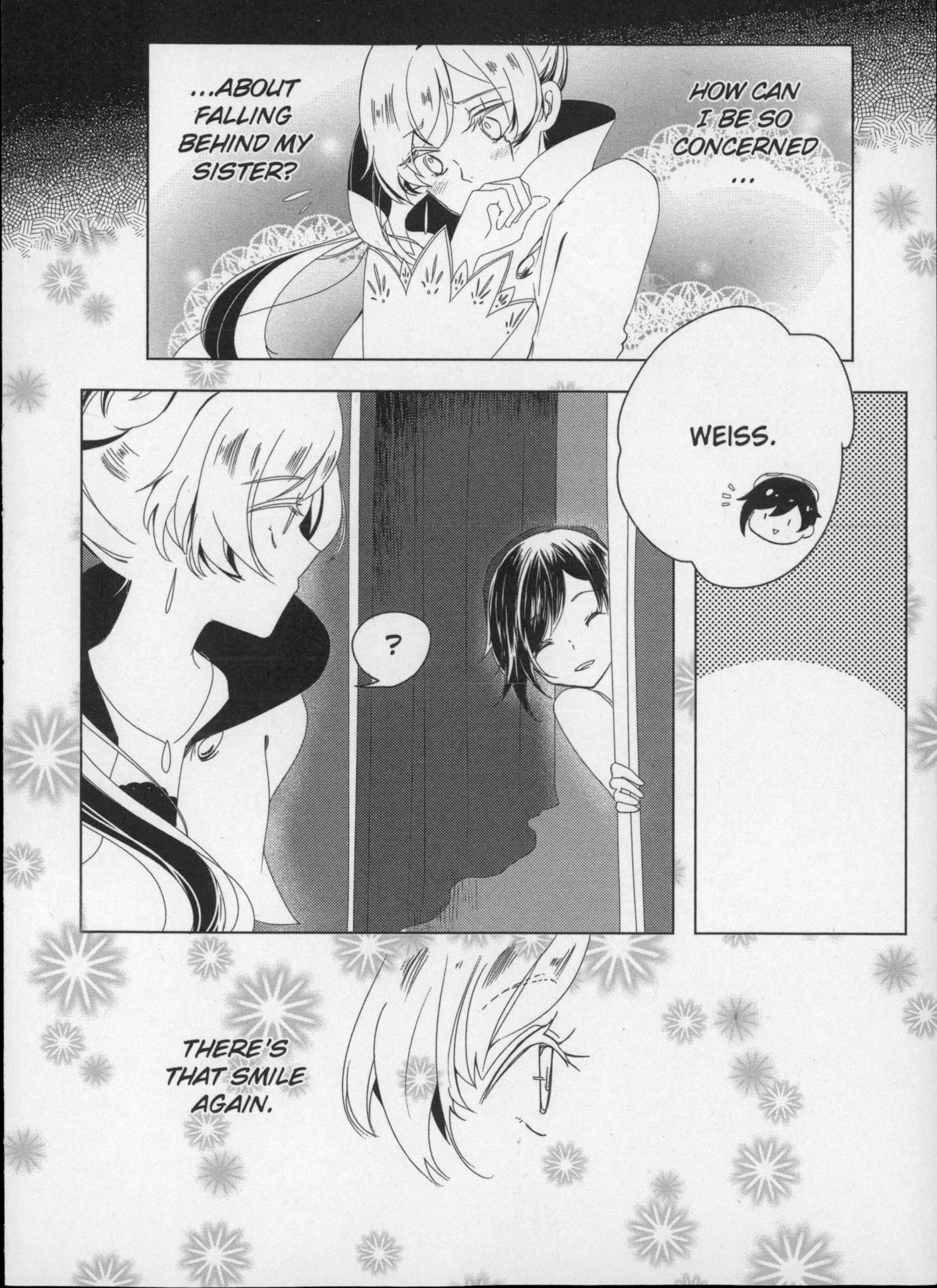
HOW CAN I BE SO CONCERNED ...
...ABOUT FALLING BEHIND MY SISTER?
WEISS.
?
THERE'S THAT SMILE AGAIN.

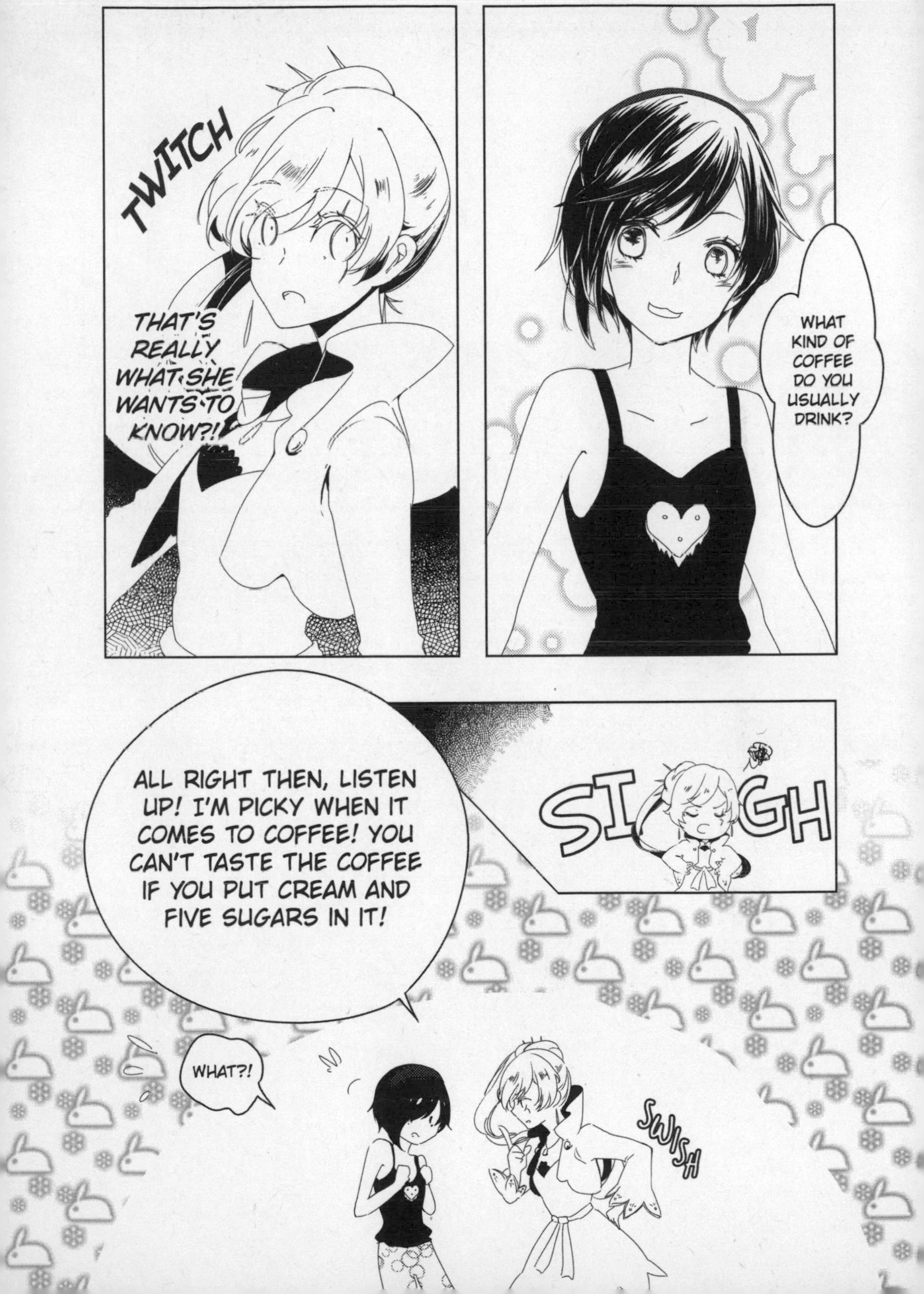
WHAT KIND OF COFFEE DO YOU USUALLY DRINK?
TWITCH
THAT'S REALLY WHAT SHE WANTS TO KNOW?!
SIGH
ALL RIGHT THEN, LISTEN UP! I'M PICKY WHEN IT COMES TO COFFEE! YOU CAN'T TASTE THE COFFEE IF YOU PUT CREAM AND FIVE SUGARS IN IT!
SWISH
WHAT?!

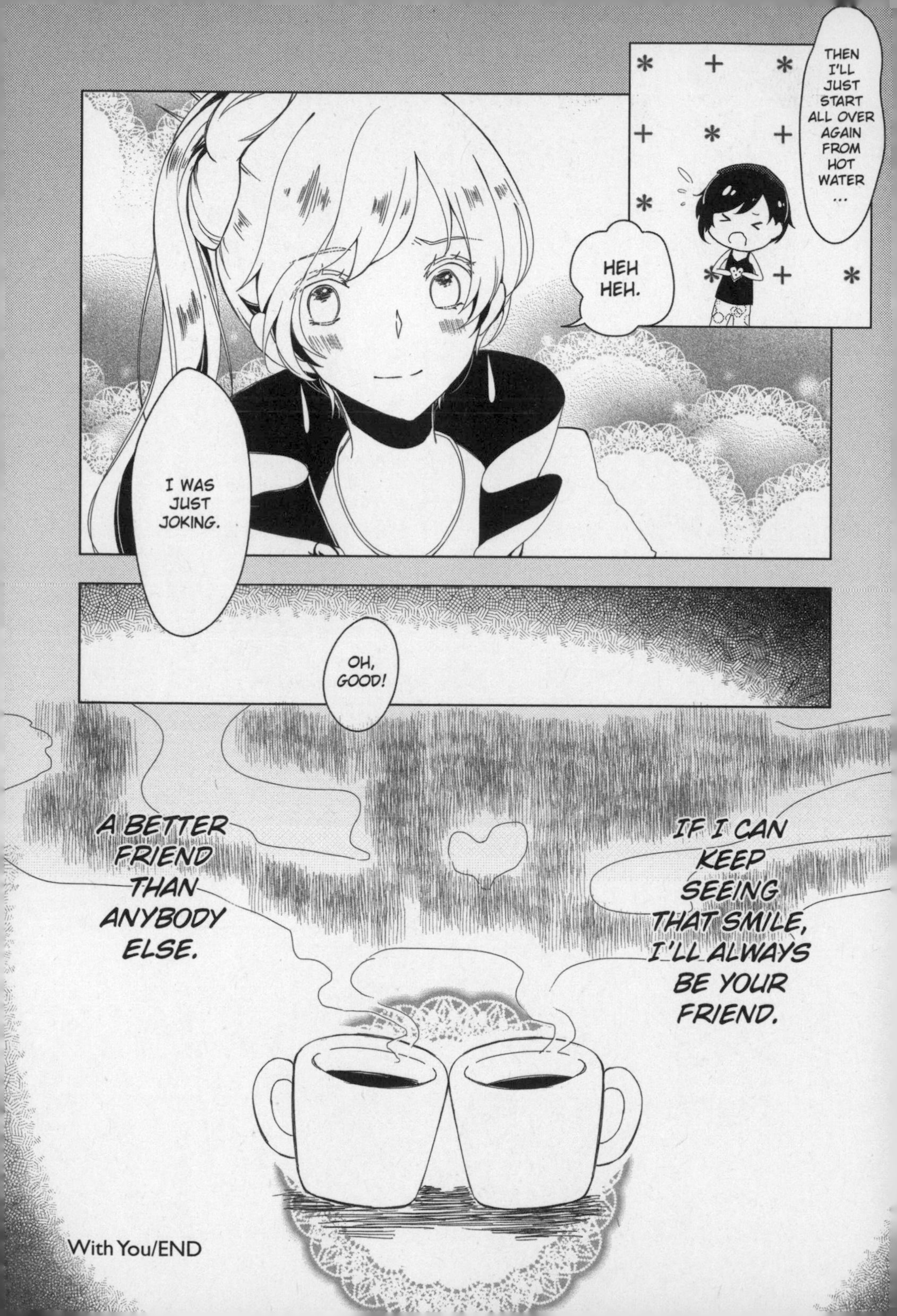
THEN I'LL JUST START ALL OVER AGAIN FROM HOT WATER...
HEH HEH.
I WAS JUST JOKING.
OH, GOOD!
IF I CAN KEEP SEEING THAT SMILE, I'LL ALWAYS BE YOUR FRIEND.
A BETTER FRIEND THAN ANYBODY ELSE.

With You/END

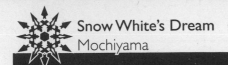

MIRROR, MIRROR ON THE WALL. WHO IS THE LONELIEST OF THEM ALL?

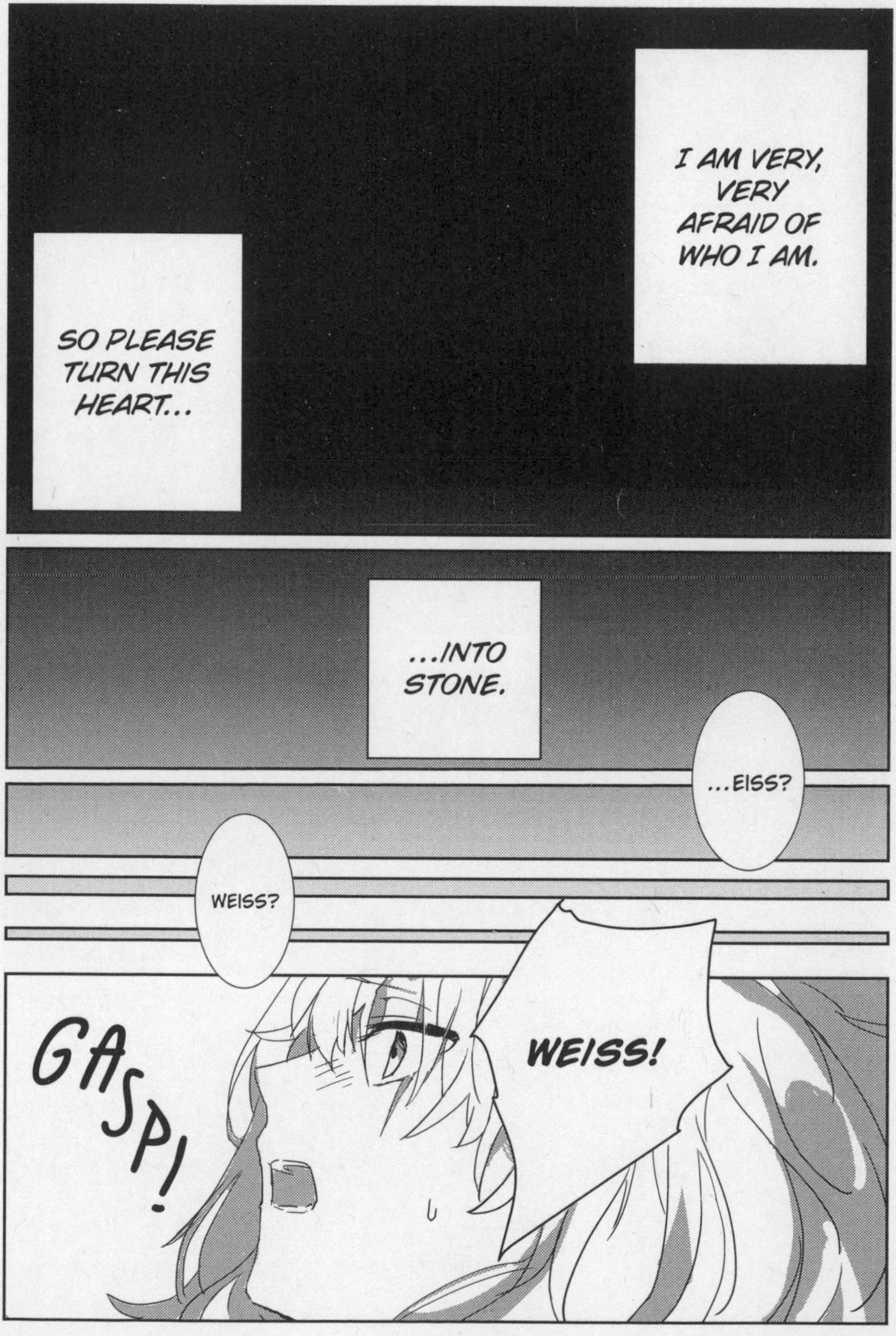
I AM VERY, VERY AFRAID OF WHO I AM.
SO PLEASE TURN THIS HEART...
...INTO STONE.
...EISS?
WEISS?
WEISS!
GASP!

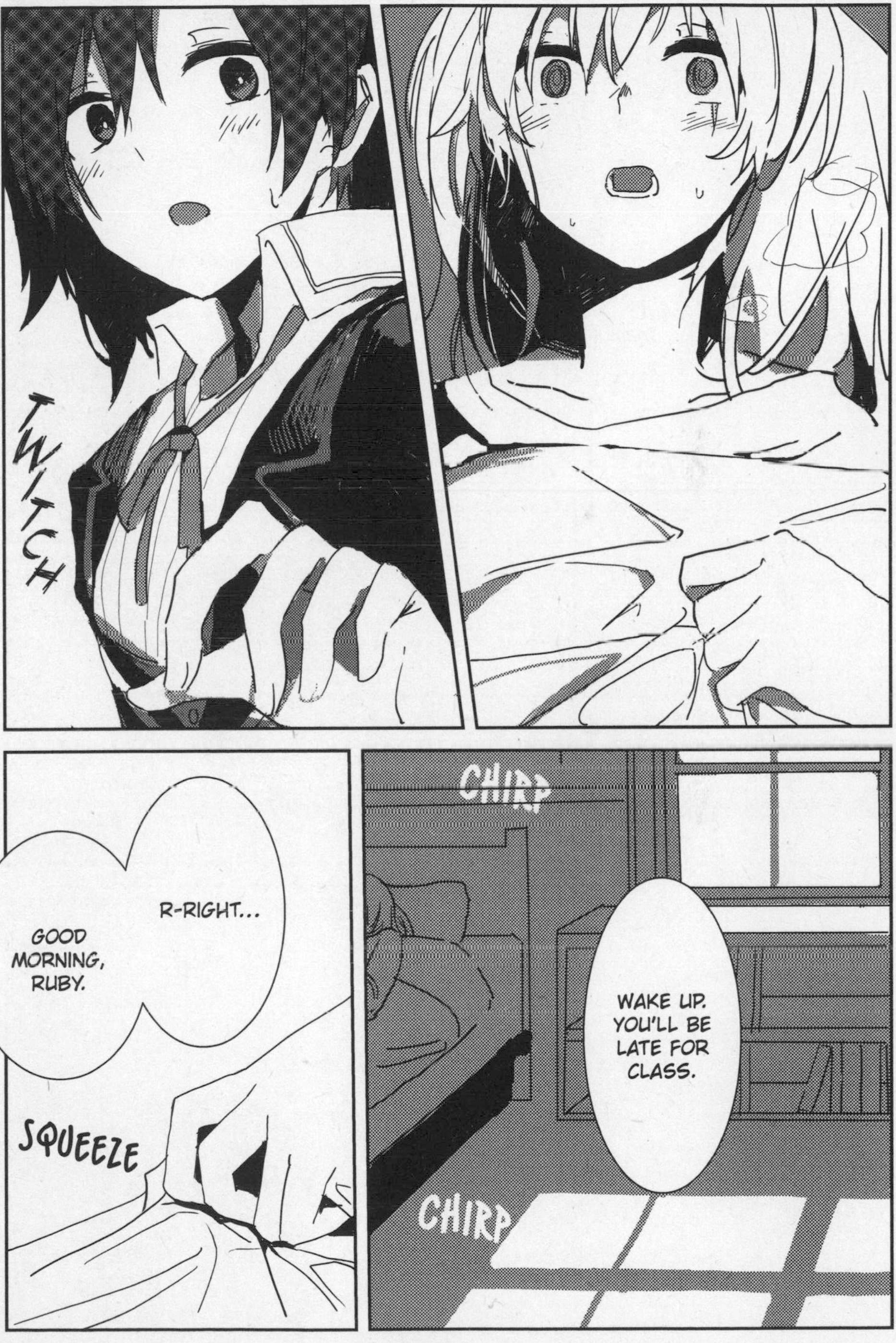
TWITCH
CHIRP
WAKE UP. YOU'LL BE LATE FOR CLASS.
CHIRP
R-RIGHT...
GOOD MORNING, RUBY.
SQUEEZE

BUZZ BUZZ BUZZ BUZZ

IF YOU'RE NOT GONNA EAT THAT, CAN I?

HEY, WEISS?

Cafeteria

?!

??

DAZE

HUH? OH, SURE...

I'M DONE.

SHE'D USUALLY SNAP AT ME FOR EVEN ASKING. I WONDER WHAT'S WRONG...

HMM...

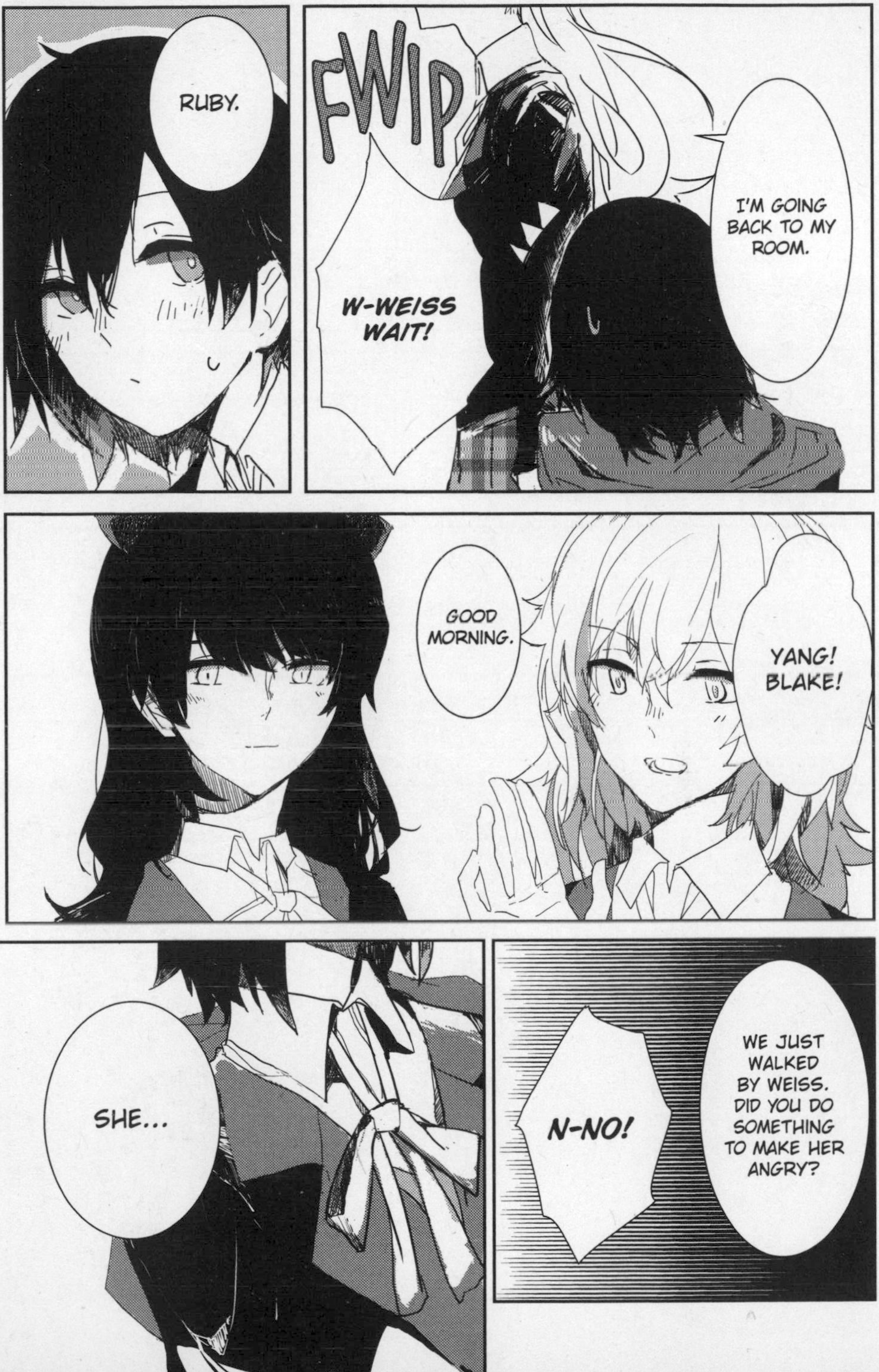
I'M GOING BACK TO MY ROOM.
FWIP
W-WEISS WAIT!
RUBY.
YANG! BLAKE!
GOOD MORNING.
WE JUST WALKED BY WEISS. DID YOU DO SOMETHING TO MAKE HER ANGRY?
N-NO!
SHE...

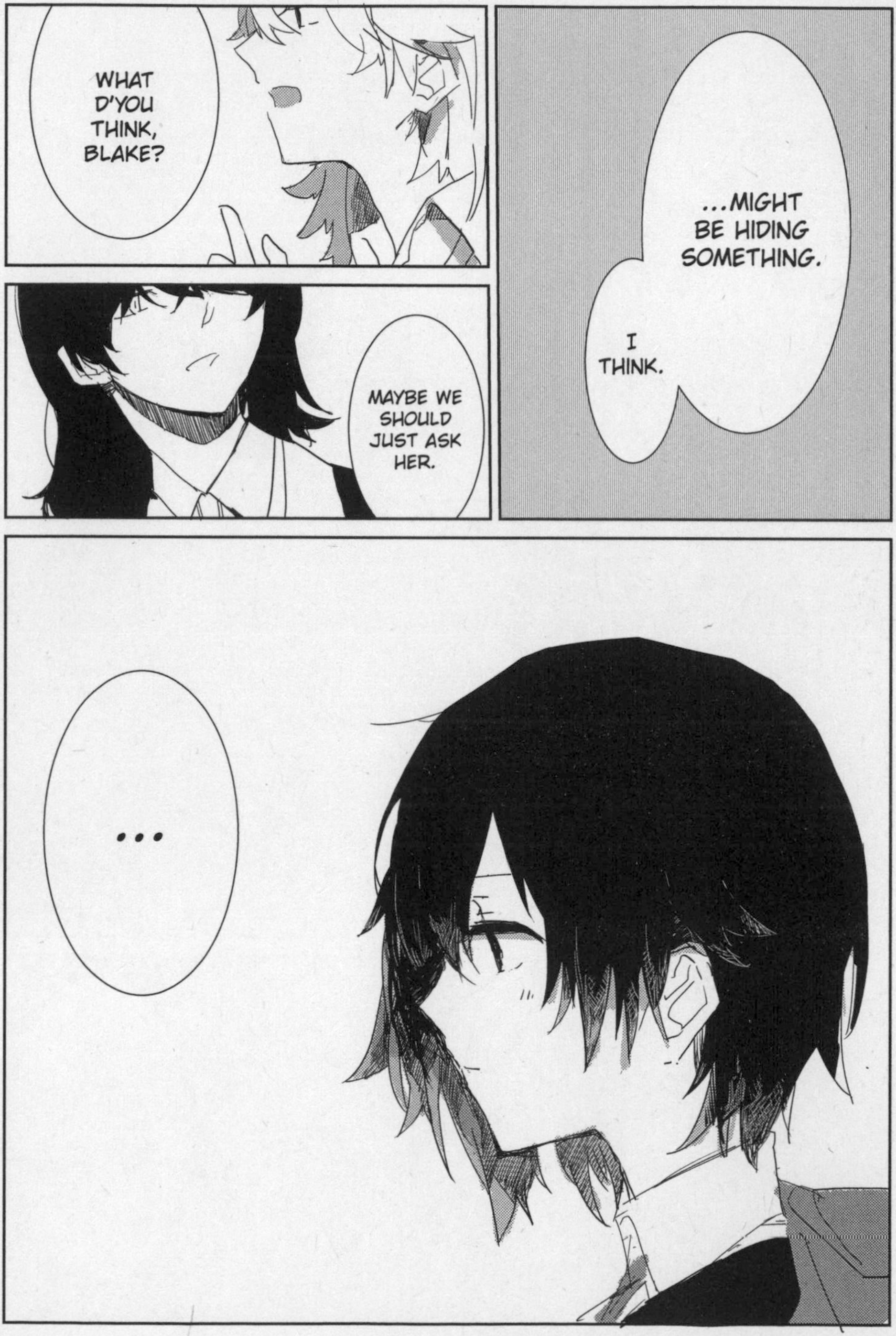
...MIGHT BE HIDING SOMETHING.
I THINK.
WHAT D'YOU THINK, BLAKE?
MAYBE WE SHOULD JUST ASK HER.
...

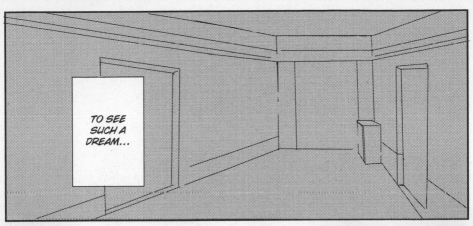

TO SEE
SUCH A
DREAM...

AM I
LONELY?

K-
CHIK
...

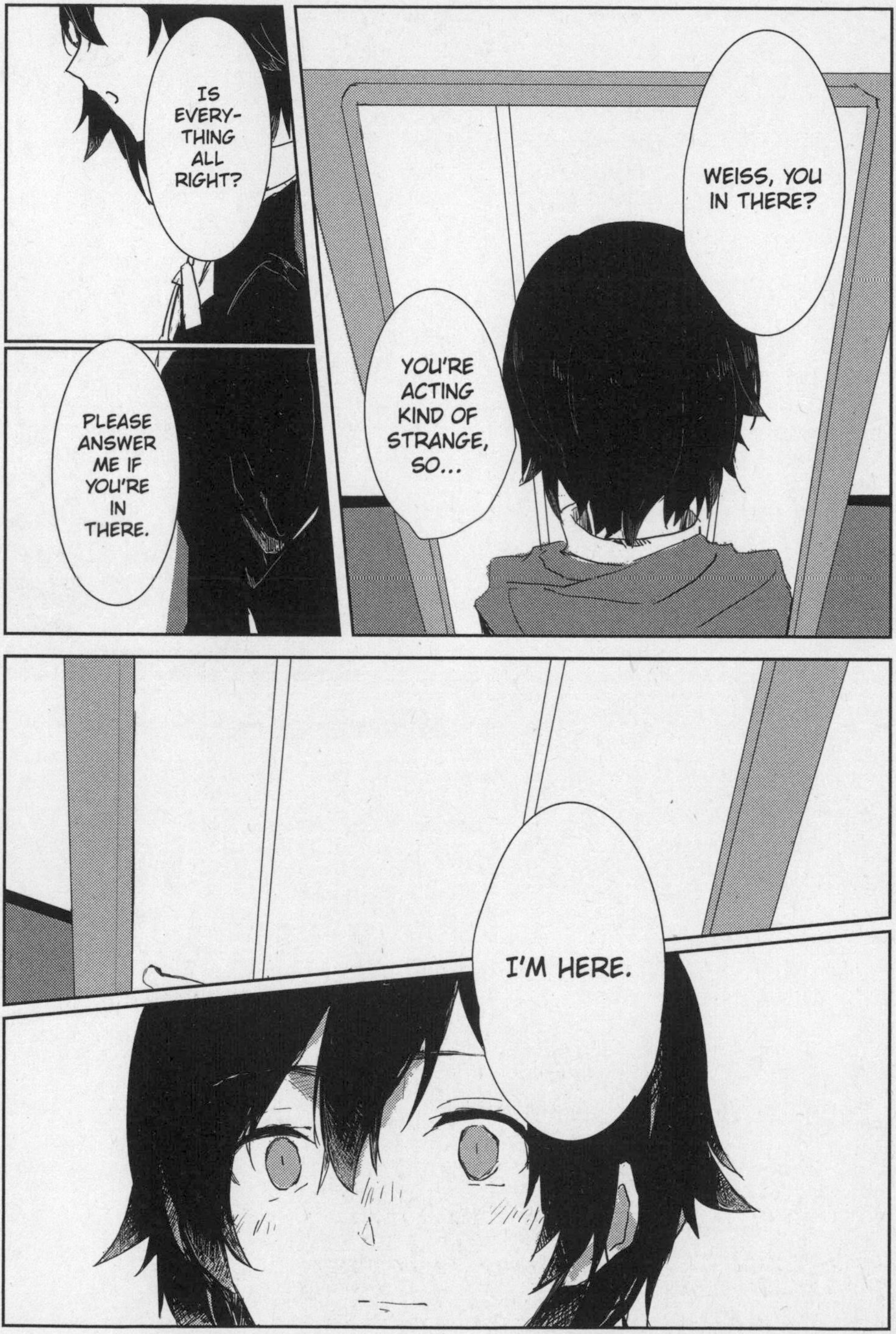
WEISS, YOU IN THERE?
YOU'RE ACTING KIND OF STRANGE, SO...
IS EVERY-THING ALL RIGHT?
PLEASE ANSWER ME IF YOU'RE IN THERE.
I'M HERE.

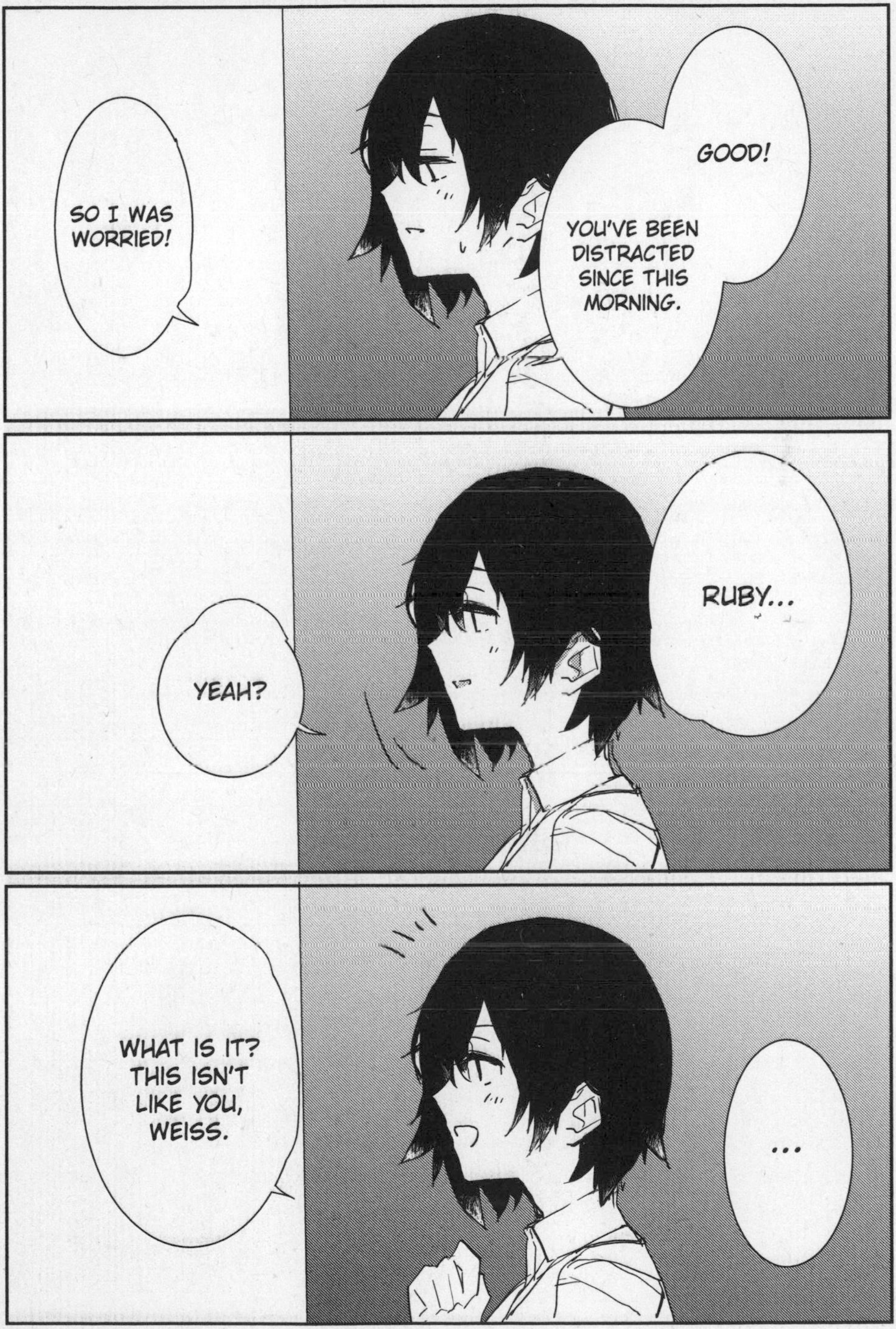
GOOD!
YOU'VE BEEN DISTRACTED SINCE THIS MORNING.
SO I WAS WORRIED!
RUBY...
YEAH?
...
WHAT IS IT? THIS ISN'T LIKE YOU, WEISS.

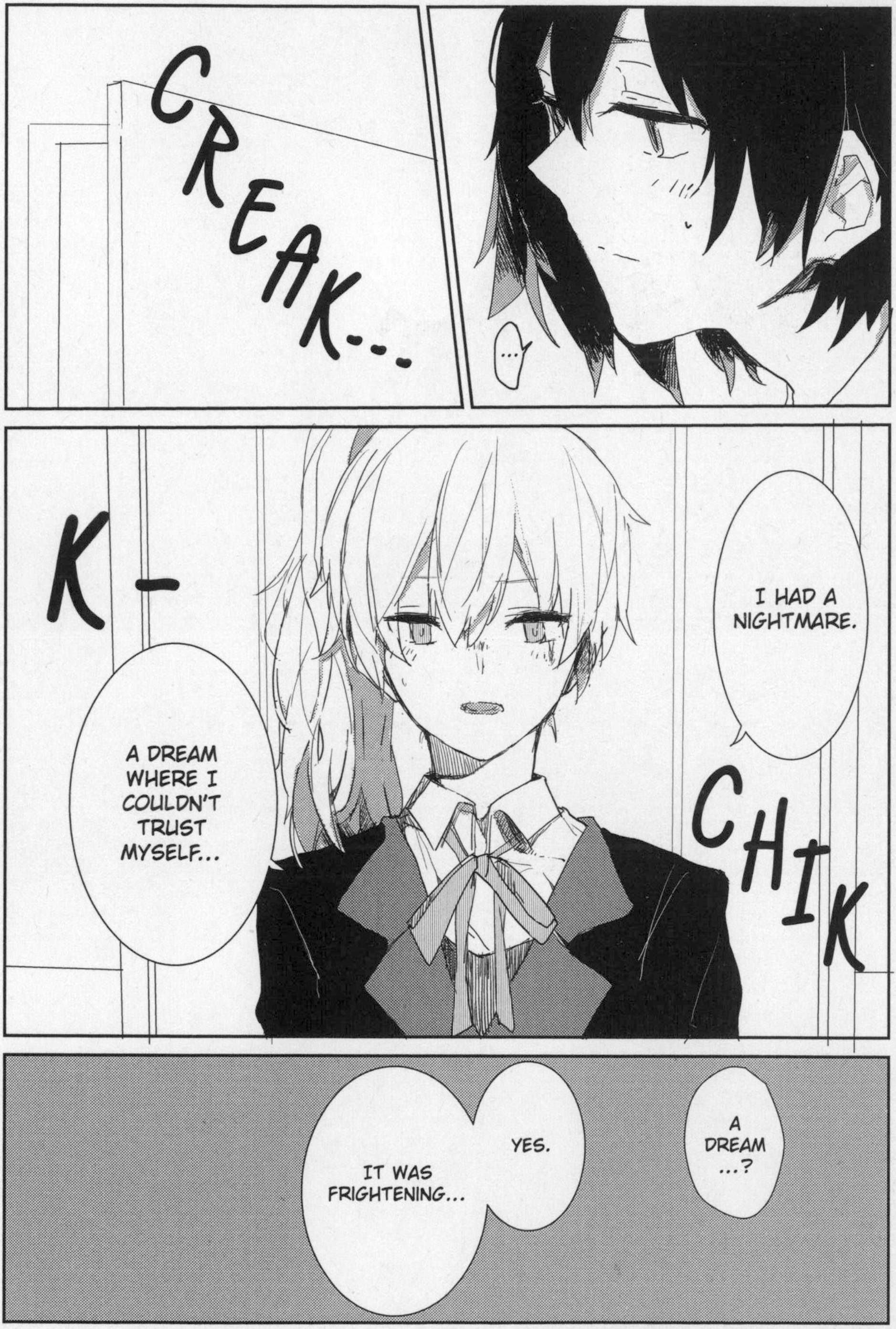
...
CREAK...
I HAD A NIGHTMARE.
K-
A DREAM WHERE I COULDN'T TRUST MYSELF...
CHIK
A DREAM ...?
YES.
IT WAS FRIGHTENING...

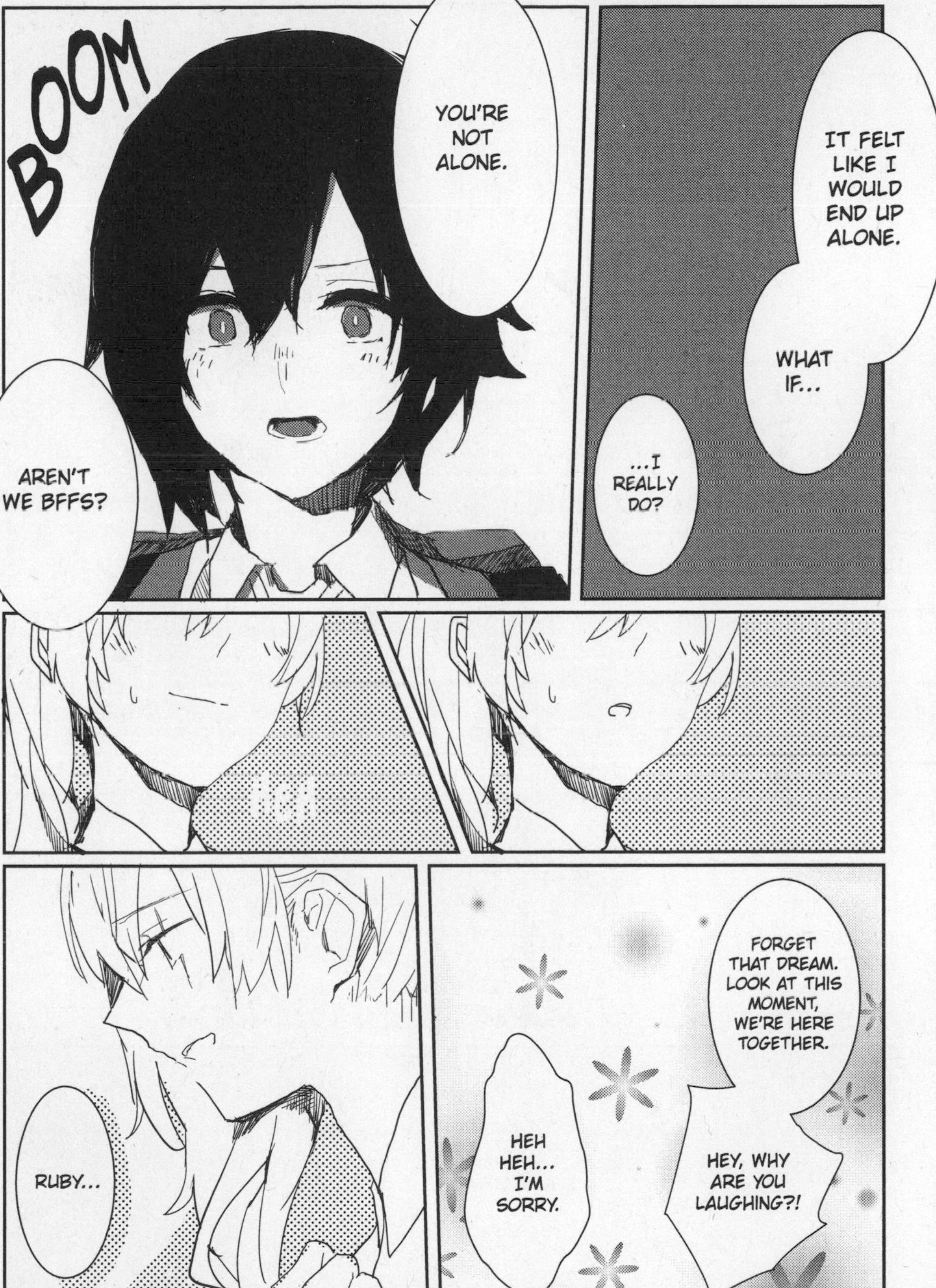
IT FELT LIKE I WOULD END UP ALONE.
WHAT IF...
...I REALLY DO?
YOU'RE NOT ALONE.
BOOM
AREN'T WE BFFS?
Heh
FORGET THAT DREAM. LOOK AT THIS MOMENT, WE'RE HERE TOGETHER.
HEY, WHY ARE YOU LAUGHING?!
HEH HEH... I'M SORRY.
RUBY...

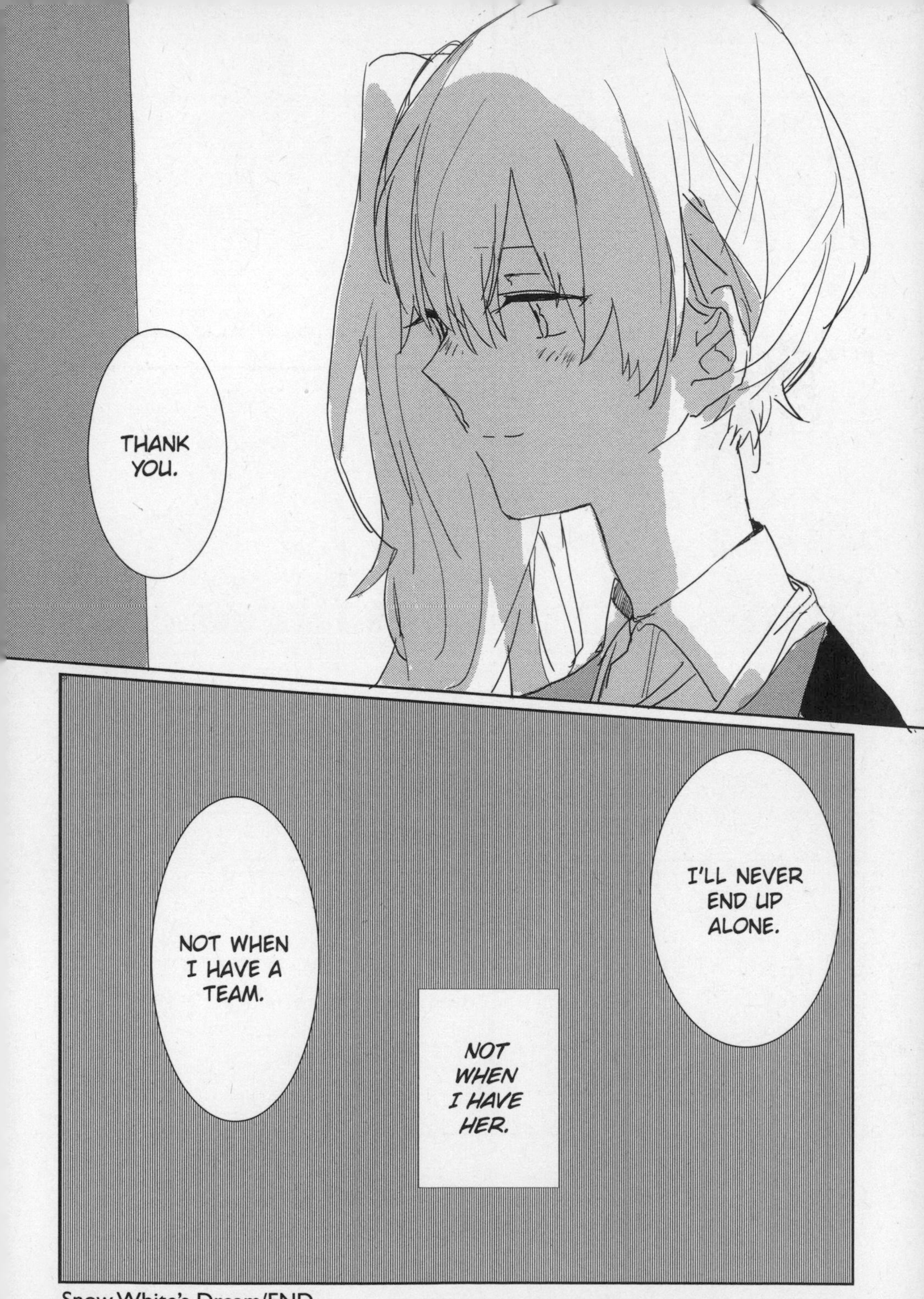
THANK YOU.
I'LL NEVER END UP ALONE.
NOT WHEN I HAVE A TEAM.
NOT WHEN I HAVE HER.

Snow White's Dream/END

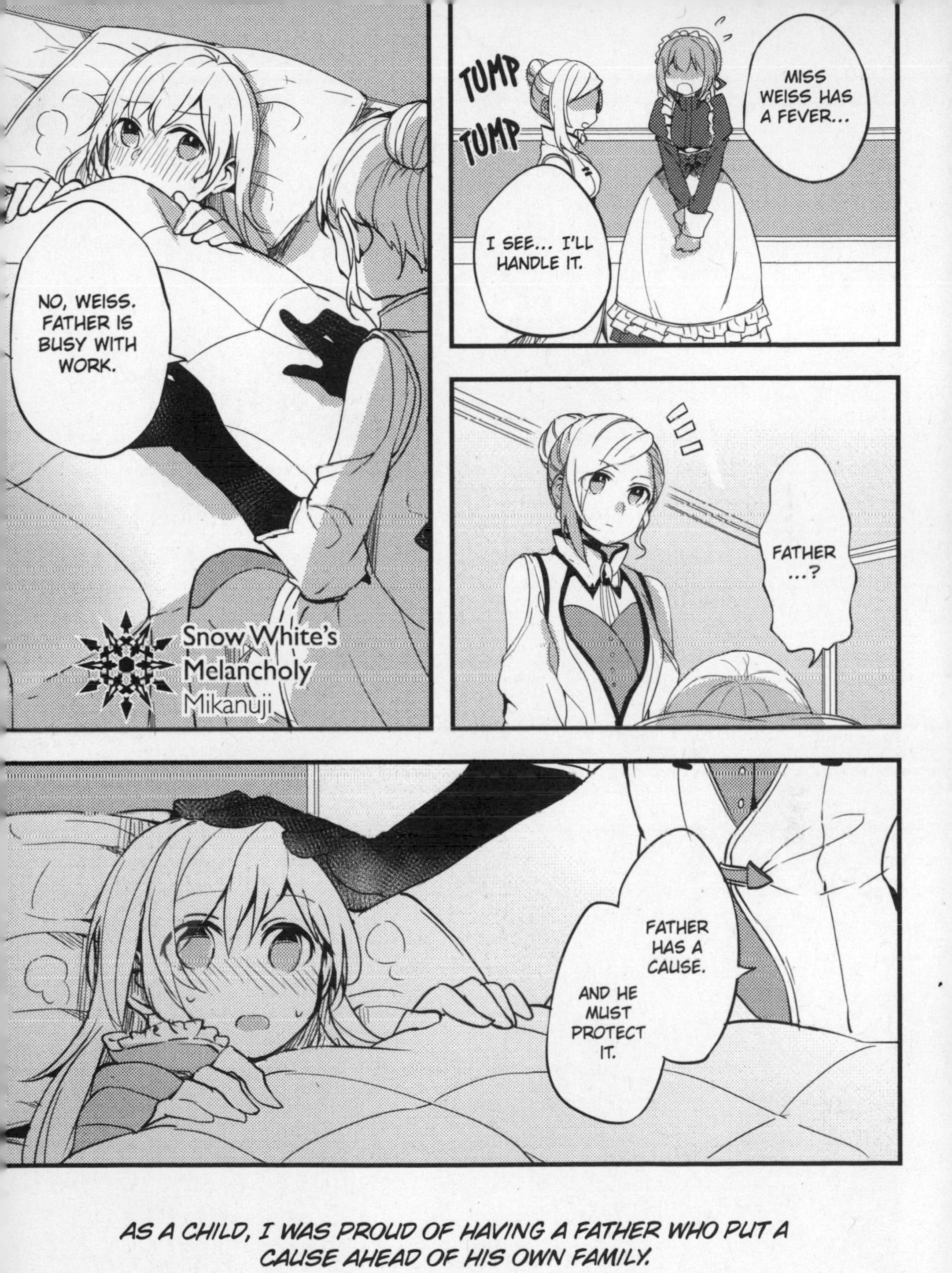
MISS WEISS HAS A FEVER...
TUMP
TUMP
I SEE... I'LL HANDLE IT.
FATHER ...?
NO, WEISS. FATHER IS BUSY WITH WORK.
Snow White's Melancholy
Mikanuji
FATHER HAS A CAUSE.
AND HE MUST PROTECT IT.

AS A CHILD, I WAS PROUD OF HAVING A FATHER WHO PUT A CAUSE AHEAD OF HIS OWN FAMILY.

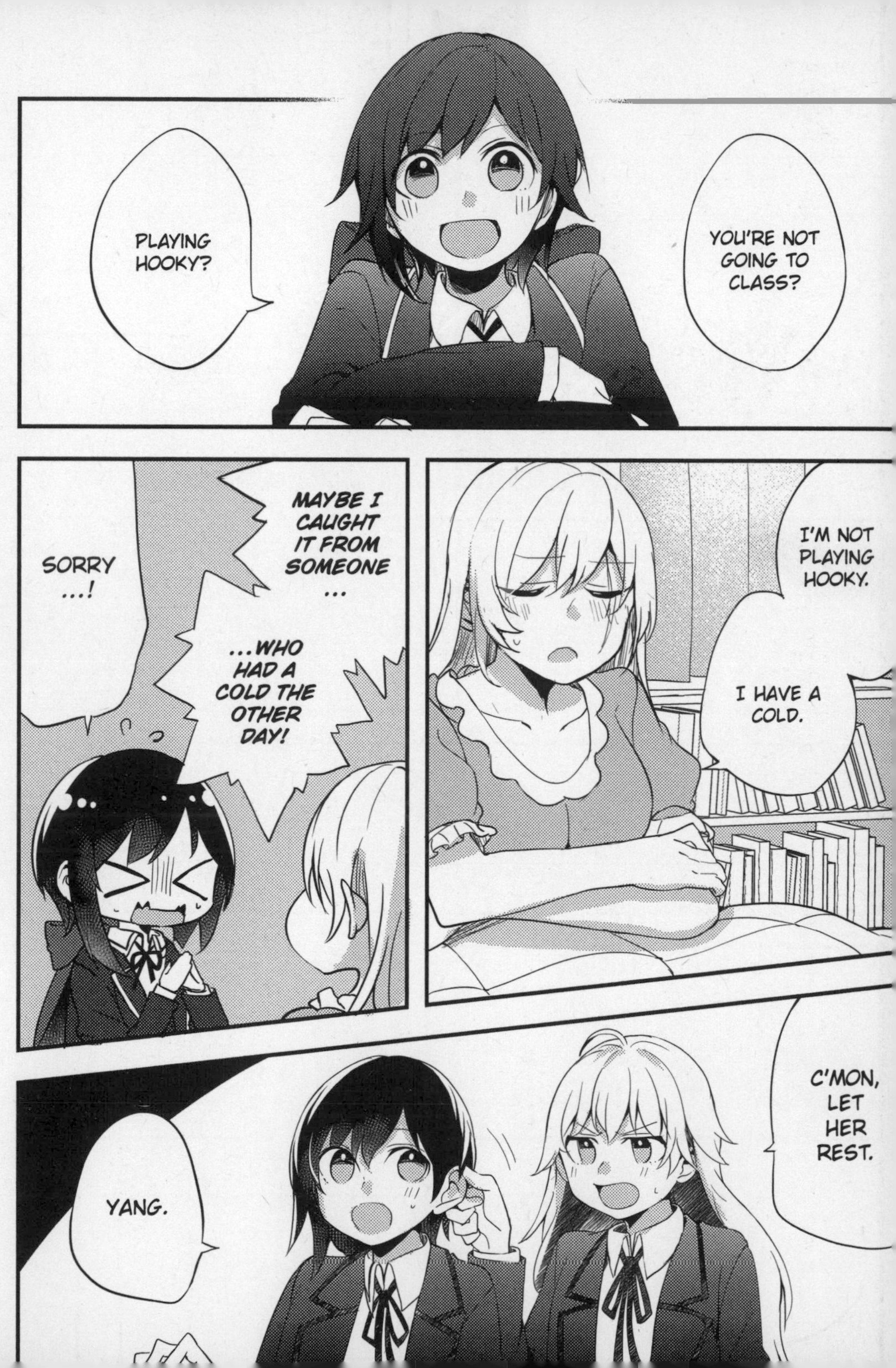
YOU'RE NOT GOING TO CLASS?
PLAYING HOOKY?
I'M NOT PLAYING HOOKY.
I HAVE A COLD.
MAYBE I CAUGHT IT FROM SOMEONE ...
...WHO HAD A COLD THE OTHER DAY!
SORRY ...!
C'MON, LET HER REST.
YANG.

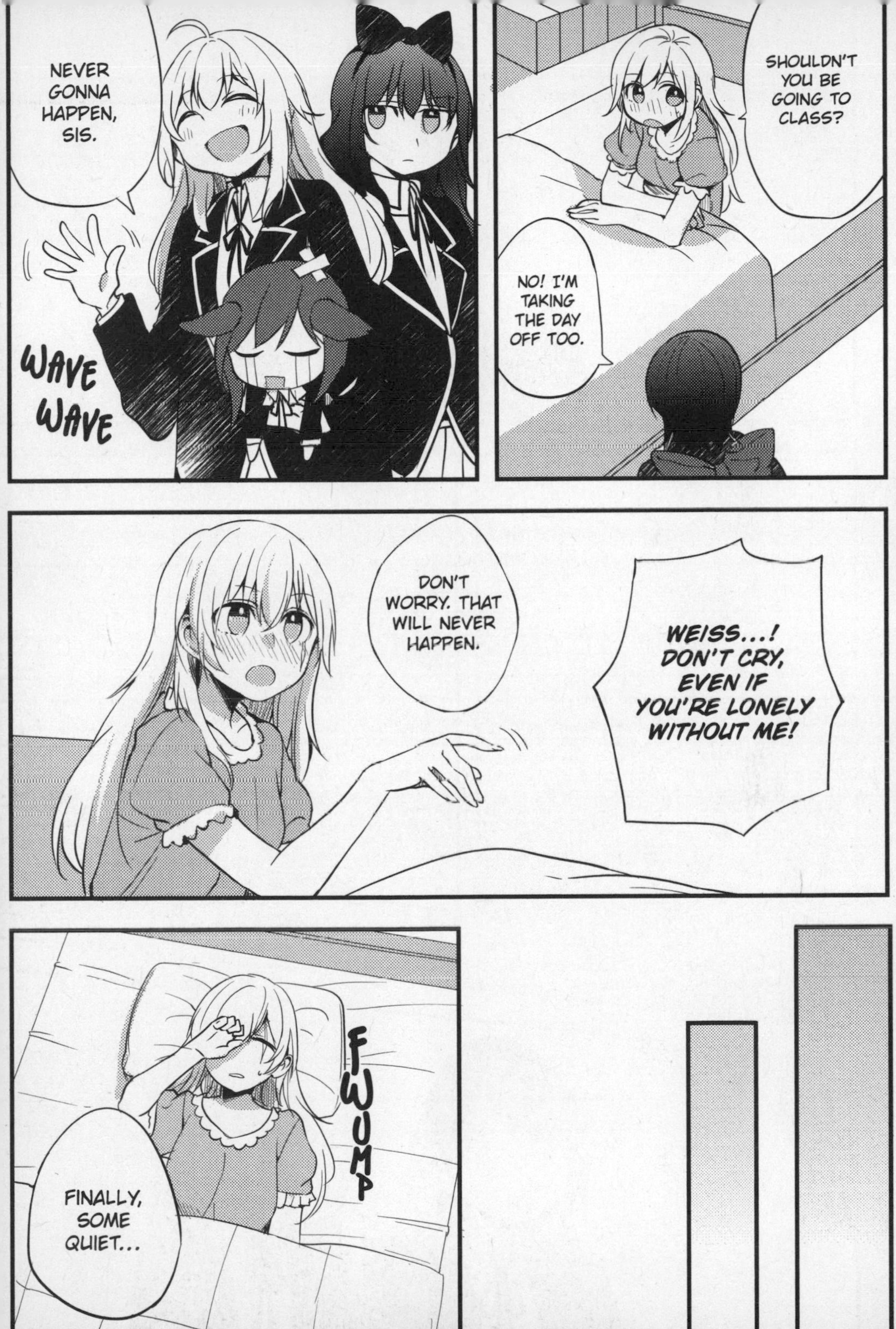
SHOULDN'T YOU BE GOING TO CLASS?
NO! I'M TAKING THE DAY OFF TOO.
NEVER GONNA HAPPEN, SIS.
WAVE WAVE
WEISS...! DON'T CRY, EVEN IF YOU'RE LONELY WITHOUT ME!
DON'T WORRY. THAT WILL NEVER HAPPEN.
FWUMP
FINALLY, SOME QUIET...

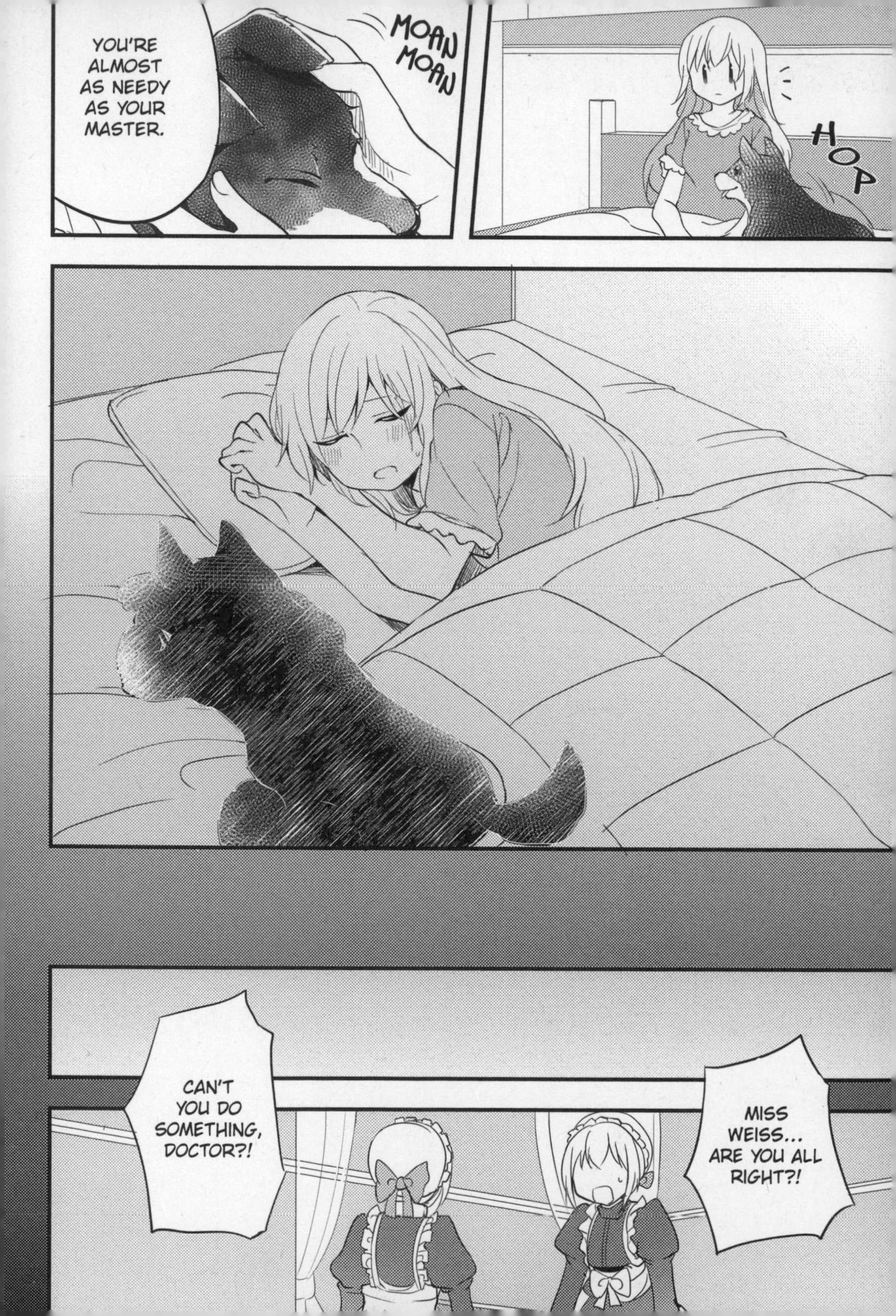
HOP
YOU'RE ALMOST AS NEEDY AS YOUR MASTER.
MOAN MOAN
MISS WEISS... ARE YOU ALL RIGHT?!
CAN'T YOU DO SOMETHING, DOCTOR?!

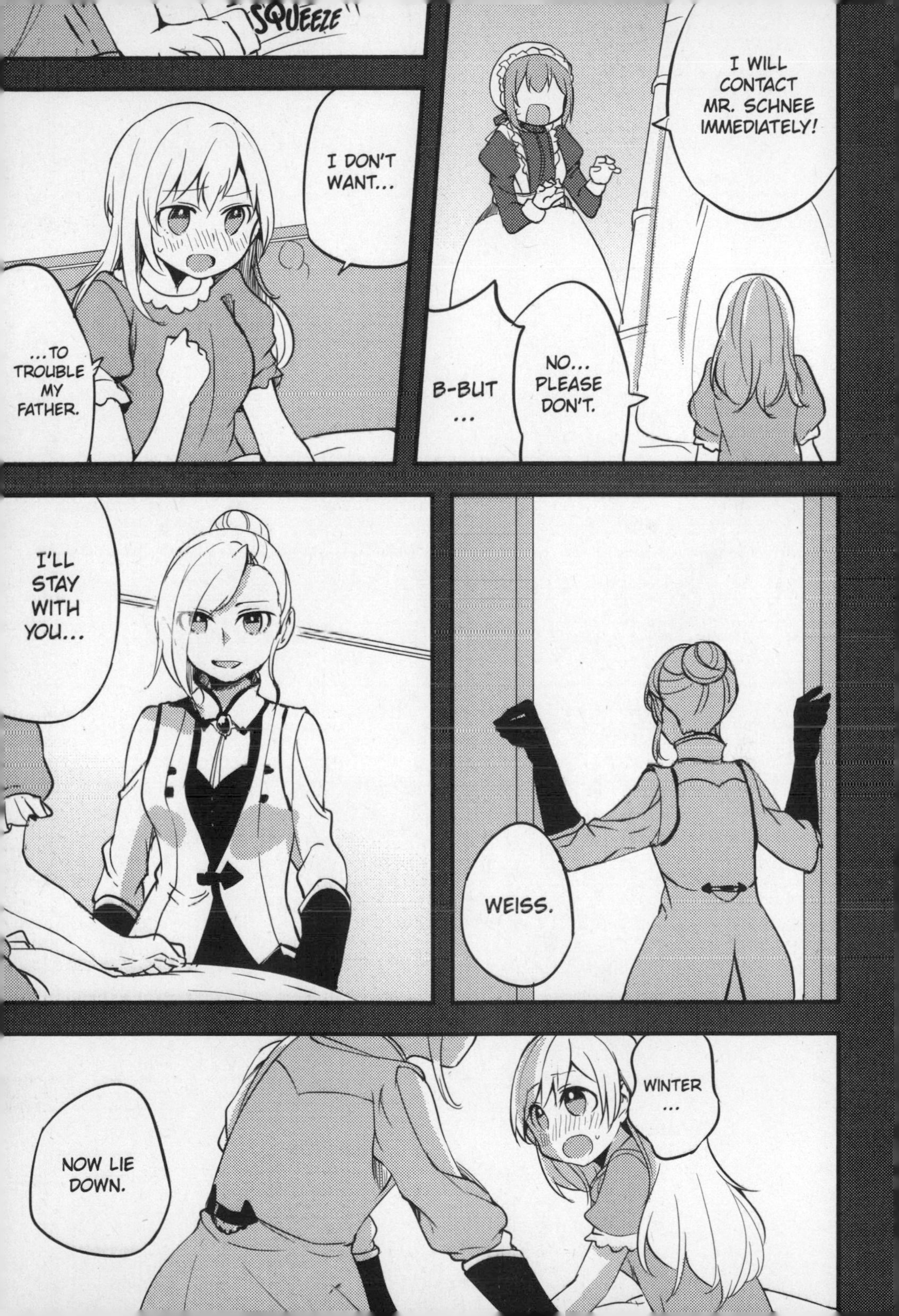
I WILL CONTACT MR. SCHNEE IMMEDIATELY!
NO... PLEASE DON'T.
B-BUT ...
SQUEEZE
I DON'T WANT...
...TO TROUBLE MY FATHER.
WEISS.
I'LL STAY WITH YOU...
WINTER ...
NOW LIE DOWN.

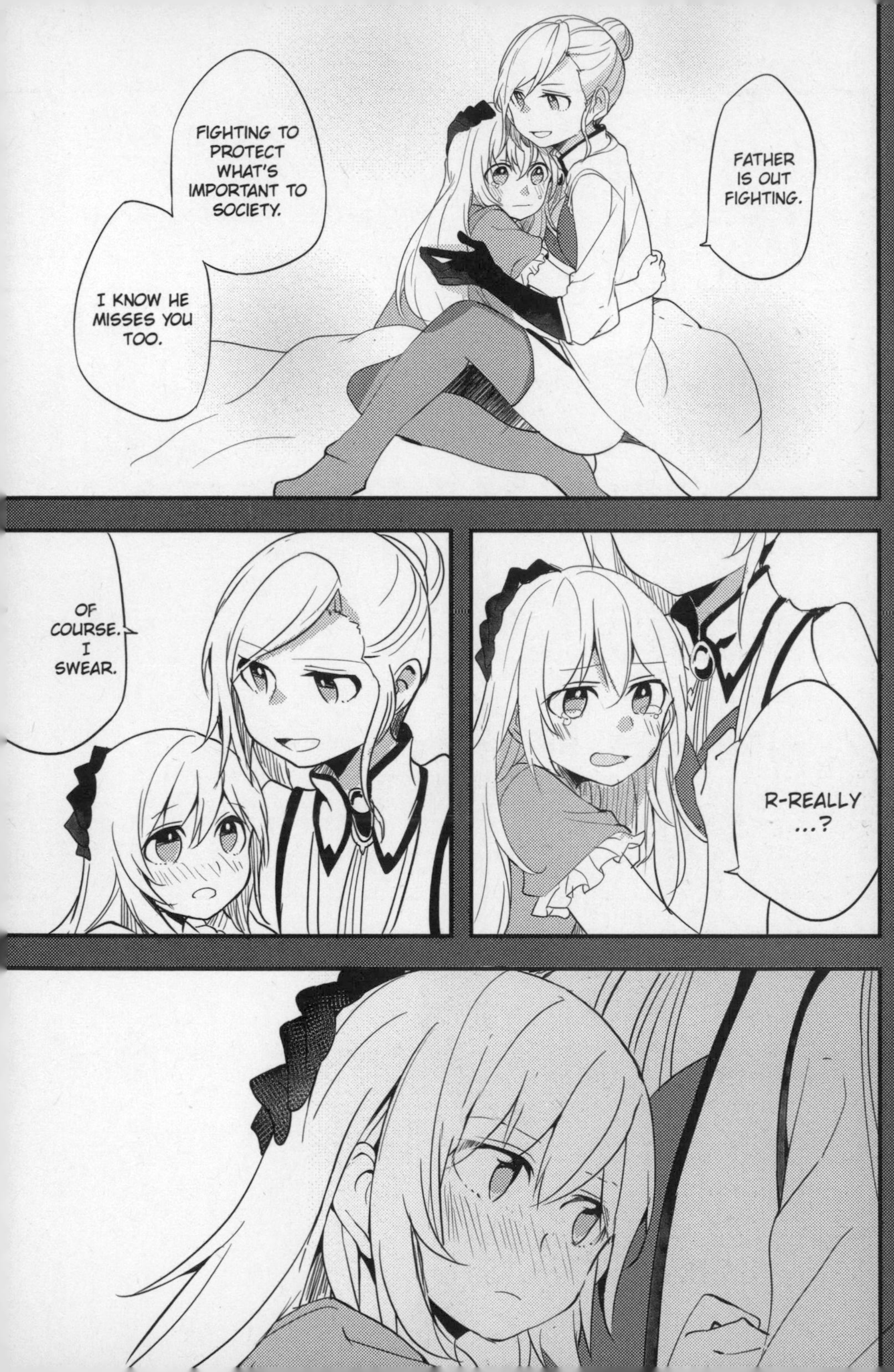
FATHER IS OUT FIGHTING.
FIGHTING TO PROTECT WHAT'S IMPORTANT TO SOCIETY.
I KNOW HE MISSES YOU TOO.
R-REALLY ...?
OF COURSE. I SWEAR.

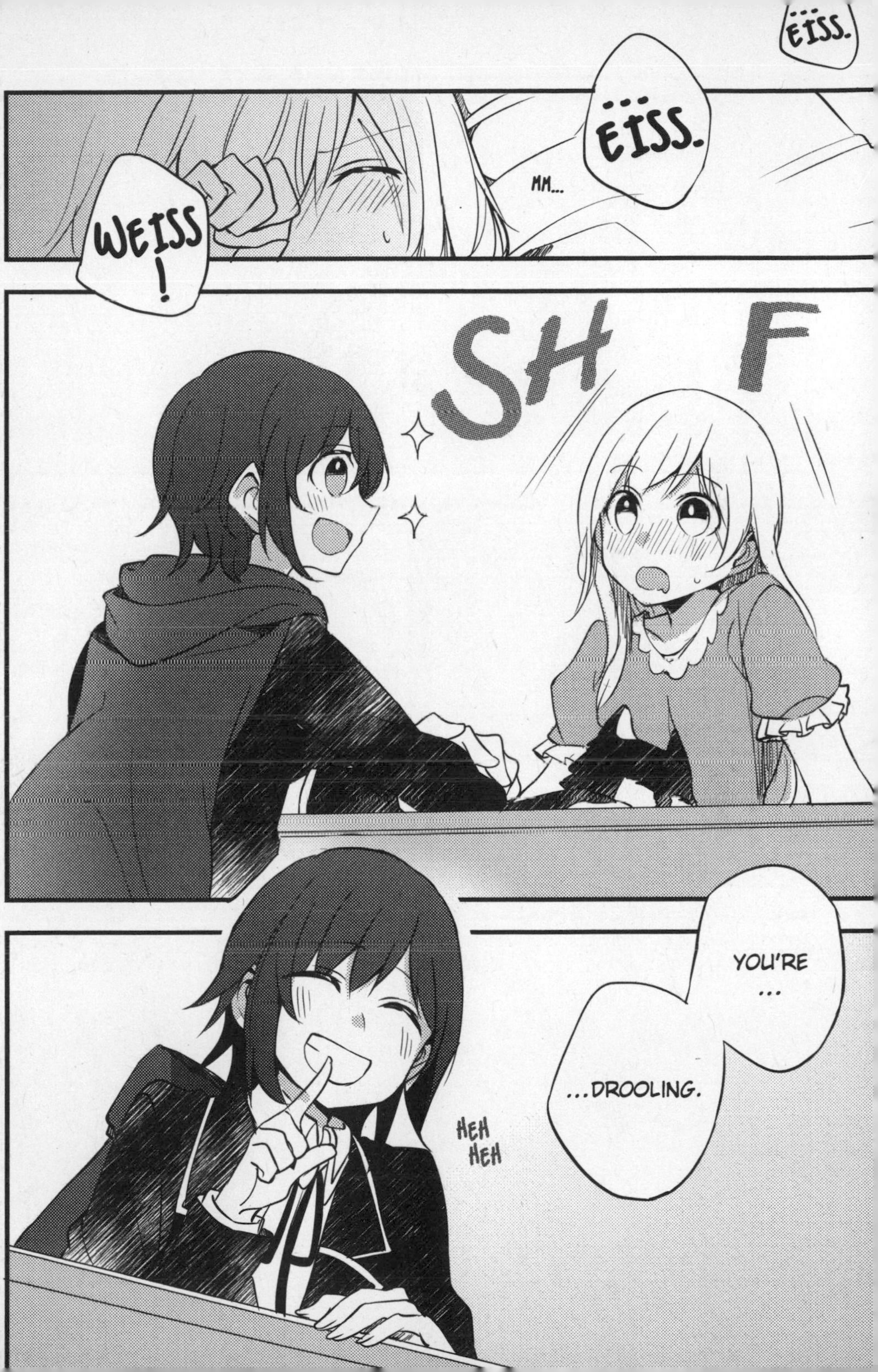
...EISS.
...EISS.
MM...
WEISS!
SH F
YOU'RE...
...DROOLING.
HEH HEH

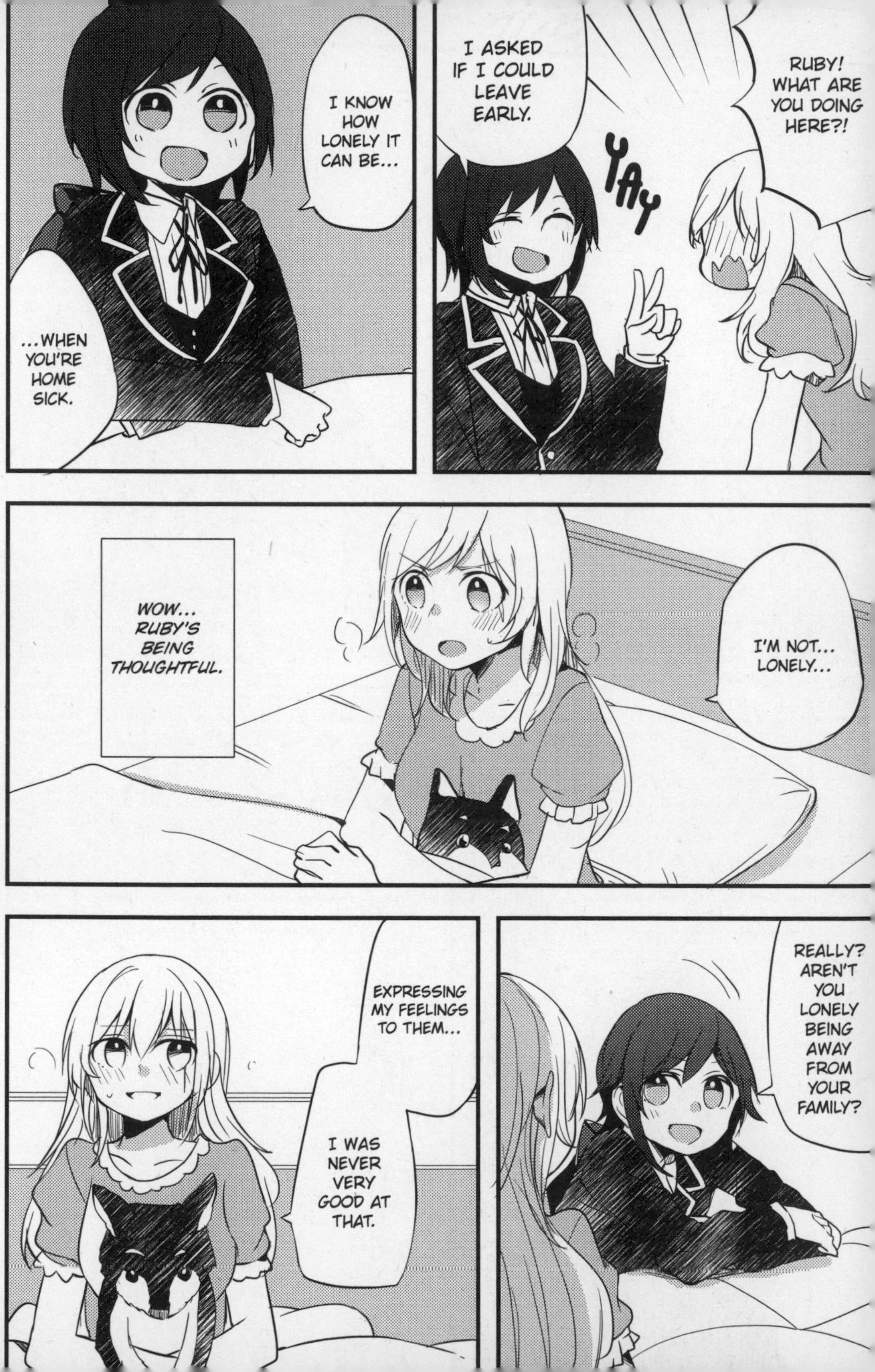
RUBY! WHAT ARE YOU DOING HERE?!
I ASKED IF I COULD LEAVE EARLY.
YAY
I KNOW HOW LONELY IT CAN BE...
...WHEN YOU'RE HOME SICK.
I'M NOT... LONELY...
WOW... RUBY'S BEING THOUGHTFUL.
REALLY? AREN'T YOU LONELY BEING AWAY FROM YOUR FAMILY?
EXPRESSING MY FEELINGS TO THEM...
I WAS NEVER VERY GOOD AT THAT.

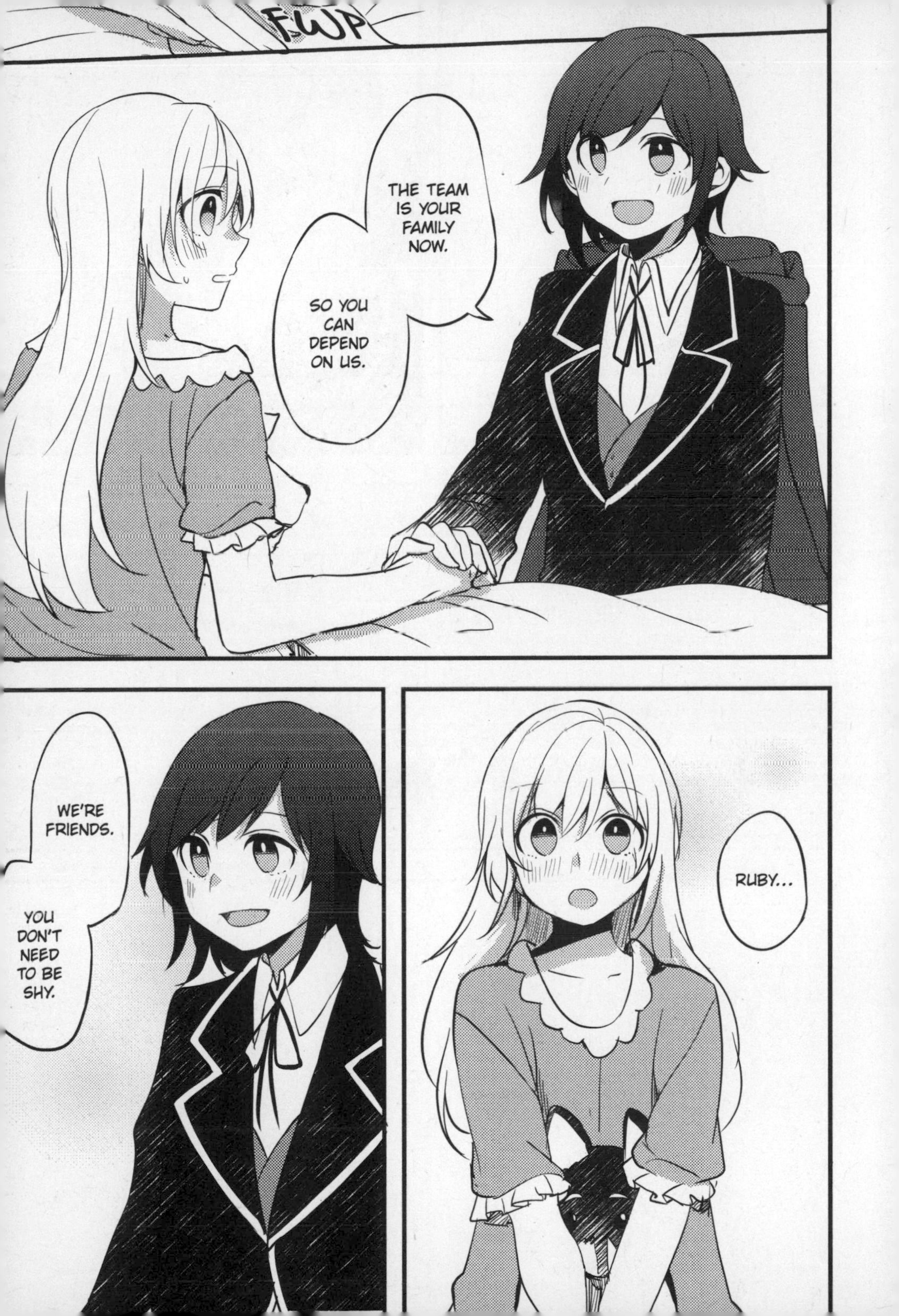
FWP
THE TEAM IS YOUR FAMILY NOW.
SO YOU CAN DEPEND ON US.
RUBY...
WE'RE FRIENDS.
YOU DON'T NEED TO BE SHY.

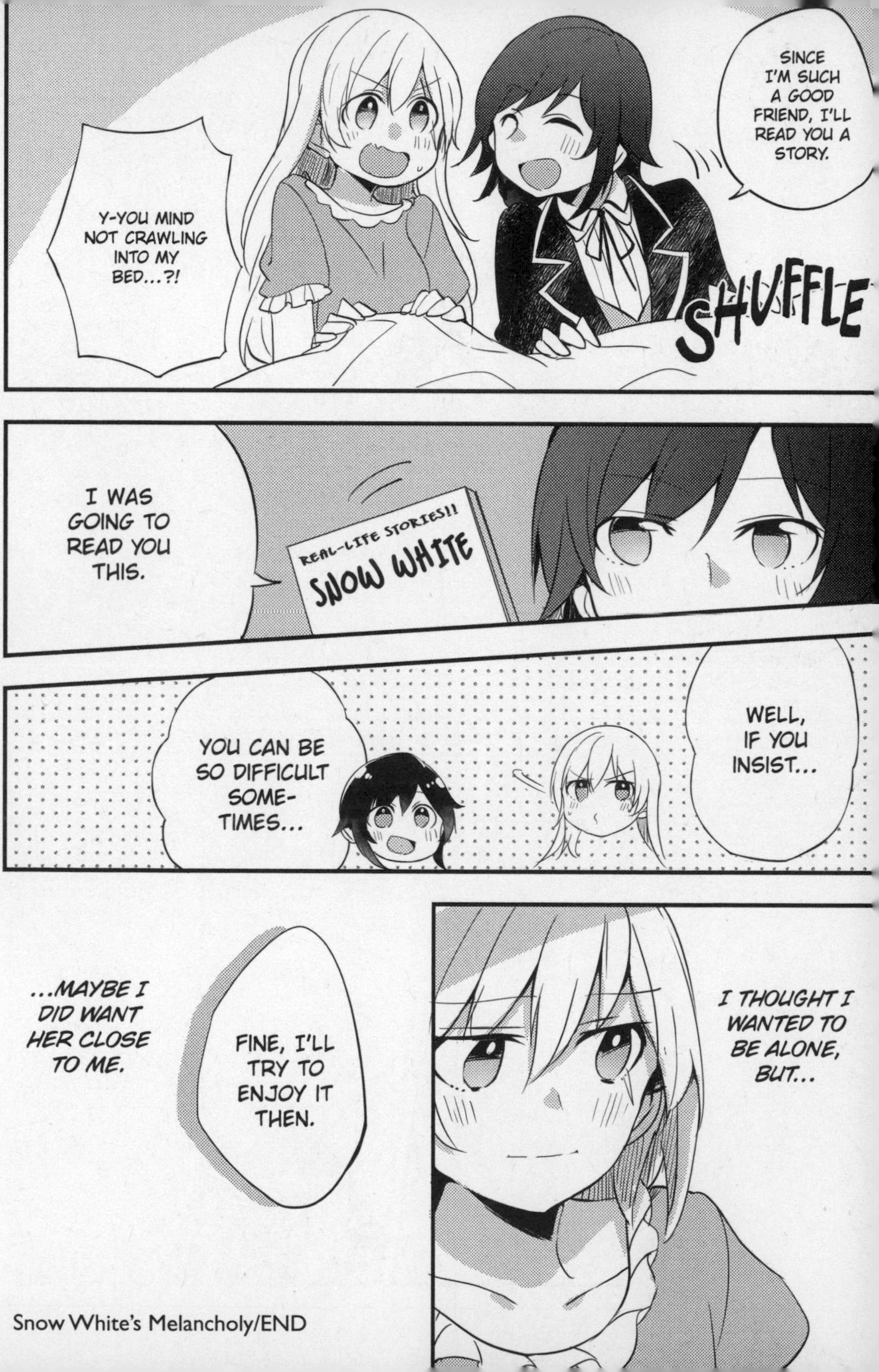
SINCE I'M SUCH A GOOD FRIEND, I'LL READ YOU A STORY.
SHUFFLE
Y-YOU MIND NOT CRAWLING INTO MY BED...?!
REAL-LIFE STORIES!!
SNOW WHITE
I WAS GOING TO READ YOU THIS.
WELL, IF YOU INSIST...
YOU CAN BE SO DIFFICULT SOME-TIMES...
I THOUGHT I WANTED TO BE ALONE, BUT...
FINE, I'LL TRY TO ENJOY IT THEN.
...MAYBE I DID WANT HER CLOSE TO ME.

Snow White's Melancholy/END

Who Is the Ice Queen Meeting?

Tsutanoha

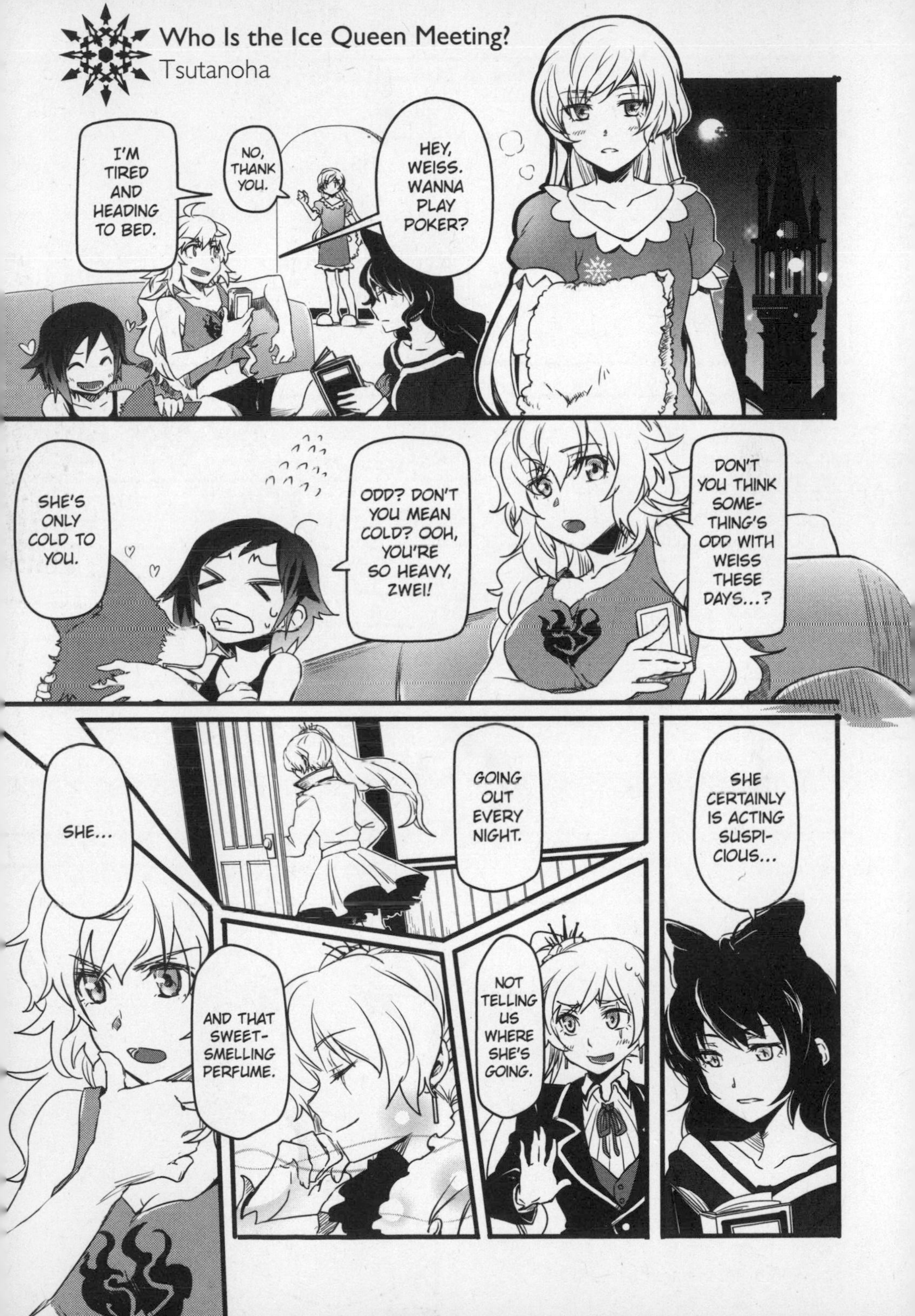
HEY, WEISS. WANNA PLAY POKER?
NO, THANK YOU.
I'M TIRED AND HEADING TO BED.
DON'T YOU THINK SOME-THING'S ODD WITH WEISS THESE DAYS...?
ODD? DON'T YOU MEAN COLD? OOH, YOU'RE SO HEAVY, ZWEI!
SHE'S ONLY COLD TO YOU.
SHE CERTAINLY IS ACTING SUSPI-CIOUS...
GOING OUT EVERY NIGHT.
NOT TELLING US WHERE SHE'S GOING.
AND THAT SWEET-SMELLING PERFUME.
SHE...

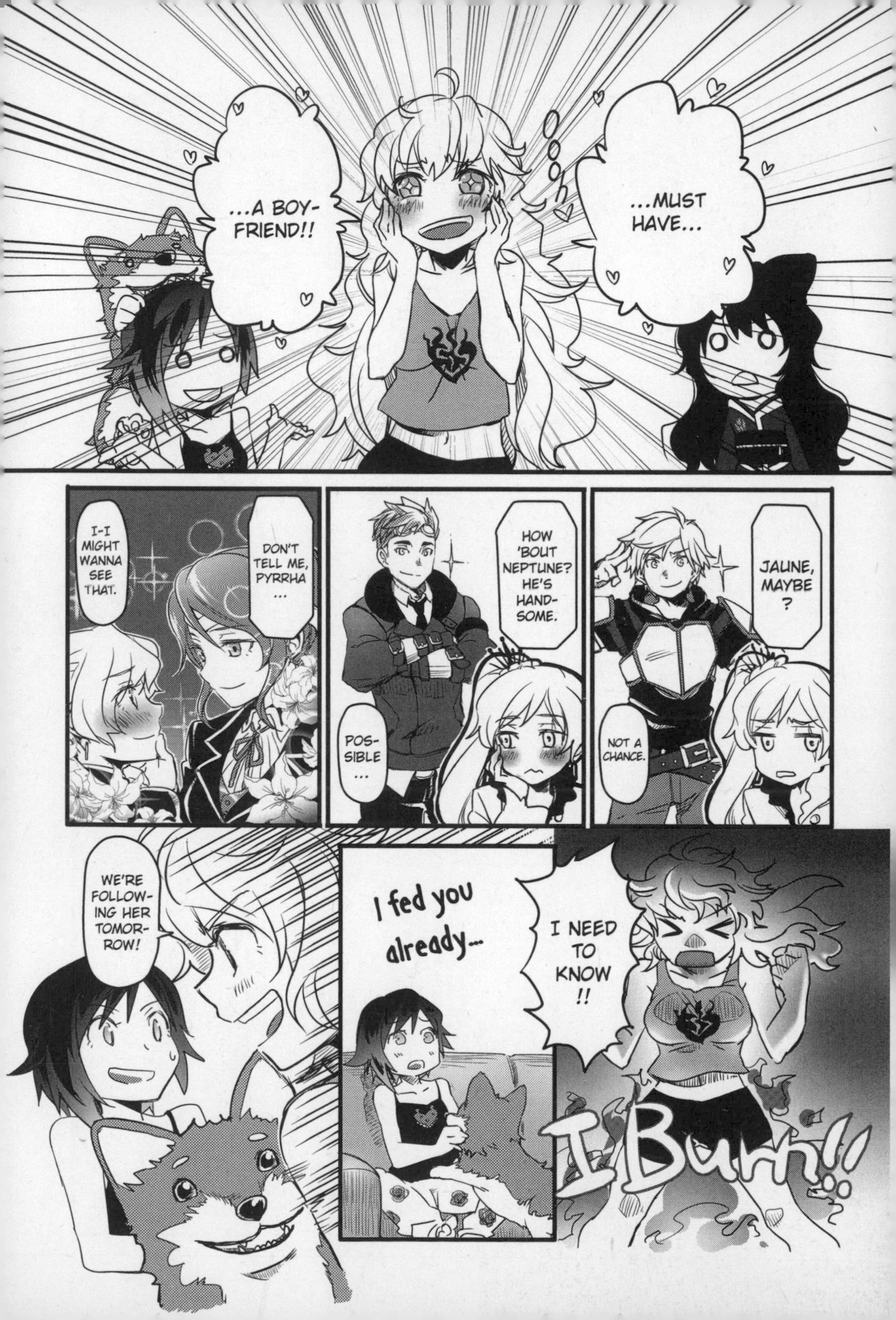
...MUST HAVE...
Oooh
...A BOY-FRIEND!!
JAUNE, MAYBE?
NOT A CHANCE.
HOW 'BOUT NEPTUNE? HE'S HAND-SOME.
POS-SIBLE...
DON'T TELL ME, PYRRHA...
I-I MIGHT WANNA SEE THAT.
I NEED TO KNOW!!
I Burn!!
I fed you already...
WE'RE FOLLOW-ING HER TOMOR-ROW!

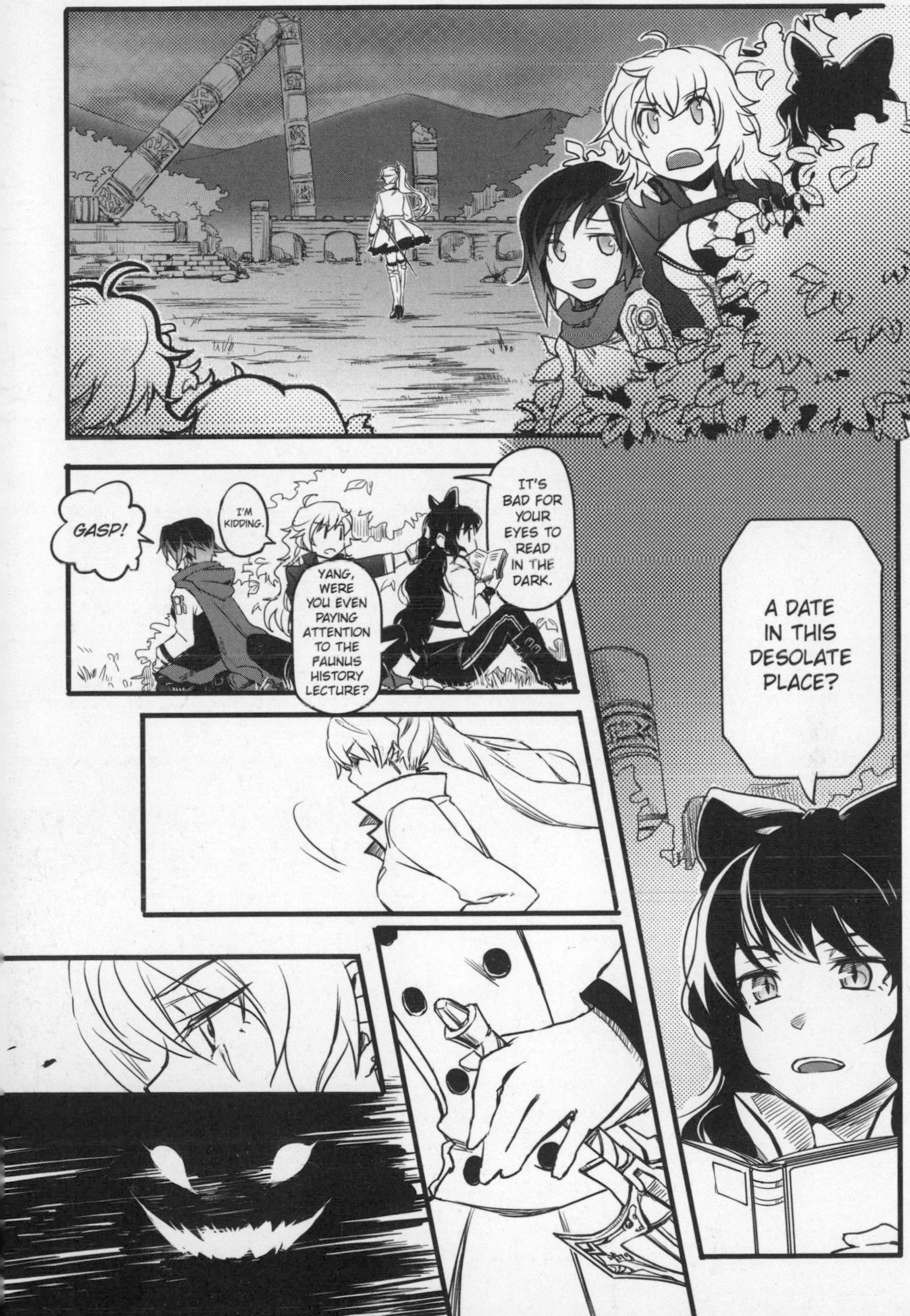
A DATE IN THIS DESOLATE PLACE?
IT'S BAD FOR YOUR EYES TO READ IN THE DARK.
YANG, WERE YOU EVEN PAYING ATTENTION TO THE FAUNUS HISTORY LECTURE?
I'M KIDDING.
GASP!

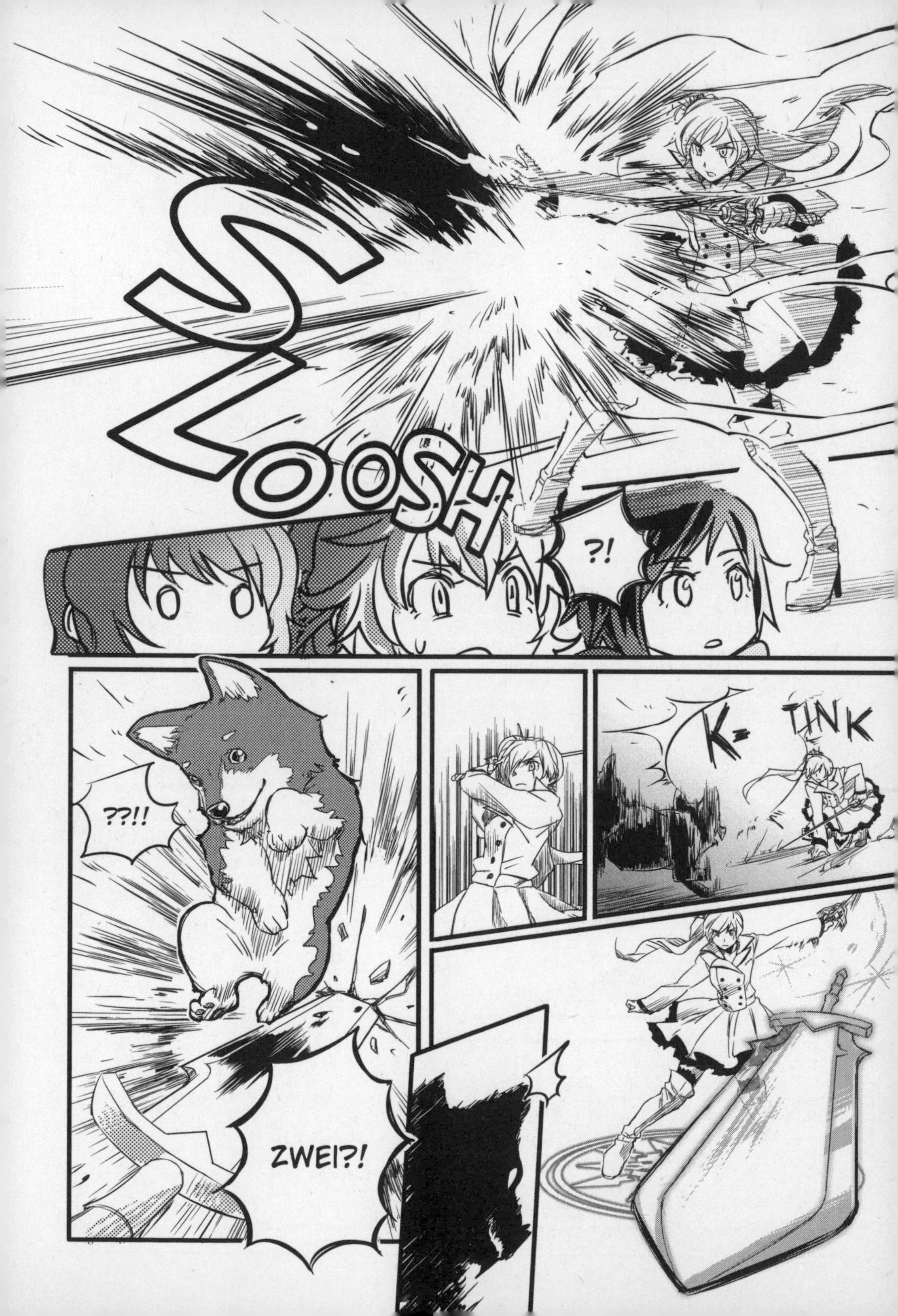
SWOOSH
?!
K-TINK
??!!
ZWEI?!

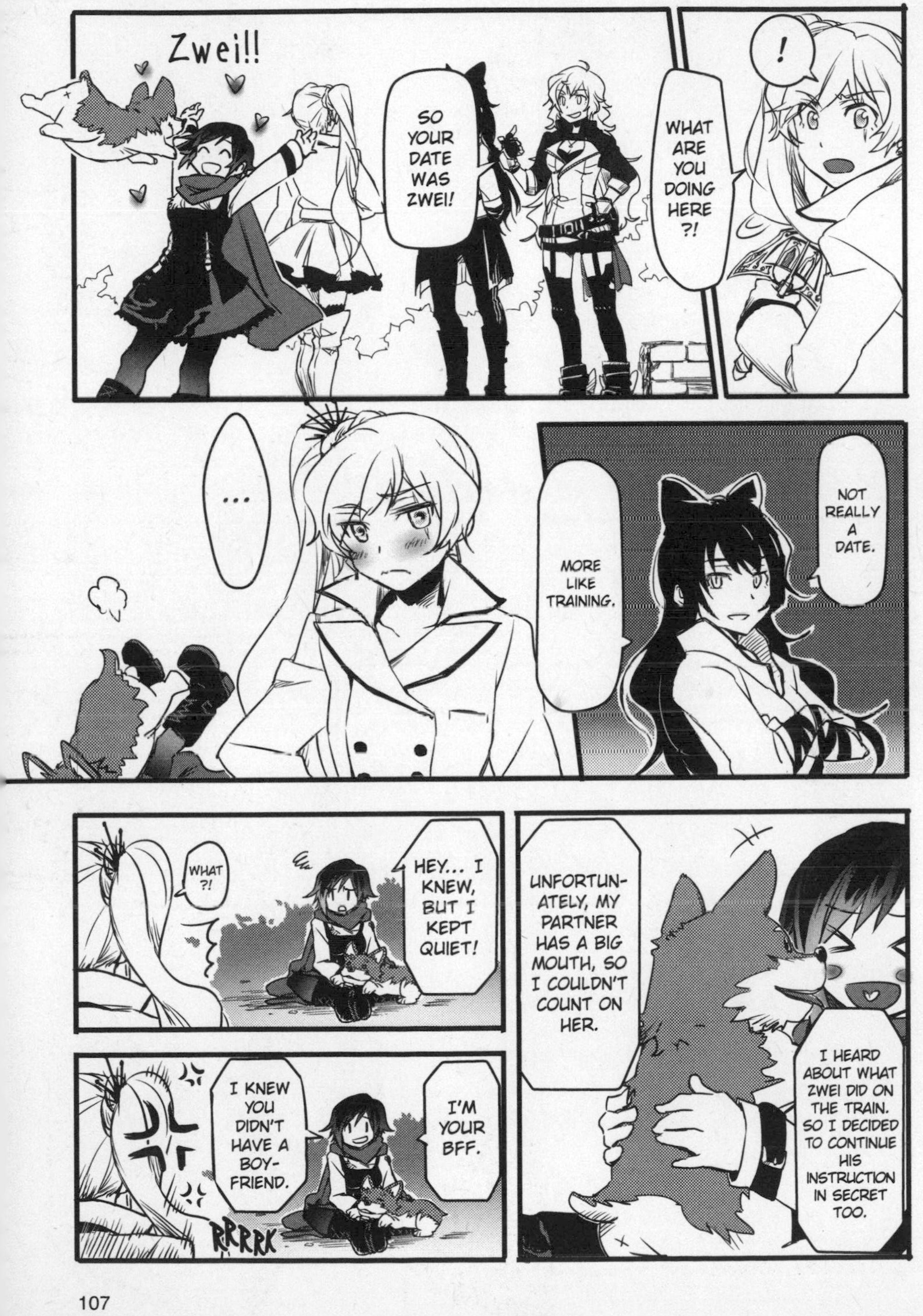
!
WHAT ARE YOU DOING HERE?!
Zwei!!
SO YOUR DATE WAS ZWEI!
NOT REALLY A DATE.
MORE LIKE TRAINING.
...
I HEARD ABOUT WHAT ZWEI DID ON THE TRAIN. SO I DECIDED TO CONTINUE HIS INSTRUCTION IN SECRET TOO.
UNFORTUNATELY, MY PARTNER HAS A BIG MOUTH, SO I COULDN'T COUNT ON HER.
HEY... I KNEW, BUT I KEPT QUIET!
WHAT?!
I'M YOUR BFF.
I KNEW YOU DIDN'T HAVE A BOY-FRIEND.
RRRRK

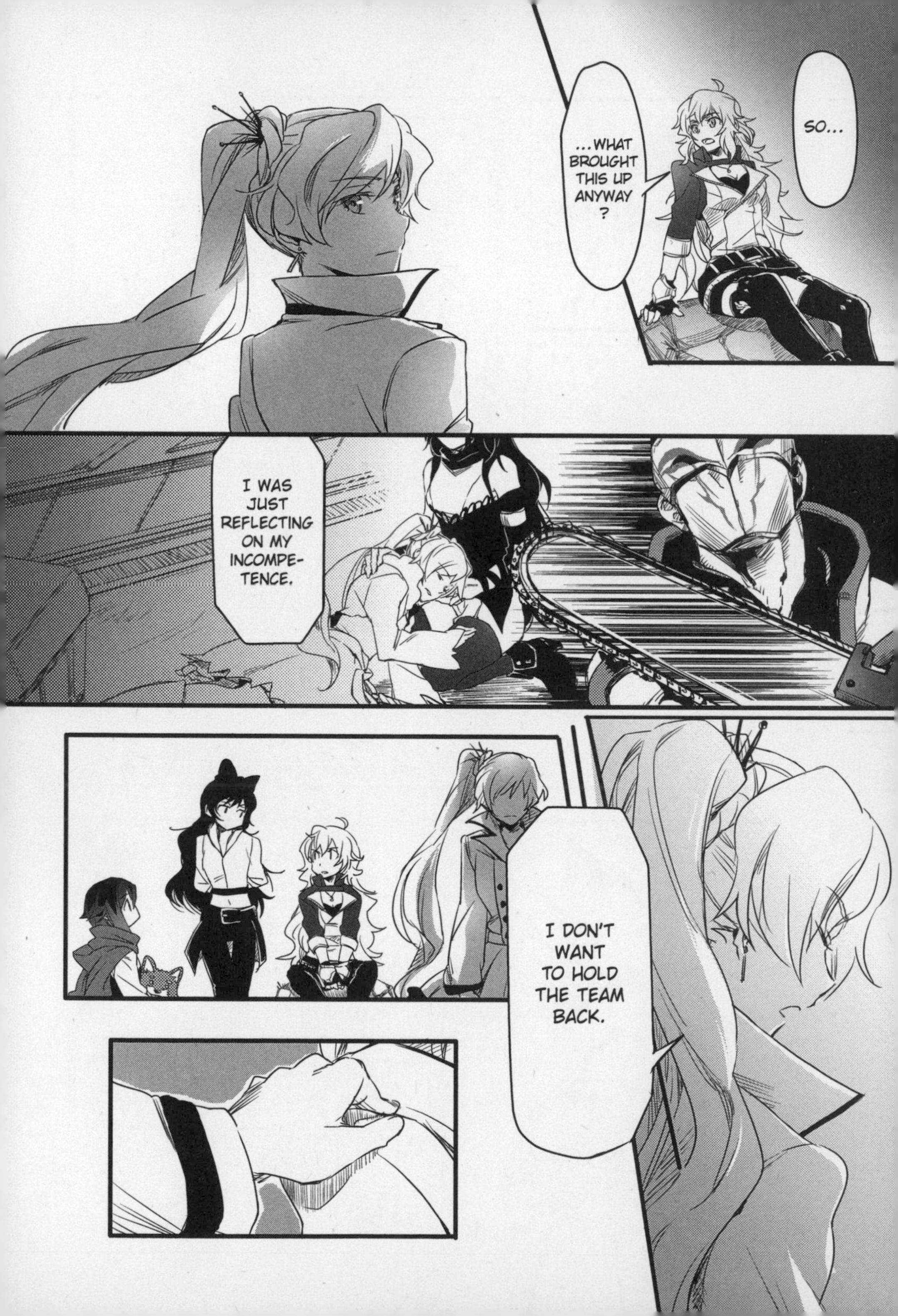
SO...
...WHAT BROUGHT THIS UP ANYWAY?
I WAS JUST REFLECTING ON MY INCOMPETENCE.
I DON'T WANT TO HOLD THE TEAM BACK.

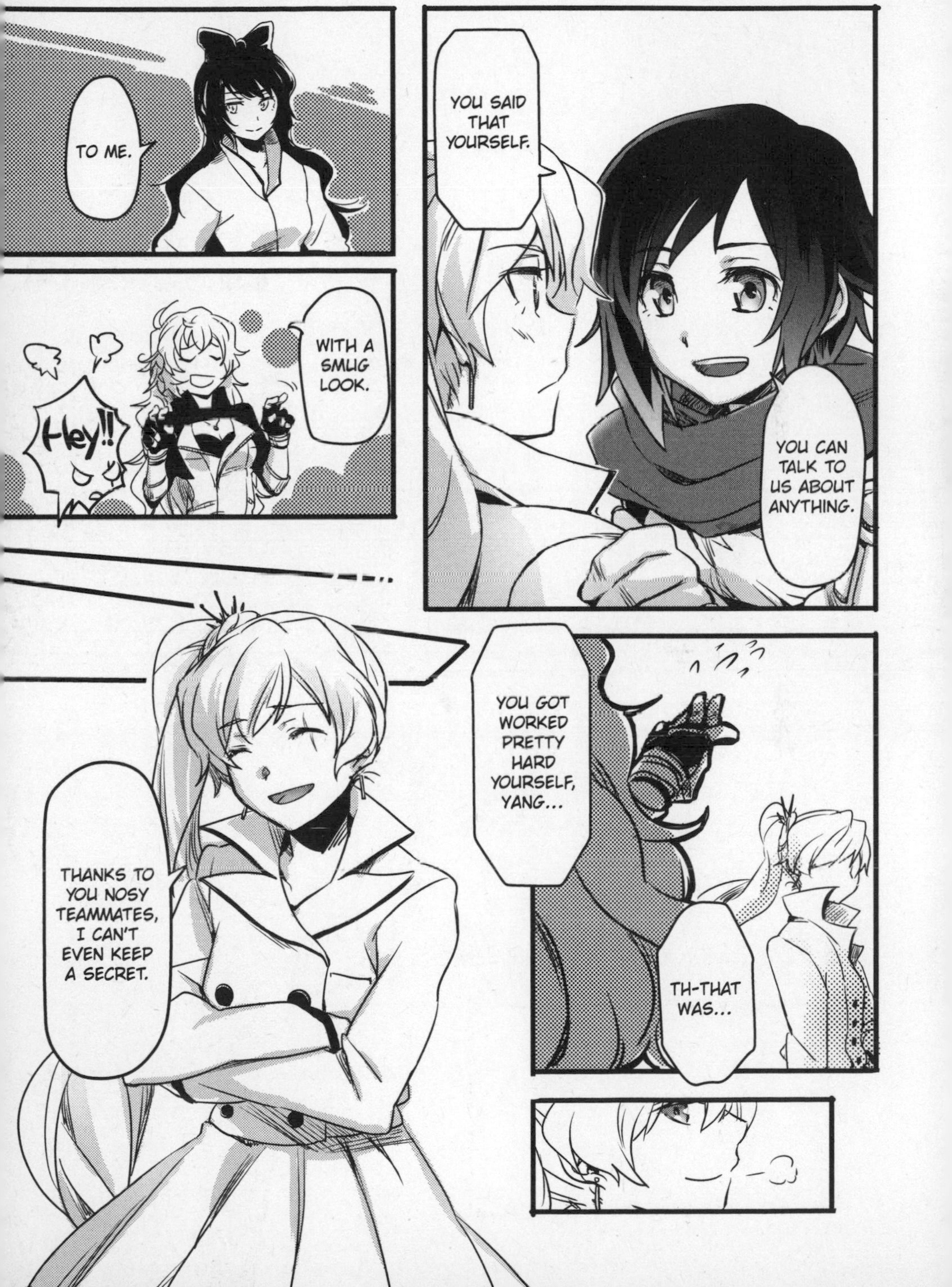
YOU SAID THAT YOURSELF.
YOU CAN TALK TO US ABOUT ANYTHING.
TO ME.
WITH A SMUG LOOK.
Hey!!
YOU GOT WORKED PRETTY HARD YOURSELF, YANG...
TH-THAT WAS...
THANKS TO YOU NOSY TEAMMATES, I CAN'T EVEN KEEP A SECRET.

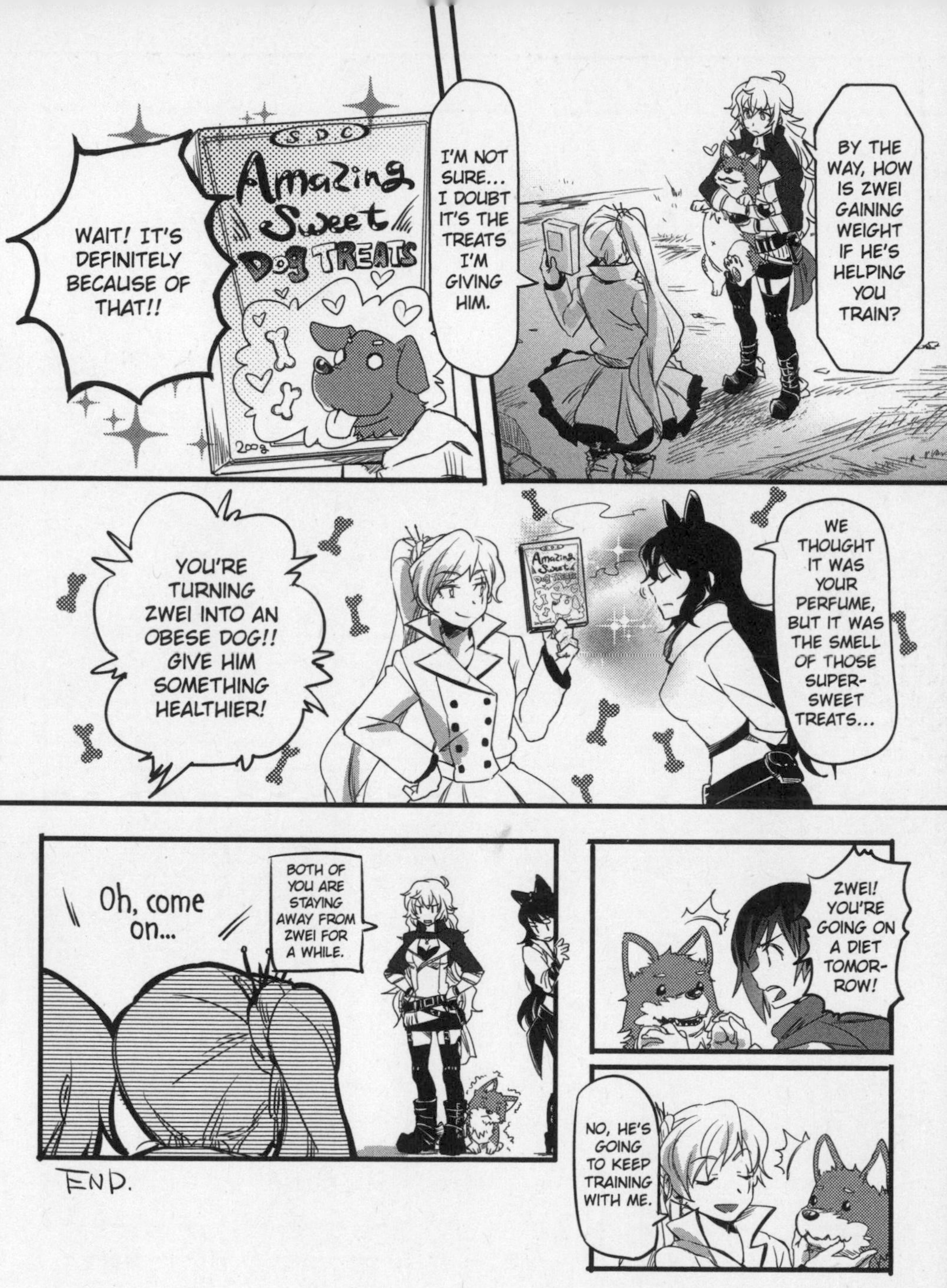
BY THE WAY, HOW IS ZWEI GAINING WEIGHT IF HE'S HELPING YOU TRAIN?
I'M NOT SURE... I DOUBT IT'S THE TREATS I'M GIVING HIM.
SDC
Amazing Sweet Dog TREATS
200g
WAIT! IT'S DEFINITELY BECAUSE OF THAT!!
WE THOUGHT IT WAS YOUR PERFUME, BUT IT WAS THE SMELL OF THOSE SUPER-SWEET TREATS...
YOU'RE TURNING ZWEI INTO AN OBESE DOG!! GIVE HIM SOMETHING HEALTHIER!
ZWEI! YOU'RE GOING ON A DIET TOMORROW!
NO, HE'S GOING TO KEEP TRAINING WITH ME.
BOTH OF YOU ARE STAYING AWAY FROM ZWEI FOR A WHILE.
Oh, come on...
END.

Who Is the Ice Queen Meeting?/END

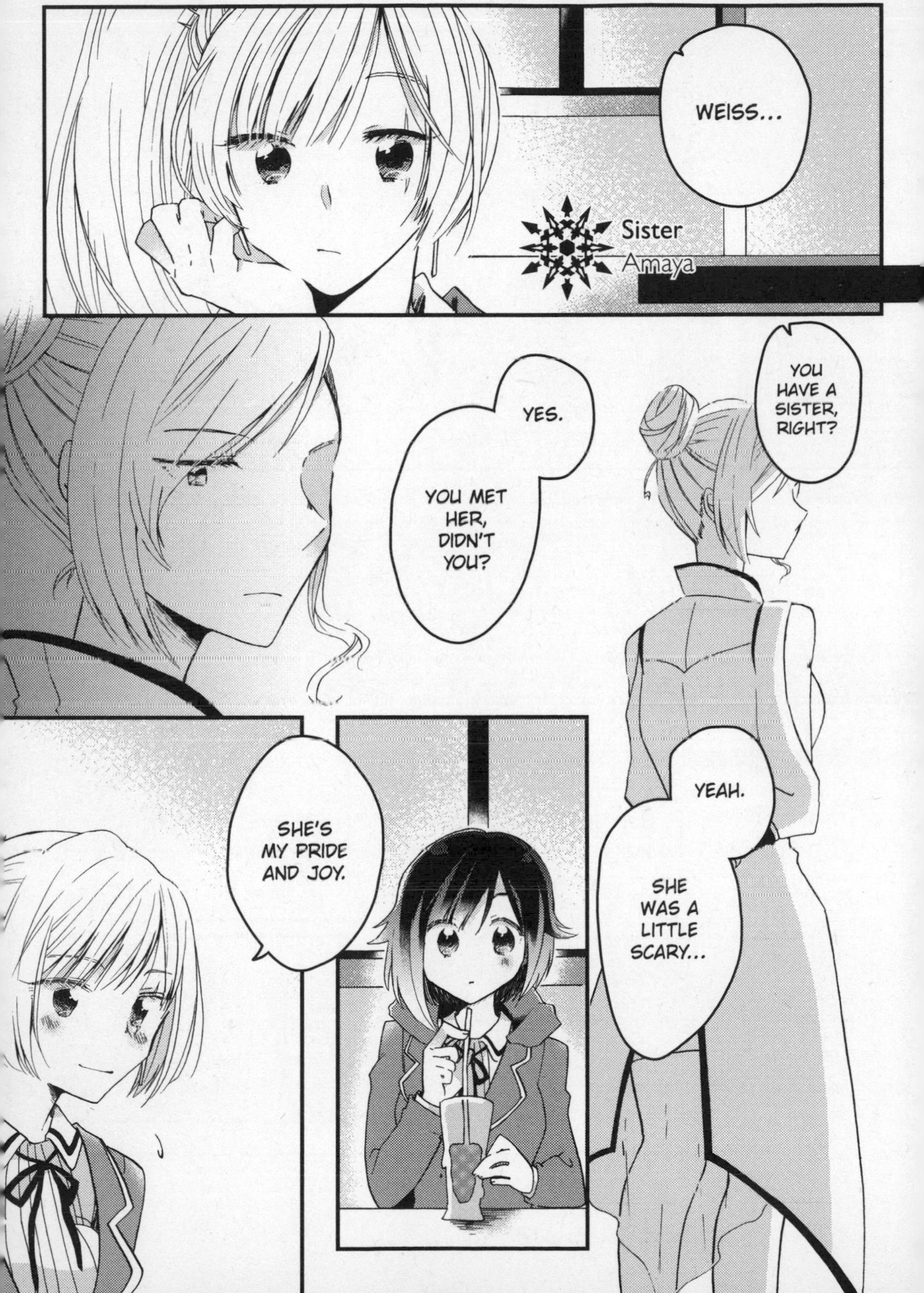
WEISS...
Sister
Amaya
YOU HAVE A SISTER, RIGHT?
YES.
YOU MET HER, DIDN'T YOU?
YEAH.
SHE WAS A LITTLE SCARY...
SHE'S MY PRIDE AND JOY.

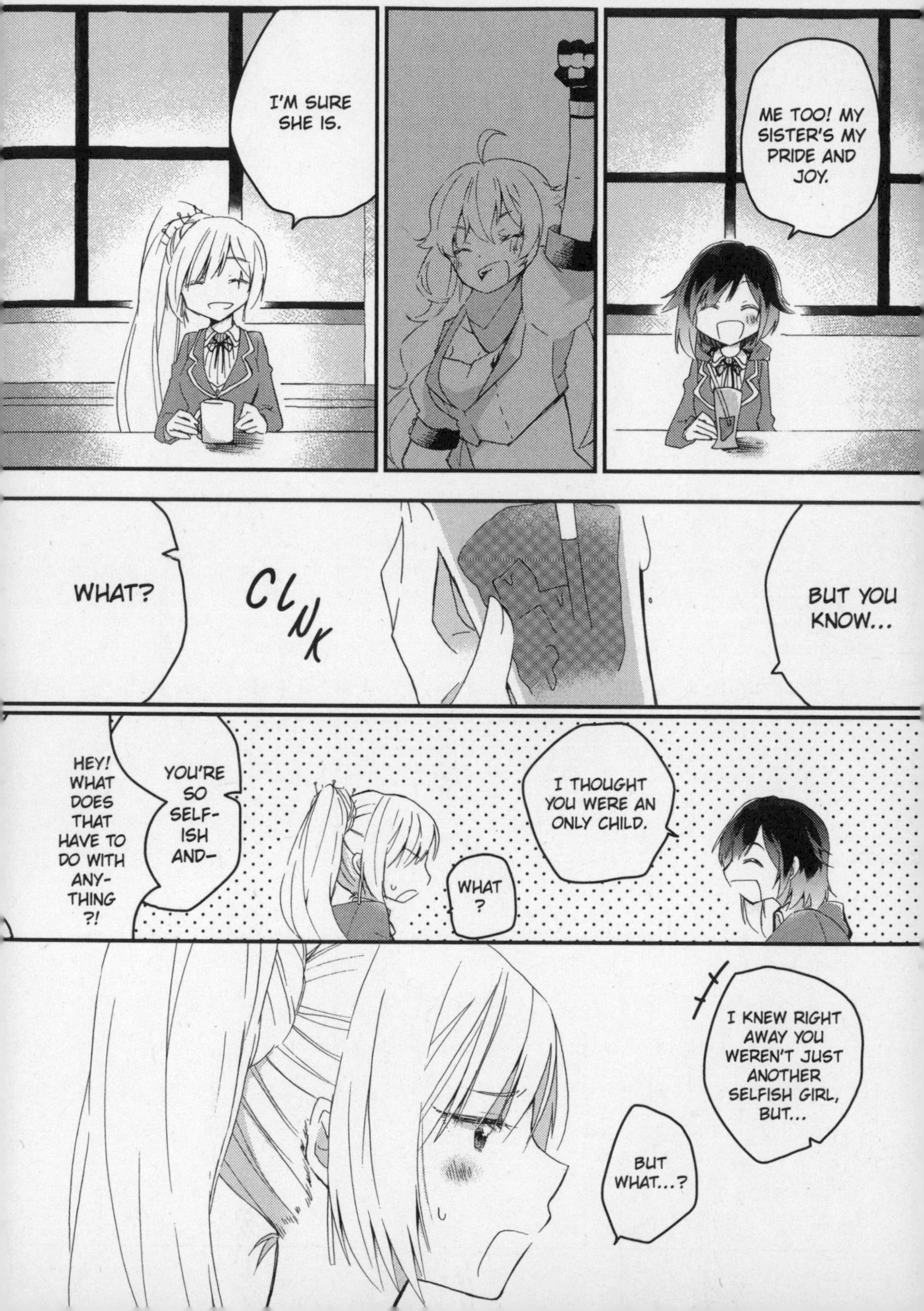
ME TOO! MY SISTER'S MY PRIDE AND JOY.
I'M SURE SHE IS.
BUT YOU KNOW...
CLINK
WHAT?
I THOUGHT YOU WERE AN ONLY CHILD.
WHAT?
YOU'RE SO SELF-ISH AND—
HEY! WHAT DOES THAT HAVE TO DO WITH ANY-THING?!
I KNEW RIGHT AWAY YOU WEREN'T JUST ANOTHER SELFISH GIRL, BUT...
BUT WHAT...?

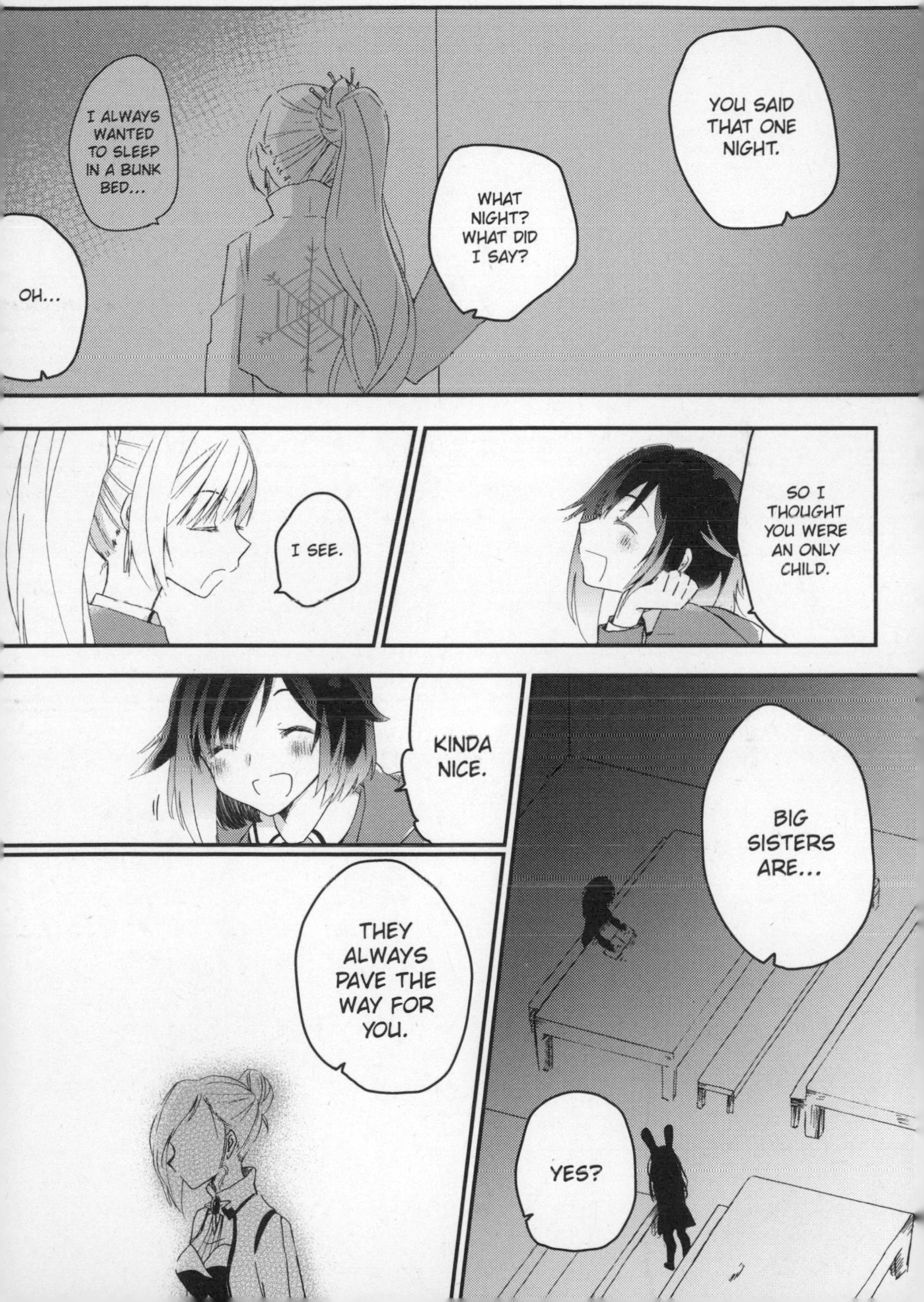
YOU SAID THAT ONE NIGHT.
WHAT NIGHT? WHAT DID I SAY?
I ALWAYS WANTED TO SLEEP IN A BUNK BED...
OH...
SO I THOUGHT YOU WERE AN ONLY CHILD.
I SEE.
BIG SISTERS ARE...
YES?
KINDA NICE.
THEY ALWAYS PAVE THE WAY FOR YOU.

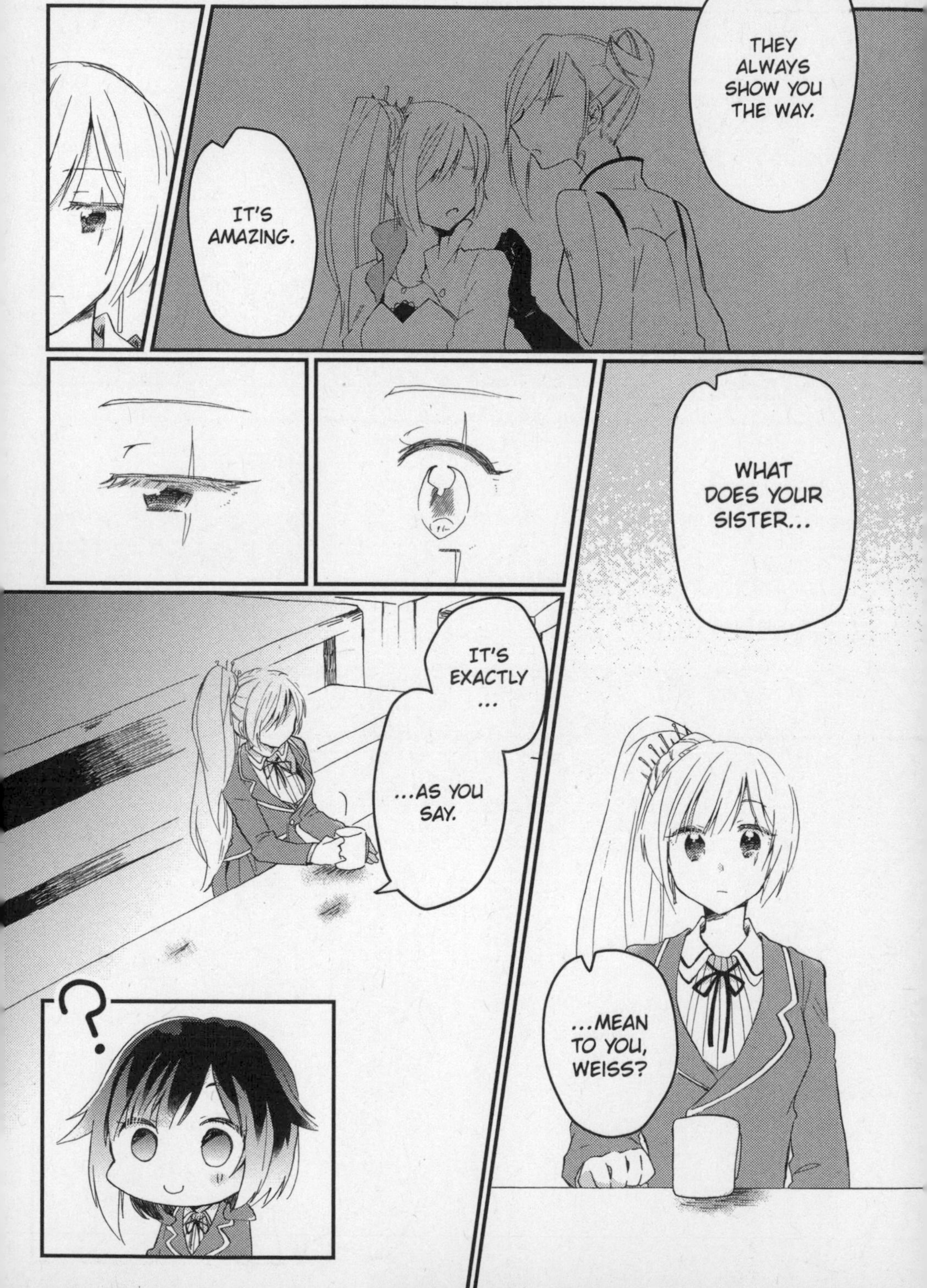
THEY ALWAYS SHOW YOU THE WAY.
IT'S AMAZING.
WHAT DOES YOUR SISTER...
...MEAN TO YOU, WEISS?
IT'S EXACTLY ...
...AS YOU SAY.
?

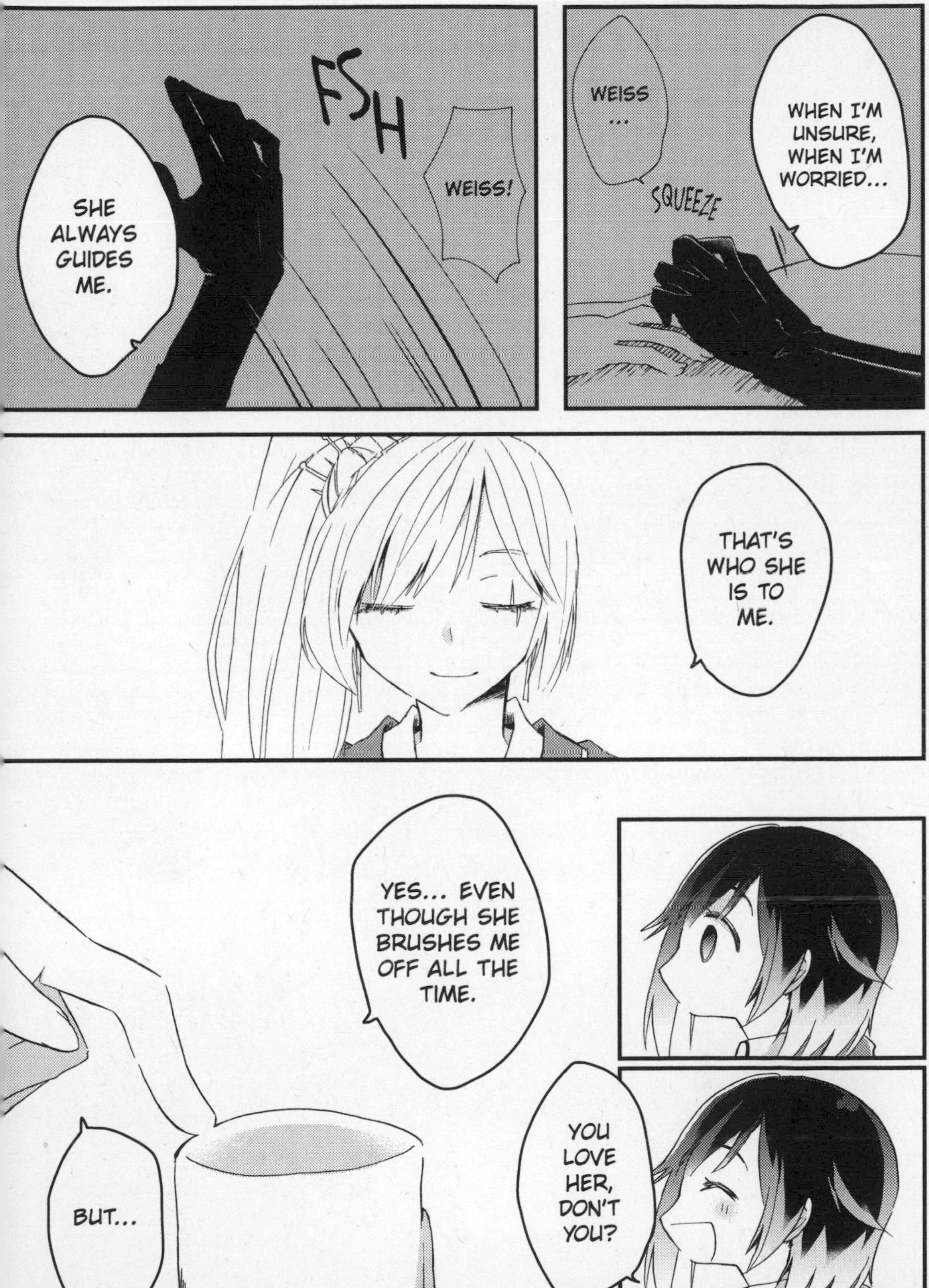
WHEN I'M UNSURE, WHEN I'M WORRIED...
WEISS ...
SQUEEZE
FSH
WEISS!
SHE ALWAYS GUIDES ME.
THAT'S WHO SHE IS TO ME.
YOU LOVE HER, DON'T YOU?
YES... EVEN THOUGH SHE BRUSHES ME OFF ALL THE TIME.
BUT...

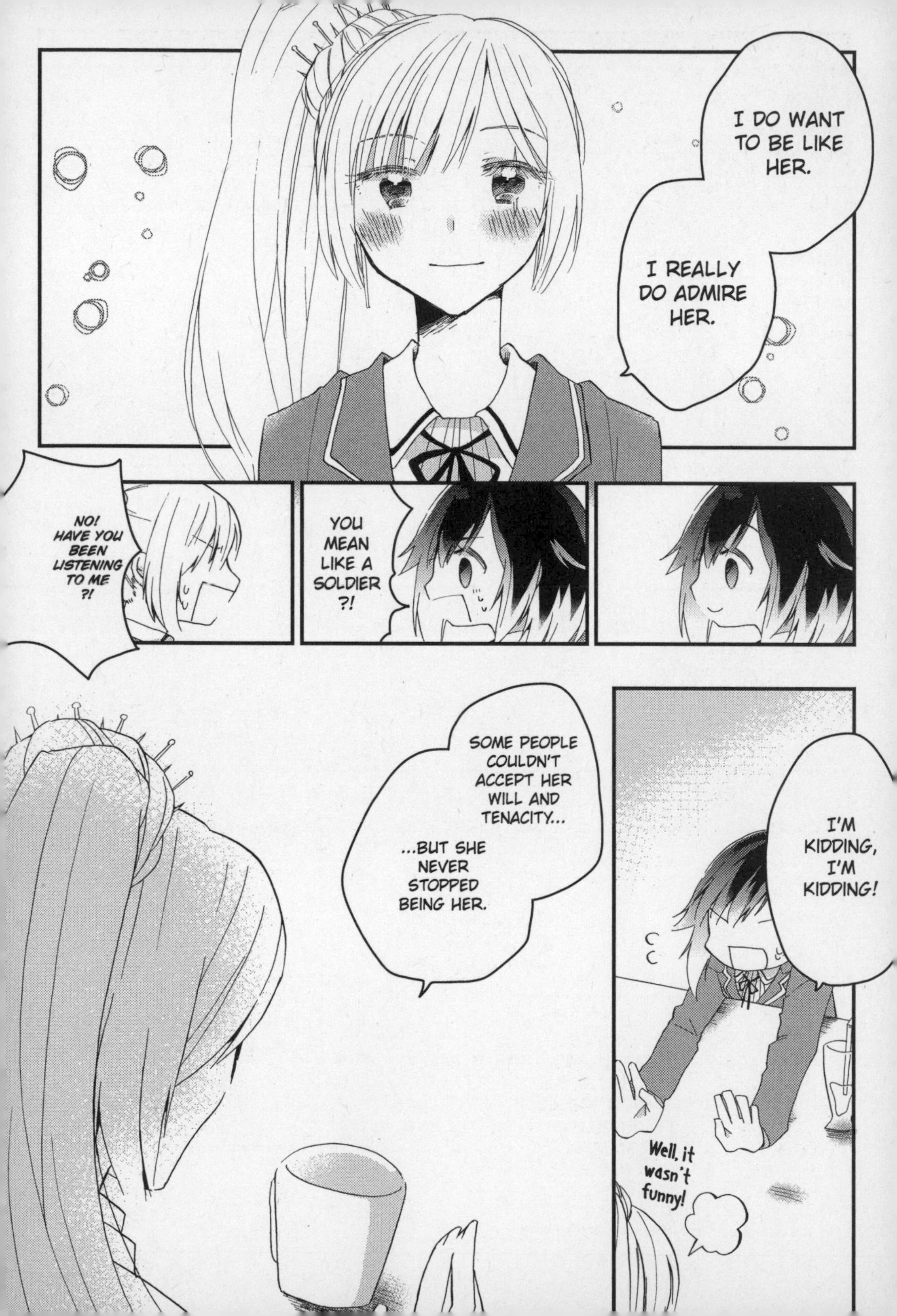
I DO WANT TO BE LIKE HER.
I REALLY DO ADMIRE HER.
YOU MEAN LIKE A SOLDIER?!
NO! HAVE YOU BEEN LISTENING TO ME?!
I'M KIDDING, I'M KIDDING!
Well, it wasn't funny!
SOME PEOPLE COULDN'T ACCEPT HER WILL AND TENACITY...
...BUT SHE NEVER STOPPED BEING HER.

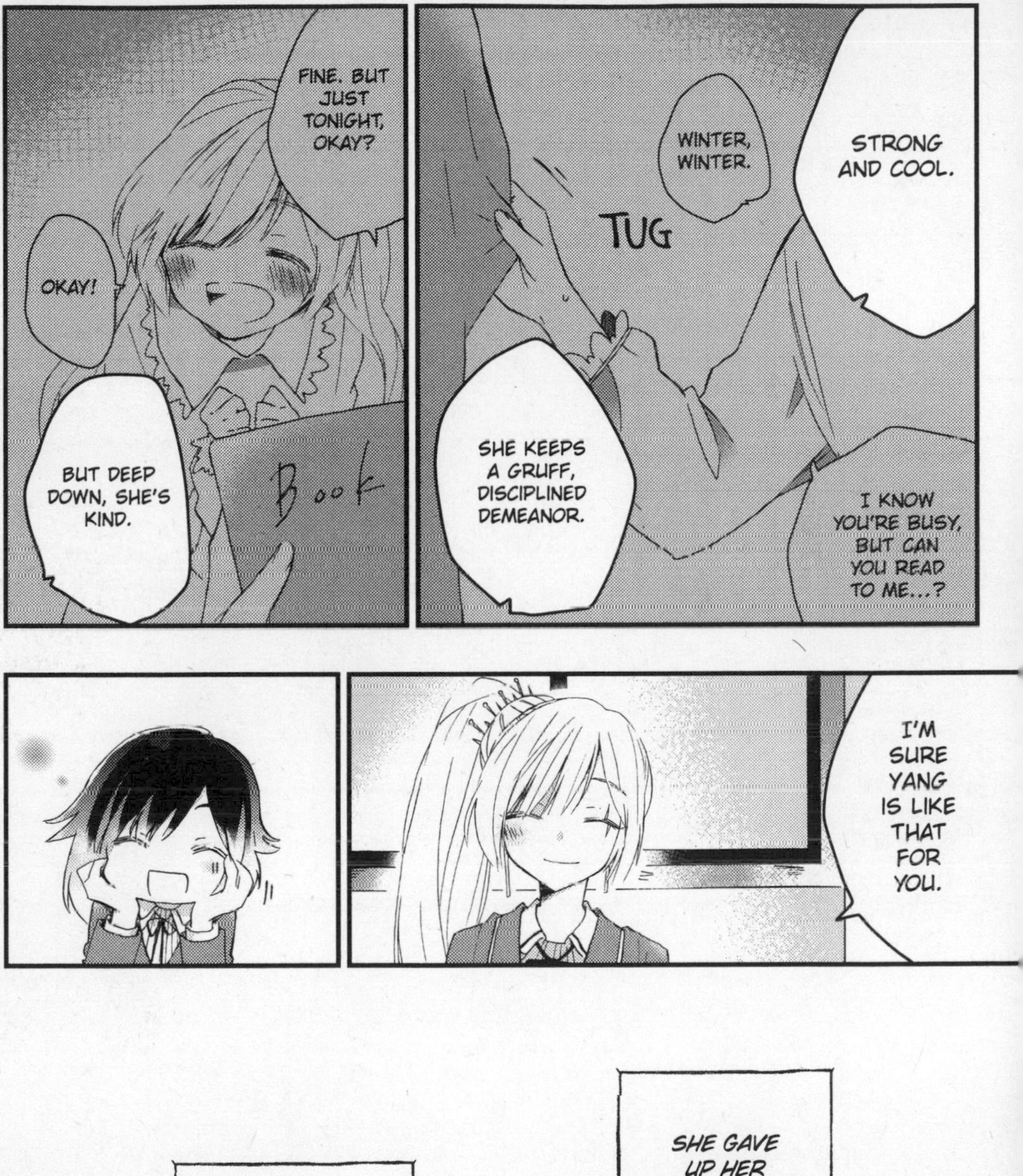
STRONG AND COOL.
WINTER, WINTER.
TUG
SHE KEEPS A GRUFF, DISCIPLINED DEMEANOR.
I KNOW YOU'RE BUSY, BUT CAN YOU READ TO ME...?
FINE. BUT JUST TONIGHT, OKAY?
OKAY!
Book
BUT DEEP DOWN, SHE'S KIND.
I'M SURE YANG IS LIKE THAT FOR YOU.
SHE GAVE UP HER INHERITANCE TO JOIN ATLAS ACADEMY.
I DID THE SAME TO JOIN BEACON, BUT I WONDER IF I'LL EVER BELIEVE IN MYSELF THE WAY SHE DOES...

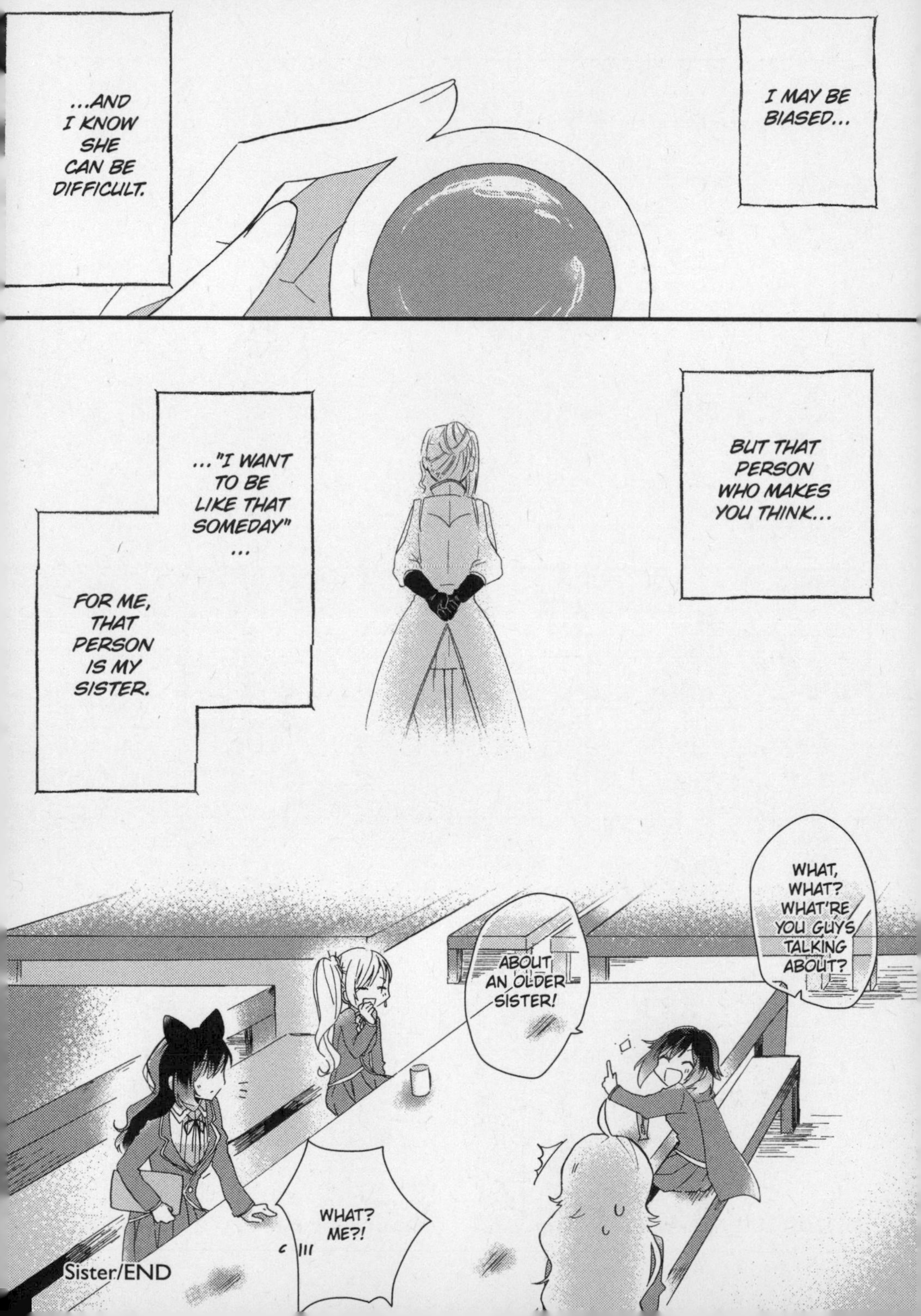
I MAY BE BIASED...
...AND I KNOW SHE CAN BE DIFFICULT.
BUT THAT PERSON WHO MAKES YOU THINK...
..."I WANT TO BE LIKE THAT SOMEDAY"...
FOR ME, THAT PERSON IS MY SISTER.
WHAT, WHAT? WHAT'RE YOU GUYS TALKING ABOUT?
ABOUT AN OLDER SISTER!
WHAT? ME?!
Sister/END

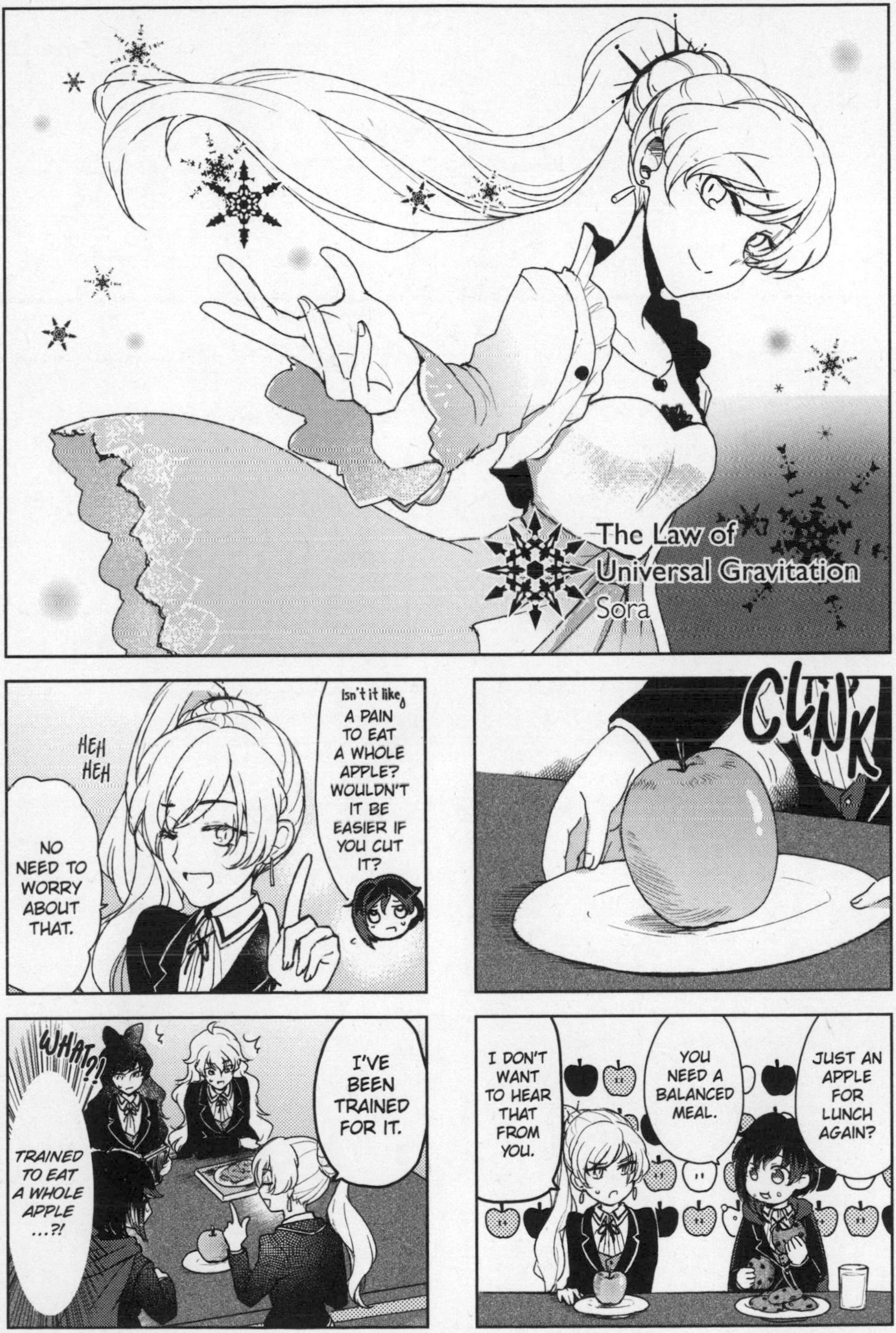

The Law of Universal Gravitation
Sora
CLINK
Isn't it like, A PAIN TO EAT A WHOLE APPLE? WOULDN'T IT BE EASIER IF YOU CUT IT?
HEH HEH
NO NEED TO WORRY ABOUT THAT.
JUST AN APPLE FOR LUNCH AGAIN?
YOU NEED A BALANCED MEAL.
I DON'T WANT TO HEAR THAT FROM YOU.
I'VE BEEN TRAINED FOR IT.
WHAT?!
TRAINED TO EAT A WHOLE APPLE ...?!

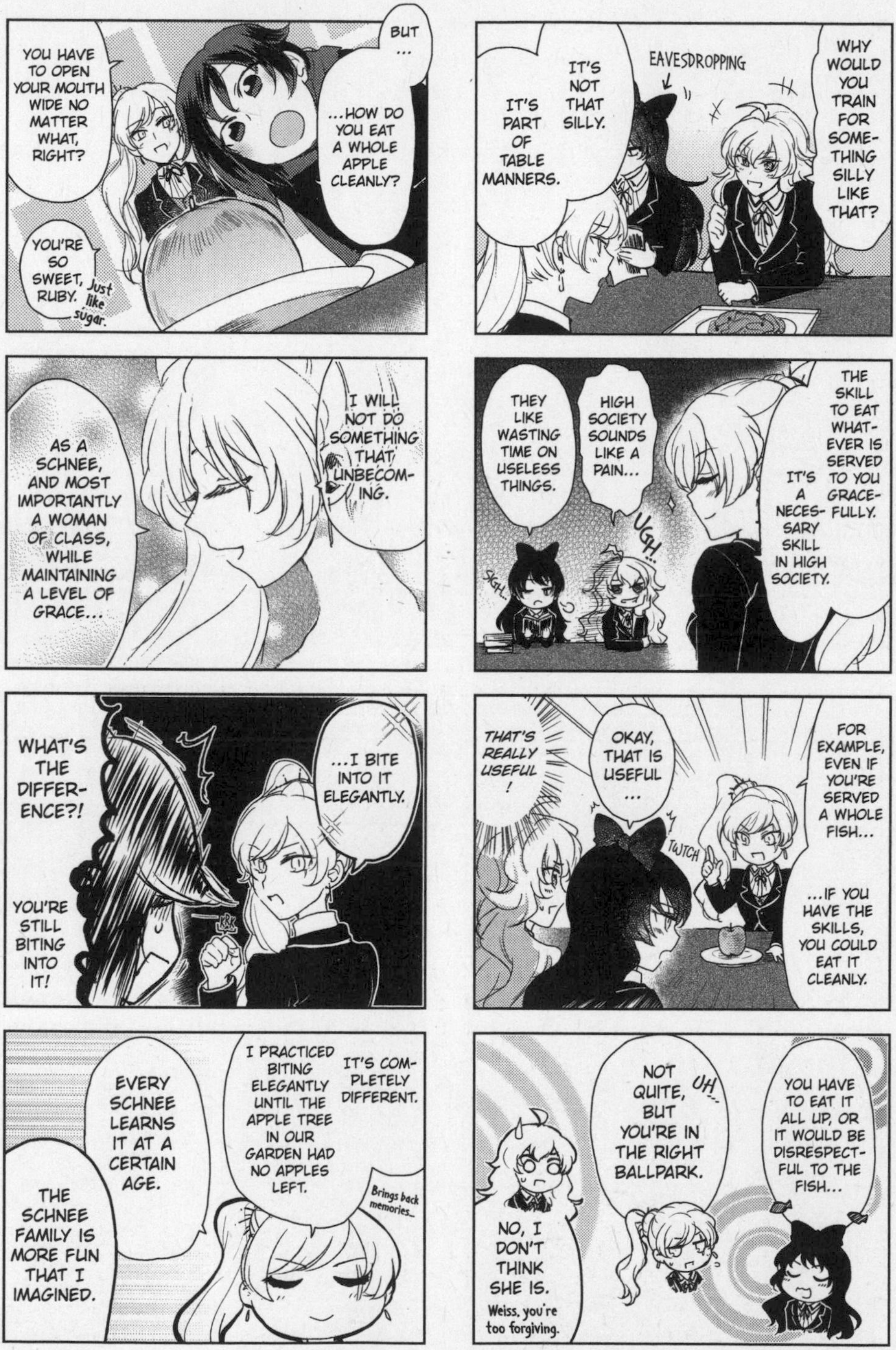
WHY WOULD YOU TRAIN FOR SOMETHING SILLY LIKE THAT?
EAVESDROPPING
IT'S NOT THAT SILLY.
IT'S PART OF TABLE MANNERS.
THE SKILL TO EAT WHATEVER IS SERVED TO YOU GRACEFULLY.
IT'S A NECESSARY SKILL IN HIGH SOCIETY.
HIGH SOCIETY SOUNDS LIKE A PAIN...
THEY LIKE WASTING TIME ON USELESS THINGS.
UGH...
SIGH...
FOR EXAMPLE, EVEN IF YOU'RE SERVED A WHOLE FISH...
OKAY, THAT IS USEFUL...
THAT'S REALLY USEFUL!
TWITCH
...IF YOU HAVE THE SKILLS, YOU COULD EAT IT CLEANLY.
YOU HAVE TO EAT IT ALL UP, OR IT WOULD BE DISRESPECTFUL TO THE FISH...
UH...
NOT QUITE, BUT YOU'RE IN THE RIGHT BALLPARK.
NO, I DON'T THINK SHE IS.
Weiss, you're too forgiving.
BUT...
...HOW DO YOU EAT A WHOLE APPLE CLEANLY?
YOU HAVE TO OPEN YOUR MOUTH WIDE NO MATTER WHAT, RIGHT?
YOU'RE SO SWEET, RUBY.
Just like sugar.
I WILL NOT DO SOMETHING THAT UNBECOMING.
AS A SCHNEE, AND MOST IMPORTANTLY A WOMAN OF CLASS, WHILE MAINTAINING A LEVEL OF GRACE...
...I BITE INTO IT ELEGANTLY.
WHAT'S THE DIFFERENCE?!
YOU'RE STILL BITING INTO IT!
IT'S COMPLETELY DIFFERENT.
I PRACTICED BITING ELEGANTLY UNTIL THE APPLE TREE IN OUR GARDEN HAD NO APPLES LEFT.
Brings back memories...
EVERY SCHNEE LEARNS IT AT A CERTAIN AGE.
THE SCHNEE FAMILY IS MORE FUN THAT I IMAGINED.

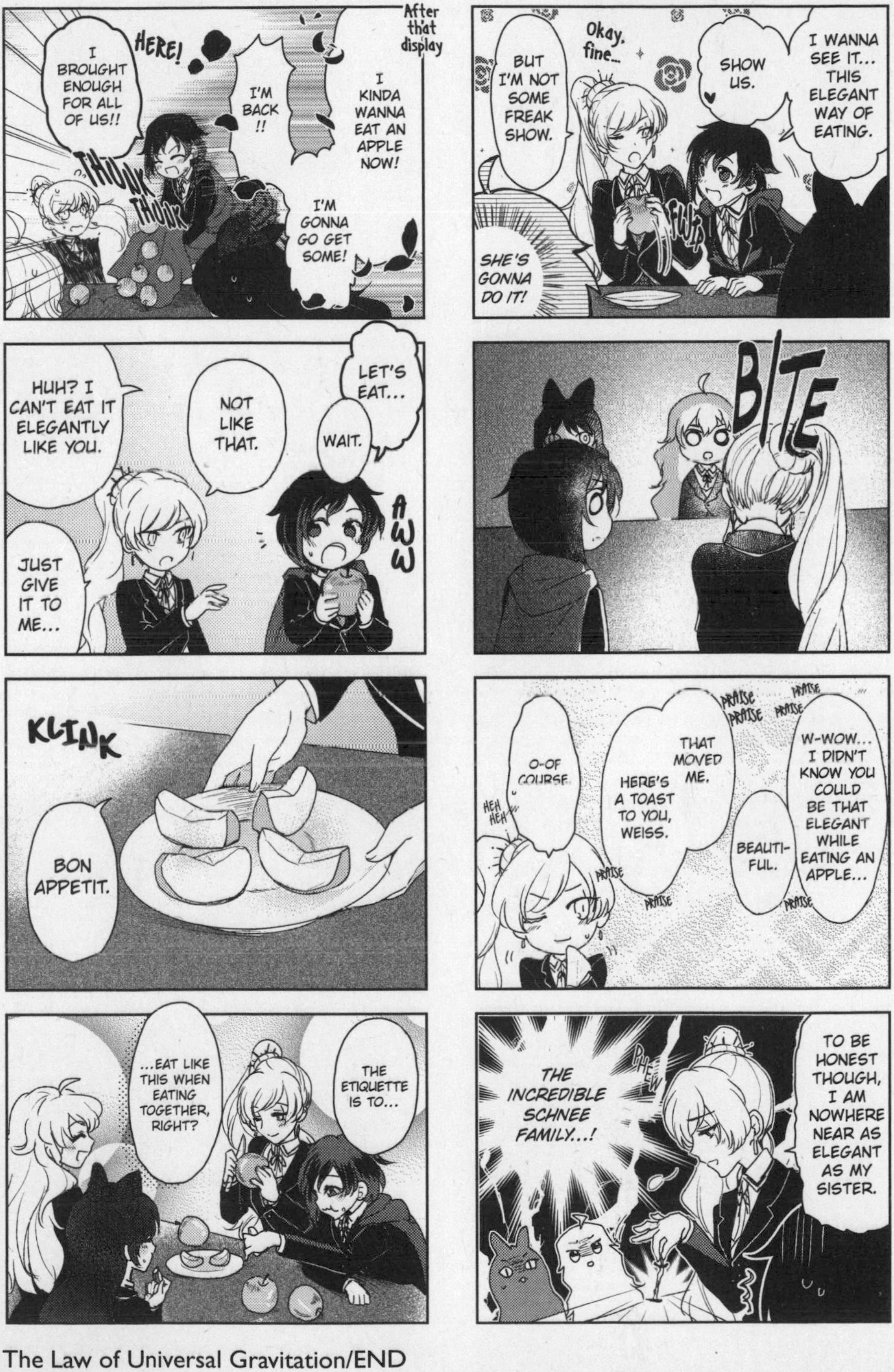

I WANNA SEE IT... THIS ELEGANT WAY OF EATING.
SHOW US.
Okay. fine...
BUT I'M NOT SOME FREAK SHOW.
FWIP
SHE'S GONNA DO IT!
BITE
PRAISE PRAISE PRAISE PRAISE
W-WOW... I DIDN'T KNOW YOU COULD BE THAT ELEGANT WHILE EATING AN APPLE...
THAT MOVED ME.
BEAUTIFUL.
HERE'S A TOAST TO YOU, WEISS.
PRAISE
PRAISE
PRAISE
O-OF COURSE.
HEH HEH
TO BE HONEST THOUGH, I AM NOWHERE NEAR AS ELEGANT AS MY SISTER.
PHEW
THE INCREDIBLE SCHNEE FAMILY...!
After that display
I KINDA WANNA EAT AN APPLE NOW!
I'M GONNA GO GET SOME!
I'M BACK!!
HERE!
I BROUGHT ENOUGH FOR ALL OF US!!
THUNK THUNK
LET'S EAT...
WAIT.
NOT LIKE THAT.
HUH? I CAN'T EAT IT ELEGANTLY LIKE YOU.
AWW
JUST GIVE IT TO ME...
KLINK
BON APPETIT.
THE ETIQUETTE IS TO...
...EAT LIKE THIS WHEN EATING TOGETHER, RIGHT?

The Law of Universal Gravitation/END

RWBY

OFFICIAL MANGA ANTHOLOGY
VOLUME 2 Mirror, Mirror

METEO

Snow White's Grim Prospects

Kaogeimoai

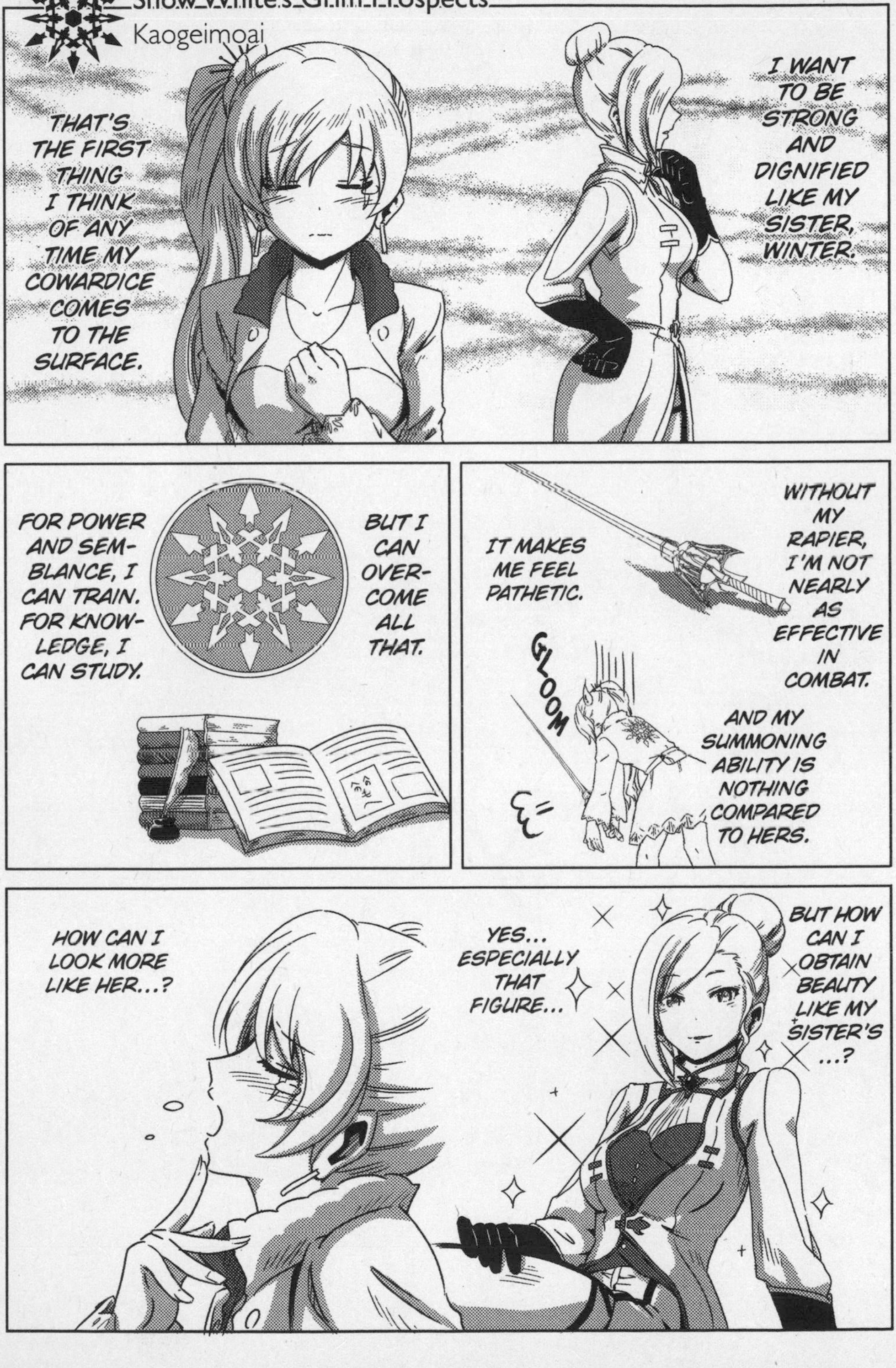
I WANT TO BE STRONG AND DIGNIFIED LIKE MY SISTER, WINTER.
THAT'S THE FIRST THING I THINK OF ANY TIME MY COWARDICE COMES TO THE SURFACE.
WITHOUT MY RAPIER, I'M NOT NEARLY AS EFFECTIVE IN COMBAT.
IT MAKES ME FEEL PATHETIC.
GLOOM
AND MY SUMMONING ABILITY IS NOTHING COMPARED TO HERS.
BUT I CAN OVERCOME ALL THAT.
FOR POWER AND SEMBLANCE, I CAN TRAIN. FOR KNOWLEDGE, I CAN STUDY.
BUT HOW CAN I OBTAIN BEAUTY LIKE MY SISTER'S ...?
YES... ESPECIALLY THAT FIGURE...
HOW CAN I LOOK MORE LIKE HER...?

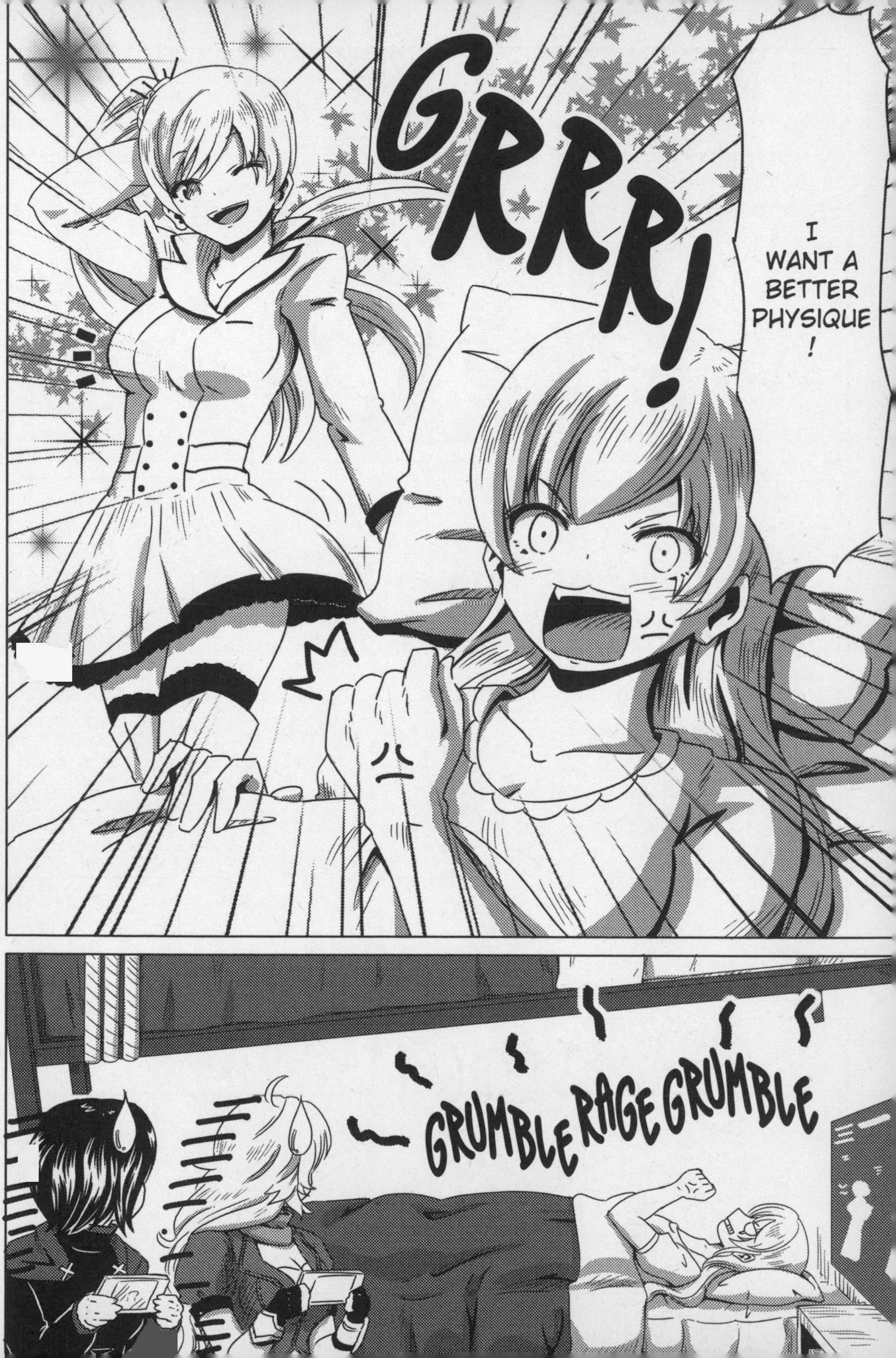
I WANT A BETTER PHYSIQUE!
GRRR!
GRUMBLE RAGE GRUMBLE

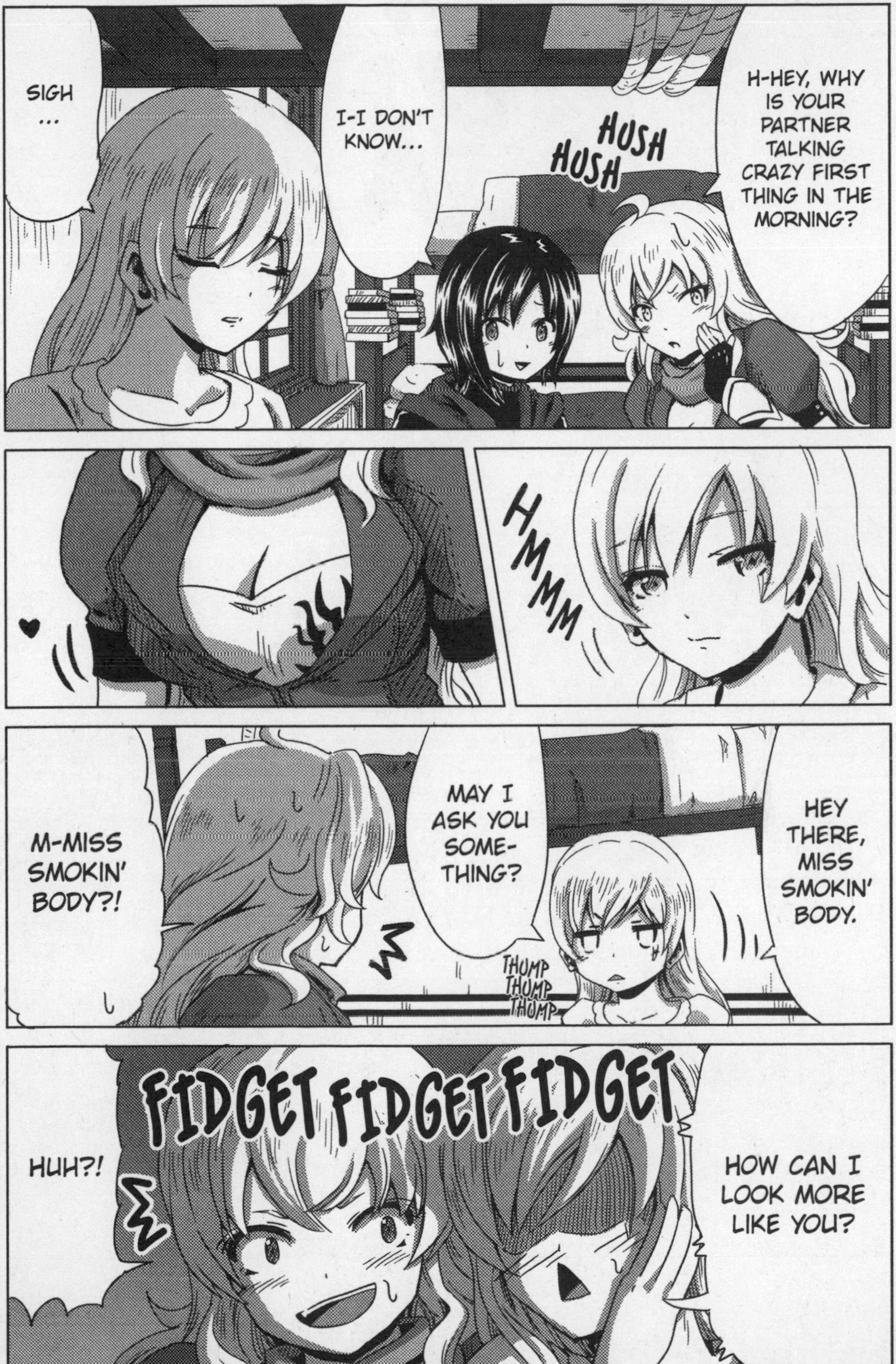
H-HEY, WHY IS YOUR PARTNER TALKING CRAZY FIRST THING IN THE MORNING?
HUSH HUSH
I-I DON'T KNOW...
SIGH ...
HMMM
HEY THERE, MISS SMOKIN' BODY.
THUMP THUMP THUMP
MAY I ASK YOU SOME-THING?
M-MISS SMOKIN' BODY?!
HOW CAN I LOOK MORE LIKE YOU?
FIDGET FIDGET FIDGET
HUH?!

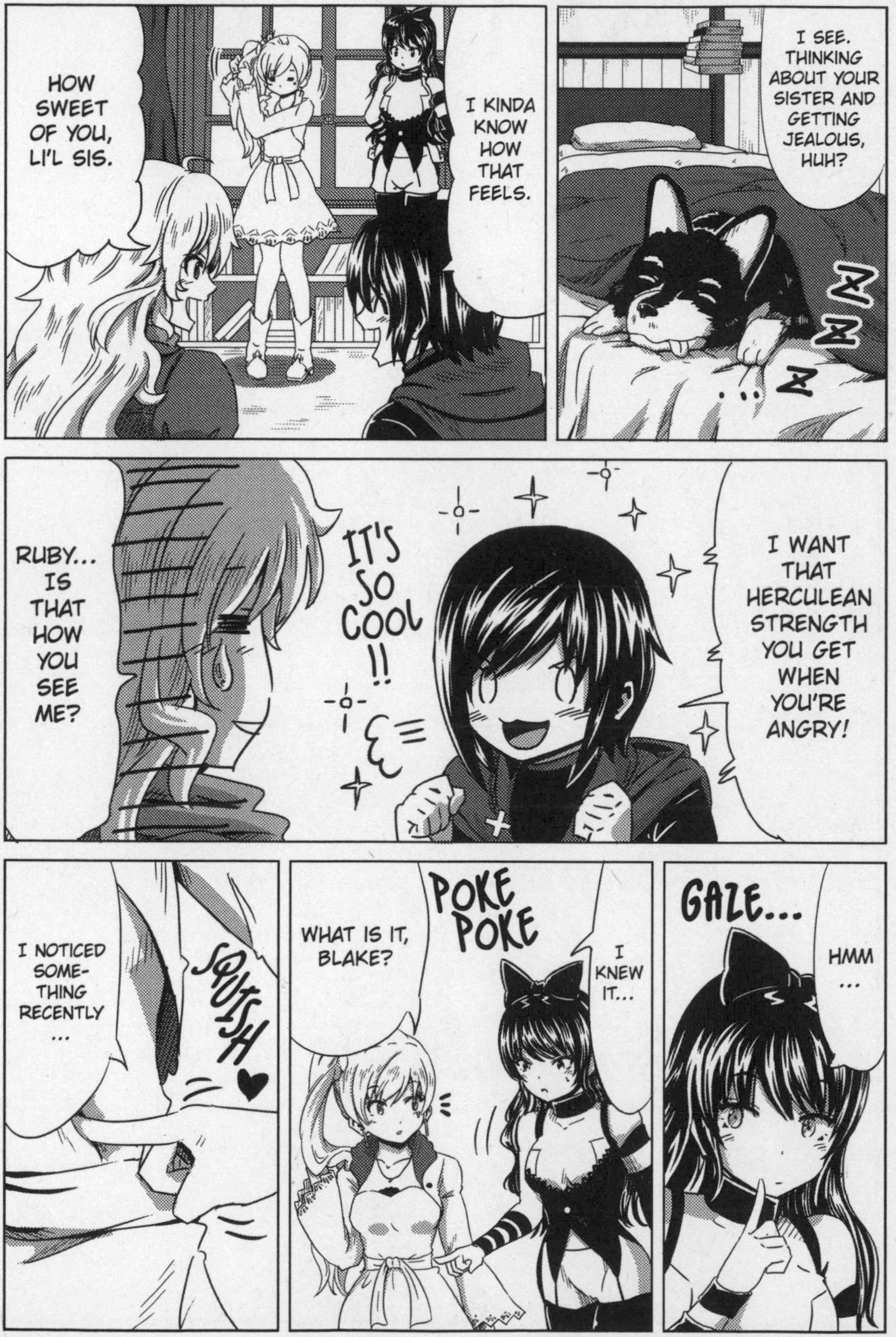
I SEE. THINKING ABOUT YOUR SISTER AND GETTING JEALOUS, HUH?
Z Z Z
...
I KINDA KNOW HOW THAT FEELS.
HOW SWEET OF YOU, LI'L SIS.
I WANT THAT HERCULEAN STRENGTH YOU GET WHEN YOU'RE ANGRY!
IT'S SO COOL!!
RUBY... IS THAT HOW YOU SEE ME?
GAZE...
HMM ...
I KNEW IT...
POKE POKE
WHAT IS IT, BLAKE?
SQUISH ♥
I NOTICED SOME-THING RECENTLY ...

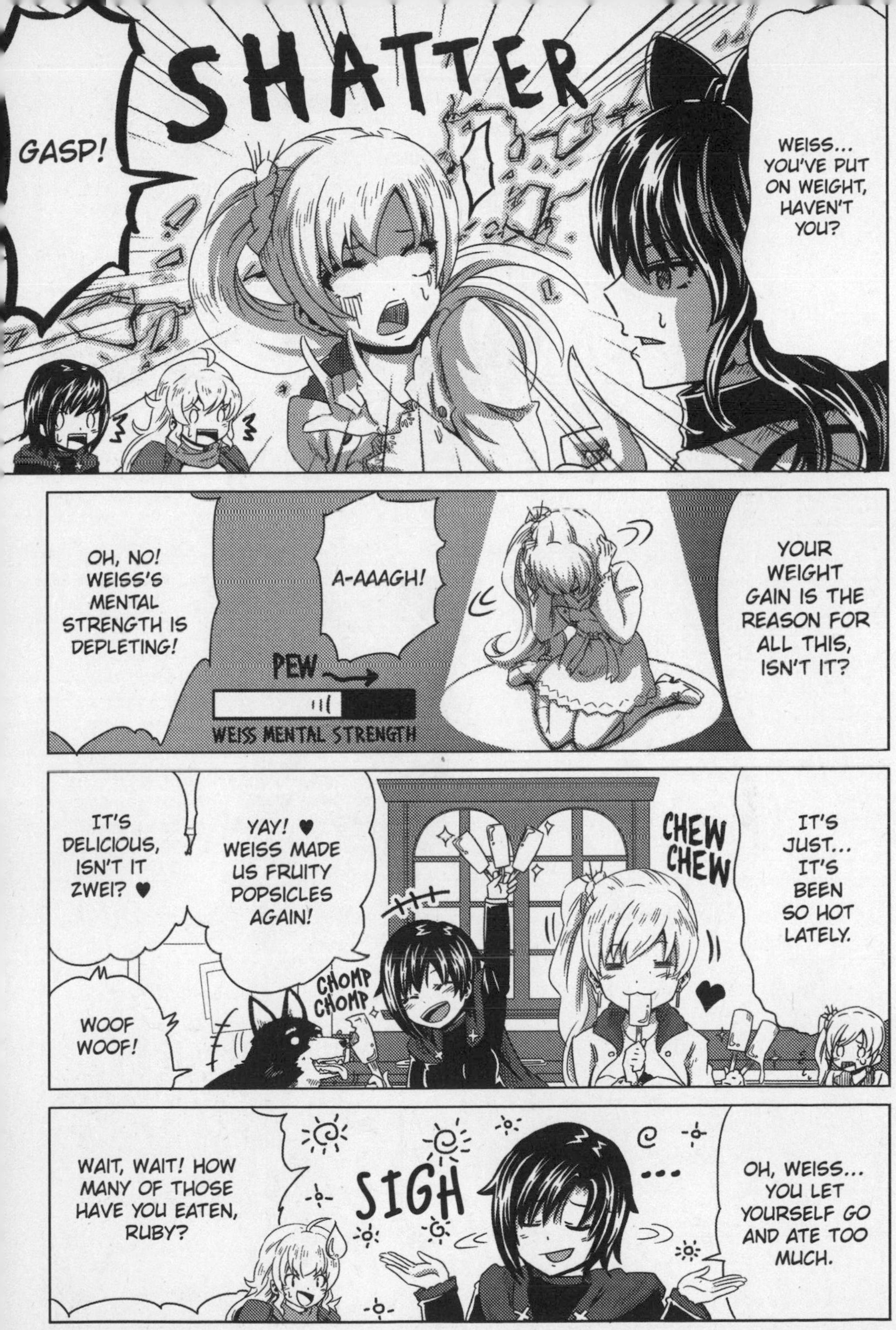
WEISS... YOU'VE PUT ON WEIGHT, HAVEN'T YOU?
SHATTER
GASP!
YOUR WEIGHT GAIN IS THE REASON FOR ALL THIS, ISN'T IT?
A-AAAGH!
OH, NO! WEISS'S MENTAL STRENGTH IS DEPLETING!
PEW
WEISS MENTAL STRENGTH
IT'S JUST... IT'S BEEN SO HOT LATELY.
CHEW CHEW
YAY! ♥ WEISS MADE US FRUITY POPSICLES AGAIN!
IT'S DELICIOUS, ISN'T IT ZWEI? ♥
CHOMP CHOMP
WOOF WOOF!
OH, WEISS... YOU LET YOURSELF GO AND ATE TOO MUCH.
...
SIGH
WAIT, WAIT! HOW MANY OF THOSE HAVE YOU EATEN, RUBY?

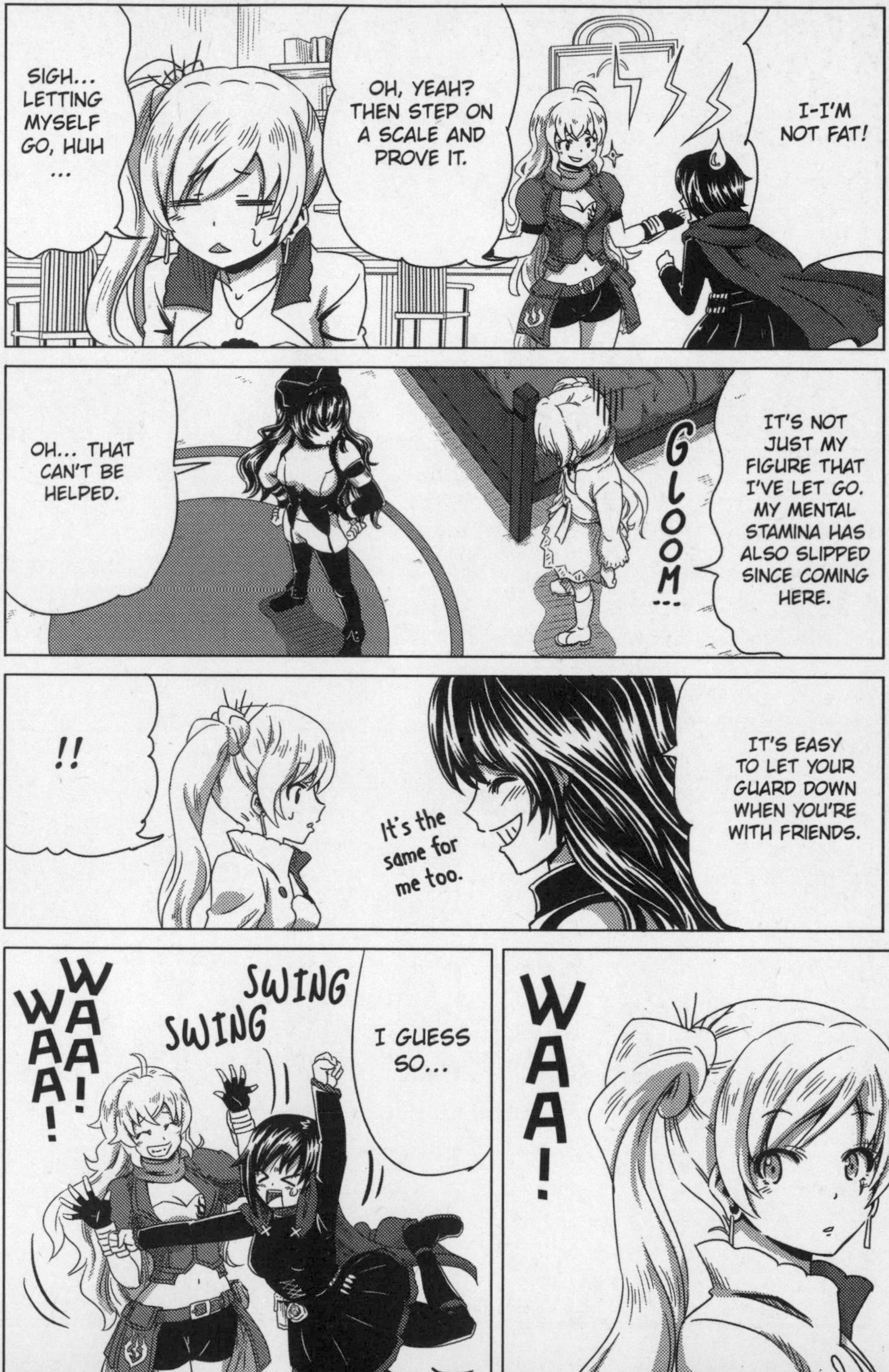
I-I'M NOT FAT!
OH, YEAH? THEN STEP ON A SCALE AND PROVE IT.
SIGH... LETTING MYSELF GO, HUH ...
IT'S NOT JUST MY FIGURE THAT I'VE LET GO. MY MENTAL STAMINA HAS ALSO SLIPPED SINCE COMING HERE.
GLOOM...
OH... THAT CAN'T BE HELPED.
IT'S EASY TO LET YOUR GUARD DOWN WHEN YOU'RE WITH FRIENDS.
It's the same for me too.
!!
WAAA!
I GUESS SO...
SWING
SWING
WAA!
WAA!

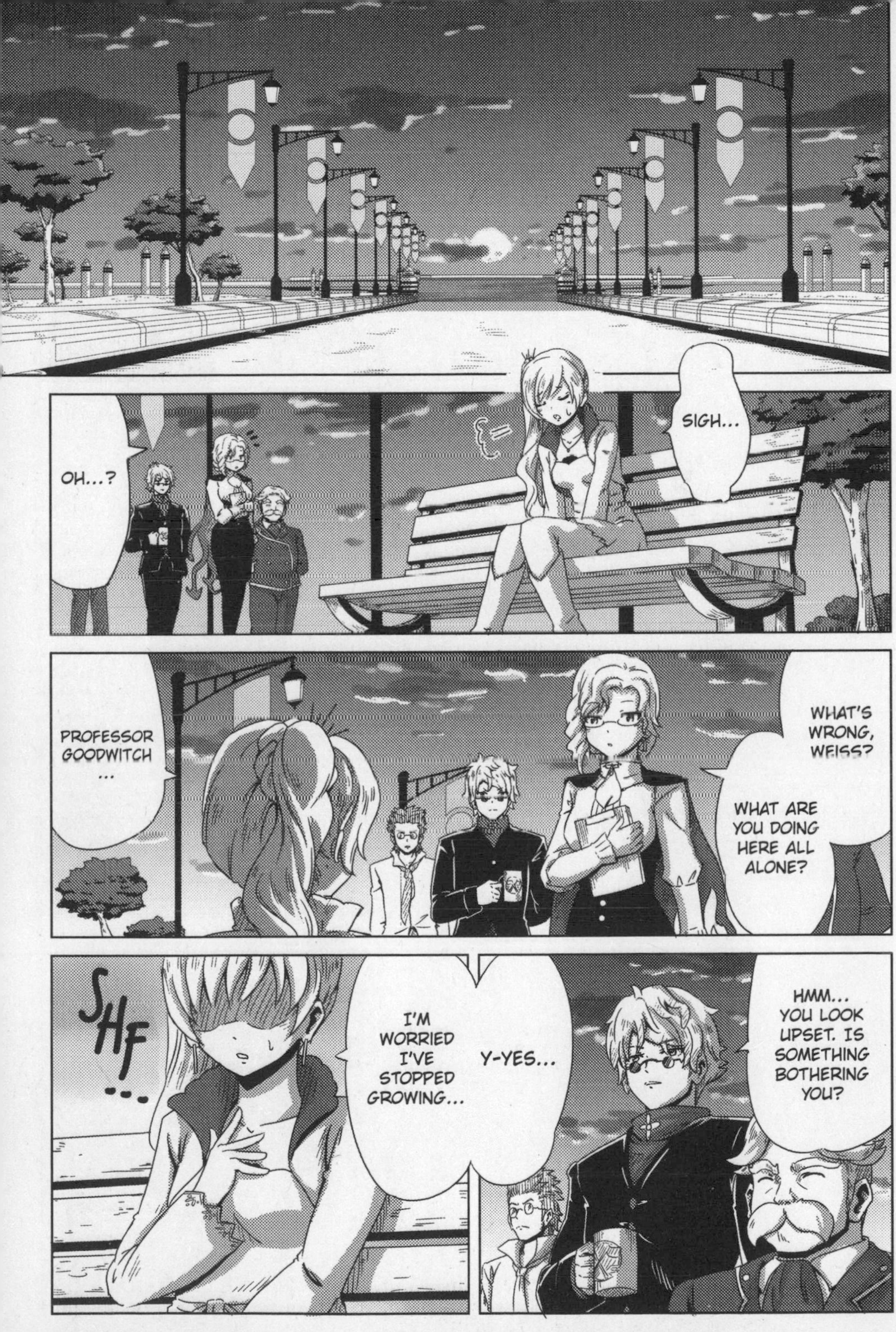
SIGH...
OH...?
WHAT'S WRONG, WEISS?
WHAT ARE YOU DOING HERE ALL ALONE?
PROFESSOR GOODWITCH ...
HMM... YOU LOOK UPSET. IS SOMETHING BOTHERING YOU?
Y-YES...
I'M WORRIED I'VE STOPPED GROWING...
SHF ...

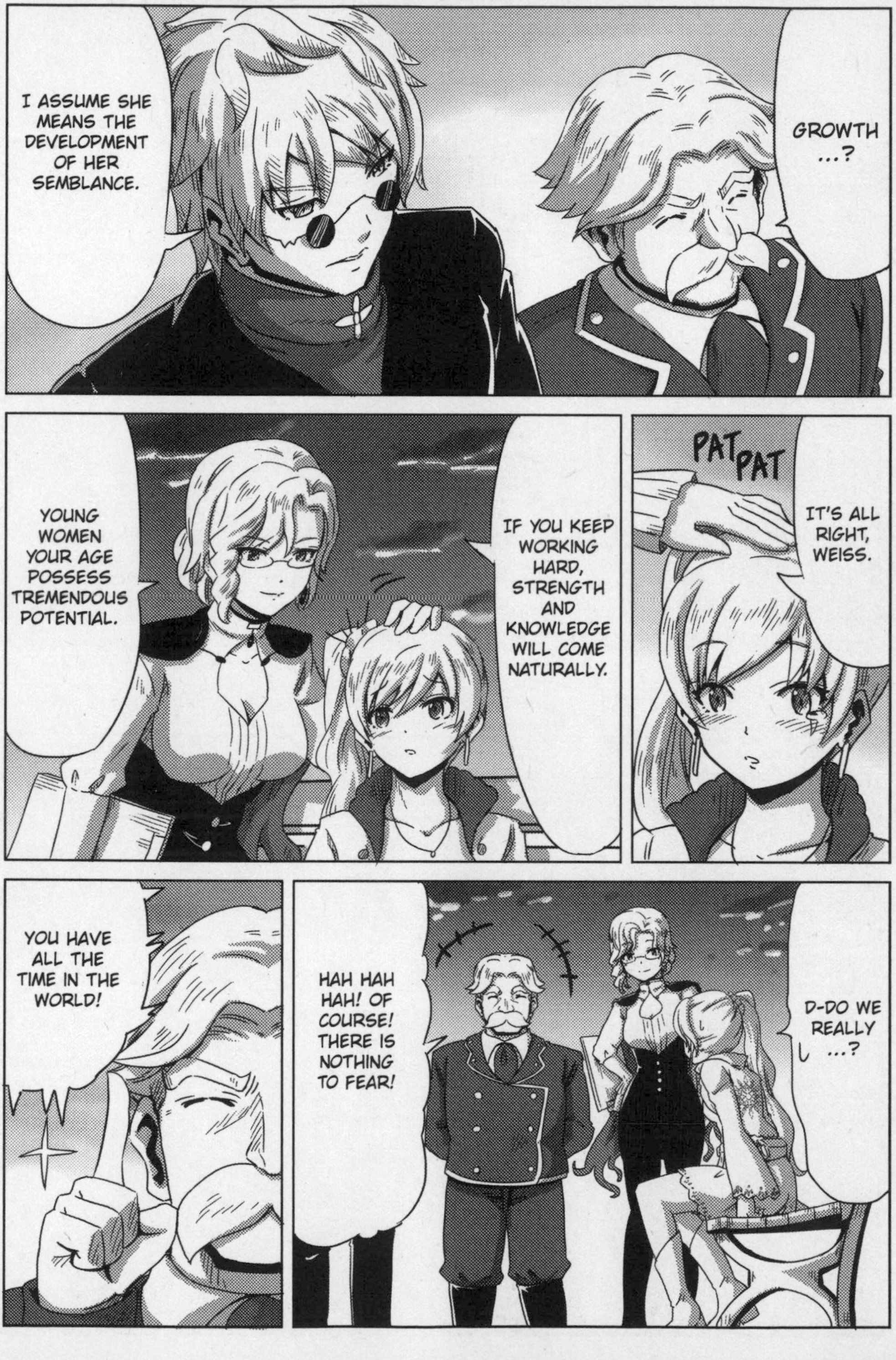
GROWTH ...?
I ASSUME SHE MEANS THE DEVELOPMENT OF HER SEMBLANCE.
PAT PAT
IT'S ALL RIGHT, WEISS.
IF YOU KEEP WORKING HARD, STRENGTH AND KNOWLEDGE WILL COME NATURALLY.
YOUNG WOMEN YOUR AGE POSSESS TREMENDOUS POTENTIAL.
D-DO WE REALLY ...?
HAH HAH HAH! OF COURSE! THERE IS NOTHING TO FEAR!
YOU HAVE ALL THE TIME IN THE WORLD!

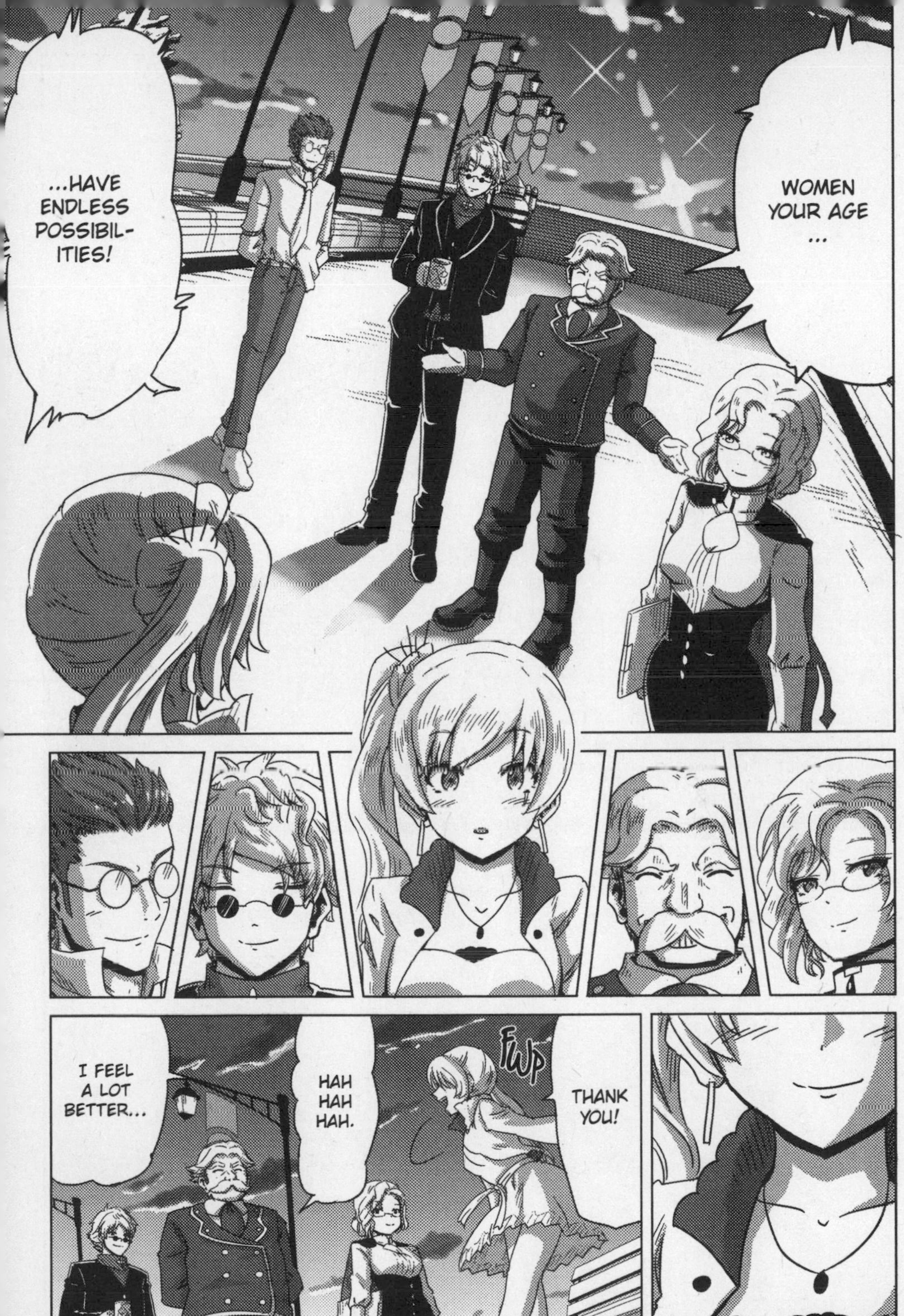
WOMEN YOUR AGE ...
...HAVE ENDLESS POSSIBIL-ITIES!
THANK YOU!
FWP
HAH HAH HAH.
I FEEL A LOT BETTER...

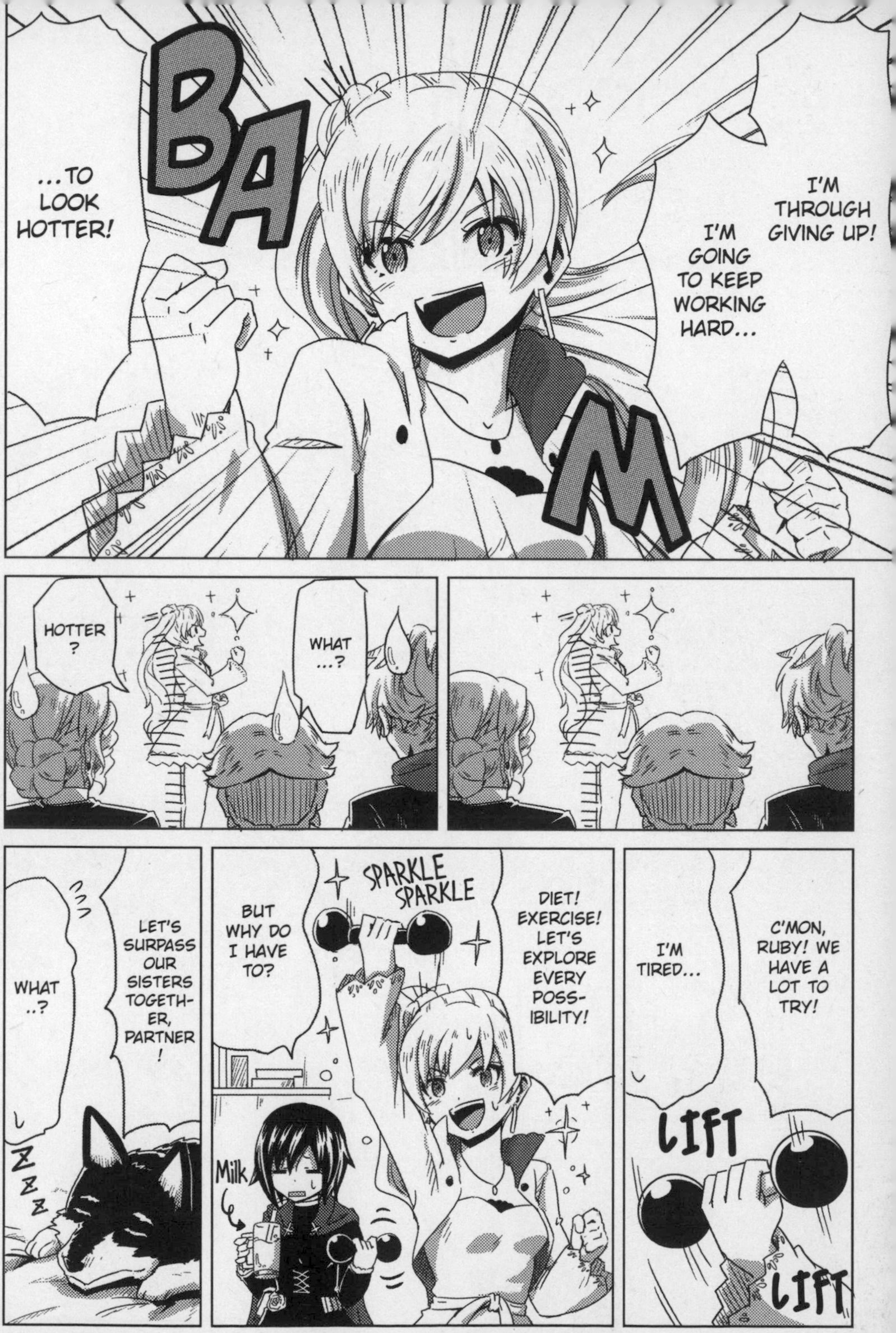
I'M THROUGH GIVING UP!
I'M GOING TO KEEP WORKING HARD...
BAM
...TO LOOK HOTTER!
WHAT ...?
HOTTER ?
C'MON, RUBY! WE HAVE A LOT TO TRY!
I'M TIRED...
LIFT
LIFT
DIET! EXERCISE! LET'S EXPLORE EVERY POSSIBILITY!
SPARKLE SPARKLE
BUT WHY DO I HAVE TO?
Milk
LET'S SURPASS OUR SISTERS TOGETHER, PARTNER!
WHAT ..?
ZZZ

Snow White's Grim Prospects/END

Chapter 4.5: Day

ryuga

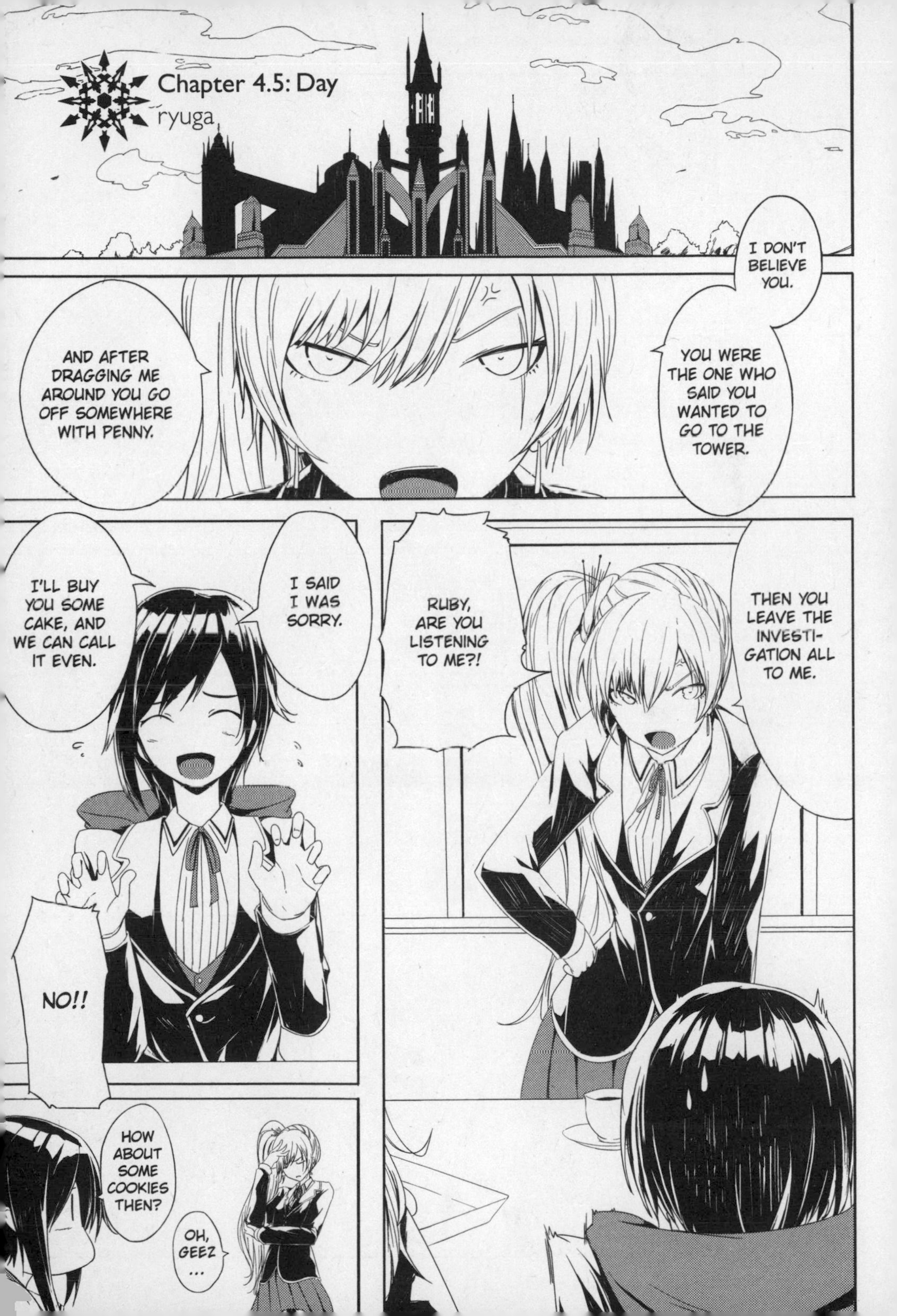
I DON'T BELIEVE YOU.
YOU WERE THE ONE WHO SAID YOU WANTED TO GO TO THE TOWER.
AND AFTER DRAGGING ME AROUND YOU GO OFF SOMEWHERE WITH PENNY.
THEN YOU LEAVE THE INVESTIGATION ALL TO ME.
RUBY, ARE YOU LISTENING TO ME?!
I SAID I WAS SORRY.
I'LL BUY YOU SOME CAKE, AND WE CAN CALL IT EVEN.
NO!!
HOW ABOUT SOME COOKIES THEN?
OH, GEEZ ...

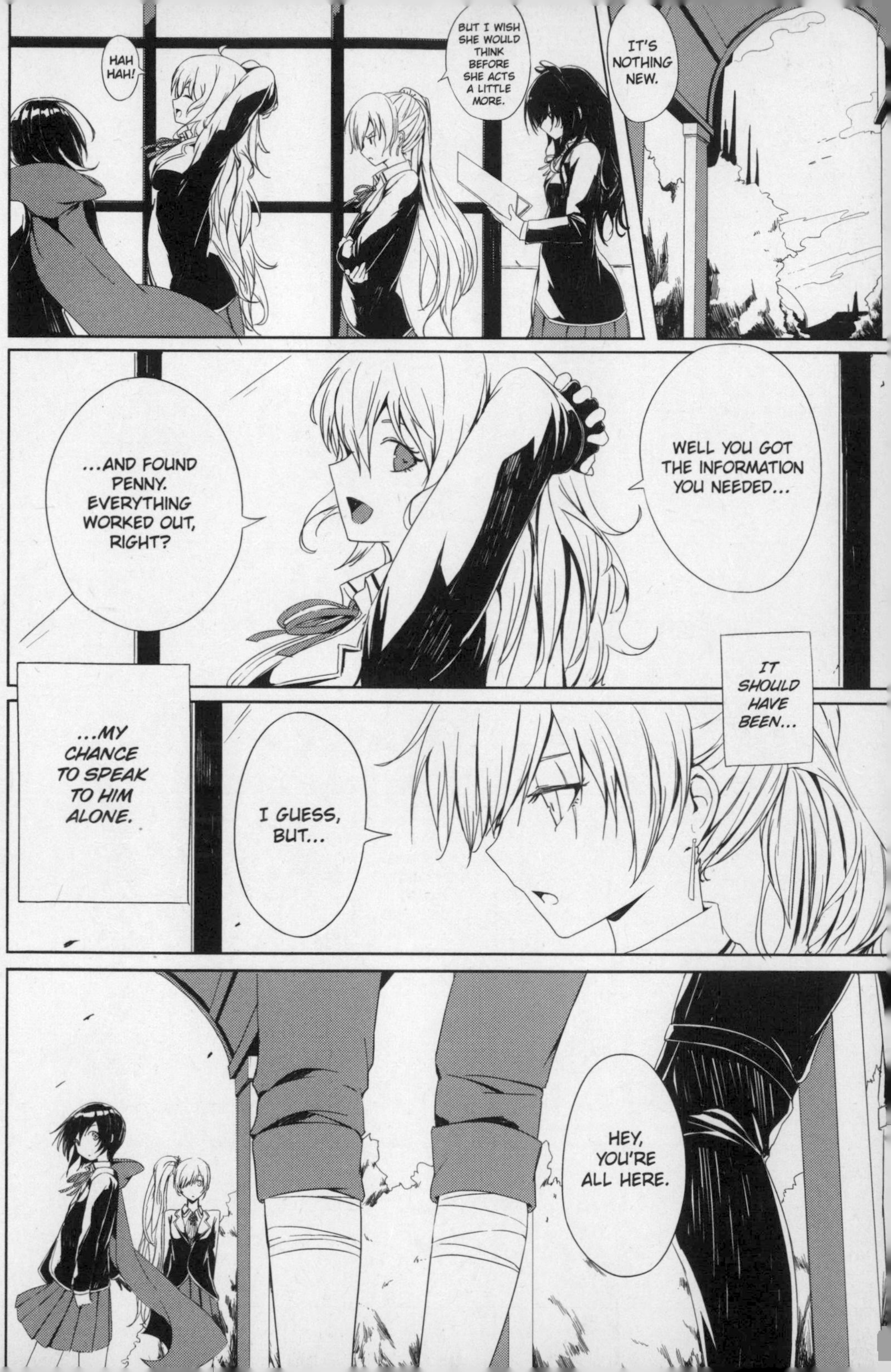
IT'S NOTHING NEW.
BUT I WISH SHE WOULD THINK BEFORE SHE ACTS A LITTLE MORE.
HAH HAH!
WELL YOU GOT THE INFORMATION YOU NEEDED...
...AND FOUND PENNY. EVERYTHING WORKED OUT, RIGHT?
IT SHOULD HAVE BEEN...
I GUESS, BUT...
...MY CHANCE TO SPEAK TO HIM ALONE.
HEY, YOU'RE ALL HERE.

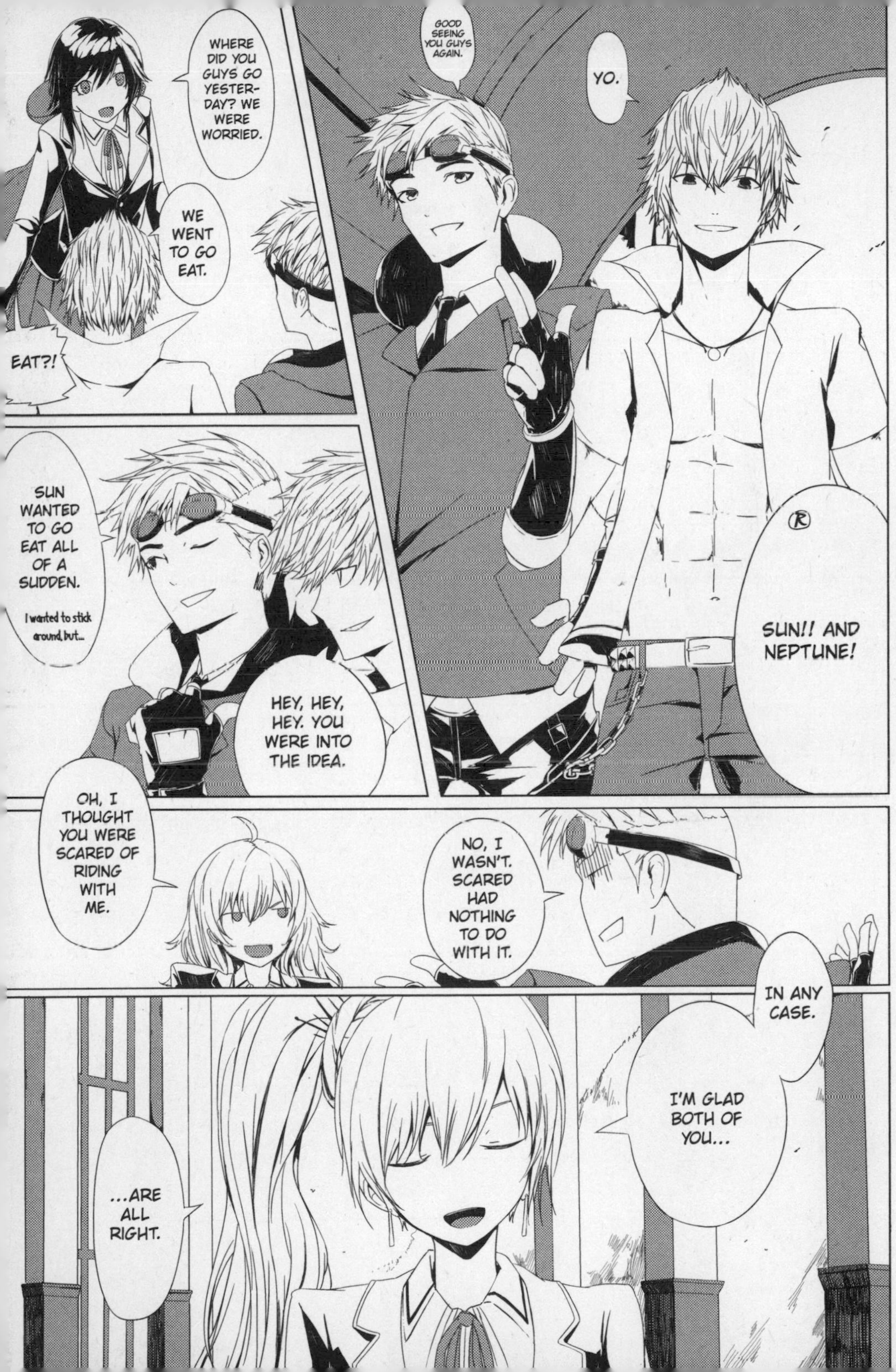
YO.
GOOD SEEING YOU GUYS AGAIN.
SUN!! AND NEPTUNE!
WHERE DID YOU GUYS GO YESTER-DAY? WE WERE WORRIED.
WE WENT TO GO EAT.
EAT?!
SUN WANTED TO GO EAT ALL OF A SUDDEN.
I wanted to stick around, but...
HEY, HEY, HEY. YOU WERE INTO THE IDEA.
NO, I WASN'T. SCARED HAD NOTHING TO DO WITH IT.
OH, I THOUGHT YOU WERE SCARED OF RIDING WITH ME.
IN ANY CASE.
I'M GLAD BOTH OF YOU...
...ARE ALL RIGHT.

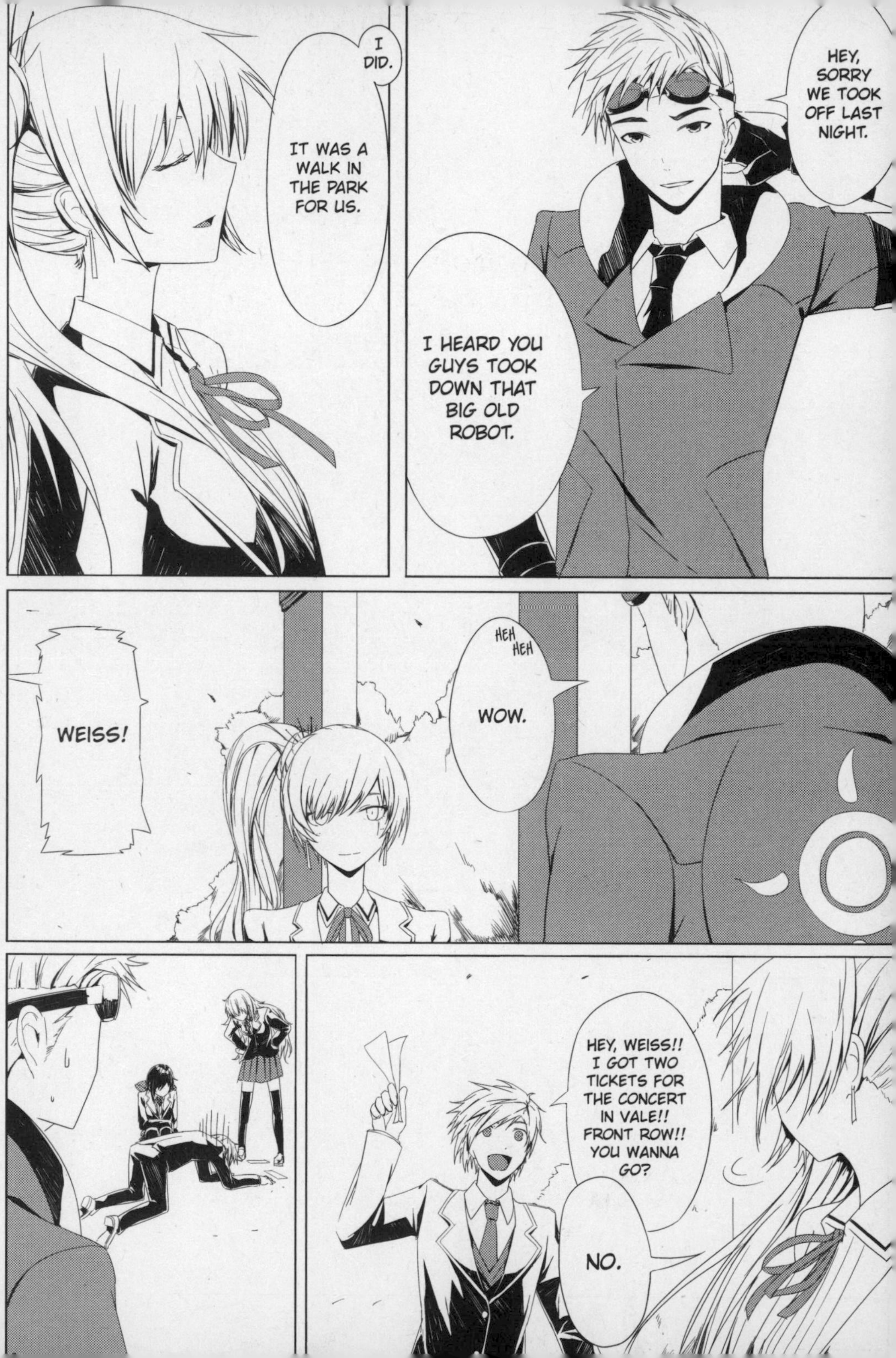
HEY, SORRY WE TOOK OFF LAST NIGHT.
I HEARD YOU GUYS TOOK DOWN THAT BIG OLD ROBOT.
I DID.
IT WAS A WALK IN THE PARK FOR US.
HEH HEH
WOW.
WEISS!
HEY, WEISS!! I GOT TWO TICKETS FOR THE CONCERT IN VALE!! FRONT ROW!! YOU WANNA GO?
NO.

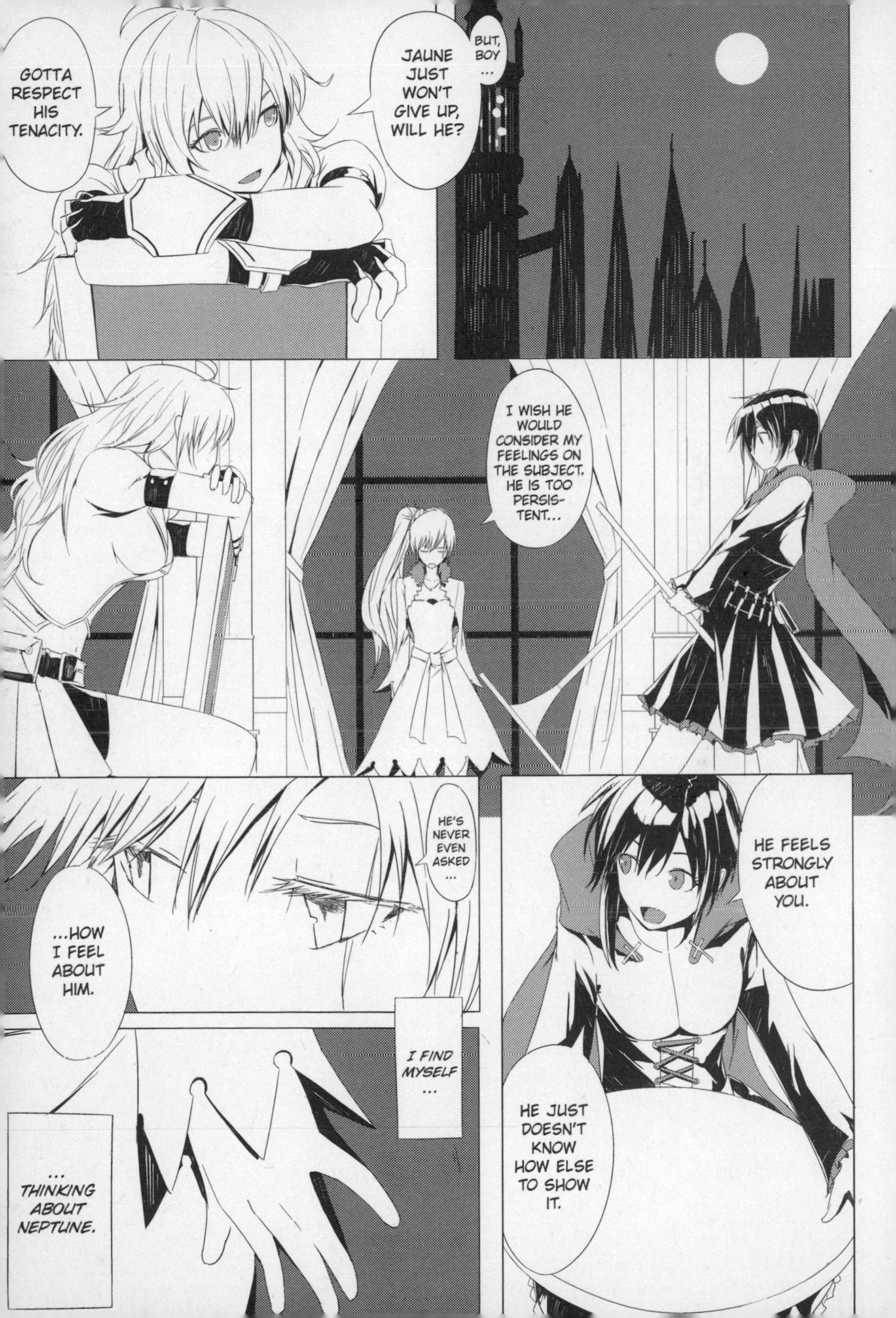
BUT, BOY ...
JAUNE JUST WON'T GIVE UP, WILL HE?
GOTTA RESPECT HIS TENACITY.
I WISH HE WOULD CONSIDER MY FEELINGS ON THE SUBJECT. HE IS TOO PERSIS-TENT...
HE FEELS STRONGLY ABOUT YOU.
HE JUST DOESN'T KNOW HOW ELSE TO SHOW IT.
HE'S NEVER EVEN ASKED ...
...HOW I FEEL ABOUT HIM.
I FIND MYSELF ...
... THINKING ABOUT NEPTUNE.

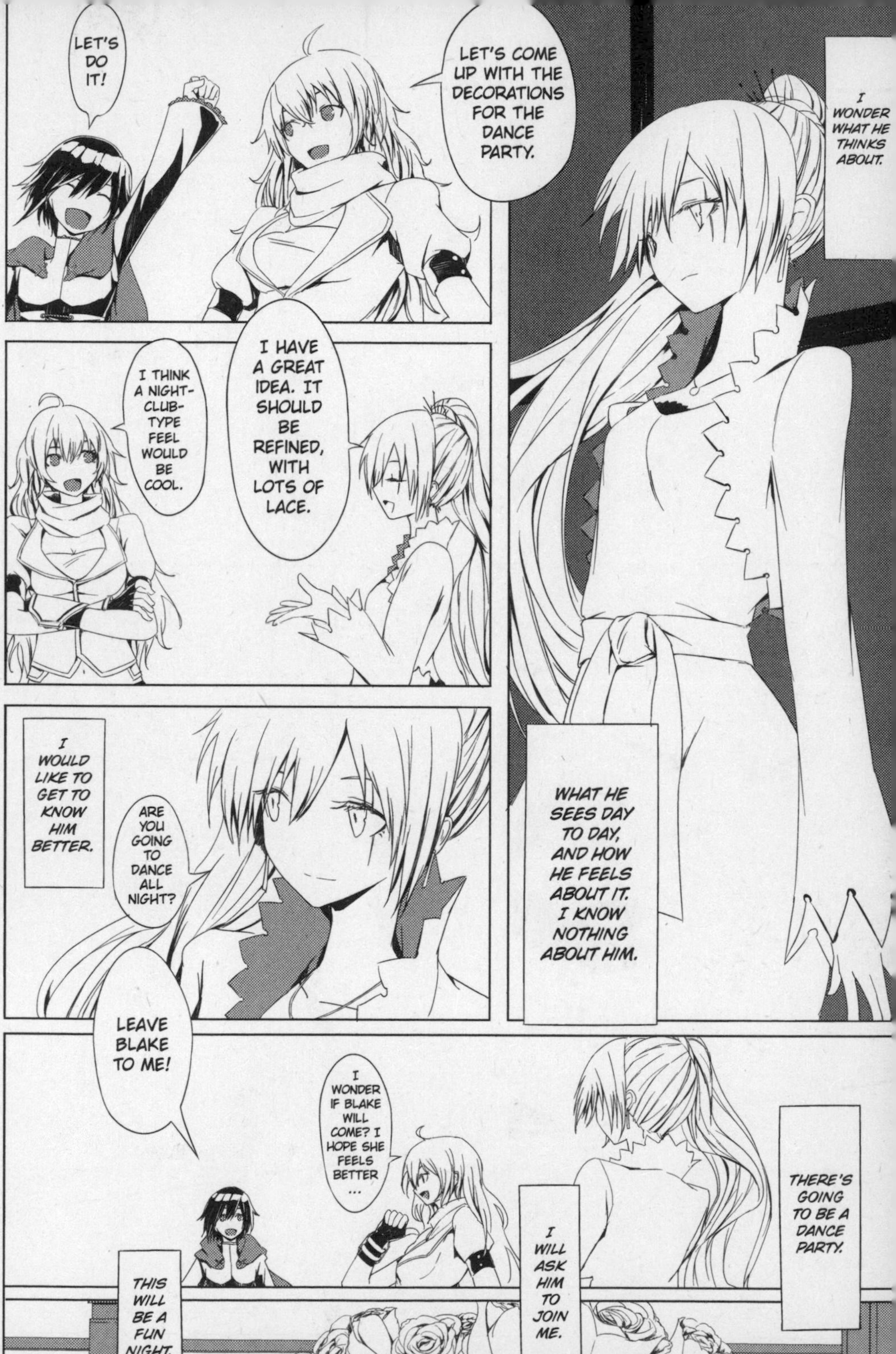
I WONDER WHAT HE THINKS ABOUT.
WHAT HE SEES DAY TO DAY, AND HOW HE FEELS ABOUT IT. I KNOW NOTHING ABOUT HIM.
LET'S COME UP WITH THE DECORATIONS FOR THE DANCE PARTY.
LET'S DO IT!
I HAVE A GREAT IDEA. IT SHOULD BE REFINED, WITH LOTS OF LACE.
I THINK A NIGHT-CLUB-TYPE FEEL WOULD BE COOL.
I WOULD LIKE TO GET TO KNOW HIM BETTER.
ARE YOU GOING TO DANCE ALL NIGHT?
LEAVE BLAKE TO ME!
THERE'S GOING TO BE A DANCE PARTY.
I WILL ASK HIM TO JOIN ME.
I WONDER IF BLAKE WILL COME? I HOPE SHE FEELS BETTER ...
THIS WILL BE A FUN NIGHT.
Chapter 4.5: Day/END

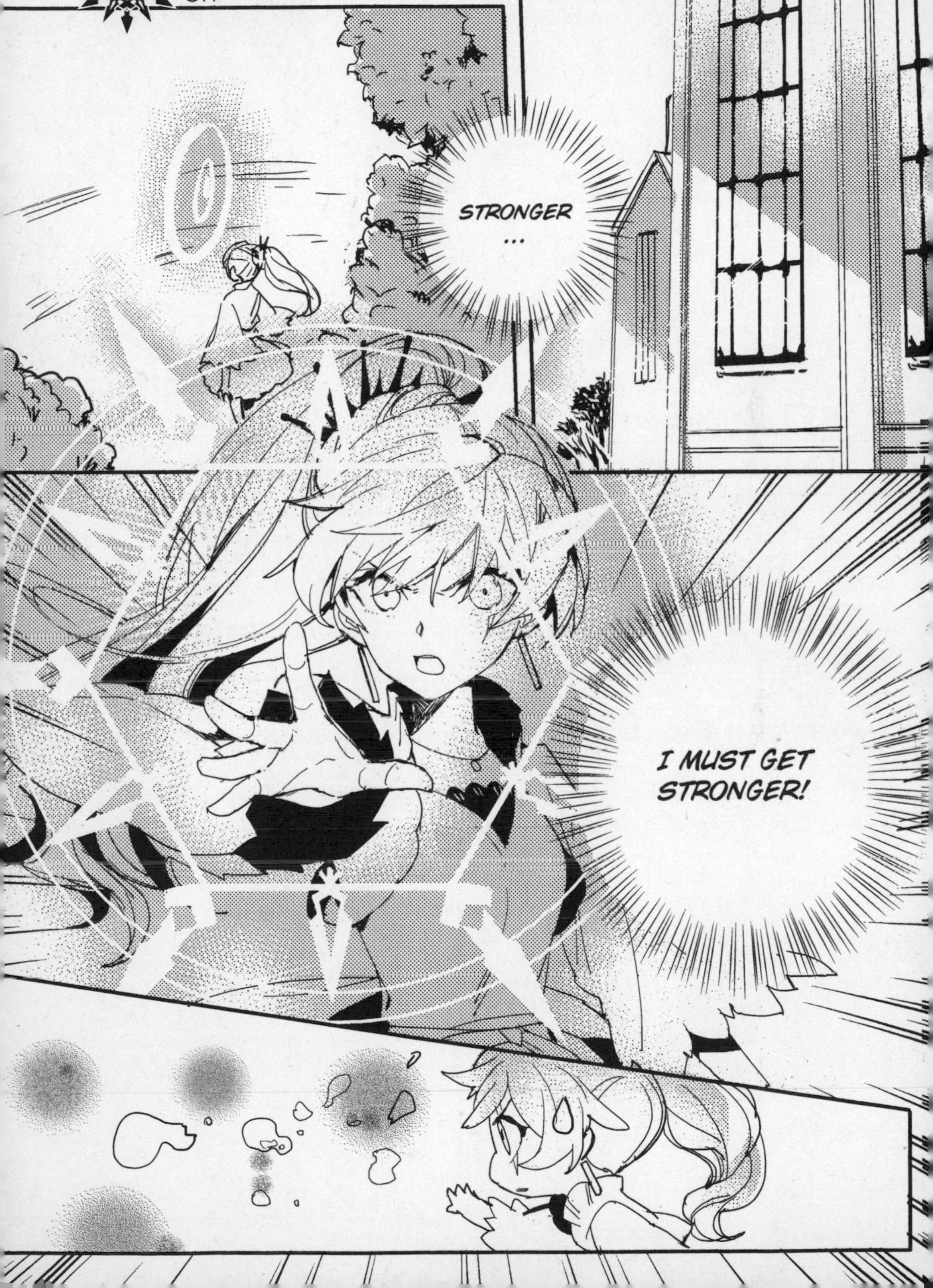
STRONGER ...
I MUST GET STRONGER!

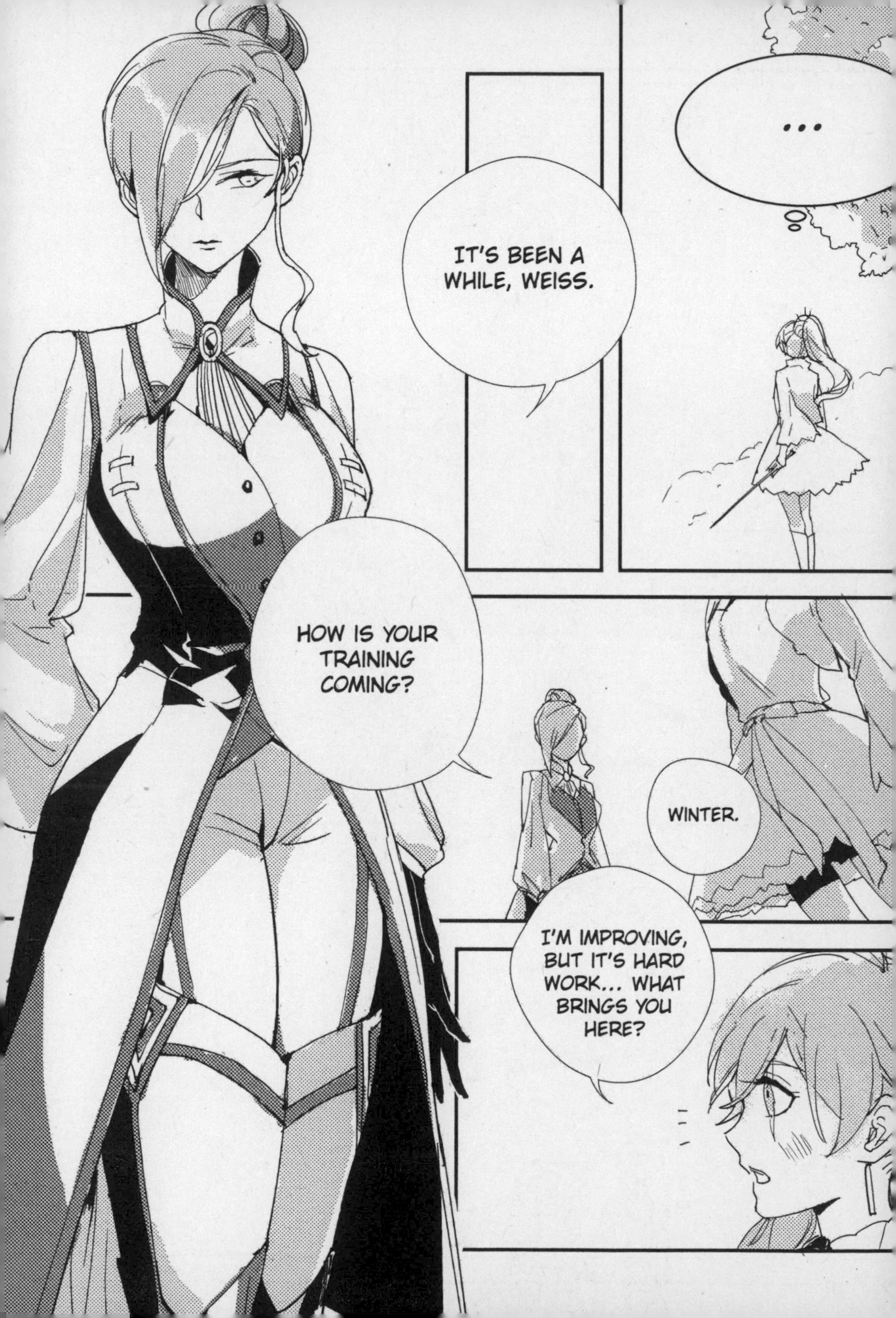
...
IT'S BEEN A WHILE, WEISS.
WINTER.
HOW IS YOUR TRAINING COMING?
I'M IMPROVING, BUT IT'S HARD WORK... WHAT BRINGS YOU HERE?

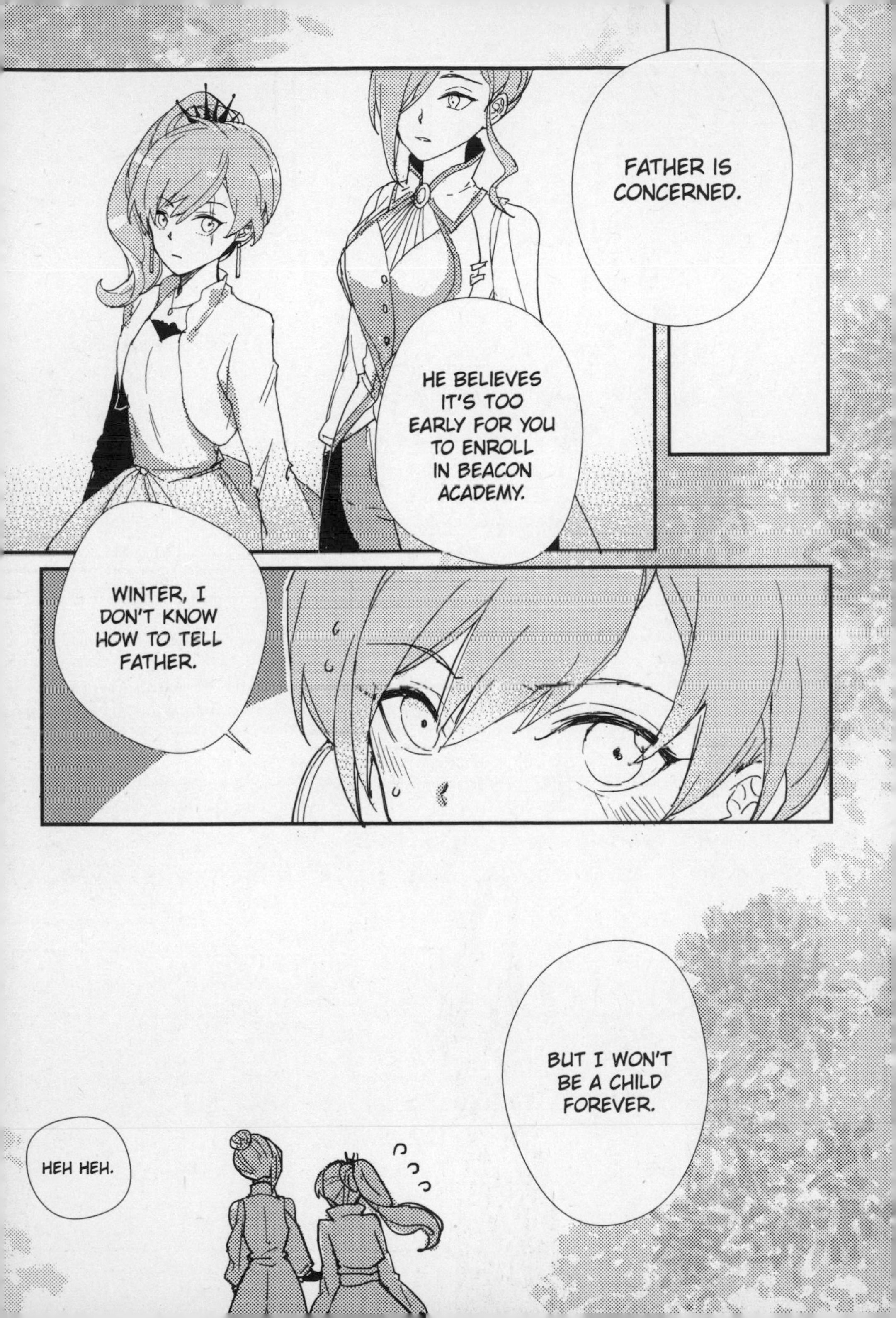
FATHER IS CONCERNED.
HE BELIEVES IT'S TOO EARLY FOR YOU TO ENROLL IN BEACON ACADEMY.
WINTER, I DON'T KNOW HOW TO TELL FATHER.
BUT I WON'T BE A CHILD FOREVER.
HEH HEH.

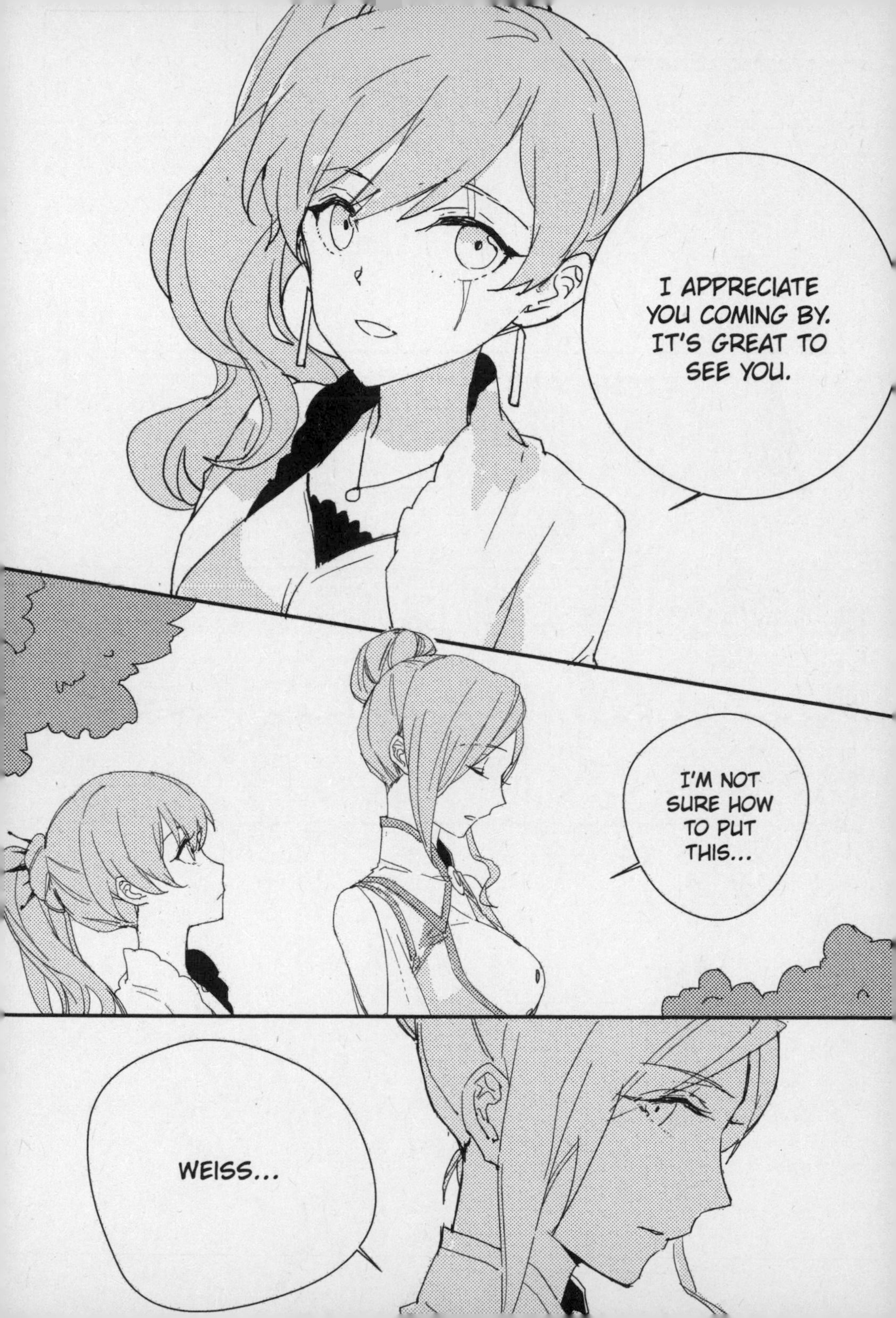
I APPRECIATE YOU COMING BY. IT'S GREAT TO SEE YOU.
I'M NOT SURE HOW TO PUT THIS...
WEISS...

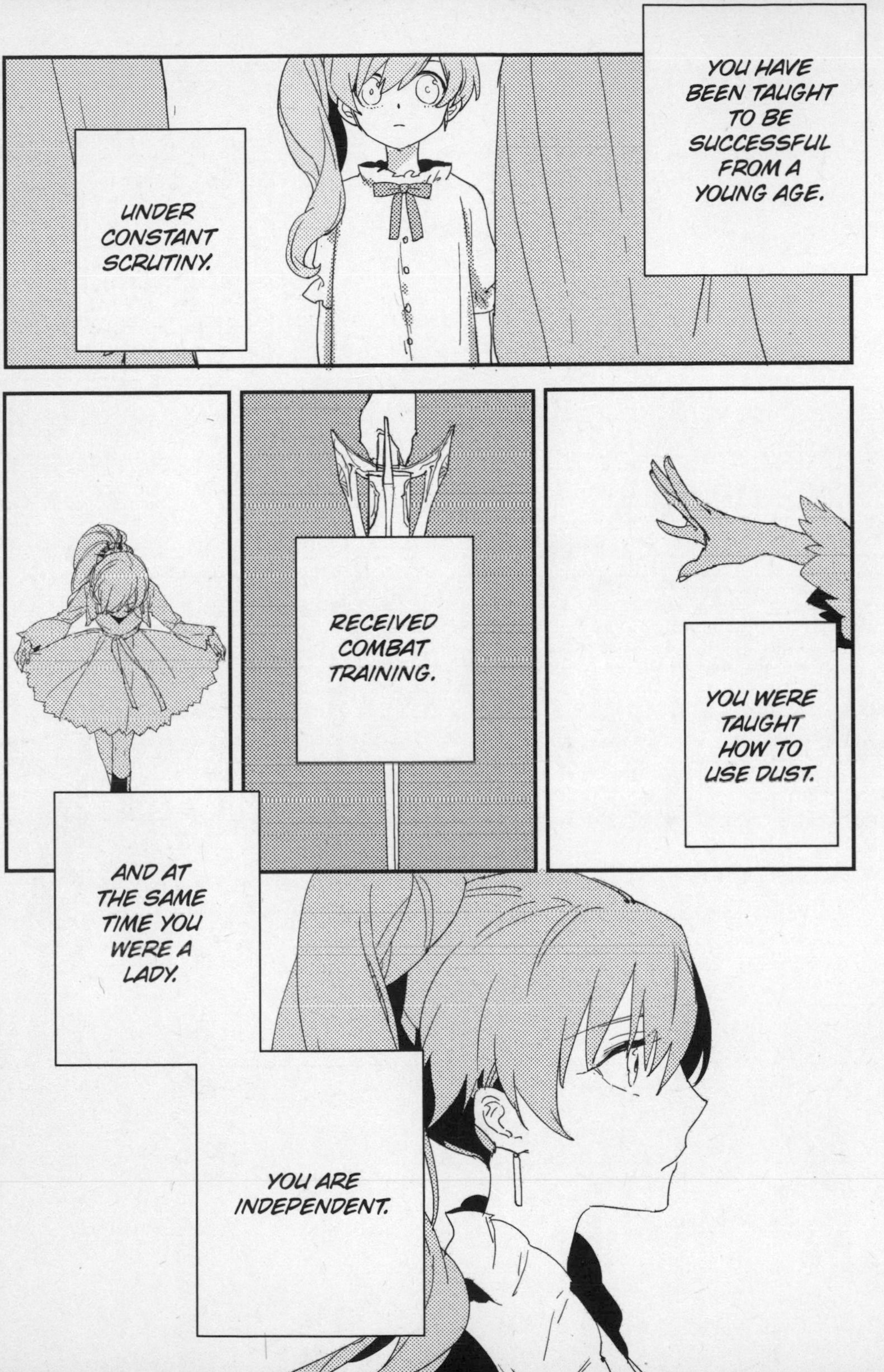
YOU HAVE BEEN TAUGHT TO BE SUCCESSFUL FROM A YOUNG AGE.
UNDER CONSTANT SCRUTINY.
YOU WERE TAUGHT HOW TO USE DUST.
RECEIVED COMBAT TRAINING.
AND AT THE SAME TIME YOU WERE A LADY.
YOU ARE INDEPENDENT.

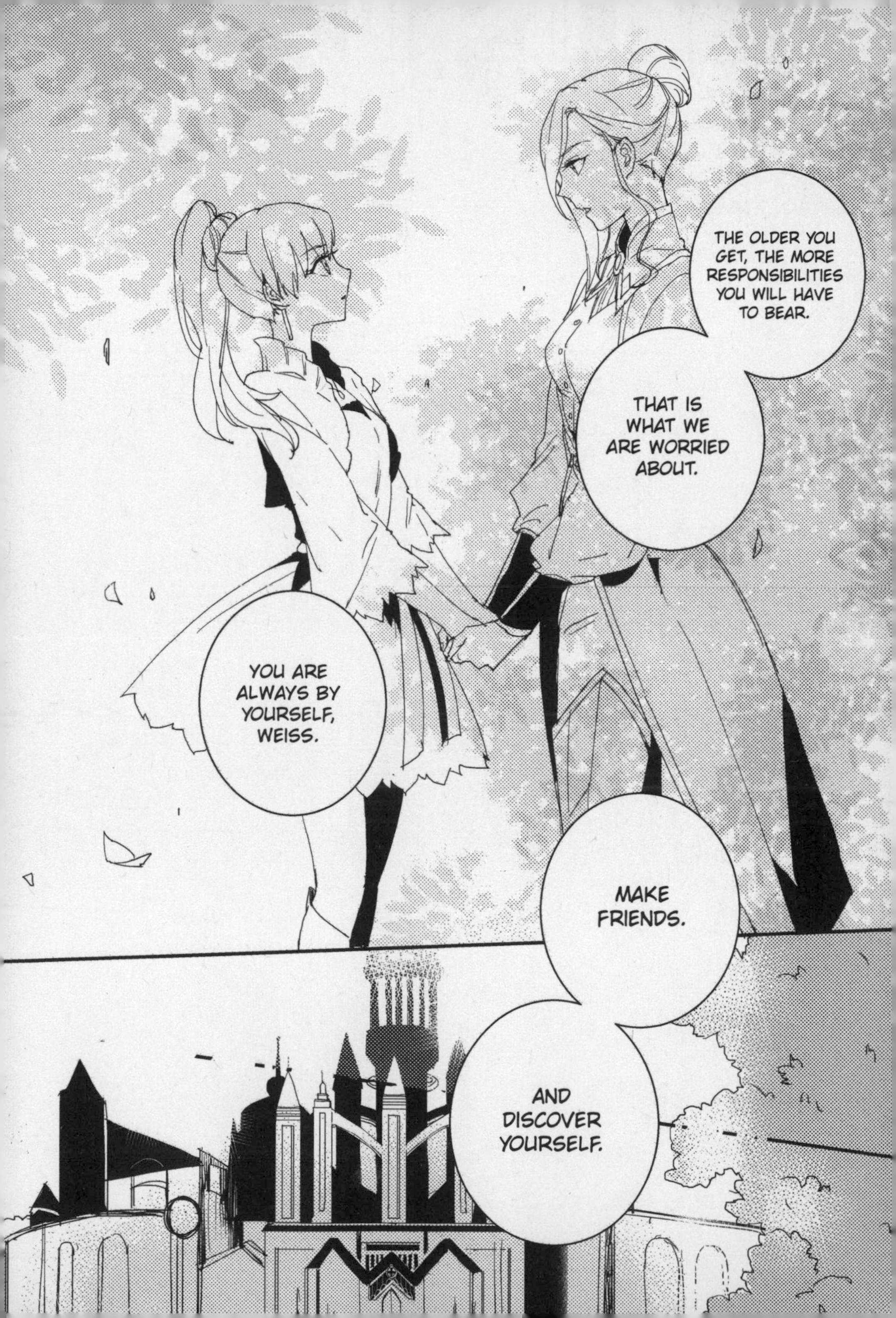
THE OLDER YOU GET, THE MORE RESPONSIBILITIES YOU WILL HAVE TO BEAR.
THAT IS WHAT WE ARE WORRIED ABOUT.
YOU ARE ALWAYS BY YOURSELF, WEISS.
MAKE FRIENDS.
AND DISCOVER YOURSELF.

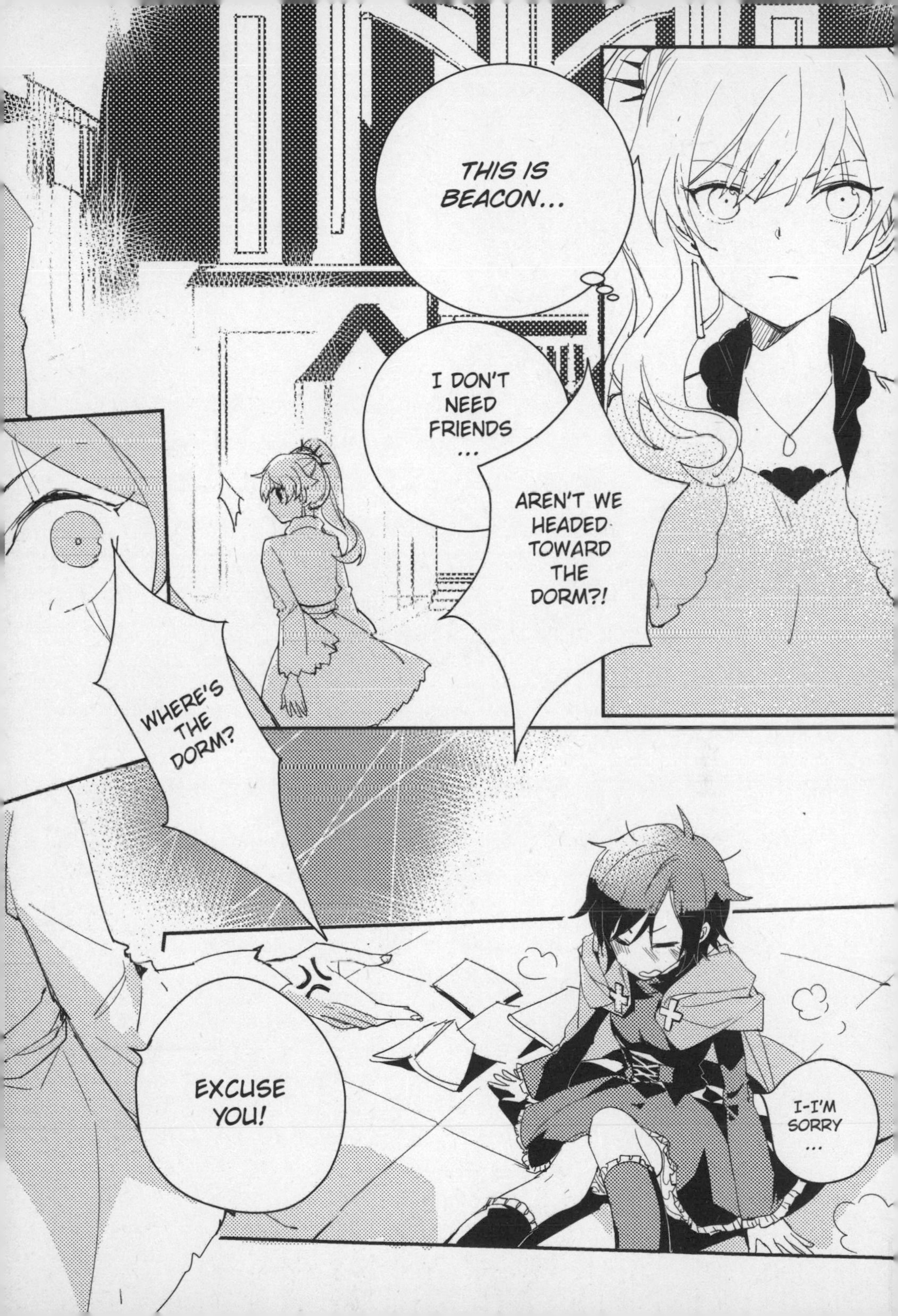
THIS IS BEACON...
I DON'T NEED FRIENDS ...
AREN'T WE HEADED TOWARD THE DORM?!
WHERE'S THE DORM?
EXCUSE YOU!
I-I'M SORRY ...

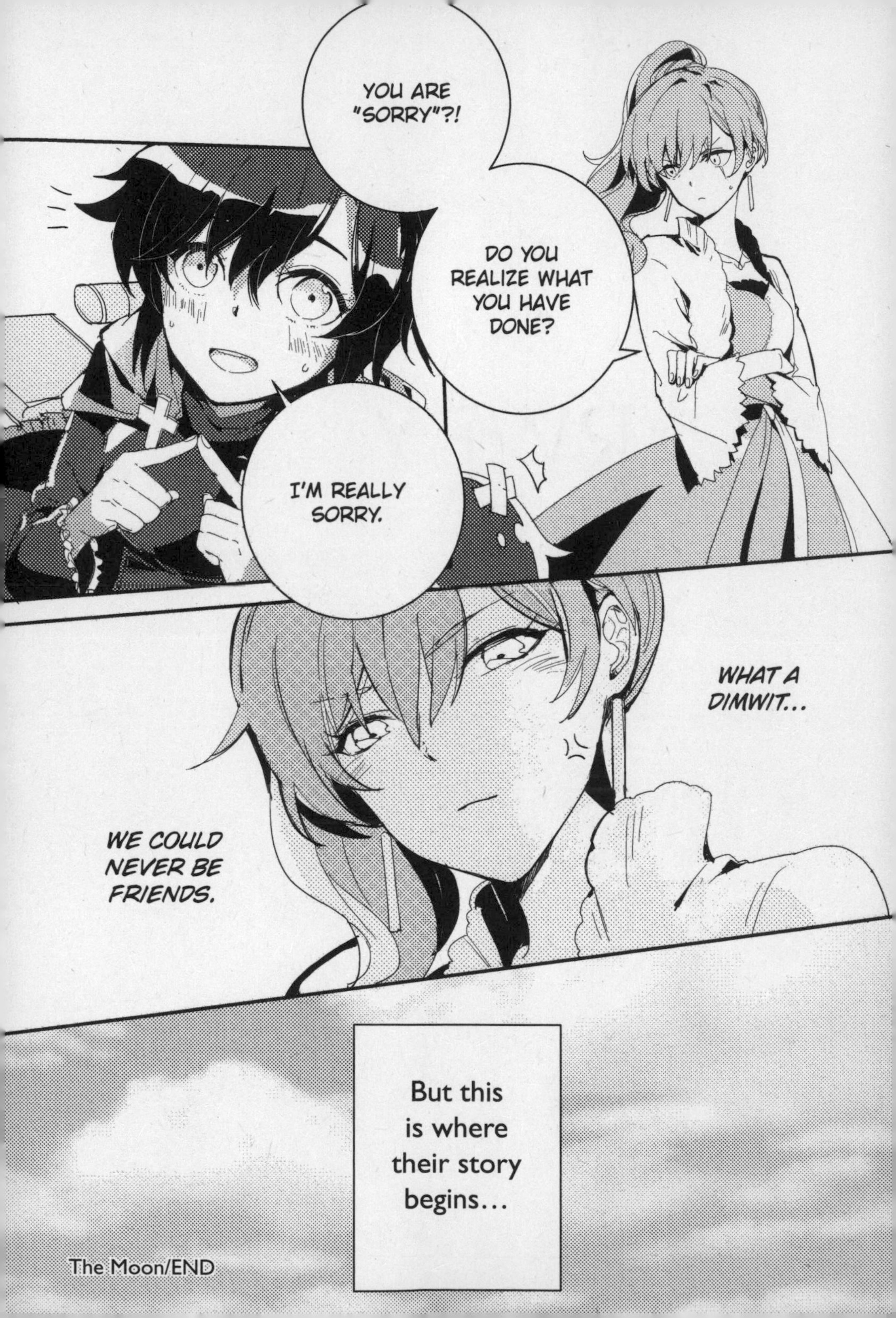
YOU ARE "SORRY"?!
DO YOU REALIZE WHAT YOU HAVE DONE?
I'M REALLY SORRY.
WHAT A DIMWIT...
WE COULD NEVER BE FRIENDS.
But this is where their story begins...
The Moon/END

RWBY

OFFICIAL MANGA ANTHOLOGY
VOLUME 2 Mirror, Mirror

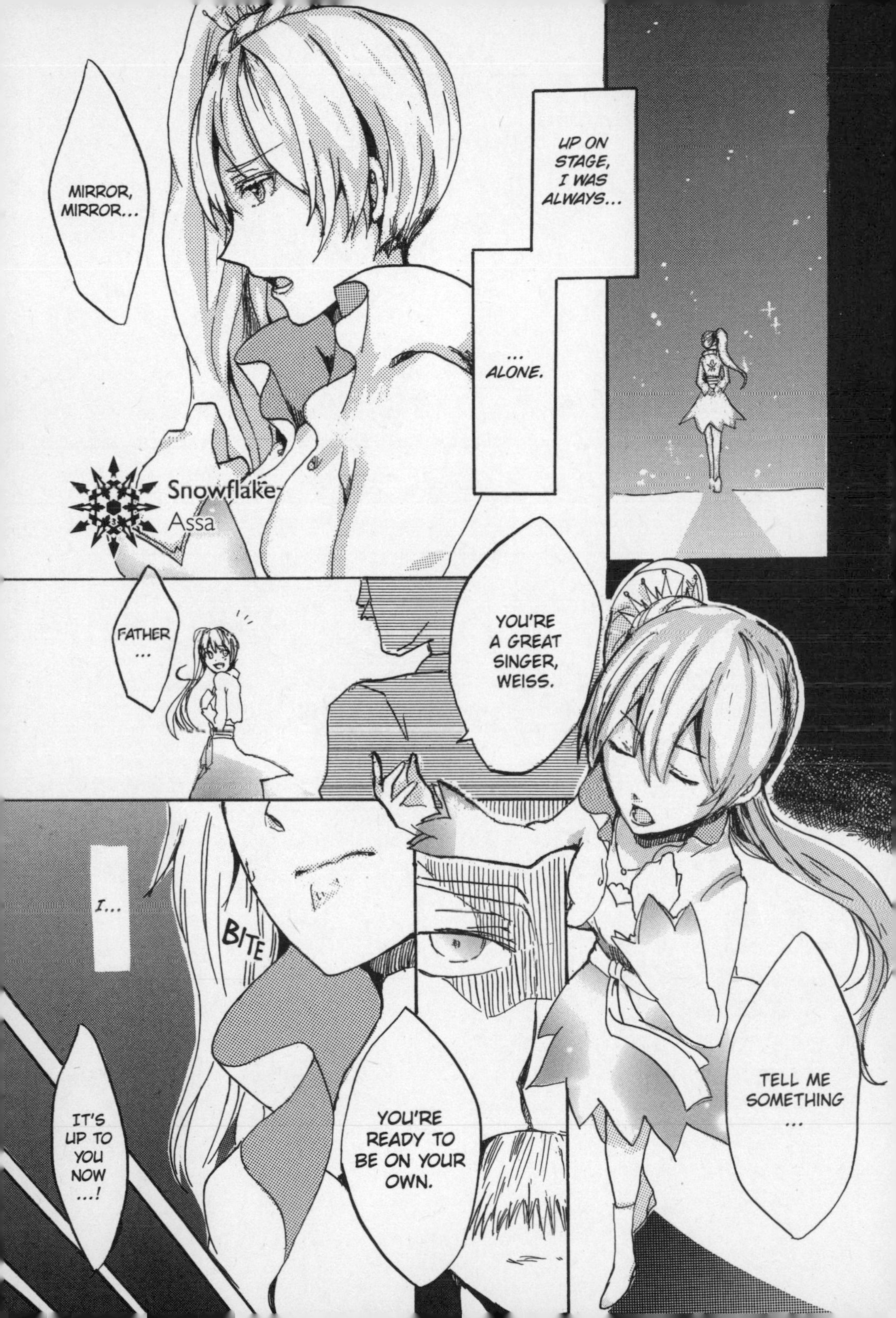
UP ON STAGE, I WAS ALWAYS...
... ALONE.
MIRROR, MIRROR...
Snowflake
Assa
YOU'RE A GREAT SINGER, WEISS.
FATHER ...
TELL ME SOMETHING ...
I...
BITE
YOU'RE READY TO BE ON YOUR OWN.
IT'S UP TO YOU NOW ...!

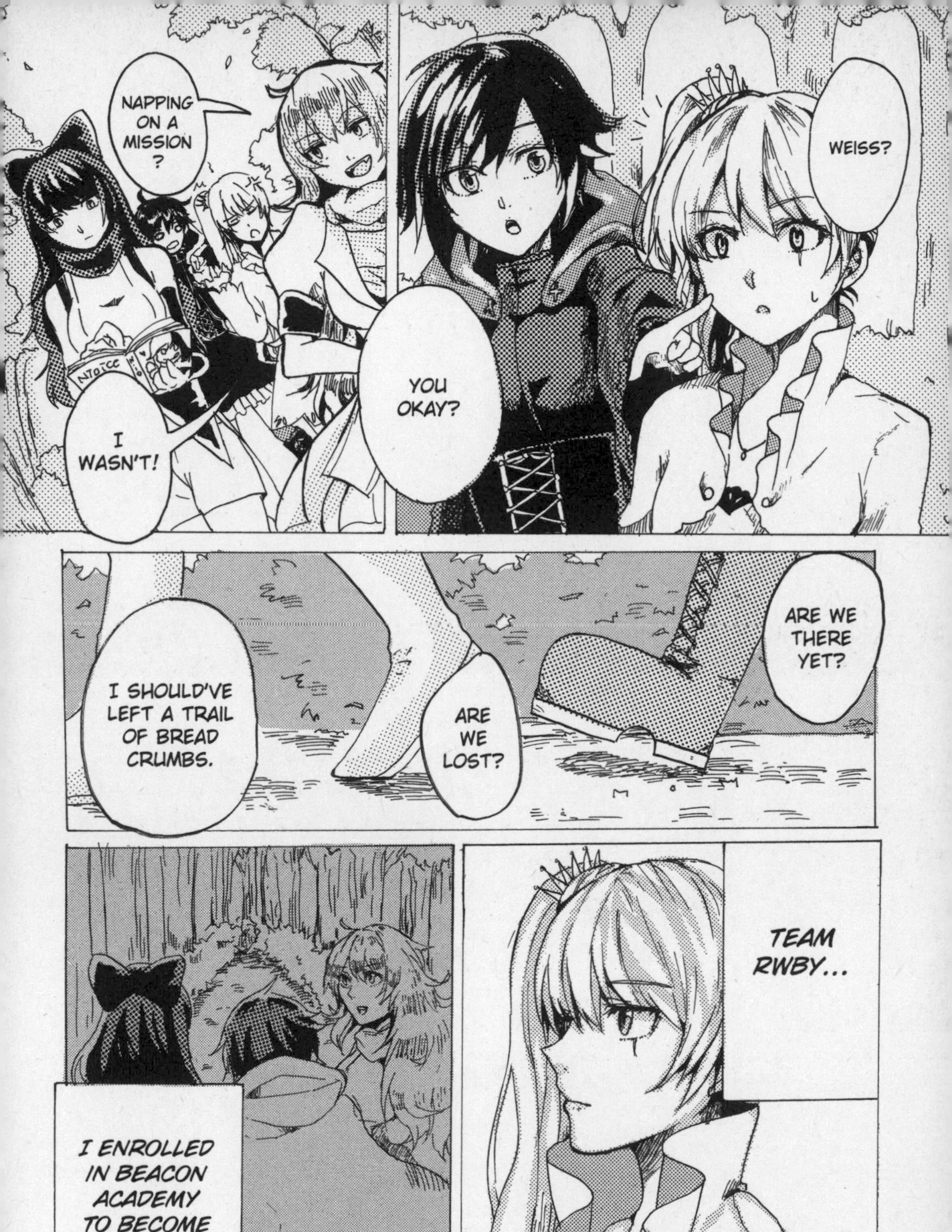
WEISS?
YOU OKAY?
NAPPING ON A MISSION ?
I WASN'T!
ARE WE THERE YET?
ARE WE LOST?
I SHOULD'VE LEFT A TRAIL OF BREAD CRUMBS.
TEAM RWBY...
I ENROLLED IN BEACON ACADEMY TO BECOME A CAPABLE HUNTRESS.

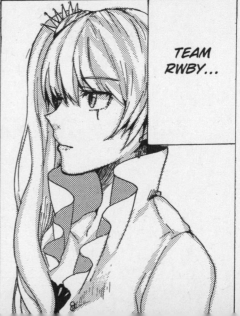

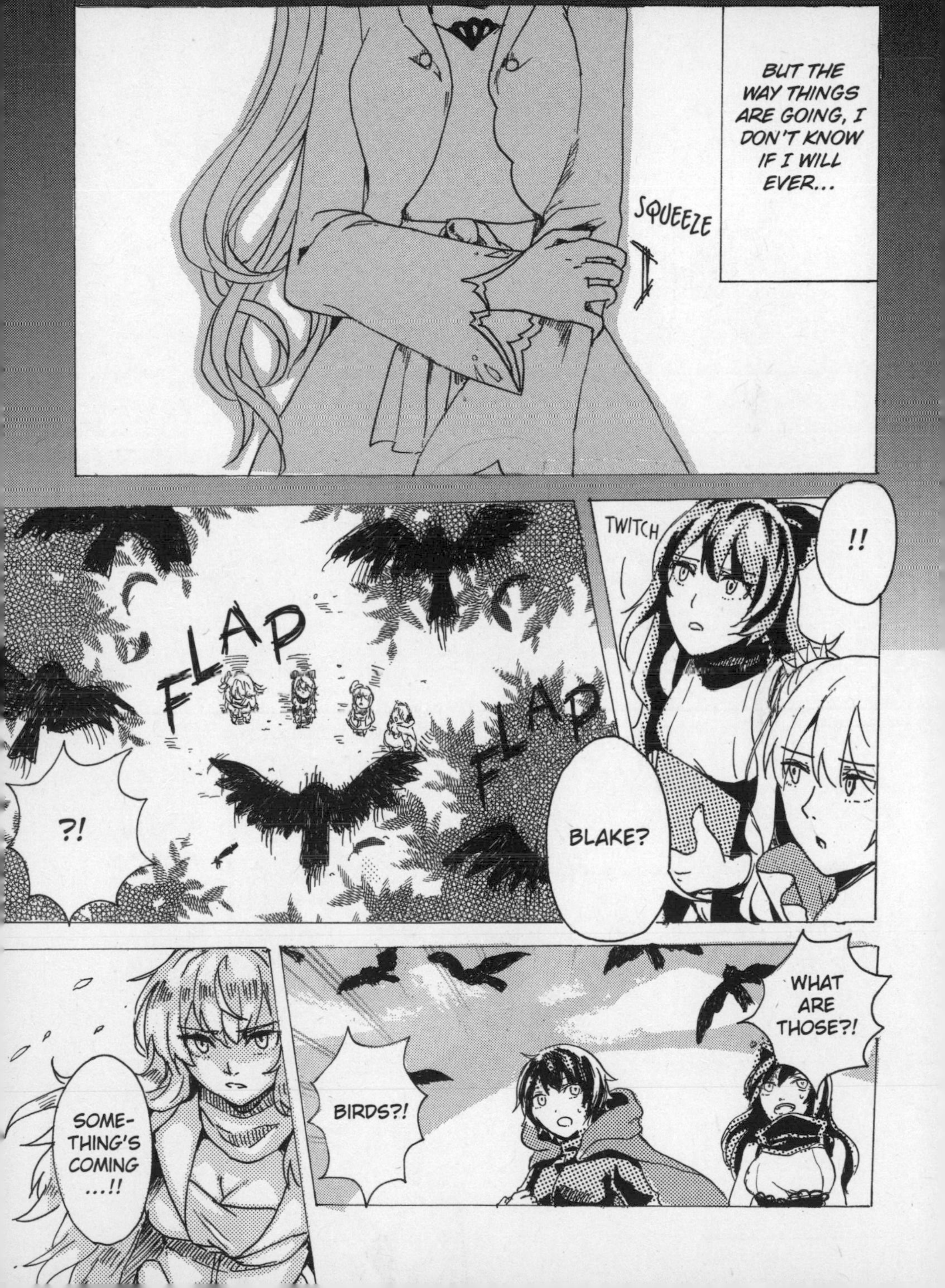
BUT THE WAY THINGS ARE GOING, I DON'T KNOW IF I WILL EVER...
SQUEEZE
!!
TWITCH
BLAKE?
FLAP
FLAP
?!
WHAT ARE THOSE?!
BIRDS?!
SOME-THING'S COMING ...!!

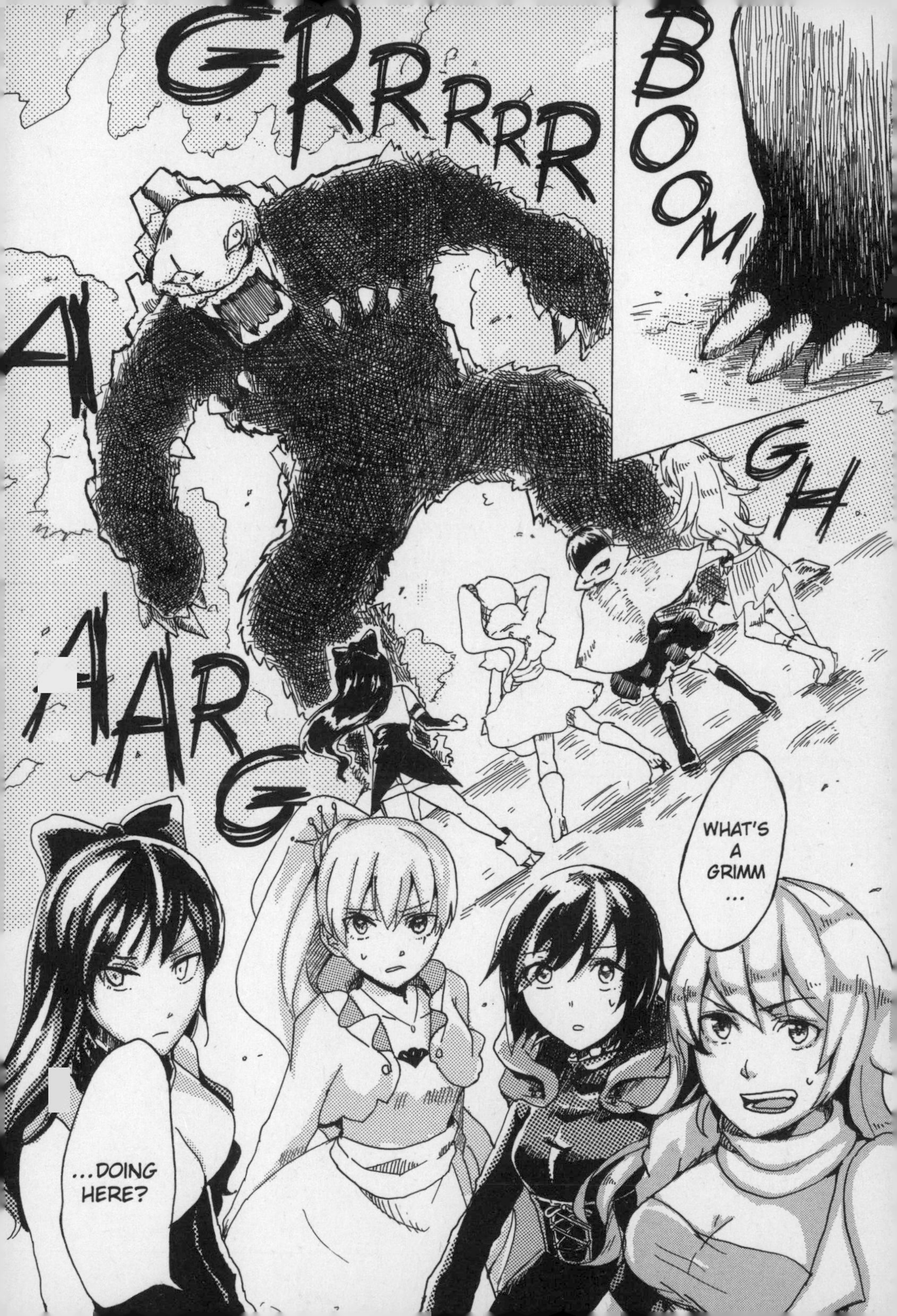
BOOM
GRRRRRR
GH
AAARG
WHAT'S A GRIMM ...
...DOING HERE?

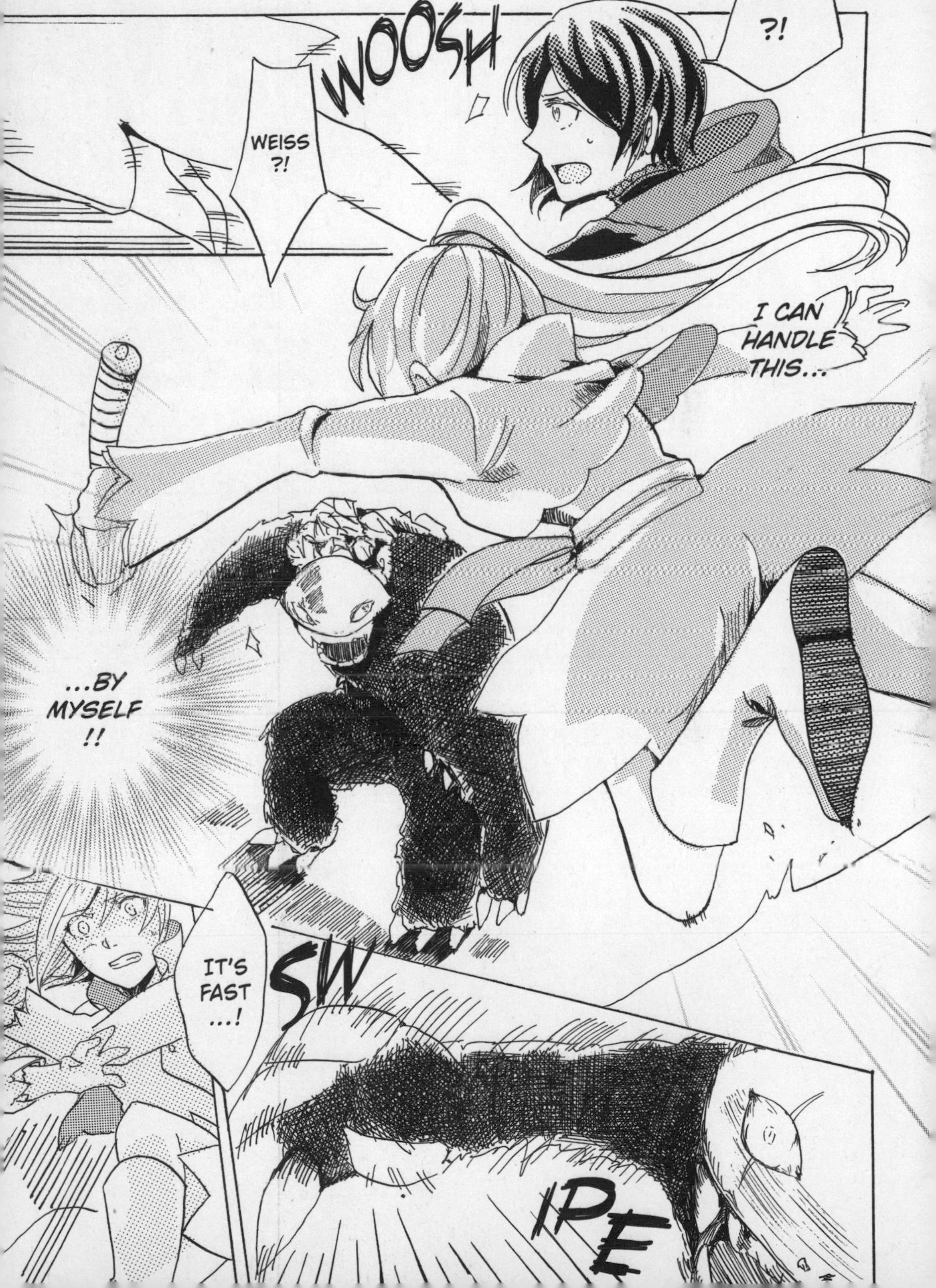
?!
WOOSH
WEISS ?!
I CAN HANDLE THIS...
...BY MYSELF !!
SW
IPE
IT'S FAST ...!

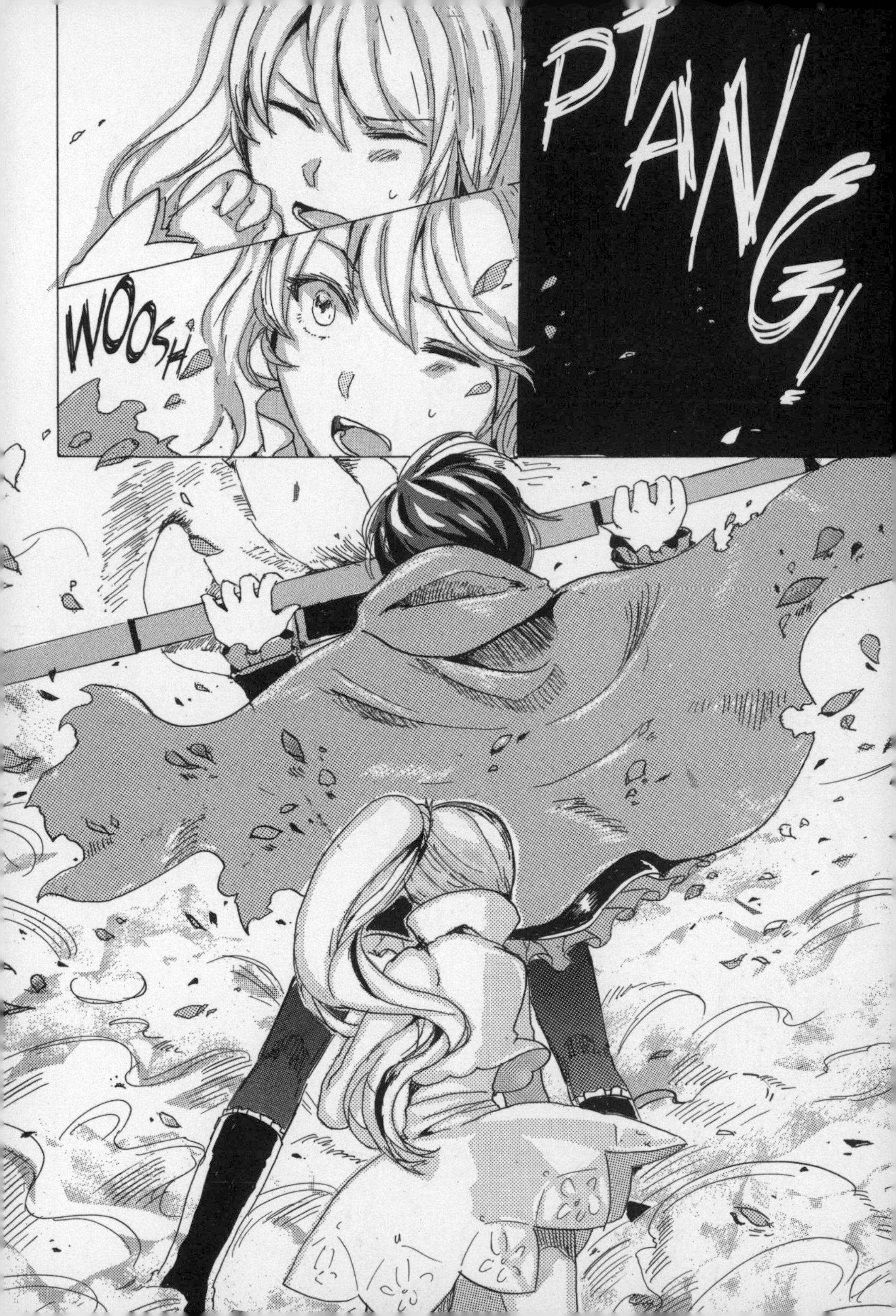
PTANG!
WOOSH

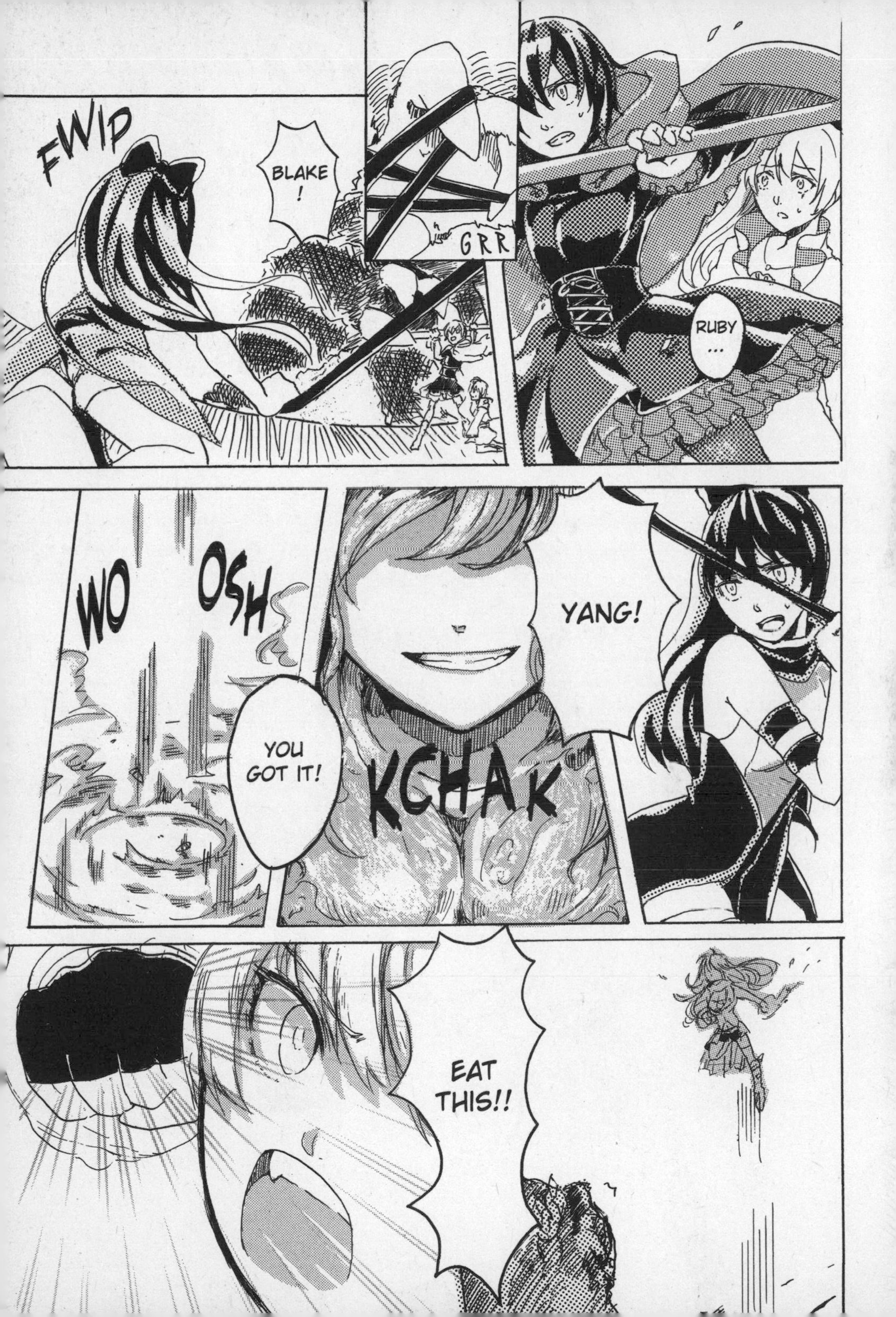
RUBY ...
GRR
FWIP
BLAKE!
YANG!
KCHAK
YOU GOT IT!
WOOSH
EAT THIS!!

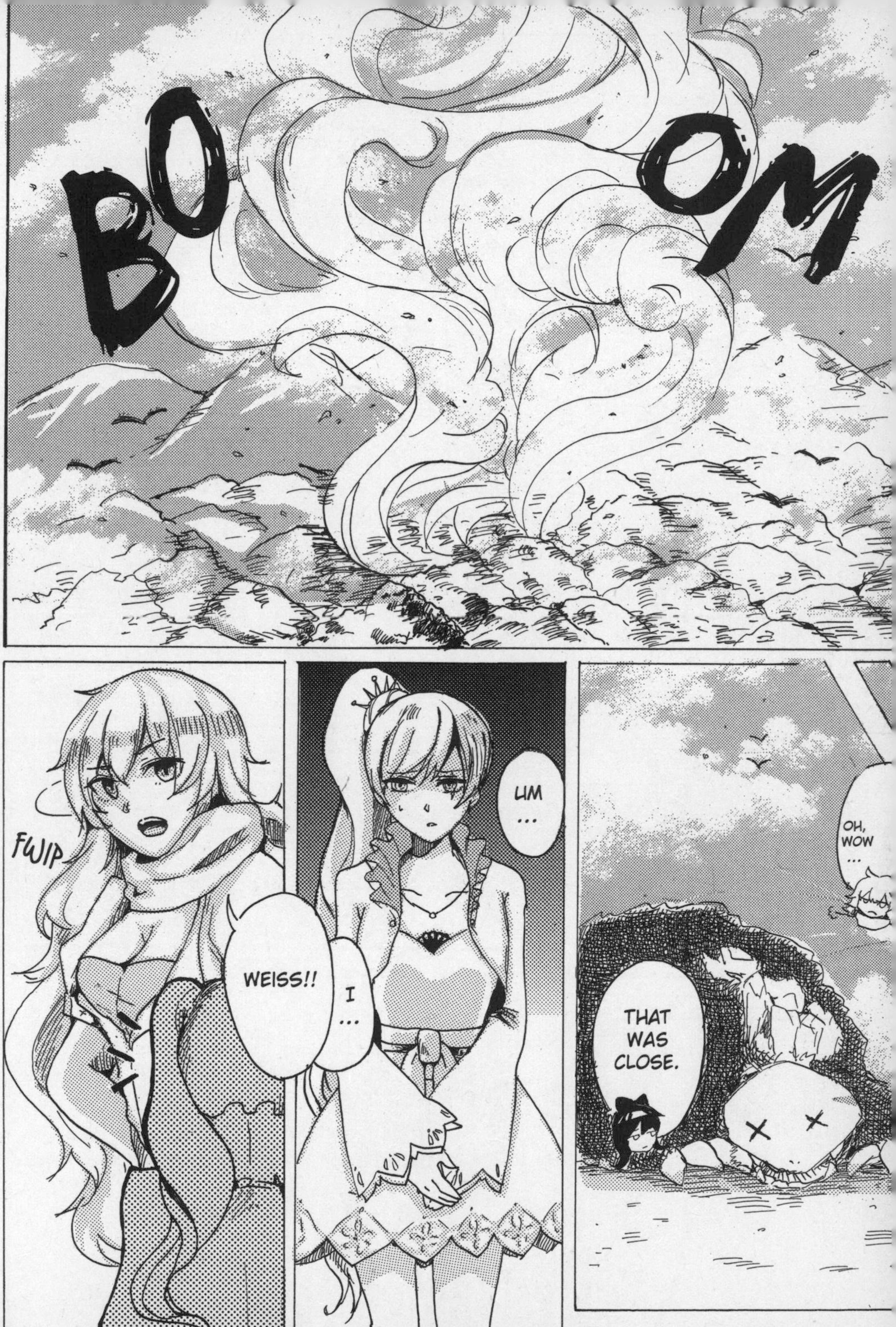
BOOM
OH, WOW ...
THAT WAS CLOSE.
UM ...
I ...
WEISS!!
FWIP

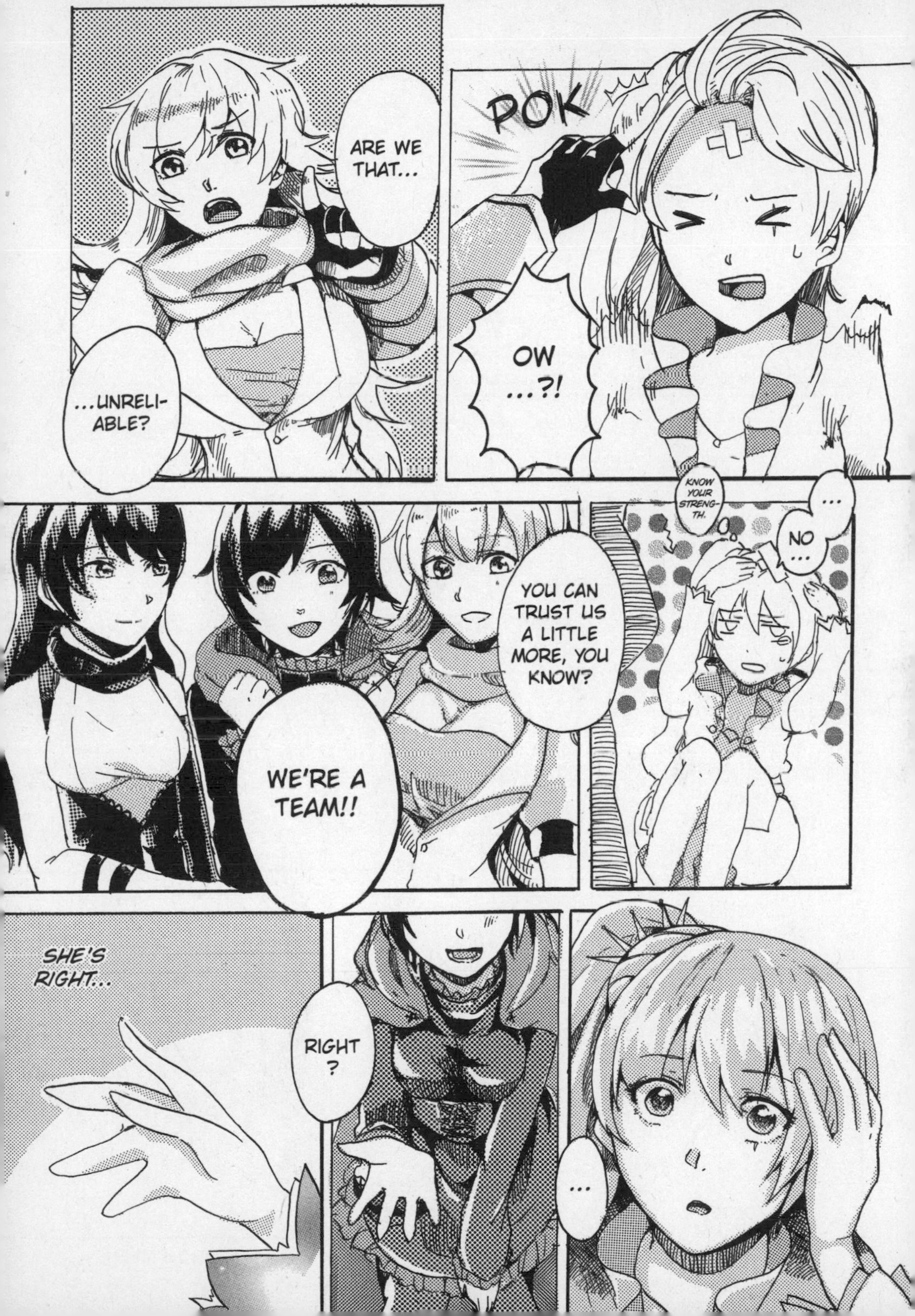
POK
OW ...?!
ARE WE THAT...
...UNRELI-ABLE?
...
NO ...
KNOW YOUR STRENGTH.
YOU CAN TRUST US A LITTLE MORE, YOU KNOW?
WE'RE A TEAM!!
...
RIGHT ?
SHE'S RIGHT...

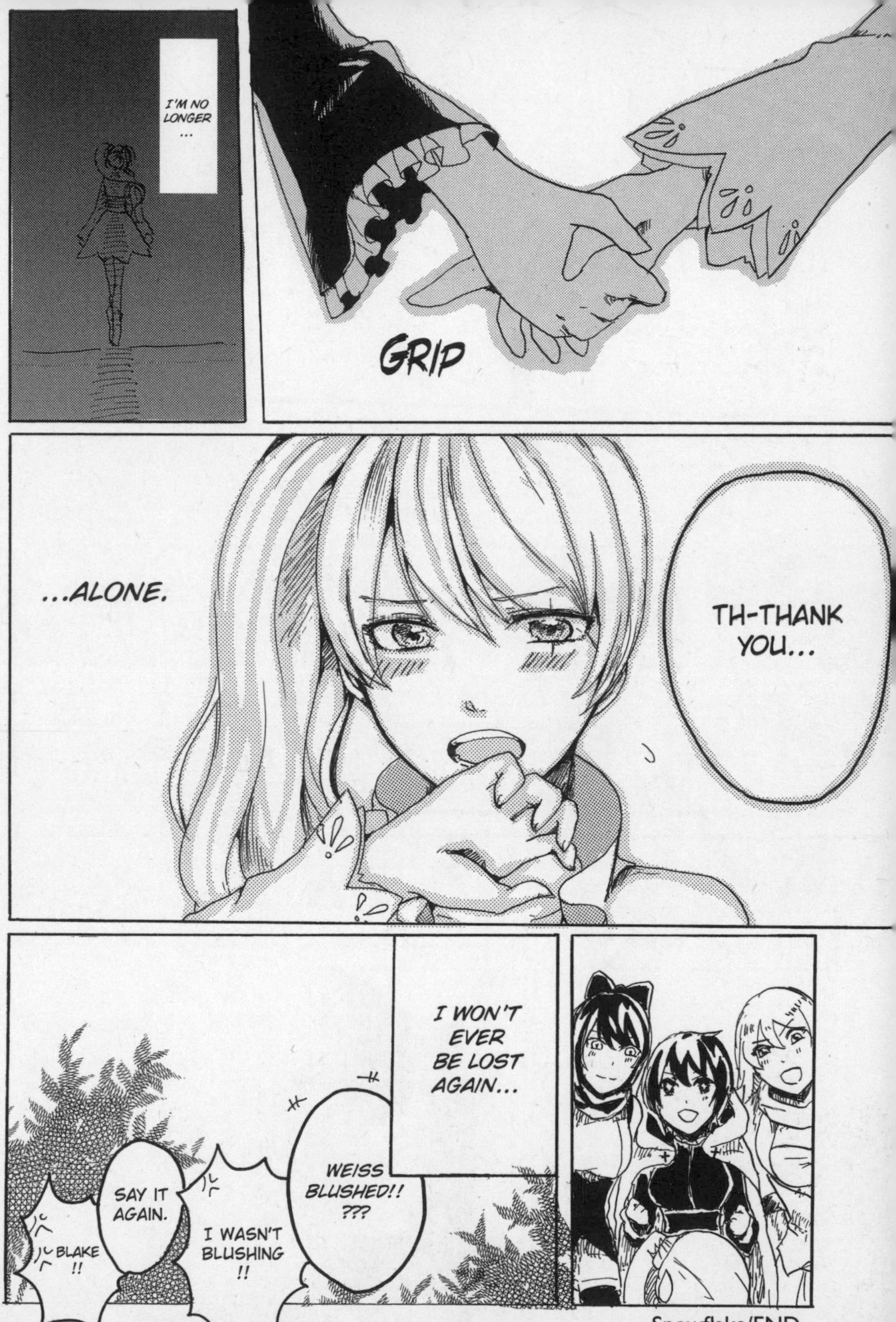
GRIP
I'M NO LONGER ...
TH-THANK YOU...
...ALONE.
I WON'T EVER BE LOST AGAIN...
WEISS BLUSHED!! ???
I WASN'T BLUSHING !!
SAY IT AGAIN.
BLAKE !!

Snowflake/END

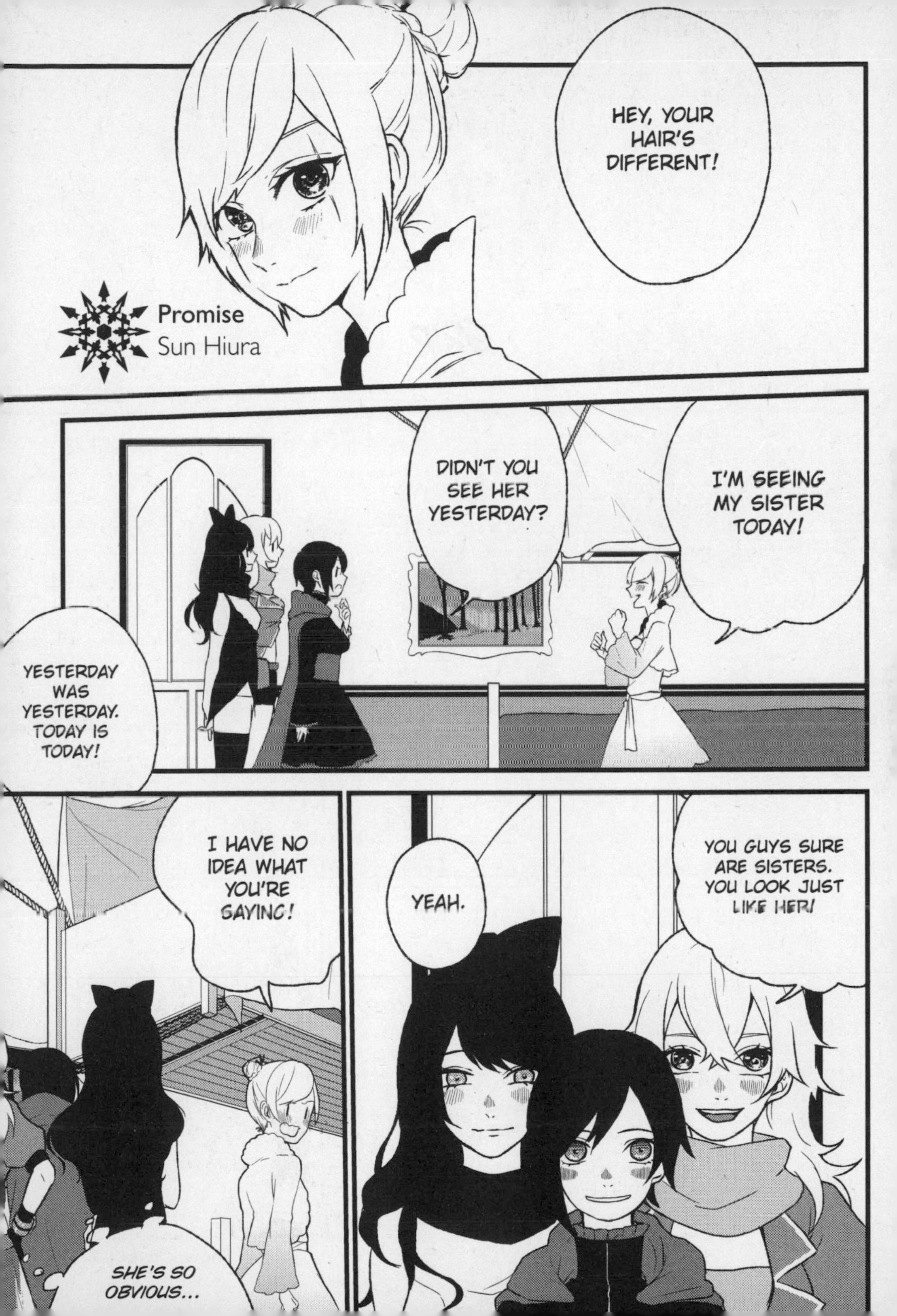
HEY, YOUR HAIR'S DIFFERENT!
Promise
Sun Hiura
I'M SEEING MY SISTER TODAY!
DIDN'T YOU SEE HER YESTERDAY?
YESTERDAY WAS YESTERDAY. TODAY IS TODAY!
YOU GUYS SURE ARE SISTERS. YOU LOOK JUST LIKE HER!
YEAH.
I HAVE NO IDEA WHAT YOU'RE SAYING!
SHE'S SO OBVIOUS...

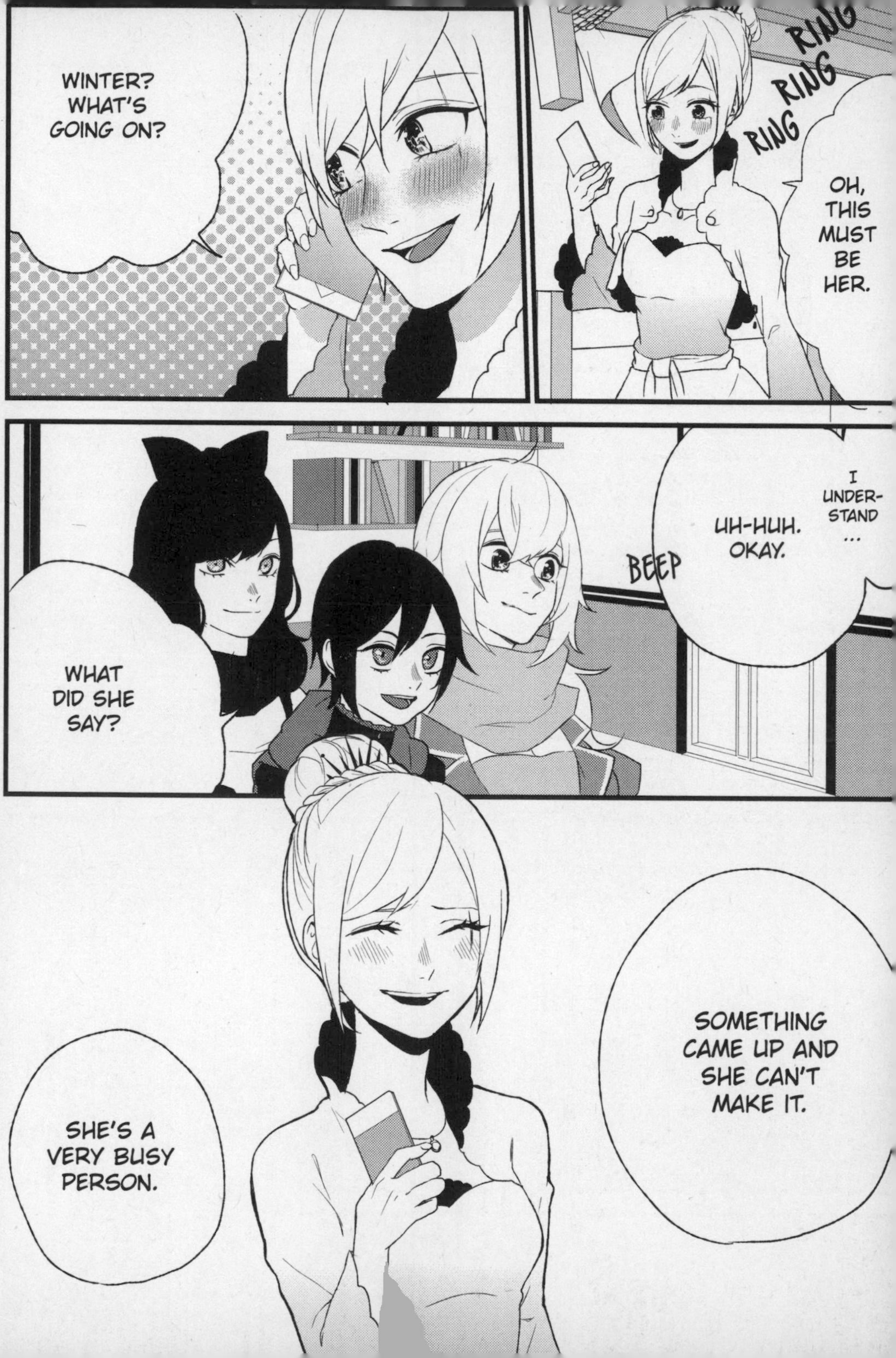
RING RING RING
OH, THIS MUST BE HER.
WINTER? WHAT'S GOING ON?
I UNDER-STAND ...
UH-HUH. OKAY.
BEEP
WHAT DID SHE SAY?
SOMETHING CAME UP AND SHE CAN'T MAKE IT.
SHE'S A VERY BUSY PERSON.

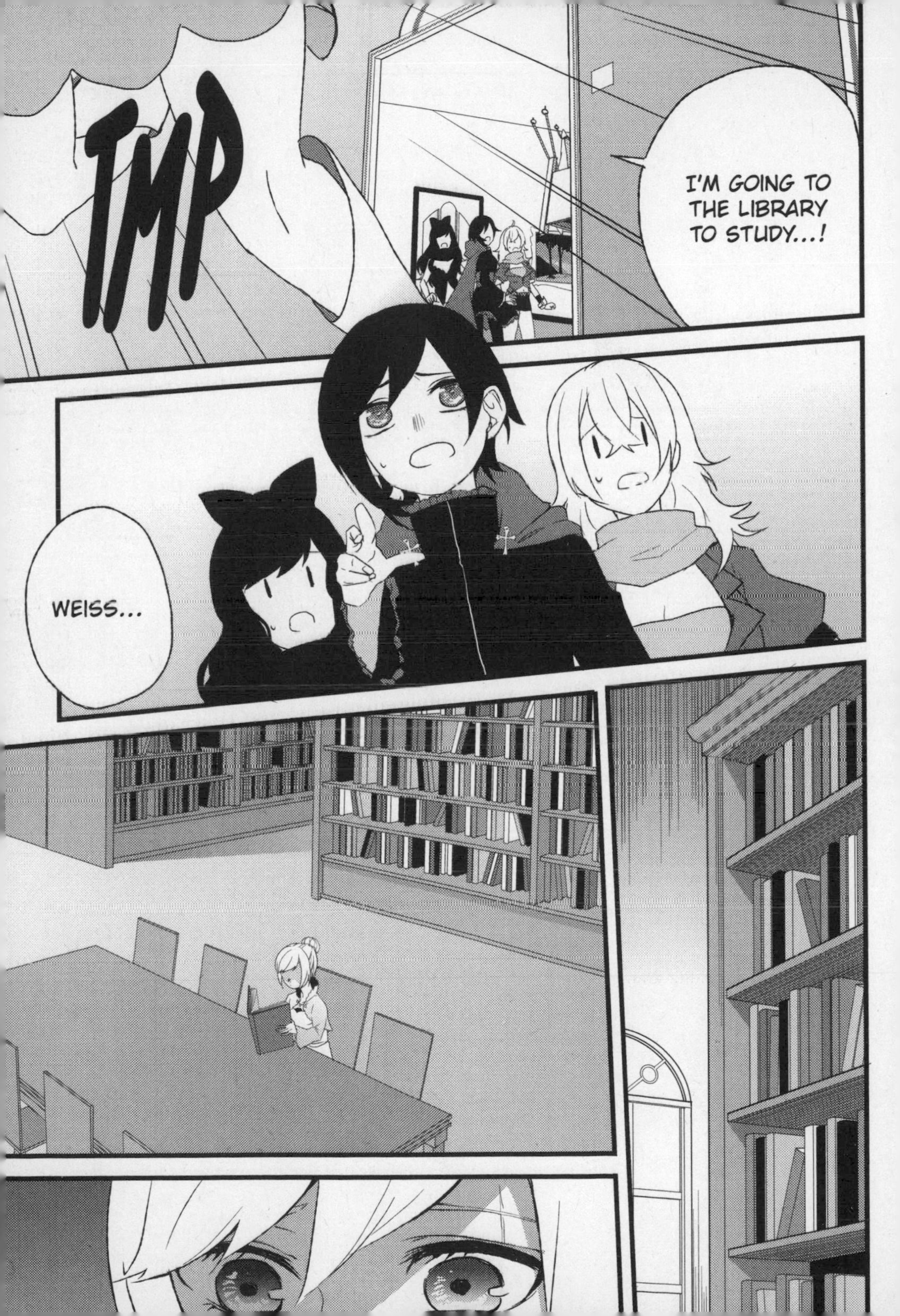
I'M GOING TO THE LIBRARY TO STUDY...!
TMP
WEISS...

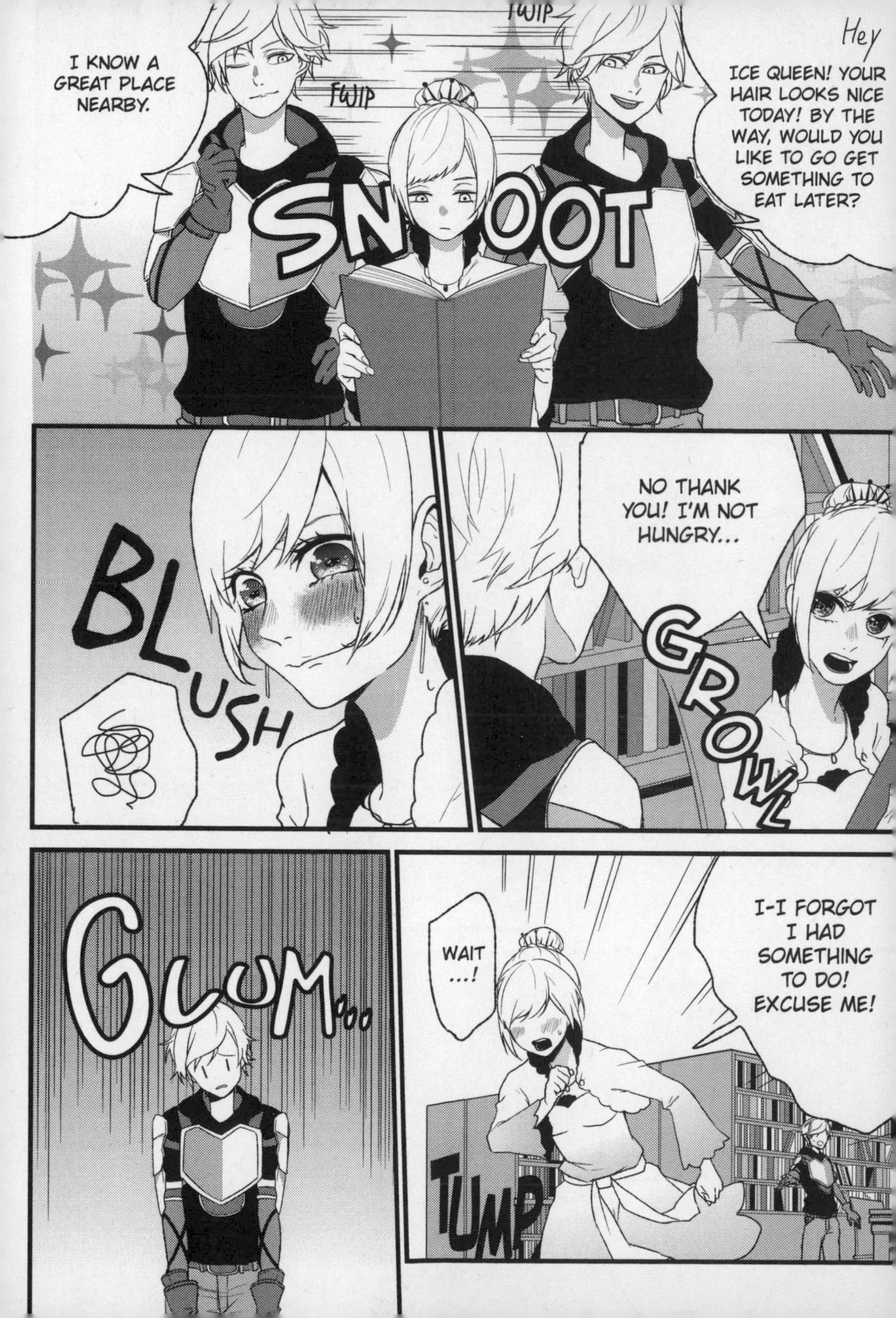

Hey
ICE QUEEN! YOUR HAIR LOOKS NICE TODAY! BY THE WAY, WOULD YOU LIKE TO GO GET SOMETHING TO EAT LATER?
FWIP
FWIP
I KNOW A GREAT PLACE NEARBY.
SNOOT
NO THANK YOU! I'M NOT HUNGRY...
GROWL
BLUSH
I-I FORGOT I HAD SOMETHING TO DO! EXCUSE ME!
WAIT ...!
TUMP
GLUM...

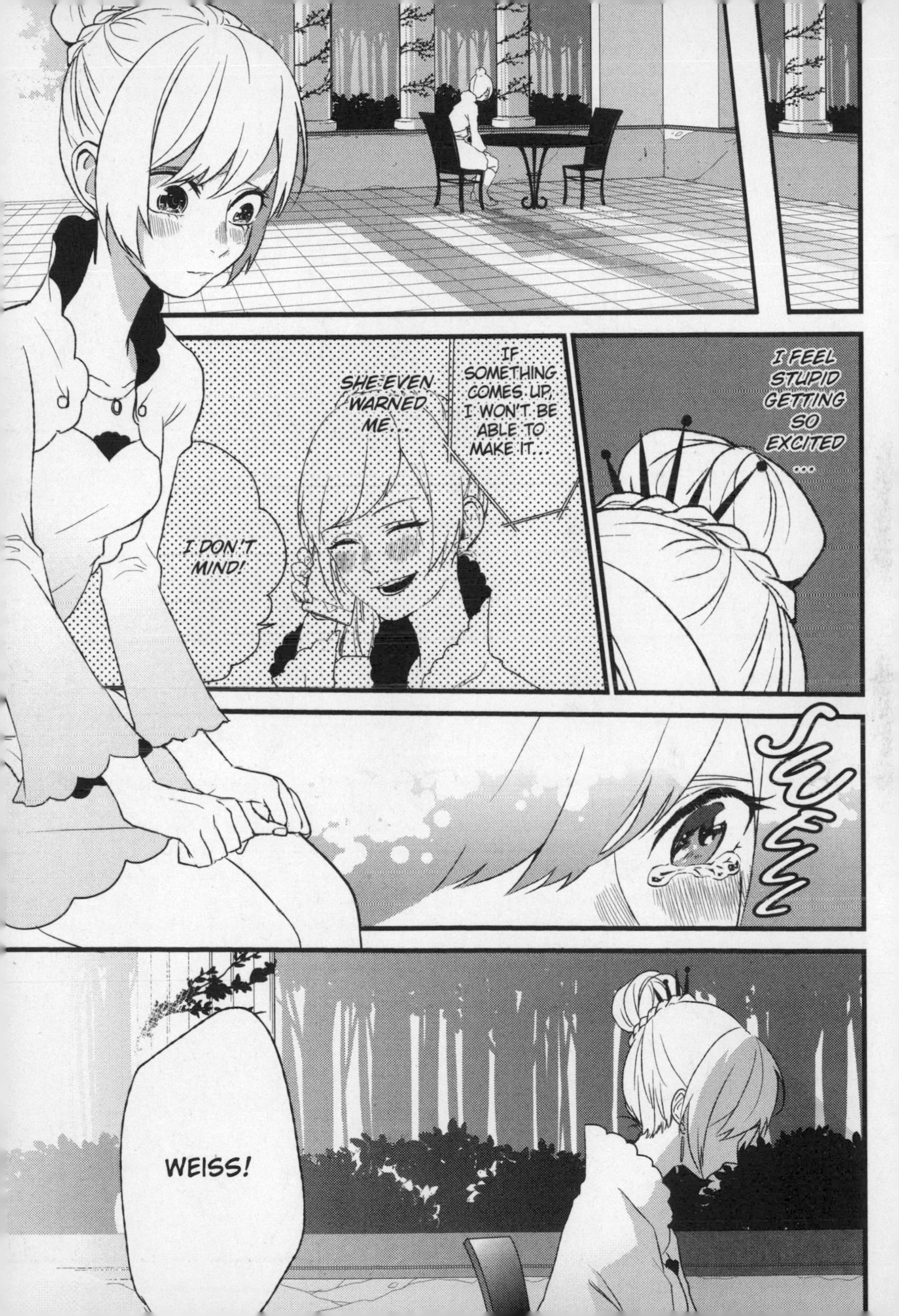
I FEEL STUPID GETTING SO EXCITED...
IF SOMETHING COMES UP, I WON'T BE ABLE TO MAKE IT...
SHE EVEN WARNED ME...
I DON'T MIND!
WEISS!

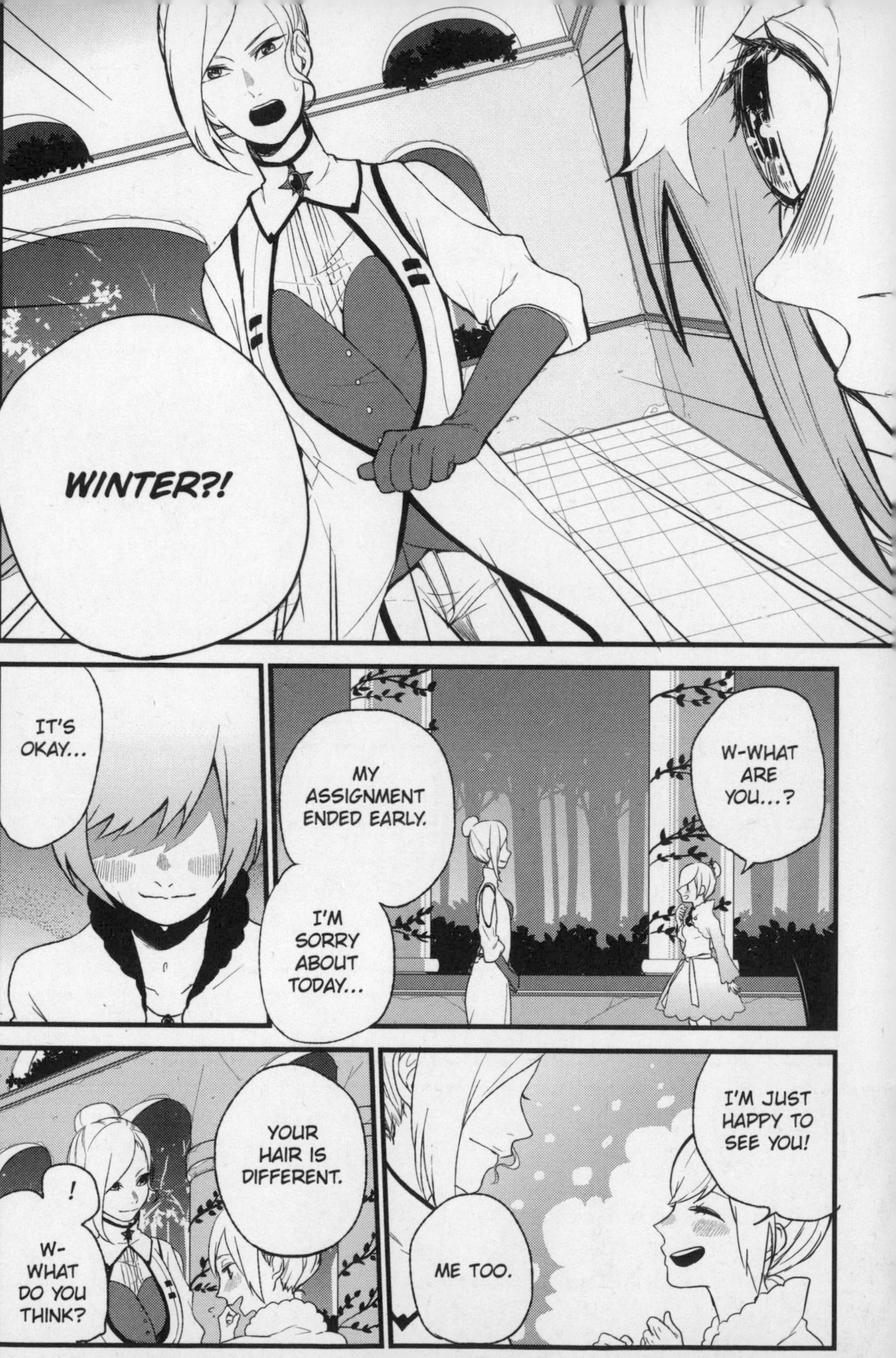
WINTER?!
W-WHAT ARE YOU...?
MY ASSIGNMENT ENDED EARLY.
I'M SORRY ABOUT TODAY...
IT'S OKAY...
I'M JUST HAPPY TO SEE YOU!
ME TOO.
YOUR HAIR IS DIFFERENT.
!
W-WHAT DO YOU THINK?

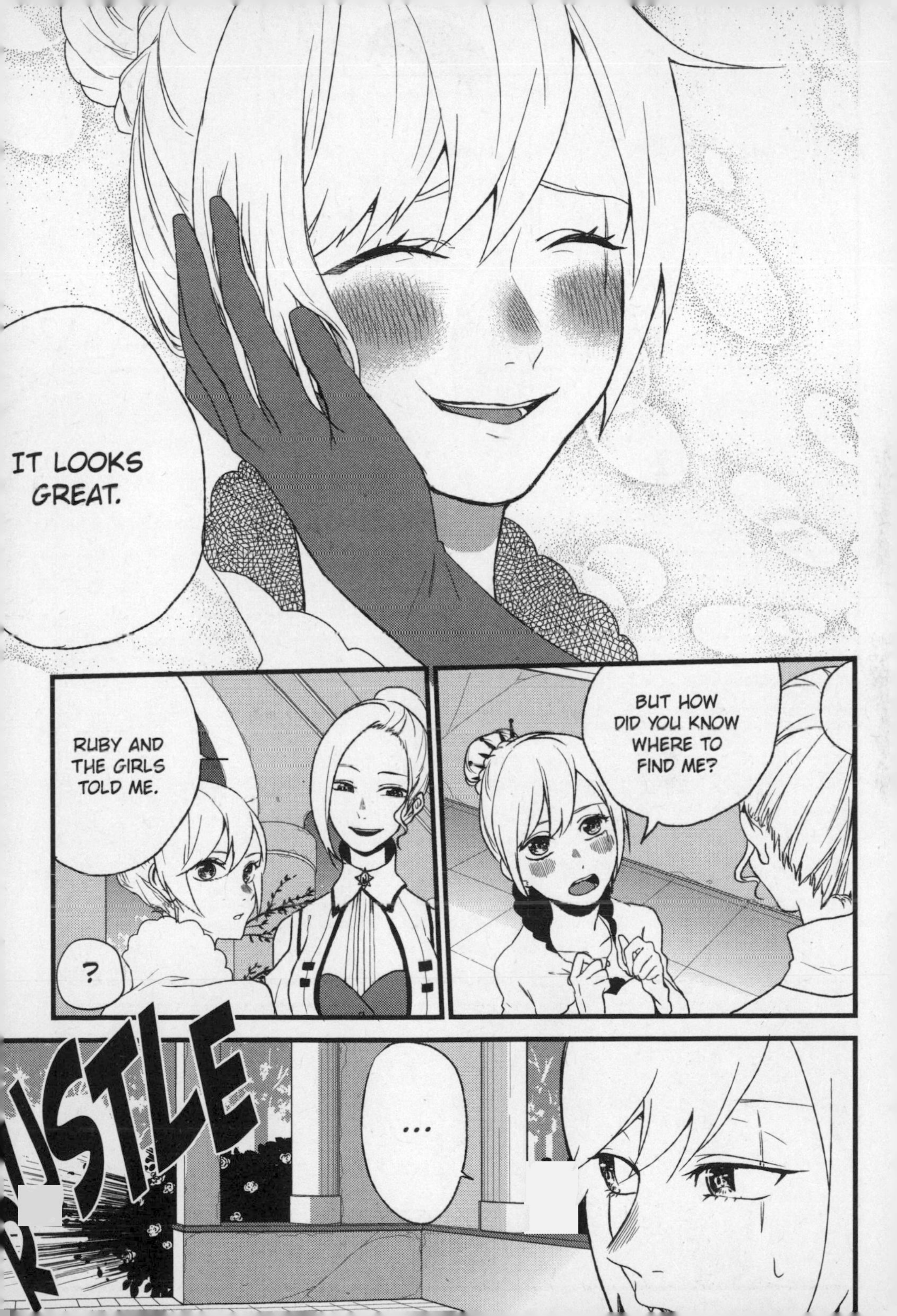
IT LOOKS GREAT.
BUT HOW DID YOU KNOW WHERE TO FIND ME?
RUBY AND THE GIRLS TOLD ME.
?
...
RUSTLE

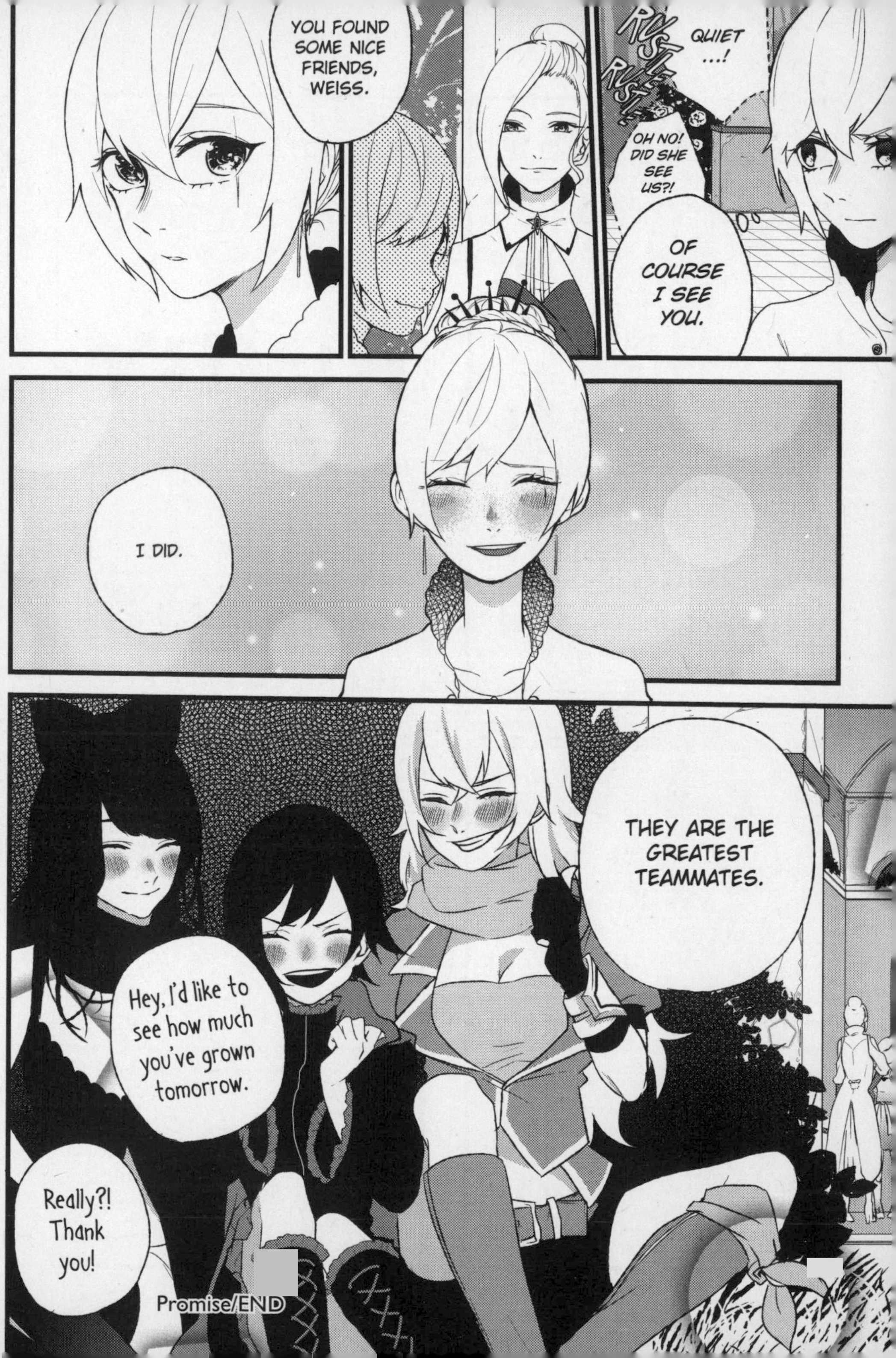
RUSTLE RUSTLE
QUIET ...!
OH NO! DID SHE SEE US?!
OF COURSE I SEE YOU.
YOU FOUND SOME NICE FRIENDS, WEISS.
I DID.
THEY ARE THE GREATEST TEAMMATES.
Hey, I'd like to see how much you've grown tomorrow.
Really?! Thank you!
Promise/END

It's Weiss

UN

DEUX

TROIS

RWBY No Doubt: Weiss

RWBY No Doubt: Weiss

Umiya

Fall

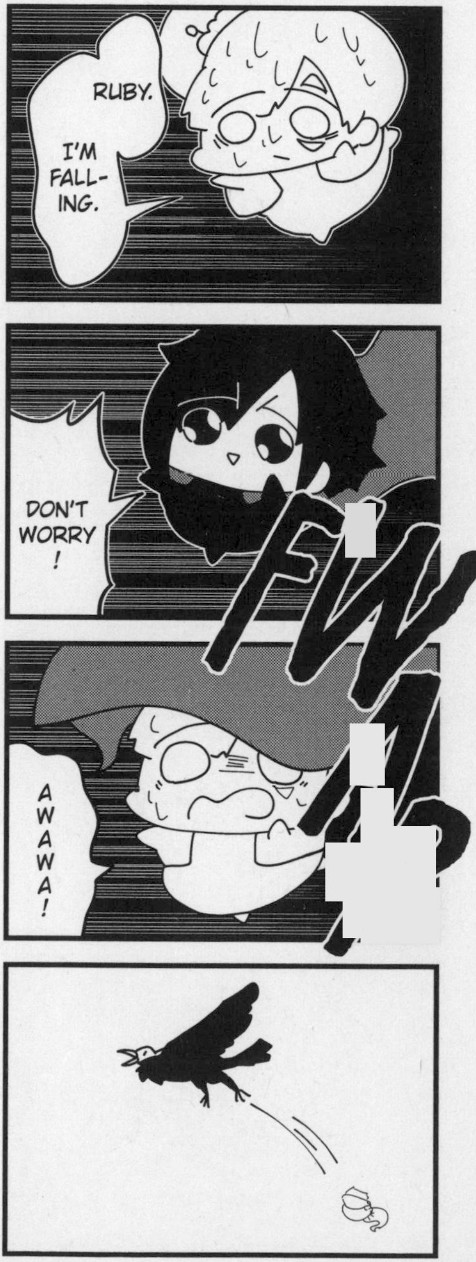
RUBY.
I'M FALL-ING.
DON'T WORRY!
FW
AWAWAWA!

Even a Flower Blushes

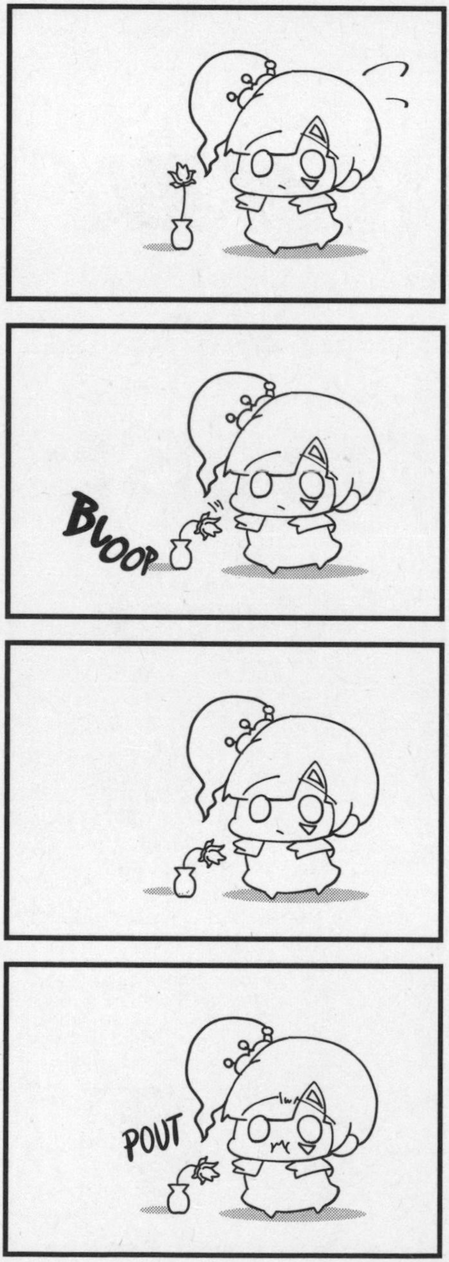
BLOOP
POUT

Ice Queen

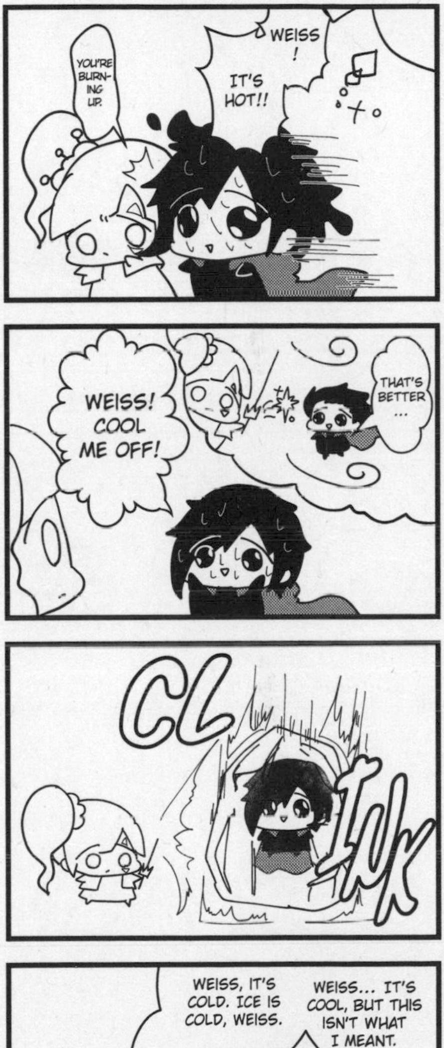
WEISS!
IT'S HOT!!
YOU'RE BURNING UP.
THAT'S BETTER ...
WEISS! COOL ME OFF!
CL
INK
WEISS... IT'S COOL, BUT THIS ISN'T WHAT I MEANT.
WEISS, IT'S COLD. ICE IS COLD, WEISS.
WEISS?
?

Let's Study

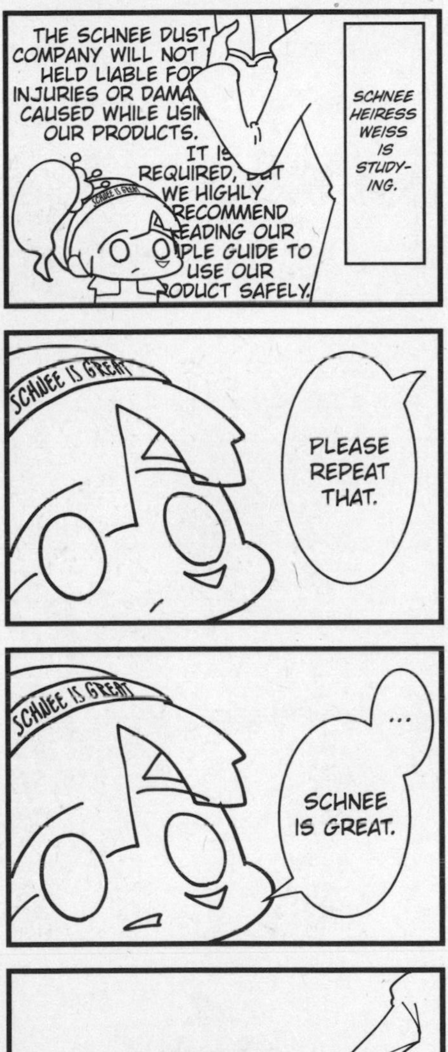
SCHNEE HEIRESS WEISS IS STUDYING.
THE SCHNEE DUST COMPANY WILL NOT HELD LIABLE FOR INJURIES OR DAMA CAUSED WHILE USIN OUR PRODUCTS.
IT IS REQUIRED, BUT WE HIGHLY RECOMMEND EADING OUR PLE GUIDE TO USE OUR ODUCT SAFELY.
SCHNEE IS GREAT
PLEASE REPEAT THAT.
SCHNEE IS GREAT
...
SCHNEE IS GREAT.
I'M SORRY.

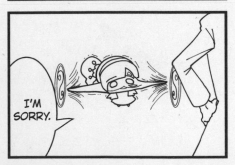

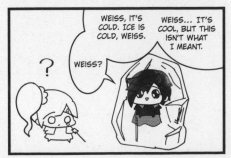

Black vs. White

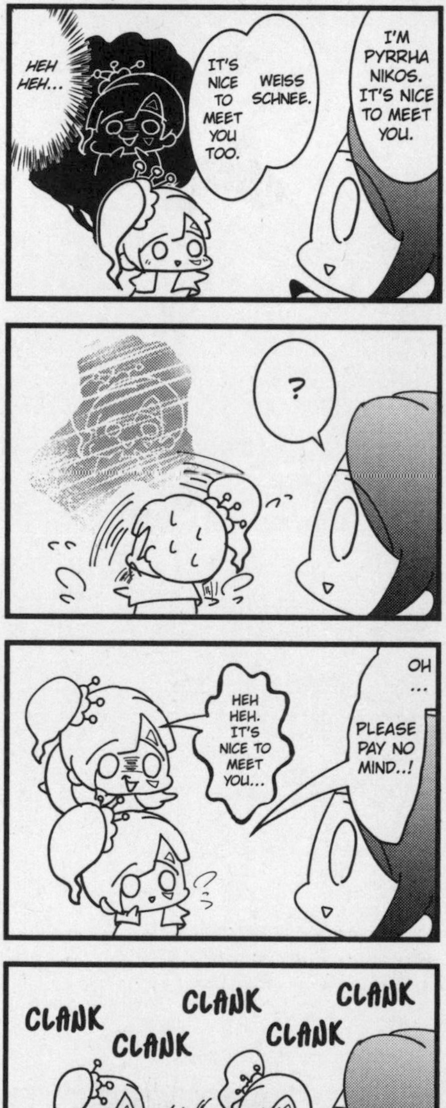
I'M PYRRHA NIKOS. IT'S NICE TO MEET YOU.
WEISS SCHNEE.
IT'S NICE TO MEET YOU TOO.
HEH HEH...
?
OH ... PLEASE PAY NO MIND..!
HEH HEH. IT'S NICE TO MEET YOU...
CLANK
CLANK
CLANK
CLANK
CLANK
CLANK
CLANK
CLANK

Can You Say Your Name?

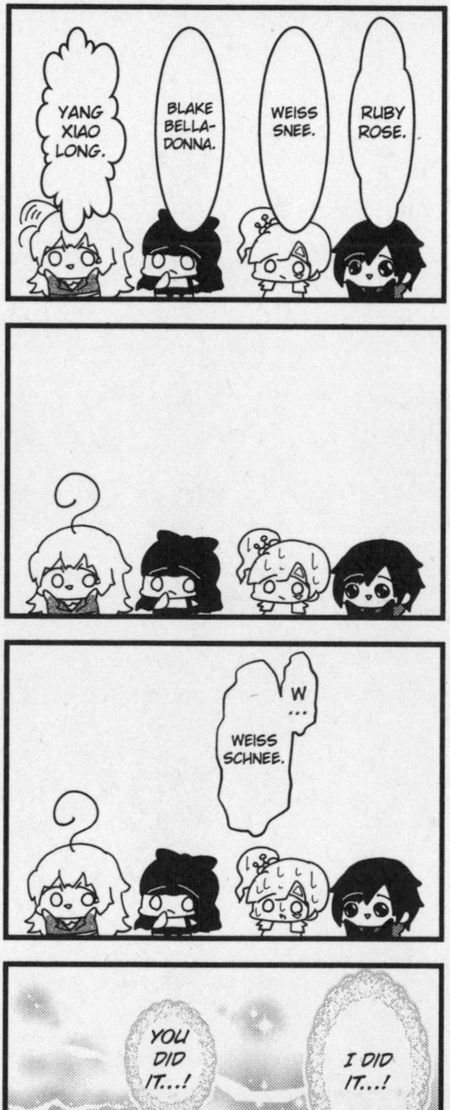
RUBY ROSE.
WEISS SNEE.
BLAKE BELLA-DONNA.
YANG XIAO LONG.
W ...
WEISS SCHNEE.
I DID IT...!
YOU DID IT...!

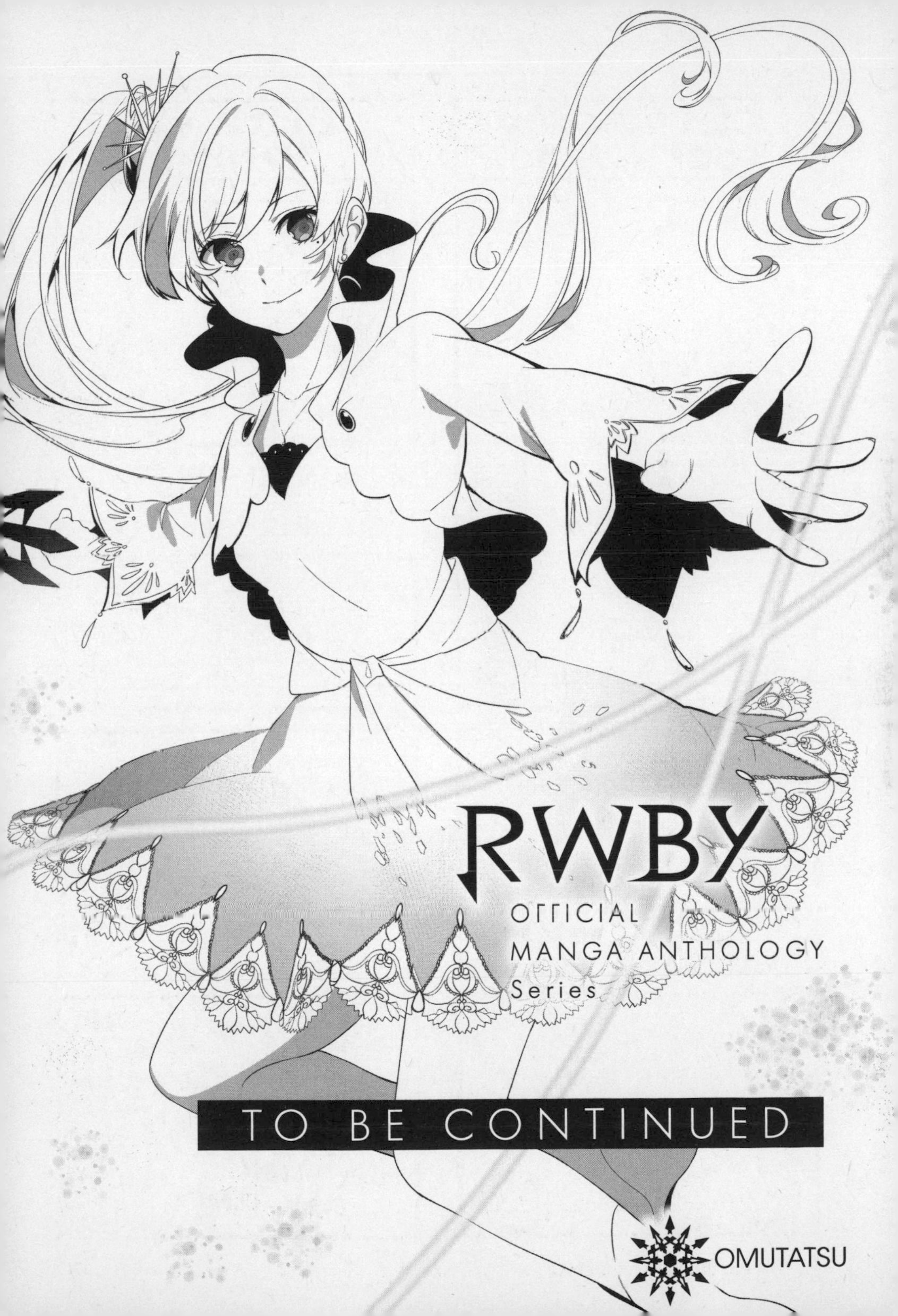
RWBY
OFFICIAL
MANGA ANTHOLOGY
Series
TO BE CONTINUED
OMUTATSU

Messages From Illustrators & Mangaka

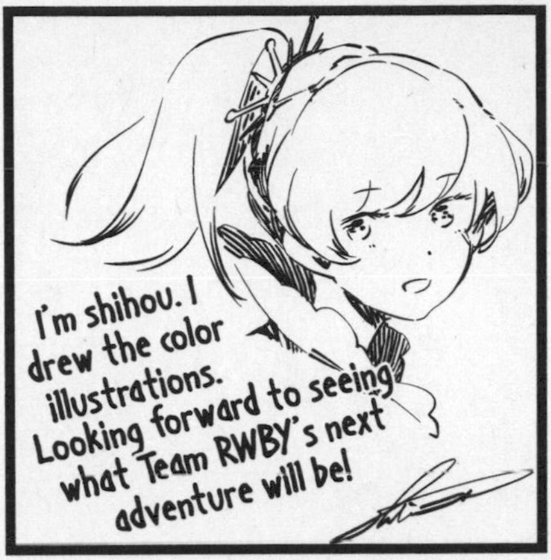
I'm shihou. I drew the color illustrations.
Looking forward to seeing what Team RWBY's next adventure will be!

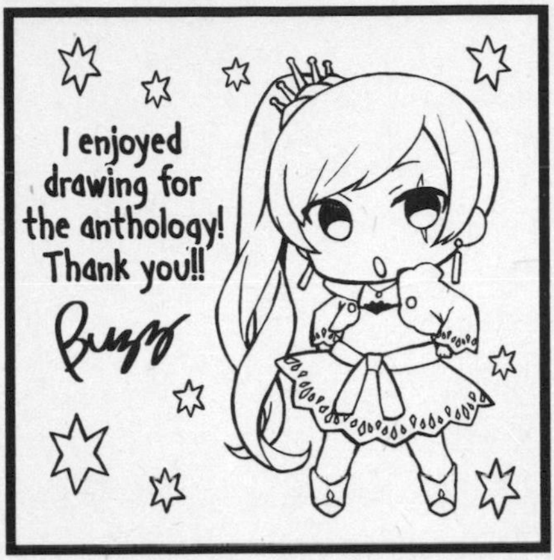
I enjoyed drawing for the anthology! Thank you!!

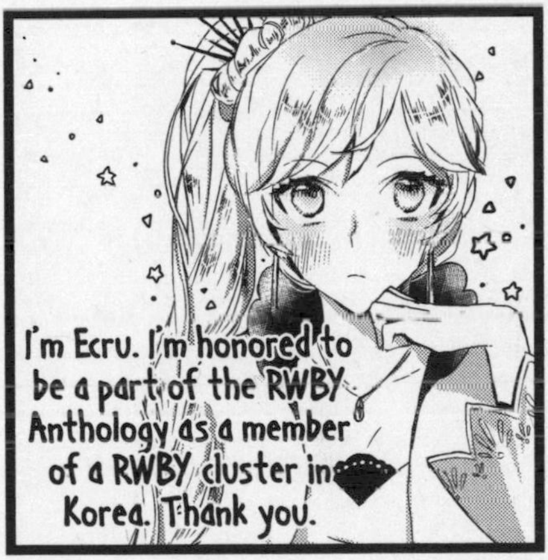
I'm Ecru. I'm honored to be a part of the RWBY Anthology as a member of a RWBY cluster in Korea. Thank you.

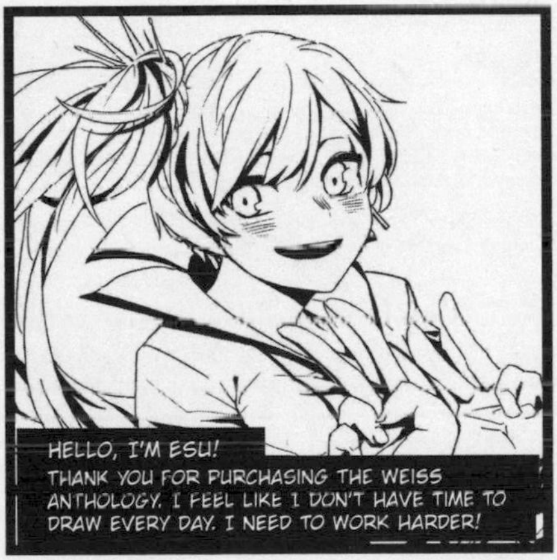
HELLO, I'M ESU!
THANK YOU FOR PURCHASING THE WEISS ANTHOLOGY. I FEEL LIKE I DON'T HAVE TIME TO DRAW EVERY DAY. I NEED TO WORK HARDER!

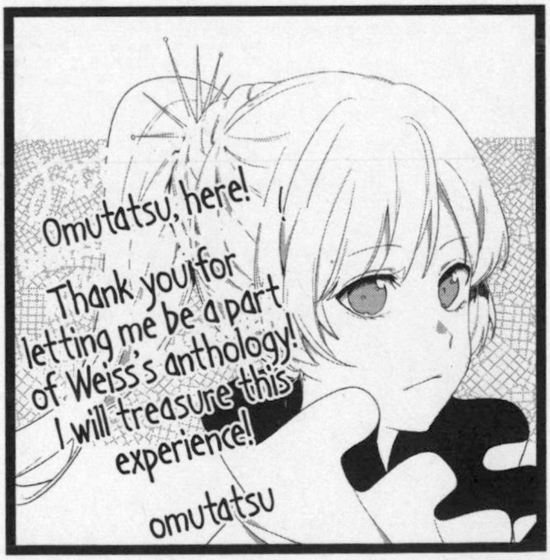
Omutatsu, here!
Thank you for letting me be a part of Weiss's anthology! I will treasure this experience!
omutatsu

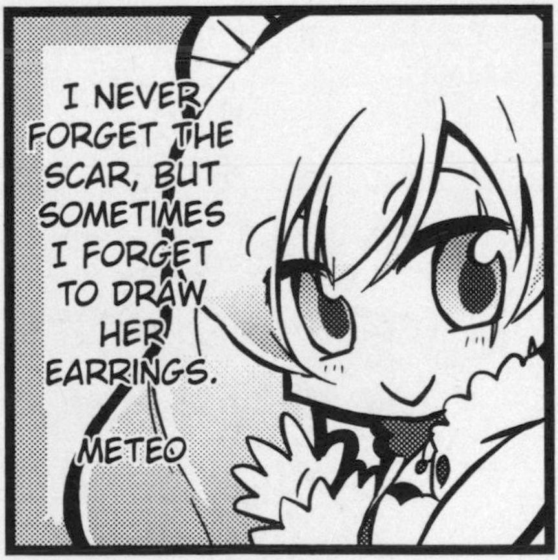
I NEVER FORGET THE SCAR, BUT SOMETIMES I FORGET TO DRAW HER EARRINGS.
METEO

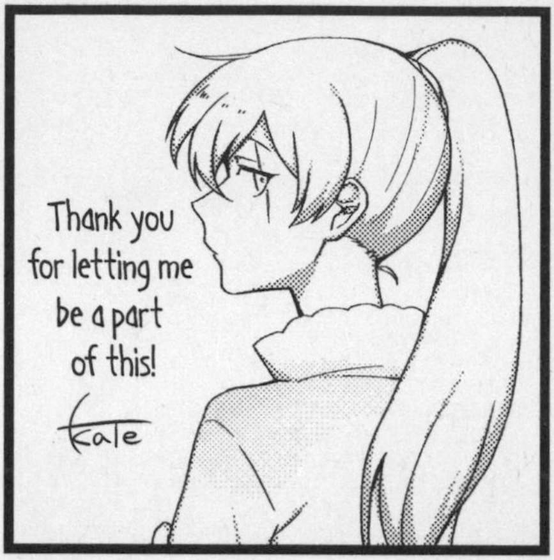
Thank you for letting me be a part of this!
Kate

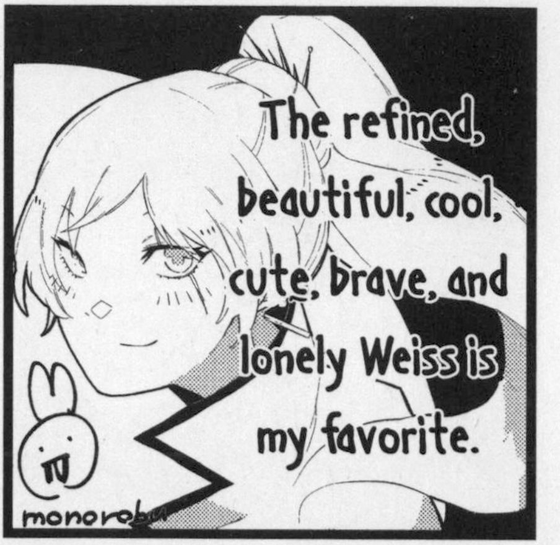
The refined, beautiful, cool, cute, brave, and lonely Weiss is my favorite.
monorobu

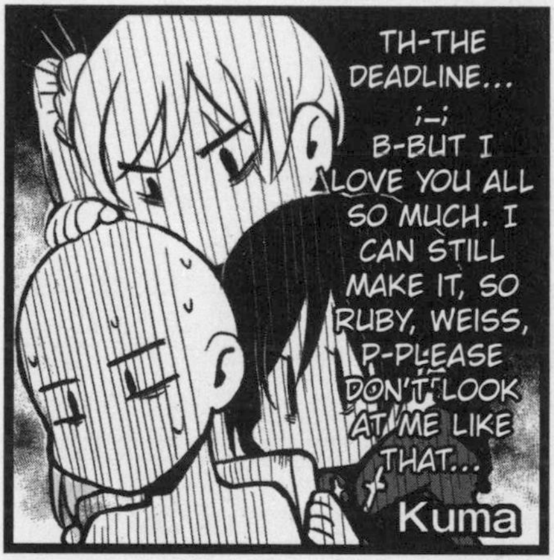
TH-THE DEADLINE... ;_;
B-BUT I LOVE YOU ALL SO MUCH. I CAN STILL MAKE IT, SO RUBY, WEISS, P-PLEASE DON'T LOOK AT ME LIKE THAT...
Kuma

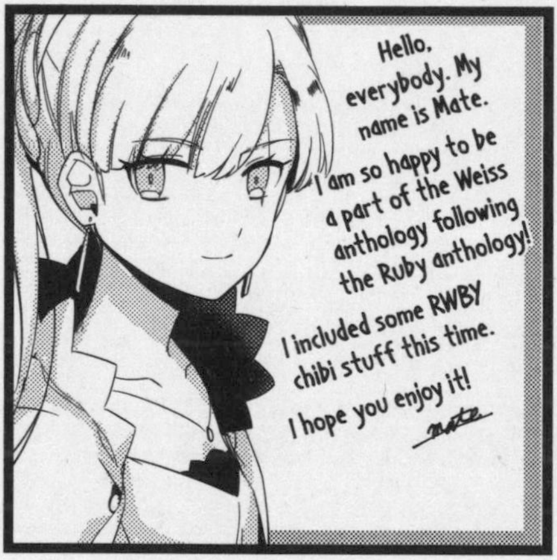
Hello, everybody. My name is Mate. I am so happy to be a part of the Weiss anthology following the Ruby anthology! I included some RWBY chibi stuff this time. I hope you enjoy it!

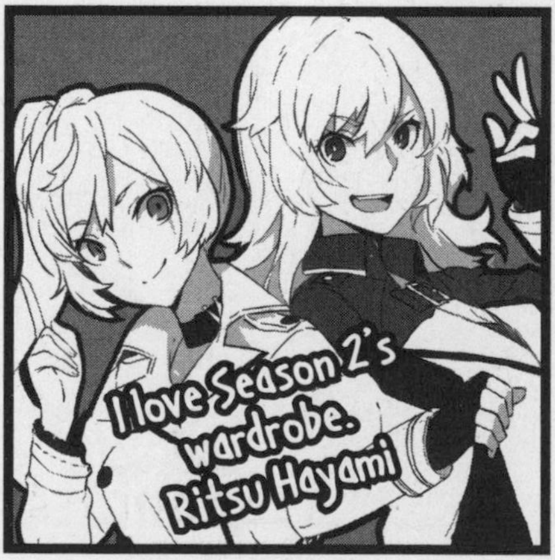
I love Season 2's wardrobe.
Ritsu Hayami

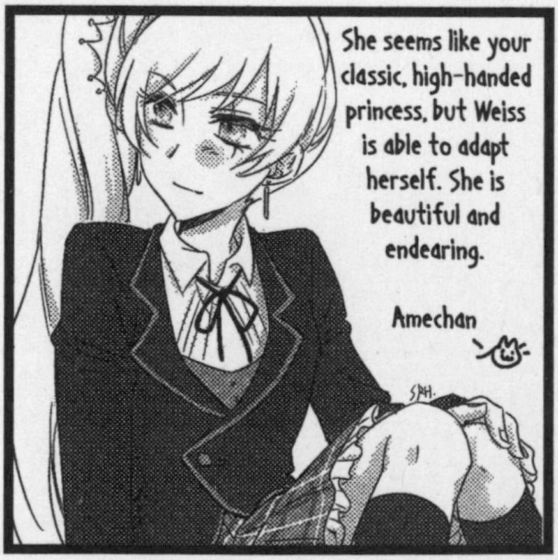
She seems like your classic, high-handed princess, but Weiss is able to adapt herself. She is beautiful and endearing.
Amechan

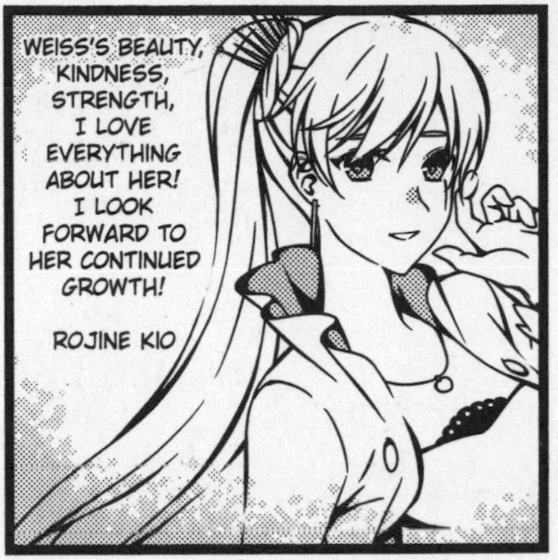
WEISS'S BEAUTY, KINDNESS, STRENGTH, I LOVE EVERYTHING ABOUT HER! I LOOK FORWARD TO HER CONTINUED GROWTH!
ROJINE KIO

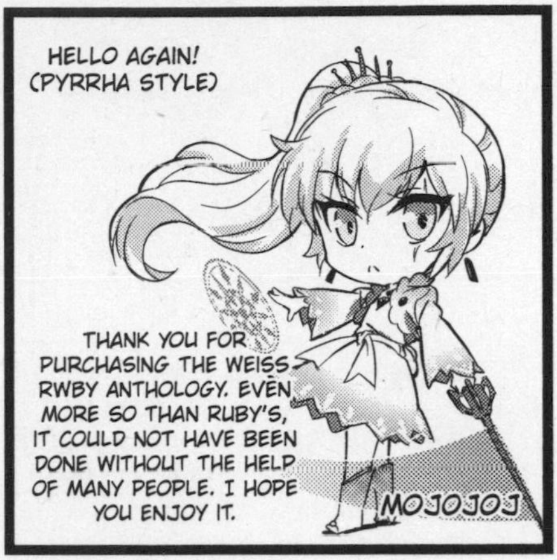
HELLO AGAIN! (PYRRHA STYLE)
THANK YOU FOR PURCHASING THE WEISS RWBY ANTHOLOGY. EVEN MORE SO THAN RUBY'S, IT COULD NOT HAVE BEEN DONE WITHOUT THE HELP OF MANY PEOPLE. I HOPE YOU ENJOY IT.
MOJOJOJ

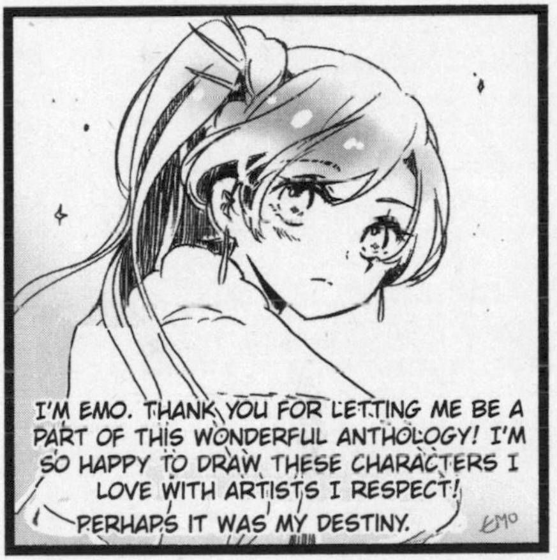
I'M EMO. THANK YOU FOR LETTING ME BE A PART OF THIS WONDERFUL ANTHOLOGY! I'M SO HAPPY TO DRAW THESE CHARACTERS I LOVE WITH ARTISTS I RESPECT!
PERHAPS IT WAS MY DESTINY.
EMO

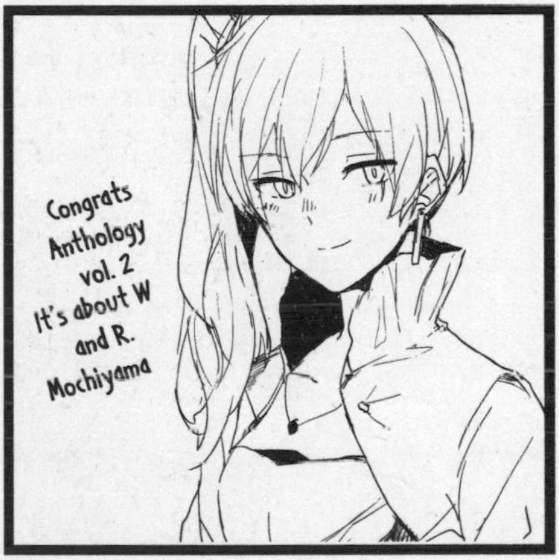
Congrats Anthology vol. 2 It's about W and R.
Mochiyama

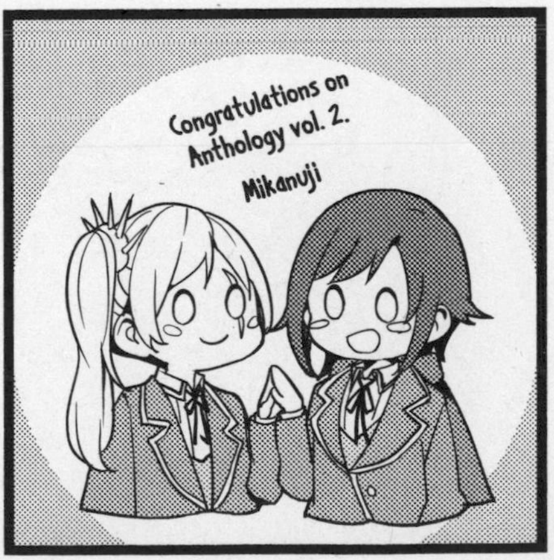
Congratulations on Anthology vol. 2.
Mikanuji

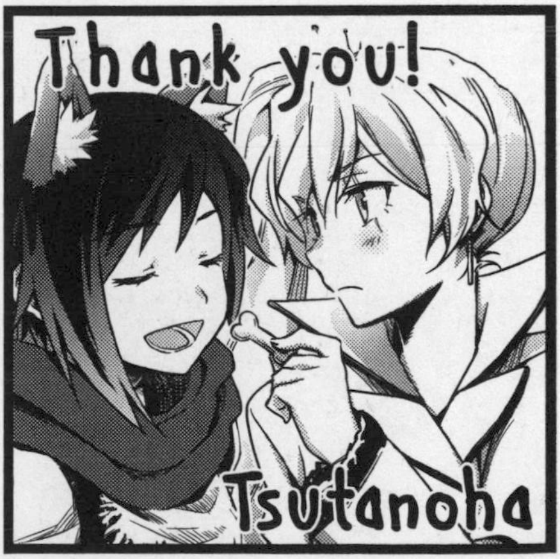
Thank you!
Tsutanoha

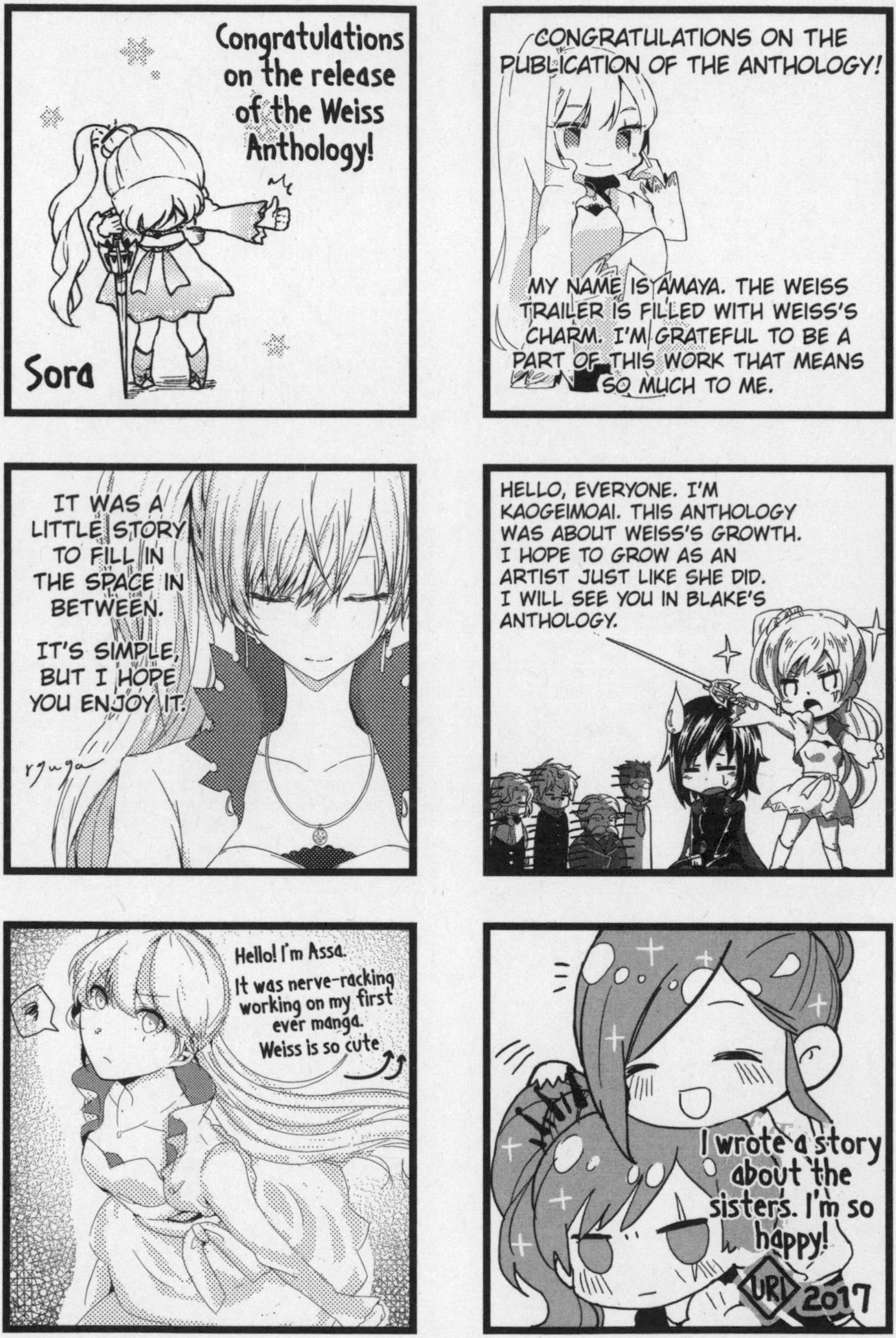
CONGRATULATIONS ON THE PUBLICATION OF THE ANTHOLOGY!
MY NAME IS AMAYA. THE WEISS TRAILER IS FILLED WITH WEISS'S CHARM. I'M GRATEFUL TO BE A PART OF THIS WORK THAT MEANS SO MUCH TO ME.
Congratulations on the release of the Weiss Anthology!
Sora
HELLO, EVERYONE. I'M KAOGEIMOAI. THIS ANTHOLOGY WAS ABOUT WEISS'S GROWTH. I HOPE TO GROW AS AN ARTIST JUST LIKE SHE DID. I WILL SEE YOU IN BLAKE'S ANTHOLOGY.
IT WAS A LITTLE STORY TO FILL IN THE SPACE IN BETWEEN.
IT'S SIMPLE, BUT I HOPE YOU ENJOY IT.
ryuga
I wrote a story about the sisters. I'm so happy!
URI 2017
Hello! I'm Assa.
It was nerve-racking working on my first ever manga. Weiss is so cute

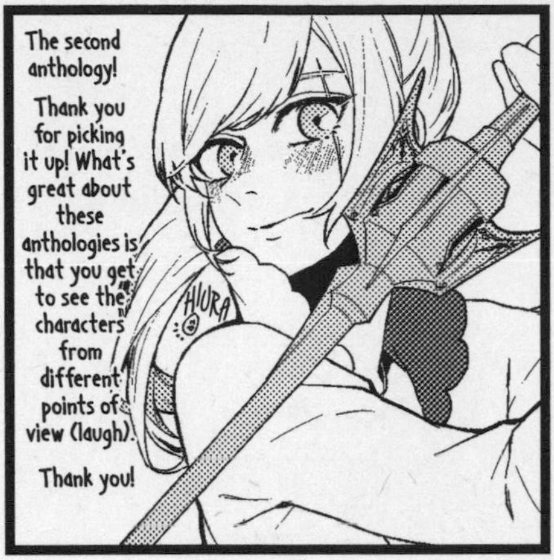
The second anthology!
Thank you for picking it up! What's great about these anthologies is that you get to see the characters from different points of view (laugh).
Thank you!
HIURA

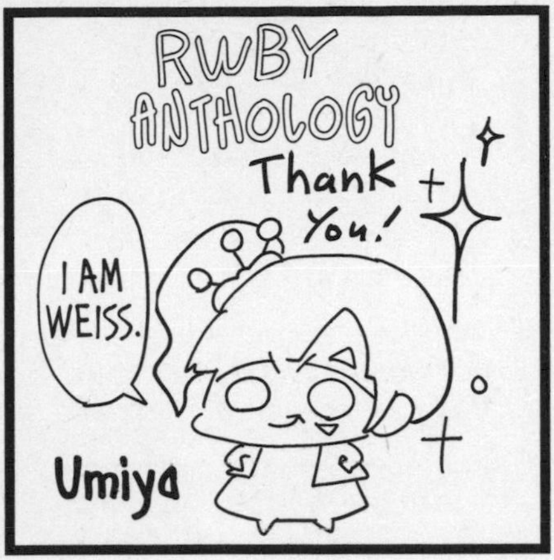
RWBY ANTHOLOGY
Thank You!
I AM WEISS.
Umiya

Much appreciated.
Thank you for getting this anthology.

HAVE FUN!

About Weiss

Ein Lee

Among all of Team RWBY, Weiss's design and personality is my favorite. Despite how I may seem, I too am timid. Maybe that's why I relate to her. I got excited when Monty wanted an ice princess–like character. Not only do I feel that I excel at it, I really love drawing characters dressed in beautiful clothing.

By drawing her ponytail flowing to the side, I tried to render her with a more asymmetrical look. Like a snowflake, Weiss is definitely not perfect. She's lacking in certain areas and has her own gamut of internal conflicts to confront. The scar on her eye is an important detail that, hopefully, shatters the traditional image of a princess.

Unlike, say, Ruby's cape, Weiss doesn't have any large items or equipment that defines the majority of her character design. With that in mind I added effects like glittering glyphs and deliberately exaggerated the flow of her hair to make her appear more glamorous. Initially I was worried that all of the pale colors would make her appear a bit flat, but I'm happy with how her final design turned out.

Her pose (in the rough sketch) was based on Ruby's illustration. Both pieces are intended to be viewed together. If you place them side by side, Ruby would be in the bottom left and Weiss in the upper right, each sketch complementing the other.

To prevent the background from being potentially perceived as too plain, I scattered some blue flourishes that contribute to the softer, romantic mood and the periwinkle petals around her.

Dear friend,

As a proud member of team *RWBY*, I sincerely appreciate the talented artists and storytellers that contributed to this exciting new manga series! Life is not always easy as a Schnee, but it is also never boring. This special manga collection shows us the difficulties of living under the Schnee family name. With the help of her sister and team, Weiss learns that she can create her own Schnee legacy.

Thank you for all your loyal support and remember to always use proper form.

Kara Eberle

Kara ♡
-weiss-

RWBY

RWBY

We *RWBY* fans love you, Monty.

Thank you for continuing *RWBY* and providing us
a magical experience, Rooster Teeth!

RWBY OFFICIAL MANGA ANTHOLOGY 2

Mirror, Mirror

VIZ Signature Edition
Official Manga Anthology Vol. 2
MIRROR MIRROR
Based on the Rooster Teeth Series Created by MONTY OUM.

©2017 Rooster Teeth Productions, LLC
©2017 Warner Bros. Japan LLC All rights reserved.
©2017 Home-sha

TRANSLATION Joe Yamazaki
ENGLISH ADAPTATION Jeremy Haun & Jason A. Hurley
TOUCH-UP ART AND LETTERING Evan Waldinger
DESIGN Shawn Carrico
EDITOR Joel Enos

COVER ILLUSTRATION Ein Lee/Meteo
ORIGINAL COVER DESIGN Tsuyoshi Kusano

SPECIAL THANKS
Ken Takizawa (Home-sha)
Takanori Inoue (Home-sha)
Misato Kaneko
Yoshihiko Wakanabe (Editor/Planner of RWBY OFFICIAL MANGA ANTHOLOGY)

Printed in the U.S.A.

Published by VIZ Media, LLC
P.O. Box 77010
San Francisco, CA 94107

10 9 8 7 6 5 4 3 2
First printing, August 2018
Second printing, October 2019

VIZ SIGNATURE
vizsignature.com

VIZ MEDIA
viz.com

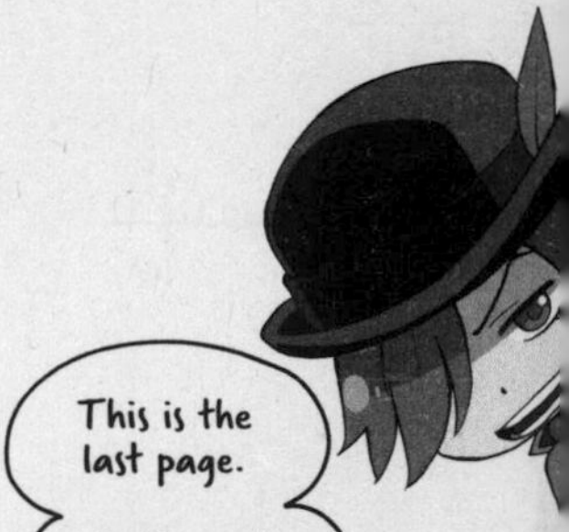
This is the last page.
RWBY reads right to left.

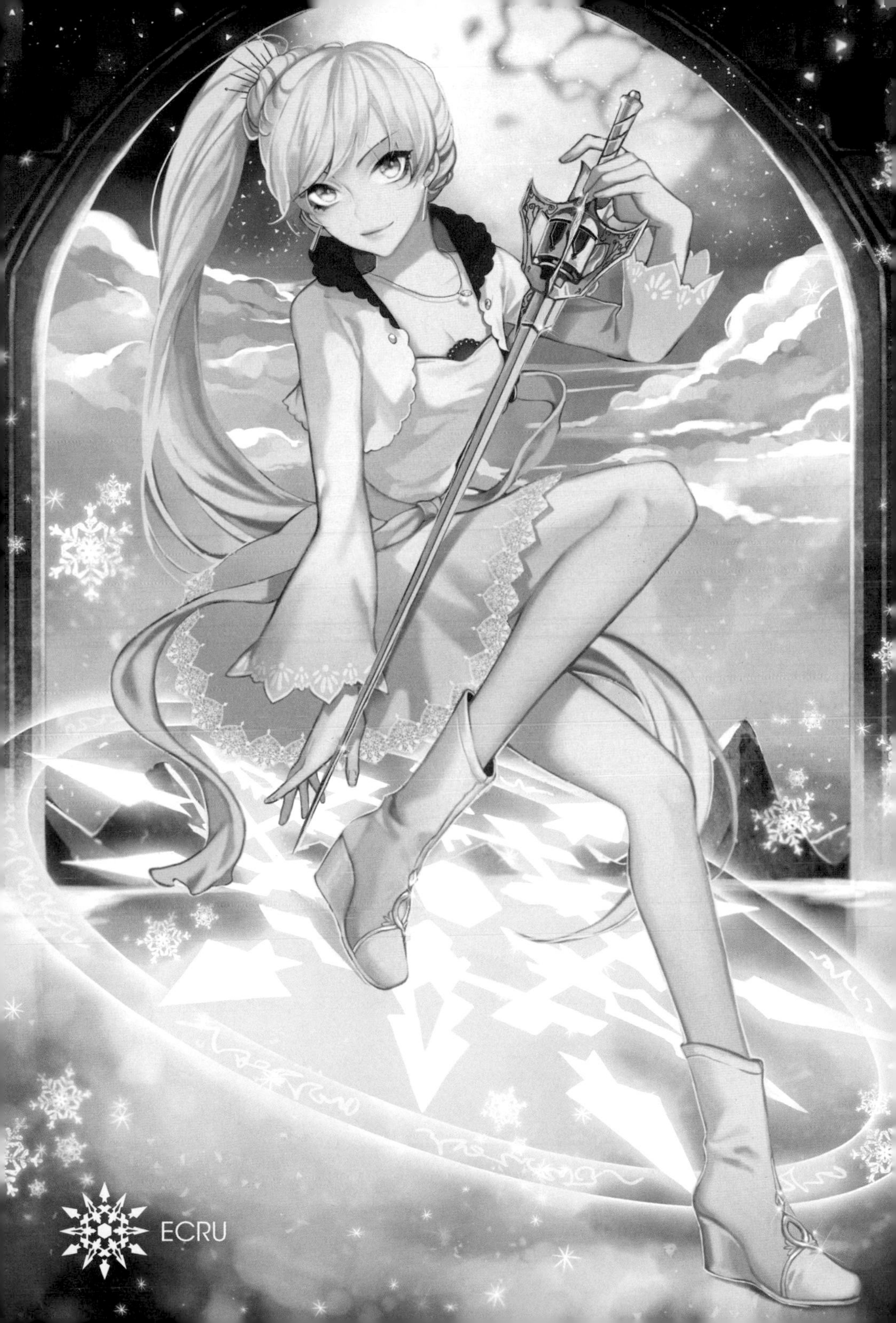
ECRU

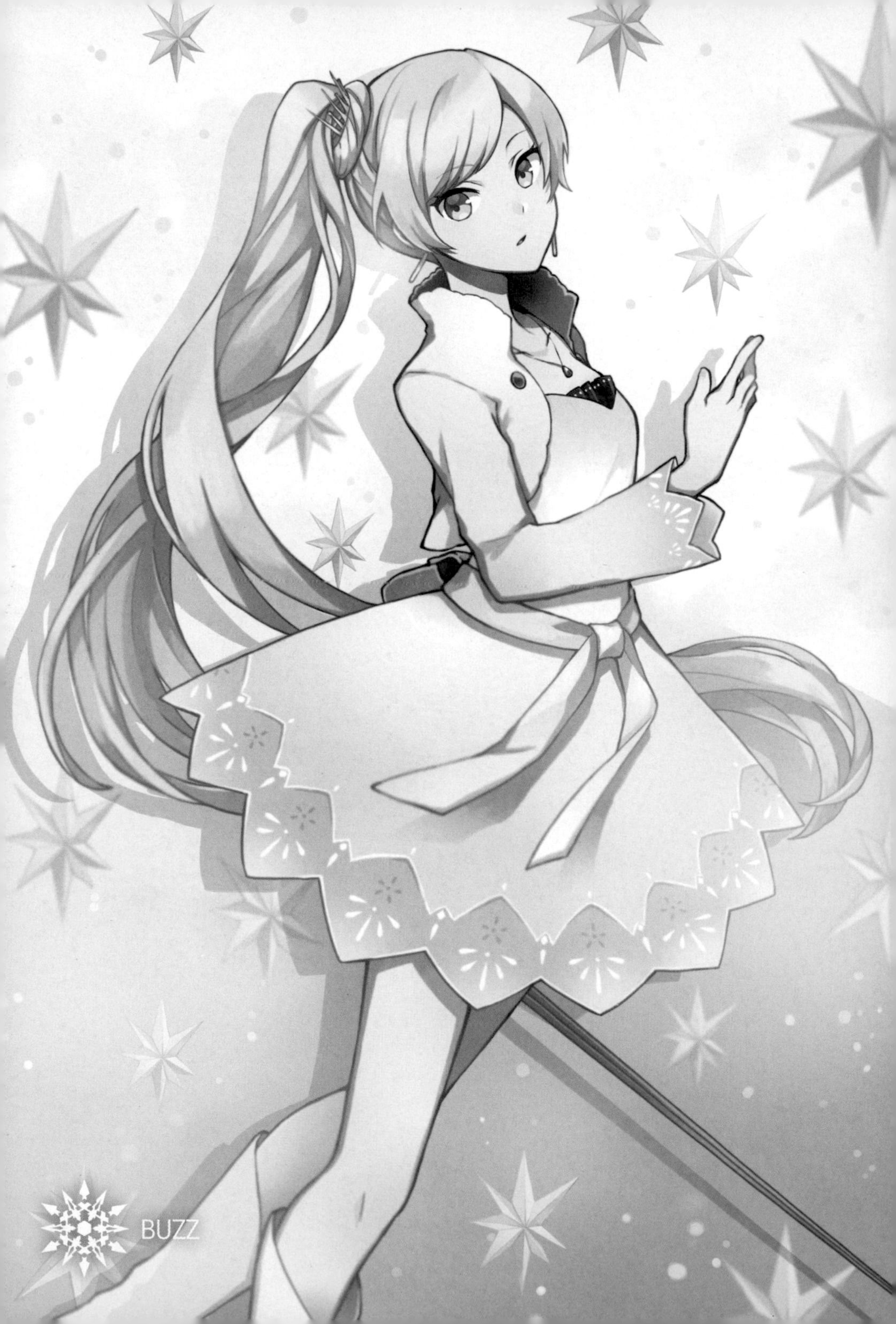
BUZZ